QuickBooks® 2012

FOR

DUMMIES®

UK EDITION

QuickBooks® 2012
FOR
DUMMIES®

UK EDITION

**by Stephen L. Nelson, CPA, MBA (finance),
MS (taxation)
and Loredana Stroup, DPhil, MBA**

WILEY

A John Wiley and Sons, Ltd, Publication

QuickBooks® 2012 For Dummies,® UK Edition

Published by
John Wiley & Sons, Ltd.
The Atrium
Southern Gate
Chichester
West Sussex
PO19 8SQ
England

Email (for orders and customer service enquires): cs-books@wiley.co.uk
Visit our home page on www.wiley.com
Copyright © 2012 John Wiley & Sons, Ltd, Chichester, West Sussex, England
Published by John Wiley & Sons Ltd, Chichester, West Sussex, England

For general information on our other products and services, please contact our Customer Care Department within the U.S. at 877-762-2974, outside the U.S. at 317-572-3993, or fax 317-572-4002.

For technical support, please visit www.wiley.com/techsupport.

Wiley also publishes its books in a variety of electronic formats and by print-on-demand. Some content that appears in standard print versions of this book may not be available in other formats. For more information about Wiley products, visit us at www.wiley.com.

British Library Cataloguing in Publication Data: A catalogue record for this book is available from the British Library.

ISBN 978-1-119-96894-8 (paperback); ISBN 978-1-119-94064-7 (ebook); 978-1-119-94065-4 (ebook); 978-1-119-94066-1 (ebook)

Printed and bound in Great Britain by TJ International, Padstow, Cornwall

10 9 8 7 6 5 4 3 2 1

WILEY

About the Authors

Stephen L. Nelson, CPA, MBA (finance), MS (taxation), has a simple purpose in life: He wants to help you (and people like you) manage your business finances by using computers. Oh, sure, this personal mandate won't win him a Nobel Prize or anything, but it's his own little contribution to the world.

Steve's experiences mesh nicely with his special purpose. A CPA in Redmond, Washington, his past small business experience includes a stint as an adjunct professor of taxation (S corporations and limited liability companies) at Golden Gate University graduate tax school and a few years working as a senior consultant and CPA with Arthur Andersen & Co. (er, yeah, *that* Arthur Andersen — but, hey, it was nearly 30 years ago). Steve, whose books have sold more than 4 million copies in English and have been translated into 11 other languages, is also the bestselling author of *Quicken 2012 For Dummies*.

Loredana Stroup, DPhil (Oxon), MBA, has over a decade of experience working with businesses in various capacities including management consulting, software training, and technology systems design and integration. Her passion is to help people run their businesses more efficiently and effectively, especially through the use of proven digital technologies. She founded and runs Alta Training Limited which specialises in QuickBooks setups, training, and troubleshooting. Intuit, the maker of QuickBooks, has recognised her expertise and tapped it in the development, testing and launching of QuickBooks (UK), and also in engaging her to write training materials and deliver training programmes across the country.

Dedications

To the entrepreneurs and small-business people of the world. You folks create most of the new jobs.

– Stephen L. Nelson

To my family.

– Loredana Stroup

Authors' Acknowledgments

Hey, reader, lots of folks spent lots of time working on this book to make QuickBooks easier for you. You should know who these people are. You may just possibly meet one of them someday at a produce shop, squeezing cantaloupe, eating grapes, and looking for the perfect peach.

First, a huge thanks to the wonderful folks at Intuit who helped me by providing the beta software and other friendly assistance for this and past editions of this book.

Another big thank-you goes to the editorial folks at Wiley Publishing, Inc., including Kevin Kirschner (project editor), Teresa Artman (copy editor), and Bob Woerner (executive editor). Thanks also to David Ringstrom for his technical assistance and superb attention to detail. Finally, thanks, too, to the composition staff.

– Stephen L. Nelson

Firstly, my wholehearted and affectionate thanks to Saxby and Saskia for their patience, to George for his enthusiasm and strong support, and to Carmen and Aurel for their special practical help that made this book possible.

Secondly, a huge thank you to the team at John Wiley & Sons, especially Sara Shlaer (senior project editor), Shena Deuchars (copy editor), and Chris Webb (associate publisher). Thank you to Antony Stemp for his technical assistance, and to the very helpful team at Intuit for supporting this project in many ways.

– Loredana Stroup

Publisher's Acknowledgments

We're proud of this book; please send us your comments at http://dummies.custhelp.com. For other comments, please contact our Customer Care Department within the U.S. at 877-762-2974, outside the U.S. at 317-572-3993, or fax 317-572-4002.

Some of the people who helped bring this book to market include the following:

Acquisitions, Editorial

Project Editor:

Associate Publisher: Chris Webb

Assistant Editor: Ellie Scott

Copy Editor: Shena Deuchars

Technical Editor: Antony Stemp

Editorial Manager: Jodi Jensen

Senior Project Editor: Sara Shlaer

Editorial Assistant: Leslie Saxman

Cartoons: Rich Tennant
(www.the5thwave.com)

Marketing

Associate Marketing Director: Louise Breinholt

Senior Marketing Executive: Kate Parrett

Composition Services

Senior Project Coordinator: Kristie Rees

Layout and Graphics: Lavonne Roberts

Proofreaders: Jessica Kramer, Linda Seifert

Indexer: BIM Indexing & Proofreading

UK Tech Publishing

    VP Consumer and Technology Publishing Director: Michelle Leete

    Associate Director–Book Content Management: Martin Tribe

    Associate Publisher: Chris Webb

Publishing and Editorial for Technology Dummies

    Richard Swadley, Vice President and Executive Group Publisher

    Andy Cummings, Vice President and Publisher

    Mary Bednarek, Executive Acquisitions Director

    Mary C. Corder, Editorial Director

Publishing for Consumer Dummies

    Kathleen Nebenhaus, Vice President and Executive Publisher

Composition Services

    Debbie Stailey, Director of Composition Services

Contents at a Glance

Table of Contents

Part III: Stuff You Do from Time to Time 229

Introduction

● ●

Running or working in a small business is one of the coolest things a person can do. Really. We mean it. Sure, sometimes the environment is difficult – but it's an environment in which you have the opportunity to make a lot of money. And it's also an environment in which you can build a company or a job that fits you. In comparison, those working in the big-company, corporate world are furiously trying to fit their round pegs painfully into square holes. Yuck.

You're wondering, of course, what any of this has to do with this book or with QuickBooks. Quite a lot, actually. The whole purpose of this book is to make it easier for you to run or work in a small business by using QuickBooks.

About QuickBooks

Let us start off with a minor but useful point. QuickBooks comes in three different flavours: QuickBooks SimpleStart, QuickBooks Pro, and QuickBooks Premier. QuickBooks SimpleStart is a much simpler version of QuickBooks Pro. In fact, it's so simple you won't need much help using it. But if you do, this book can help guide you. QuickBooks Pro is a good choice for established businesses where fancier features like stock item backorders, multiple units of measure, tracking time and expenses by customer (or job) and using that information to invoice customers, are not important. And of course, QuickBooks Premier is the top of the range flavour – it has all the bells and whistles. We should also mention that up to three users can be working in QuickBooks Pro simultaneously, while up to 30 users can work with QuickBooks Premier at the same time.

To write this book, we used the QuickBooks Premier Accountant Edition, which is just QuickBooks Premier by another name. By describing how you use QuickBooks Premier, we also tell you how to use QuickBooks Pro. That's because most things we talk about in this book apply both to QuickBooks Premier and to QuickBooks Pro. Where there are differences, we point them out.

The bottom line? Yes, there are several flavours of QuickBooks, but if you're just trying to get started and want to use QuickBooks, this book works for both QuickBooks Pro and QuickBooks Premier.

About This Book

This book isn't meant to be read from cover to cover, like some Stieg Larsson page-turner. Instead, it's organised into tiny, no-sweat descriptions of how you do the things you need to do. If you're the sort of person who just doesn't feel right not reading a book from cover to cover, you can (of course) go ahead and read this thing from front to back. You can start reading Chapter 1 and continue all the way to the end (which means through Chapter 19 and the appendixes).

We don't think this from-start-to-finish approach is bad because we tell you loads of stuff (tips and tricks, for example) along the way. We tried to write the book in such a way that the experience isn't as rough as you might think, and we really do think you get will get good value from your reading.

But you can also use this book the way you'd use an encyclopaedia. If you want to know about a subject, you can look it up in the Table of Contents or the index and then you can flip to the correct chapter or page and read as much as you need or enjoy. No muss, no fuss.

We should, however, mention one thing: Accounting software programs require you to do a certain amount of preparation before you can use them to get real work done. If you haven't started to use QuickBooks yet, we recommend that you read through the first few chapters of this book to find out what you need to do first.

Hey. There's something else you should know. We fiddled a bit with the Windows display settings. For example, we messed about with the font settings and most of the colours. The benefit is that the pictures in this book are easy to read. And that's good. But the cost of all this is that our pictures look a little bit different from what you see on your screen. And that's not good. In the end, however, what the publisher found is that people are happier with increased readability. Anyway, we just thought we should mention it here, upfront, in case you have any questions about it.

What You Can Safely Ignore

Sometimes we provide step-by-step descriptions of tasks. We feel very bad about having to do this so, to make things easier for you, we describe the tasks using bold text. That way, you know exactly what you're supposed to do. We also provide a more detailed explanation in the text that follows the step. You can skip the text that accompanies the step-by-step boldface directions if you already understand the process.

Here's an example that shows what we mean:

1. **Press Enter.**

   Find the key that's labelled Enter. Extend your index finger so that it rests ever so gently on the Enter key. In one sure, fluid motion, press the Enter key with your index finger. Then remove your finger from the key.

Okay, that example is extreme. We never go into that much detail, but you get the idea. If you know how to press Enter, you can just do that and not read further. If you need help – maybe with the finger part or something else – just read the nitty-gritty details.

 Can you skip anything else? Let's see now. . . . You can skip the Technical Stuff icons, too. The information next to these icons is intended only for those of you who like that kind of technical stuff.

 For that matter, we suppose that you can safely ignore the stuff next to the Tip icons, too – even if our accumulated wisdom, gleaned from long hours slaving over a hot keyboard, can save you much weeping and gnashing of teeth. If you're someone who enjoys trying to do something another way, go ahead and read the tips.

 Sometimes, we use made-up examples (along with examples from our own experience) to help you understand how some topic or area of QuickBooks helps you and your business. We mark these examples with the Case Study icon. This is just our way of continuing the giving. But sure, you can skip them.

What You Should Not Ignore (Unless You're a Masochist)

 Don't skip the Warning icons. They're the ones flagged with the picture of a 19th century bomb. They describe some things that you *really* shouldn't do.

Out of respect for you, we don't put advice like 'Don't smoke!' next to these icons. We figure that you're an adult and you can make your own lifestyle decisions. So we reserve the Warning icons for more urgent and immediate dangers – things akin to 'Don't smoke while you're filling your car with petrol.'

 This icon is a friendly reminder to do something. Not to be too pushy, but it's probably not a good idea to ignore these icons.

Three Foolish Assumptions

We make three assumptions about you:

- ✔ **You have a PC running Microsoft Windows.** (We took pictures of the QuickBooks windows and dialog boxes while using Windows 7, in case you're interested.)
- ✔ **You know a little bit about how to work with your computer.**
- ✔ **You have or will buy a copy of QuickBooks for each computer on which you want to run the program.**

This book works for QuickBooks 2012, although in a pinch, you can probably also use it for QuickBooks 2010.

By the way, if you haven't already installed QuickBooks and need help, jump to Appendix A, which tells you how to install QuickBooks in ten easy steps.

How This Book Is Organised

This book is divided into six mostly coherent parts.

Part I: Quickly into QuickBooks

Part I covers some upfront tasks that you need to take care of before you can start using QuickBooks. We promise we don't waste your time here. We just want to make sure that you get off to a good start.

Part II: Daily Entry Tasks

The second part of this book explains how to use QuickBooks for your daily financial record keeping: preparing customer invoices, recording sales, and paying bills – that sort of stuff. Oh, and yes, multicurrency is covered here too.

Just so you know, you'll be amazed at how much easier QuickBooks makes your life. QuickBooks is a really cool program.

Part III: Stuff You Do from Time to Time

Part III talks about the kinds of things that you should do at the end of the week, the end of the month or the end of the year. This part explains, for example, how to manage your VAT, do payroll, and create a business budget.

While we're on the subject, we also want to categorically deny that Part III contains any secret messages that you can decipher by reading backwards. Yllaer.

Part IV: Housekeeping Chores

Part IV talks about some of the maintenance tasks that you need (or someone needs) to perform to keep your accounting system shipshape: account reconciliations, financial report generation, job-costing mechanics, and file management.

Part V: The Part of Tens

Gravity isn't just a good idea; it's a law.

By tradition, the same is true for this part of a *For Dummies* book. The Part of Tens provides a collection of lists: ten tricky situations and ways to handle them, ten things to do when you next visit the Canary Islands – oops, sorry, wrong book.

Also by tradition, these ten-item lists don't need to have exactly ten items. You know the concept of a baker's dozen, right? You order a dozen scones but get 13 for the same price. Well, *For Dummies* ten-item lists have *roughly* ten items. (If the Dummies Man – the bug-eyed, pale-faced guy suffering from triangle-shape-head syndrome who appears on the back cover of this book and on icons throughout these pages – were running the bakery, a 10-scone order might mean that you get anywhere from 8 to 13 scones.) So exacting that it's scary.

Part VI: Appendixes

An unwritten rule says that computer books have appendixes, so we include four. Appendix A tells you how to install QuickBooks in ten easy steps. Appendix B explains small business accounting, provides a short biography of an Italian monk, and explains double-entry bookkeeping. Appendix C describes how to set up QuickBooks for use by multiple users – and for multiple users on a network. Yikes! Last but not least, Appendix D describes how to print cheques using pre-printed cheques.

Cheat Sheet

We have also included an online Cheat Sheet packed with top secret codes to help you become a more efficient QuickBooks user. You'll find things like fast ways to open and close windows, enter dates, perform calculations, edit transactions, and so on. You can find the Cheat Sheet at this (top secret) url: www.dummies.com/cheatsheet/quickbooks2012uk.

Conventions Used in This Book

To make the best use of your time and energy, you should know about the conventions that we use in this book.

When we want you to type something, such as **Few would dispute that Marmite is an acquired taste**, it's in bold type. When we want you to type something that's short and uncomplicated, such as **Jennifer**, it still appears in boldface type.

Except for passwords, you don't have to worry about the case of the letters you type in QuickBooks. If we tell you to type **Jennifer**, you can type **JENNIFER** or follow poet e. e. cummings' lead and type **jennifer**.

Whenever we tell you to choose a command from a menu, we say something like "Choose Lists⇨Items", which simply means to first choose the Lists menu and then choose Items. The ⇨ separates one part of the command from the next part.

You can choose menus, commands, and dialog box elements with the mouse. Just click the thing you want.

Part I
Quickly into QuickBooks

The 5th Wave   By Rich Tennant

"I bought a software program that should help
us monitor and control our spending habits, and
while I was there, I picked up a few new games,
a couple of screensavers, four new mousepads,
this nifty pullout keyboard cradle..."

In this part . . .

All accounting programs – including QuickBooks – make you do a bunch of preliminary stuff. This may be a bit of a downer, but getting depressed about it won't make things go any faster. So if you want to quickly get up and go with QuickBooks, peruse the chapters in this first part. We promise that we get you through this stuff as quickly as possible.

Chapter 1

QuickBooks: The Heart of Your Business

*W*e'll start this conversation by quickly covering some basic questions concerning QuickBooks, such as "Why even use QuickBooks?", "Where and how do I start?" and, most importantly, "What should I not do?"

This little orientation shouldn't take more than a few minutes. Really. And the orientation lets you understand the *really* big picture concerning QuickBooks.

Why QuickBooks?

Okay, we know you know that you need an accounting system. Somebody, maybe your accountant, friend, or spouse, has convinced you of this. And you, the team player that you are, have just accepted this conventional viewpoint as the truth.

But just between us, why do you *really* need QuickBooks? What does QuickBooks do that you really, truly need done? And just to be truly sceptical, also ask the question "Why QuickBooks?" Why not, for example, use some other accounting software?

Why you need an accounting system

Let's start with the most basic question: why do you even need an accounting system? It's a fair question, so let us supply you with the two-part answer.

The first reason is that it is a legal requirement that you keep accounting records for tax purposes. Maintaining an accounting system – be it a paper-based ledger system, a spreadsheet or fully fledged accounting software – will help you meet your legal obligations. If you decide just to blow off this requirement – after all, you got into business so that you could throw off the shackles of bureaucracy – you might get away with your omission. But if HM Revenue & Customs (HMRC) examines your return and you cannot prove the numbers, HMRC gets to do your accounting the way *it* wants. And you can bet the HMRC way means that you pay more in taxes.

Here's the second reason for maintaining an accounting system. Our strong belief – backed by more than 35 years of business experience and close-hand observations of several hundred business clients – is that you can't successfully manage your business without a decent accounting system. Success requires accurately measuring profits or losses and reasonably estimating your financial position.

This second reason makes sense, right? If your friend Kenneth doesn't know when he's making money, which products or services are profitable, and which customers are worth keeping (and which aren't), does he really have a chance?

We don't think he does.

To summarise, your business must have a decent accounting system, no matter how you feel about accounting and regardless of how time-consuming and expensive such a system is or becomes. Successful business management depends on such an accounting system.

What QuickBooks does

Okay, let's go on to the next question that we need to discuss: what does QuickBooks do to help you maintain an accounting system that measures profits and losses and other stuff like that?

QuickBooks truly makes business accounting easy by providing windows that you use to record common business transactions. For example, QuickBooks has a window (you know, a Windows window that appears on your monitor's screen) that looks like a cheque. To record a cheque, you fill in the blanks of the window with bits of information, such as the date, the amount, and the person or business you're paying.

QuickBooks also has a handful of other windows that you use in a similar fashion. For example, QuickBooks supplies an invoice window that looks like an invoice you might use to bill a customer or client. You fill in the invoice window's blanks by recording invoice information, such as the name of the client or customer, the invoice amount and the date by which you want to be paid.

And here's the great thing about these cheque and invoice windows: when you record business transactions by filling in the blanks shown onscreen, you collect the information that QuickBooks needs to prepare the reports that summarise your profits or losses and your financial position.

For example, if you record two invoices (for £10,000 each) to show amounts that you billed your customers and then you record three cheques (for £4,000 each) for your spending on advertising, rent, and supplies, QuickBooks can (with two or three mouse clicks from you) prepare a report that shows your profit, as shown in Table 1-1.

Table 1-1	A Profit and Loss Report
	Amount
Income	£20,000
Advertising	(£4,000)
Rent	(£4,000)
Supplies	(£4,000)
Total Expenses	(£12,000)
Profit	£8,000

The brackets, by the way, indicate negative amounts. It's an accounting convention, but back to the real point of this little narrative.

Your accounting with QuickBooks can be just as simple as we described in the previous paragraphs. In other words, if you record just a handful of business transactions using the correct QuickBooks windows, you can begin to prepare reports like the one shown in Table 1-1. Such reports can be used to calculate profits or (ugh) losses for last week, last month, or last year. Such reports can also be used to calculate profits and losses for particular customers and products.

This accounting stuff is cool! (For the record, that's the only exclamation point in this chapter.) Good accounting gives you a way of managing your business profitability. And obviously, all sorts of good and wonderful things stem from operating your business profitably: a materially comfortable life for you and your employees; financial cushioning to get you through the tough patches; and profits that can be reinvested in your business, in other businesses, and in community charities.

Let us also mention a couple other handy things that QuickBooks does for you, the overworked business owner or bookkeeper:

- ✔ **E-mail invoices and payslips:** QuickBooks can e-mail invoices to your customers and payslips to your employees in a secure way. This can save you time and money.

- ✔ **Online Filing:** QuickBooks can file your VAT returns online and submit your payroll forms electronically – another timesaver.

- ✔ **Print cheques**: QuickBooks can print your supplier cheques or employee paycheques with a few mouse clicks. If you've had to write 20+ cheques by hand on a regular basis, you know what a timesaver this is.

No Really, Why QuickBooks?

No question about it – you need a good accounting system if you're in business. But you know what? That fact doesn't explain why you should use QuickBooks. (We ignore for one moment that you've probably already purchased QuickBooks.) Therefore, let us suggest to you two reasons why QuickBooks is an excellent choice to use as the foundation of your accounting system:

- ✔ **Ease of use:** QuickBooks historically has been the easiest or one of the easiest accounting software programs to use. Why? The whole just-enter-transaction-information-into-windows-that-resemble-forms thing (which we talked about earlier) makes data entry a breeze. Most business people already know how to fill in the blanks on these forms. That means that most people – that probably includes you, too – know almost everything they need to know to collect the information that they need to do their books with QuickBooks. Over time, other software programs have tended to become more QuickBooks-like in their ease of use. The team at Intuit have truly figured out how to make and keep accounting easy.

We should tell you, however, that there is a downside to the ease-of-use quality of QuickBooks. Part of the reason why QuickBooks is easy to use is because it doesn't possess all the built-in internal control mechanisms that some more traditional accounting systems have. Those internal control mechanisms, of course, make your financial data more secure, but they also make the accounting software more complicated to use.

✔ **Expense:** QuickBooks, especially compared with the hardcore accounting packages that accountants love, is pretty inexpensive. Different versions have different prices, but for a ballpark figure, you can get an excellent accounting software solution for a few hundred quid. Not to go all grandfatherly on you or anything, but not so very long ago inexpensive accounting software packages often cost several thousand quid.

So What's Next?

At this point, presumably, you know why you need accounting software and why QuickBooks is probably a reasonable and maybe even an excellent choice. In other words, you swallowed the line about QuickBooks hook, line, and sinker. That decision on your part leaves the question of what you should do next. In a nutshell, before you can begin working with QuickBooks, you need to do the following:

1. Install the QuickBooks software, as we describe in Appendix A.

2. Run through the QuickBooks Setup we describe in Chapter 2.

3. Load the master files, as we describe in Chapter 3.

If you're thinking, "Hang on, that seems like a bit more work than what's involved in installing spreadsheet software or a new word processor", you're right. You might as well hear the ugly truth about accounting software: Accounting software – all of it – requires quite a bit of setup work to get things running smoothly. For example, you need to build a list of expense categories, or accounts, to use for tracking expenses. You also need to set up a list of the customers that you invoice.

Rest assured, however, that none of the setup work is overly complex; it's just time-consuming. Also, know from the very start that QuickBooks provides a tremendous amount of hand-holding to help you step through the setup process. And remember, too, that you have your new friends – the authors of this book – to help you whenever the setup process gets a little gnarly.

How to Succeed with QuickBooks

Before wrapping up the little why, what, and how discussion of this chapter, we ought to provide a handful of ideas about how to make your experience with QuickBooks a successful one.

Budget wisely, Grasshopper

Here's the first suggestion: Please plan on spending at least a few hours to get the QuickBooks software installed, set up, and running. We know you don't really want to do that. You have a business to run, a family to take care of, a dog to walk, and so on.

But here's the reality sandwich you probably need to take a big bite of: it takes half an hour just to get the software installed on your computer. (This installation isn't complicated, of course. You'll mostly just sit there, sipping tea or whatever.)

But after the QuickBooks software is installed, unfortunately, you still have to run through the QuickBooks Setup process. Again, this work isn't difficult, but it does take time. For example, a very simple service business probably takes at least an hour. If your business keeps stock, or if you're a contractor with some serious job-costing requirements, the process can take several hours.

Therefore, do yourself a favour: Give yourself adequate time for the job at hand.

Don't focus on features

Now here's another little tidbit about getting going with QuickBooks. At the point that you install the QuickBooks software and start the program, you'll be in shock about the number of commands, whistles, bells, and buttons that the QuickBooks window provides. But you know what? You can't focus on the QuickBooks features.

Your job is simply to figure out how to record a handful – probably a small handful – of transactions with QuickBooks. Therefore, what you want to do is focus on the transactions that need to be recorded for you to keep your books.

Say you're a one-person consulting business. In that case, you might need to figure out how to record only the following three types of transaction:

- ✔ Invoices
- ✔ Payments from customers (because you invoiced them)
- ✔ Payments to suppliers (because they sent you bills)

So all you need to do is discover how to record invoices (see Chapter 4), customer payments (see Chapter 5), and write cheques (see Chapter 6). You don't need to worry about much else except maybe how to print reports, but that's easy (see Chapter 15 for the click-by-click instructions).

"Oh," you're saying, "you just intentionally picked an easy business. I'm a retailer with a much more complicated situation."

Okay, well, you're right that we picked an easy business for the first example, but we stand by the same advice for retailers. If you're a retailer, you probably need to figure out how to record only four transactions. Here they are:

- ✔ Sales receipts
- ✔ Bills from your suppliers
- ✔ Payments to your suppliers
- ✔ Employee payroll cheques

In this example, then, all you need to do is find out how to record sales receipts – probably a separate sales receipt for each day – (see Chapter 5), how to record bills from suppliers and cheques to pay your bills (see Chapter 6), and how to handle employee payroll (see Chapter 12).

Not to be cranky or careless here, but one truly good trick for getting up to speed with QuickBooks is to focus on the transactions that you need to record. If you identify those transactions and then figure out how to record them, you've done the hardest part. Really. You can focus on the other stuff (you know, the things that you do periodically like VAT returns and bank reconciliations) once you are up and running.

Get professional help

A quick point: you can probably get an accountant or QuickBooks Professional Advisor (for whom you can search on the Intuit website) to sit down with you for an hour or so and show you how to enter a handful of transactions in QuickBooks. In other words, for a cost that's probably somewhere between

£100 and £200, you can have somebody hold your hand for the first three invoices you create, the first two bills you record, the first four cheques you write, and so on.

You should try to do this if you can. You'll save yourself untold hours of headache by having someone who knows what she or he is doing provide an itty-bit of personalised training.

Use both the profit and loss statement and the balance sheet

And now, the final point: You really want to use your *profit and loss statement* (which measures your profits) and your *balance sheet* (which lists your assets, liabilities, and owner's equity) as part of managing your business. In other words, get used to producing a QuickBooks profit and loss statement each week, month or whatever. Then use that statement to determine your profitability. In a similar fashion, regularly produce a balance sheet to check your cash balances, the amounts customers or clients owe, and so on.

Maybe this advice seems obvious, but there's a semi-hidden reason for this suggestion: if you or you and the bookkeeper do the accounting correctly, both the QuickBooks profit and loss statement and the balance sheet will show numbers that make sense. In other words, the cash balance number on the balance sheet (remember that a balance sheet lists your assets, including cash) will resemble what the bank says you hold in cash. If the QuickBooks balance sheet says instead that you're holding £34 million in cash, well, you'll know something is rotten in the state of Denmark.

Chapter 2

Answering Mr Wizard

. . . .

In This Chapter

▶ Preparing for the QuickBooks Setup

▶ Walking through the QuickBooks Setup

▶ Taking care of post-Setup tasks

. . . .

We know that you're eager to get started. After all, you have a business to run. But before you can start using QuickBooks, you need to do some upfront work. Specifically, you need to prepare for the QuickBooks Setup. Then you need to walk through the Setup steps. In this chapter, we describe how you do all this.

We assume that you know how Windows works. If you don't, take the time to read Chapter 1 of your Windows user's guide or try the appropriate edition of *Windows For Dummies,* by Andy Rathbone.

Getting Ready for the QuickBooks Setup

You need to complete three tasks to get ready for the QuickBooks Setup:

✔ Make an important decision about your *conversion date* (the date you convert from your old accounting system to QuickBooks).

✔ Prepare a trial balance as of the conversion date.

✔ Go on a scavenger hunt to collect the information that you'll need.

The big decision

Before you fiddle with your computer or the QuickBooks software, you need to choose the date – the *conversion date* – on which you want to begin using QuickBooks for your financial record keeping.

This decision is hugely important because the conversion date that you choose dramatically affects both the work you have to do to get QuickBooks running smoothly and the initial usefulness of the financial information that you collect and record by using QuickBooks.

You have three basic choices:

- ✓ **The right way:** You can convert at the beginning of your accounting year (also referred to as a *financial year*). This way is the right way for two reasons. First, converting at the beginning of the year requires the least amount of work from you. Second, it means that you have all the current year's financial information in one system.

- ✓ **The slightly awkward way:** You can convert at the beginning of some interim accounting period (for example, the beginning of a VAT quarter). This approach works, but it's slightly awkward because you have to plug your year-to-date income and expenses numbers from the old system into the new system. (If you don't know what an interim accounting period is, see Appendix B.)

- ✓ **The my-way-or-the-highway way:** You can convert at some time other than what we call the right way and the slightly awkward way. Specifically, you can choose to convert whenever you jolly well feel like it. You create a lot of unnecessary work for yourself if you take this approach, and you pull out a bunch of your hair in the process, but you also have the satisfaction of knowing that through it all you did it your way – without any help from us.

We recommend choosing the right way. What this choice means is that if it's late in the accounting year, you wait until the first day of the next year to convert to QuickBooks. If it's still early in the accounting year, you can retro-actively convert from the beginning of the accounting year. If you do this, you need to enter your financial records for the first part of the current year in QuickBooks. This means entering sales, recording purchases, and so on.

If it's some time in the middle of the accounting year, you probably want to use the slightly awkward way. We are actually going to use the slightly awk-ward way in this chapter and the next chapter because if you see how to con-vert to QuickBooks by using the slightly awkward way, you know how to use both the right way and the slightly awkward way.

The trial balance of the century

After you decide when you want to convert, you need a trial balance.

"Yikes", you say. "What's a trial balance?" A *trial balance* simply lists all your assets, liabilities, and owner's equity account balances as well as the year-to-date income and expense numbers on a specified date (which, not coincidentally, happens to be the conversion date). You need this data for the QuickBooks Setup and for some fiddling around that you need to do after you complete the QuickBooks Setup.

Just to split hairs, the trial balance should show account balances at the very start of the first day that you'll begin using QuickBooks for actual accounting. For example, if the conversion date is 1/1/2012, the trial balance needs to show the account balances at one minute past midnight on 1/1/2012. This is also the very same thing as showing the account balances at the very end of the last day that you'll be using the old accounting system – in other words, at exactly midnight on 31/12/2011 if you're converting to QuickBooks on 1/1/2012.

Just for fun, we created the sample trial balance shown in Table 2-1. This table shows you what a trial balance looks like if you convert at the very beginning of the accounting year.

Table 2-1	A "Right Way" Sample Trial Balance		
Trial Balance Information		*Debit*	*Credit*
Assets			
Fixed assets		£60,000	
Accumulated depreciation (fixed assets)			£3,000
Current account		£5,000	
Accounts receivable		£8,000	
Liabilities			
Accounts payable			£6,000
VAT liability			£2,000
Loan payable			£10,000
Owner's equity			
Owner's Equity			£52,000
Totals		£73,000	£73,000

Creating a trial balance like the one in Table 2-1 need not be difficult. In fact, it may be as simple as asking your accountant for a copy of last accounting year's trial balance.

In case you're wondering what we mean by accounts receivable and accounts payable (in Table 2-1), QuickBooks calls the Trade Debtor account *accounts receivable*, and the Trade Creditor account, *accounts payable*. So accounts receivable is where QuickBooks keeps track of what customers owe you, and accounts payable is where QuickBooks tracks what you owe your suppliers.

If you are still in the first year of trading and have not reached the end of your financial year, you don't need to worry about a trial balance. Instead, you can simply enter into QuickBooks all your financial transactions, like sales, purchases, and so on, from the day you started trading.

If you're using the slightly awkward way to convert to QuickBooks – in other words, if your conversion date is some date other than the beginning of the accounting year – you also need to provide year-to-date income and expense balances. To get your income, cost of goods sold, expenses, other income, and other expense account balances, you need to calculate the year-to-date amount of each account. If you can get this information from your old accounting system, that's super. If not, you need to get it manually. (If you suddenly have images of yourself sitting at your desk late at night, tapping away on a numeric keypad, you're probably right. What's more, you probably also need to allocate half of another Saturday to getting QuickBooks up and running.)

If you're converting at some time other than the beginning of the accounting year, your trial balance looks like the one shown in Table 2-2. Notice the year-to-date income and expense balances.

Table 2-2 A "Slightly Awkward Way" Sample Trial Balance

Trial Balance Information	Debit	Credit
Assets		
Fixed assets	£60,000	
Accumulated depreciation (fixed assets)		£3,000
Current account	£5,000	
Accounts receivable	£8,000	
Liabilities		
Accounts payable		£6,000
VAT liability		£2,000

Trial Balance Information	Debit	Credit
Loan payable		£10,000
Owner's equity and income statement information		
Owner's Equity		£19,000
Sales		£60,000
Cost of goods sold	£20,000	
Supplies expense	£2,100	
Rent expense	£4,900	
Totals	£100,000	£100,000

If you have to prepare these figures manually (in other words you cannot get them from your previous accounting system), here's what you'll need to do:

- **To get your fixed asset account balances:** Know what each asset originally costs. For depreciable fixed assets, you also need to provide any accumulated depreciation that has been claimed for that asset. (*Accumulated depreciation* is the total depreciation that you've already expensed for each asset.) Your accountant may have these figures to hand.

  By the way, check out Appendix B if you have questions about accounting or accounting terminology, such as *depreciation*.

- **To get your cash balance:** Reconcile your bank account or bank accounts (if you have more than one bank account) as of the conversion date.

- **To get your accounts receivable balance:** Tally the total of all your unpaid customer invoices. To do this track down copies of all the unpaid invoices that your customers (or clients or patients or whatever) owe you as of the conversion date.

- **To get your other asset account balances:** Know the balance of any loans made by the business, and the value of stock that you hold.

- **To get your accounts payable balance:** Tally the total of all your unpaid supplier invoices. To do this track down copies of all the unpaid bills you owe your suppliers as of the conversion date.

- **To get your other liability account balances:** Know how much you owe on each liability, for example bank loans, VAT, and so on.

About those debits and credits

Don't be anxious about those debits and credits. You just need to keep them straight for a few minutes. For assets and expenses, a *debit balance* is the same thing as a positive balance. So, a cash debit balance of £5,000 means that you have £5,000 in your account, and £20,000 of cost of goods sold means that you incurred £20,000 of costs-of-goods expense. For assets and expenses, a *credit balance* is the same thing as a negative balance. So if you have a cash balance of –£5,000, your account is overdrawn by £5,000. In the sample trial balance shown in Table 2-1, the accumulated depreciation shows a credit balance of £3,000, which is, in effect, a negative account balance.

For liabilities, owner's equity accounts and income accounts, things are flip-flopped. A credit balance is the same thing as a positive balance. So an accounts payable credit balance of £6,000 means that you owe your creditors £6,000. A bank loan credit balance of £10,000 means that you owe the bank £10,000. And a sales account credit balance of £60,000 means that you've enjoyed £60,000 worth of sales.

Sorry to keep repeating it, but do remember that those income and expense account balances are year-to-date figures. They exist *only* if the conversion date is after the start of the financial year.

You don't need to worry about the owner's equity accounts. QuickBooks can calculate your owner's equity account balances for you, based on the difference between your total assets and your total liabilities. This method is a bit sloppy, and accountants may not like it, but it's a pretty good compromise. (If you do have detailed account balances for your owner's equity accounts, use these figures – and know that you're one in a million.)

The mother of all scavenger hunts

Even after you decide when you want to convert to QuickBooks and you come up with a trial balance, you still need to collect a bunch of additional information:

- ✔ **Company and VAT registration numbers:** If your business is a limited company incorporated at Companies House you will have a company registration number, and if your business is registered for VAT with HMRC, you will have a VAT registration number. QuickBooks asks for your company number and VAT registration number so have these to hand.

- ✔ **Copies of all the unpaid invoices that your customers owe you as of the conversion date:** This is probably obvious, but the total accounts receivable balance shown on your trial balance needs to match the total of the unpaid customer invoices.

- ✔ **Copies of all unpaid bills that you owe your suppliers as of the conversion date:** Again, this is probably obvious, but the total accounts payable balance shown on your trial balance needs to match the total of the unpaid supplier bills.

- ✔ **A detailed listing of any stock items you're holding for resale:** This list should include not only stock item descriptions and quantities but also the initial purchase prices and the anticipated sales prices. In other words, if you sell porcelain wombats and you have 1,200 of these beauties in stock, you need to know exactly what you paid for them (or how much they cost you to make).

- ✔ **A summary of your VAT liabilities for Boxes 1, 2, and 4 as of the conversion date:** You can get this from your old accounting system, or you can tally the figures by hand. Box 1 is the total VAT owed on sales, Box 2 is the VAT on goods bought from the EC (European Community) area (if any), and Box 4 is the total VAT to be reclaimed on purchases, as of the conversion date. And don't forget that any VAT which should have been reported in prior VAT returns but was not for whatever reason needs to be added to the VAT figures for Boxes 1, 2, or 4 as of the conversion date. Don't worry; we explain what you need to gather in more detail in Chapter 3.

- ✔ **Year-to-date P11 figures for each person employed as of the conversion date and a breakdown of payroll tax liabilities you owe as of the conversion date:** You need the information shown on the P11 forms to adequately and accurately set up the QuickBooks payroll feature. Not to scare you, but this is probably the most tedious part of setting up QuickBooks. We cover the payroll setup in Chapter 12.

- ✔ **If you're retroactively converting as of the beginning of the year, you need a list of all the transactions (sales, purchases, payroll transactions, and everything and anything else) that have occurred since the beginning of the year:** If you do the right-way conversion retroactively, you need to re-enter each of these transactions into the new system. You actually enter the information after you complete the QuickBooks Setup that we describe later in this chapter, but you might as well get all this information together now (if you can), while you're searching for the rest of the items in this scavenger hunt.

If you take the slightly awkward way, you don't need to find the last item in the preceding list. You can just use the year-to-date income and expense numbers from the trial balance.

Stepping through the QuickBooks Setup

After you decide when you want to convert, prepare a trial balance as of the conversion date and collect the additional raw data that you need, you're ready to step through the QuickBooks Setup. You need to start QuickBooks and then walk through the steps.

Starting QuickBooks

To start QuickBooks 2012, click the Windows Start button and then click the menu choice that leads to your QuickBooks software. (For example, we choose Start⇨All Programs⇨QuickBooks⇨QuickBooks Premier - Accountant Edition 2012.) Or double-click the QuickBooks program icon if you put one on the desktop during the installation.

QuickBooks comes in three flavours: QuickBooks SimpleStart, QuickBooks Pro, and QuickBooks Premier. These programs differ in several significant ways: QuickBooks SimpleStart is a special "light" version of QuickBooks, which looks completely different. QuickBooks Pro includes time-estimating features, briefly described in Chapter 16; it also includes the capability to share a QuickBooks file over a network, as we describe in Appendix C. QuickBooks Premier has features beyond the QuickBooks Pro features, including stock backorders, multiple units of measure, and features useful for accountants and auditors who want to use QuickBooks for larger small businesses.

As we mentioned earlier, we used the QuickBooks Premier – Accountant Edition to write this book. This is simply QuickBooks Premier, but instead of calling it QuickBooks Premier, Intuit (the makers of QuickBooks) decided to call it QuickBooks Premier – Accountant Edition (rolls right off the tongue, doesn't it?). Remember, you can use this book for both QuickBooks Pro and QuickBooks Premier.

If this is the first time you have started QuickBooks, QuickBooks displays the QuickBooks Setup window with the message "Let's get your business set up quickly!" (see Figure 2-1).

If you've already been using an earlier version of QuickBooks, QuickBooks should prompt you to open (and possibly convert) an existing file – and you don't need to be reading this chapter.

If you aren't starting QuickBooks for the first time but you want to step through the QuickBooks Setup to set up a new company, choose File⇨New Company.

Figure 2-1:
The first
QuickBooks
Setup
window.

The first QuickBooks Setup dialog box includes an Advanced Setup button you can use to get started. A simple bit of advice: don't fiddle with the Advanced Setup unless you're an accounting expert.

Using the Express Setup

QuickBooks 2012 provides a much accelerated setup process compared with past versions of the software. Basically, you'll fill in some boxes, click some buttons and, *voilà!*, you find that you've largely set up QuickBooks. Because we can give you some tips, identify some shortcuts and warn you of some traps you want to avoid, we're going to provide step-by-step instructions.

1. **Choose to use the Express Setup.**

   With the first QuickBooks Setup dialog box displayed (refer to Figure 2-1), click the Express Start button. QuickBooks displays the Tell Us about Your Business dialog box (see Figure 2-2).

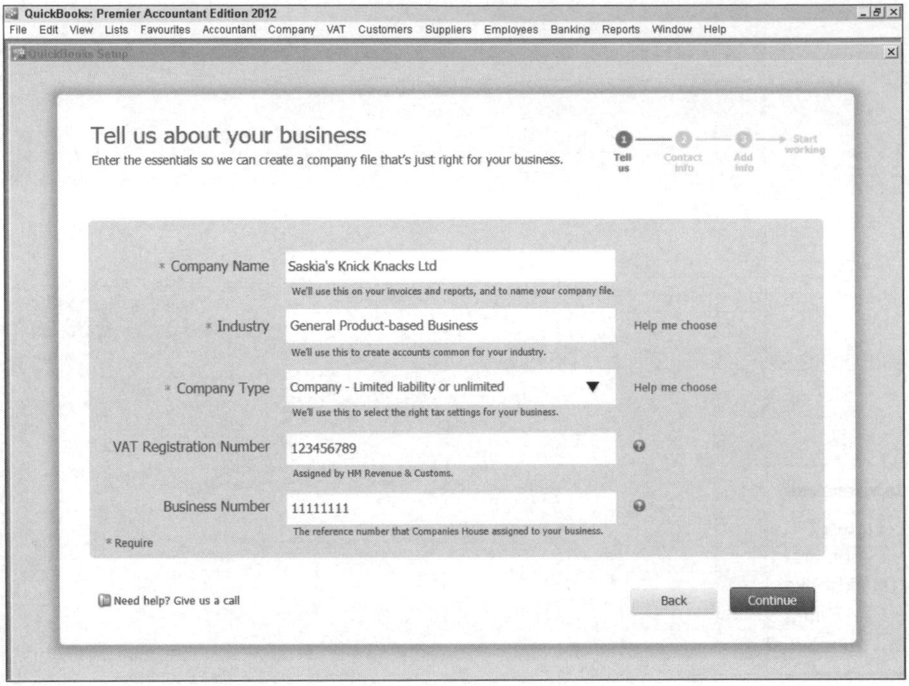

QuickBooks Setup

Tell us about your business

Enter the essentials so we can create a company file that's just right for your business.

① ─── ② ─── ③ ─➤ Start working
Tell us   Contact Info   Add Info

* Company Name   Saskia's Knick Knacks Ltd
We'll use this on your invoices and reports, and to name your company file.

* Industry   General Product-based Business   Help me choose
We'll use this to create accounts common for your industry.

* Company Type   Company - Limited liability or unlimited   ▼   Help me choose
We'll use this to select the right tax settings for your business.

VAT Registration Number   123456789   ❓
Assigned by HM Revenue & Customs.

Business Number   11111111   ❓
The reference number that Companies House assigned to your business.

* Require

🖥 Need help? Give us a call   Back   Continue

Figure 2-2:
The Tell Us about Your Business dialog box.

2. **Specify the company name.**

   The name you specify goes on QuickBooks reports and appears on invoices you send customers. Accordingly, you want to use your "real" business name. And if your business is incorporated as a limited liability company, you want to use the right suffix in your name. For example, don't use *Acme Supplies* but rather *Acme Supplies Limited* or *Acme Supplies Ltd.*

   Note: QuickBooks also uses the company name for the QuickBooks data file.

3. **Identify your industry.**

   For example, if you're in the construction business, type **construction.** When you type something into the Industry field, QuickBooks displays (below the field) a list of all the various industries that it recognises. QuickBooks will not make any suggestions if it does not have a match for your industry. What's more, if you try to move away from the industry field you will see the message "Invalid Industry. Please enter another or click Help me choose". Click Help Me Choose and select the industry closest to yours from the list. If you don't see a suitable choice, scroll to the bottom of the list and choose General Product-based Business or General Service-based Business.

Be careful about the industry you specify. QuickBooks sets up a starting chart of accounts for you based on the industry. A chart of accounts lists the asset, liability, income, and expense accounts (or categories) that QuickBooks will use to categorise your business's finances. But don't panic; you can change the chart of accounts later.

4. **Select the company type.**

   Click the drop-down arrow in this field and select from the list that QuickBooks provides.

5. **Enter a VAT registration number (optional).**

   If you are registered for VAT with HM Revenue & Customs, enter your nine-digit VAT registration number. Don't worry if you don't have it to hand; you can enter this information later (see Chapter 3).

6. **Enter a business number (optional).**

   If your business is incorporated with Companies House, type in your eight-digit registration number. Again, don't worry if you don't have it to hand; you can enter this information later (see Chapter 3).

7. **Click Continue.**

8. **Supply your business contact information.**

   When QuickBooks displays the Enter Your Business Contact Information dialog box (see Figure 2-3), verify that the correct business name shows in the Legal Name field. Then fill in the rest of the address and contact information. I hope you don't feel cheated but we won't give you instructions like "Enter your street address into the Address box" and "Please remember that your telephone number goes into the Phone box".

   If you ever decide that you want to change some piece of information that you entered on a previous page of the QuickBooks Setup dialog box, you can just click the Back button to back up.

   If you're an observant person, you may have noticed the Preview Your Settings button that appears on the Enter Your Business Contact Information dialog box. You can safely ignore this button, but if you're a truly curious cat, go ahead and click the button. QuickBooks will then display a dialog box that identifies which standard QuickBooks features the QuickBooks Setup process is turning on and which asset, liability, income and expense accounts will initially appear on your chart of accounts. You can untick any accounts you do not want included in your Chart of Accounts during the Setup process (and you can always edit, add, or delete accounts later). Oh, one other thing: The Preview Your Company Settings dialog box also provides a Company File Location tab that identifies where your QuickBooks data file will be located.

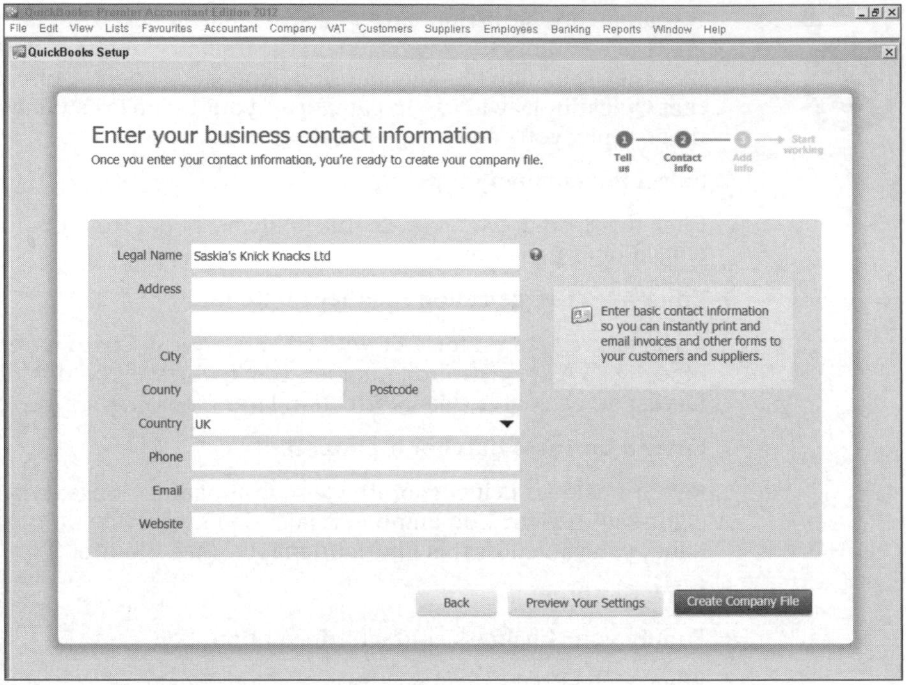

Figure 2-3:
The Enter
Your
Business
Contact
Information
dialog box.

9. **Create the QuickBooks data file.**

   After you provide the business contact information requested by QuickBooks, click the Create Company File button. QuickBooks creates the data file it will use to store your financial information. (In some versions of QuickBooks, the file creation process takes a few minutes.) When QuickBooks finishes creating your file, it displays the You've Got a Company File! dialog box (see Figure 2-4).

10. **Identify your customers and suppliers.**

   With the You've Got a Company File! dialog box displayed, click the Add More button to the right of Add the People You Do Business With. "Hang on", you say. "Why does the button show 'Add More'? Why do I see the message 'You've added 1 supplier' beneath Add the People You Do Business With? I don't remember adding any suppliers." You're right, you didn't. When QuickBooks creates the company file it always adds two suppliers (not one as the message states) – HM Revenue & Customs and HMRC VAT – to the supplier list. Anyway, when you click the Add More button, QuickBooks displays a dialog box that asks, "Perchance, are contact names and addresses stored electronically someplace else like Outlook, Yahoo, or Gmail?"

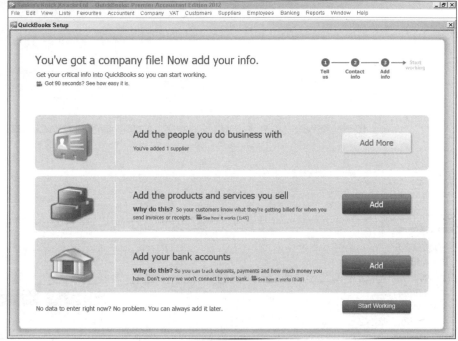

Figure 2-4:
The You've
Got a
Company
File! dialog
box.

- *If you do have contact name and address information stored some-place else that QuickBooks will retrieve:* click the appropriate button and follow the onscreen instructions.

- *Otherwise:* click the Paste from Excel or Enter Manually button and then Continue.

When QuickBooks displays the Add the People You Do Business With dialog box (see Figure 2-5), use the rows of the displayed worksheet to describe your customers and suppliers. To enter a contact into the next empty row:

   a. *Select the Customer or Supplier radio button (as appropriate).*

   b. *Describe the contact using the fields provided:* Name, Company Name, First Name, Last Name, Email, Phone, and so forth. Each contact goes into its own row.

Click the Continue button when you finish identifying your contacts.

On the following screen QuickBooks asks whether you want to enter opening balances.

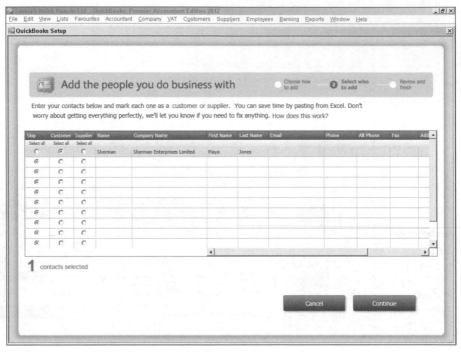

Figure 2-5:
The Add the
People You
Do Business
With dialog
box.

If your business operates with the cash-accounting VAT scheme **do not** enter opening customer and supplier balances in the QuickBooks Setup process because the VAT will not be handled correctly. You need to enter each unpaid customer invoice and each unpaid supplier bill individually as we describe in Chapters 4 and 6, respectively.

To enter opening balances, click the Enter Opening Balances link. For each

- *Customer:* tally the invoices you issued to that customer that remain unpaid as of the conversion date.

- *Supplier:* tally the bills received from that supplier that remain unpaid as of the conversion date.

Click Continue twice to return to the You've Got a Company File! dialog box.

In the Name column provide a short abbreviated name or nickname for a contact. You'll use what you specify in the Name column within QuickBooks to refer to the contact, so you want to use something short and sweet. For example, if you're working with, say, customer Maya Jones at Sherman Enterprises Limited, you might enter **Sherman** into the Name column, **Sherman Enterprises Limited** into the Company Name column, **Maya** into the First Name column, and so forth.

Each name in the customer and supplier list must be unique. If a contact is both a customer and a supplier, you can use, for example, Joe Bloggs_c (customer) and Joe Bloggs_s (supplier) in the Name column.

You may as well know now that this is the simplest way of dealing with opening customer and supplier balances if you are not VAT registered, or if you are VAT registered and use the accrual VAT reporting method. But there is a price to pay for this simplicity. The price is that you will not be able to allocate customer payments against specific invoices or specify which supplier bills you are paying. If this is a trade-off you are unwilling to make, you can enter each individual unpaid customer invoice (Chapter 4) and supplier bill (Chapter 6).

11. **Identify the items (the stuff) you sell.**

With the You've Got a Company File! dialog box displayed (Figure 2-4), click the Add button in the Add Products and Services You Sell row. QuickBooks displays another dialog box that asks what kind of stuff you want to describe: services, stock parts (stuff that you track in stock), non-stock parts (stuff that you don't track in stock), and so on. (Which items QuickBooks lists depends on the industry that you specified in Step 3.) Make the appropriate selection.

When QuickBooks displays the Add the Products and Services You Sell dialog box (see Figure 2-6), use the rows of the displayed worksheet to describe the product or service. For every item, you'll enter a name, a description and a price. For some types of item, however, you can specify more detail than just this skeletal information. Click the Continue button when you finish identifying your products and services to return to the You've Got a Company File! dialog box.

The Setup process captures limited information about each stock part item, and makes a number of assumptions on your behalf. It's a fast and simple way to get you going and it may be a good choice if you are just starting out with QuickBooks. If you are looking for more options and control, you are better off adding stock part items as we describe in Chapter 3.

12. **Describe your bank accounts.**

With the You've Got a Company File! dialog box displayed (Figure 2-4), click the Add button in the Add Your Bank Accounts row. When QuickBooks displays the Add Your Bank Accounts dialog box (see Figure 2-7), use the worksheet to describe each bank account of your business: its name, account number, bank statement balance at the conversion date and the conversion date. Click Continue when you finish identifying your bank accounts. QuickBooks then asks if you wish to return to the You've Got a Company File! dialog box.

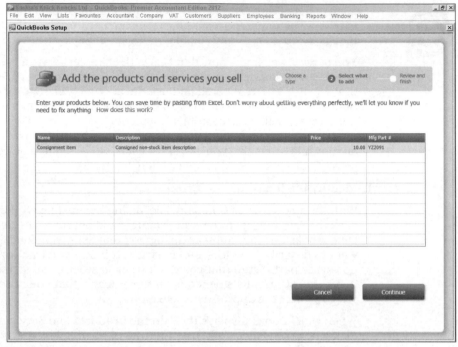

Figure 2-6:
The Add the
Products
and
Services
You Sell dia-
log box.

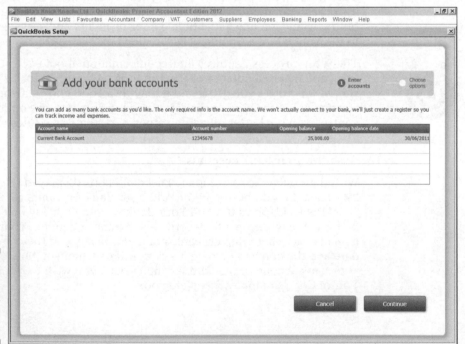

Figure 2-7:
The Add
Your Bank
Accounts
dialog box.

13. **Start working with QuickBooks.**

    With the You've Got a Company File dialog box displayed, click the Start Working button. QuickBooks displays the QuickBooks program window. You're done.

Setting Your Financial Year

The first thing you should do after you finish the QuickBooks Setup (besides celebrate) is to let QuickBooks know in what month your financial year and payroll tax year (if applicable) begins. QuickBooks needs this information to produce accurate financial reports, such as the profit and loss report for a financial year.

You do this by clicking Company:⇨Company Information. In the Report Information area of the Company Information window (see Figure 2-8), select the drop-down arrow next to the Financial Year field and choose the first month of your financial year. Next, click the down arrow next to the Tax Year field and select April. The Tax Year field refers to the payroll tax year which begins on 6 April of one year and ends on 5 April of the following year.

You can also enter your company details like address, phone number, and so on in this window if you have not already done this in the QuickBooks Setup process.

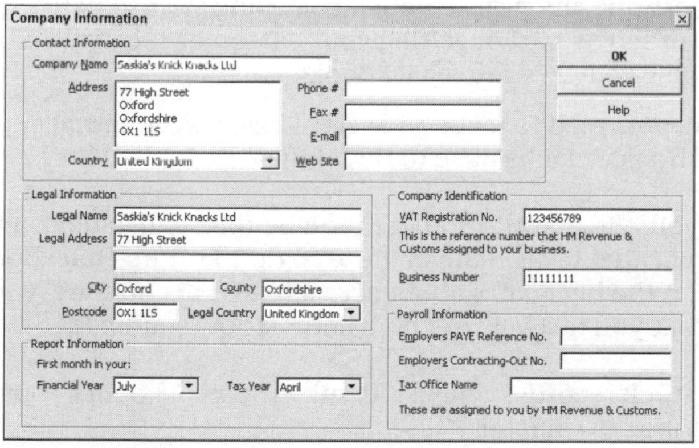

Figure 2-8: The Company Information window.

Registering QuickBooks

At some point after QuickBooks starts, you will see a message box that asks whether you want to register QuickBooks. If you don't register, you can use the product roughly a few times and then – wham! The program locks up and you can no longer access your files. Either you register it, or you can't use it. No one likes being forced to do something, but getting worked up about having to register QuickBooks is a waste of time.

The simplest option is to just register. Here's how: when QuickBooks displays the message box that asks whether you want to register, click the Online button to register online or click the Phone button to register over the phone. If you go with the Phone option, QuickBooks displays another dialog box that gives you a telephone number to call and provides a space for you to enter your registration number.

The Rest of the Story

Throughout the preceding sections in this chapter, we describe how you prepare for and then step through the QuickBooks Setup process. After you complete the QuickBooks Setup, you still have a few tasks to take care of:

- ✔ If you chose not to enter opening balances in the QuickBooks Setup, you need to describe in detail your stock, your customer receivables, and (if you choose to track supplier bills you owe) your supplier payables.

- ✔ If you are VAT registered, you need to describe your VAT liability (or refund) balance.

- ✔ You also need to load all the remaining balances in the QuickBooks trial balance, and if you are doing this the "slightly awkward way" you also need to describe any year-to-date income and year-to-date expenses that aren't recorded as part of getting your customer receivables and supplier payables entered into QuickBooks.

- ✔ At the end you need to make an accrual-based accounting adjustment to the QuickBooks trial balance to tidy things up.

We won't kid you, the first three chores can be time consuming, and they are the most complicated tasks that you need to do to set up QuickBooks. (If you aren't sure what the big deal is about accrual-basis accounting, we respectfully suggest that you take a break here and read Appendix B.)

To set up the stock records, you just identify the item counts you hold in stock, as described in Chapter 3.

To set up your customer receivables and (if necessary) supplier payables, you first need to enter customer invoices that were prepared prior to the conversion date but that are still uncollected at conversion. Similarly, you may need to enter supplier payables that were incurred prior to the conversion date but that are still unpaid at conversion. We describe how to do that in Chapter 3.

To set up your beginning VAT balances you enter the VAT amounts for Boxes 1, 2, and 4 of your VAT return, also described in Chapter 3.

So if you're still okay with doing some more installation and setup work, go ahead and flip to Chapter 3. However . . .

Should You Get Your Accountant's Help?

So, should you get help from your accountant? If you follow our directions carefully (both in this chapter and the next) and your business financial affairs aren't wildly complex, you can probably figure out all this stuff on your own.

Having said that, however, we suggest that you seriously consider getting your accountant's help at this juncture. Some of the setup tasks can be tricky to get right (like the VAT balances, for example). Your accountant probably knows your business and can keep you from making a terrible mess of things, just in case you don't follow our directions carefully. He or she can do a much better job of giving you advice specific to your situation. As mentioned before, your accountant may be able to give you beginning trial balance figures. But you may also decide that you're more comfortable (and it's more efficient) for your accountant to load your trial balance into QuickBooks.

Just so you know: one of the things that we do for our clients is help them set up QuickBooks. Because we do this we can give you a couple of pieces of useful information about getting help in setting up. The first is that if your accountant does not know QuickBooks, it's worth your while to find a local QuickBooks Professional Advisor (QPA) by searching this website: `proadvisors .quickbooks.co.uk`. The QPA should be able to guide you through the setup process in an hour or two, or do the setup much faster than you can on your own. Second, a few hours of tutoring from a QPA should mean that you get enough help to record all your usual transactions. With just this help, you can find out how to pay your bills, how to invoice customers exactly the way you want, and how to produce reports. A bit of planning and expert advice in the beginning can save you a whole lot of trouble later.

Chapter 3

Populating QuickBooks Lists

The QuickBooks Setup process (which we discuss at some length in Chapter 2) doesn't actually get QuickBooks completely ready to use. You also need to enter additional information about your products, employees, customers, and suppliers (and a handful of other items) into lists. In this chapter, we describe how you create and work with these lists. We also describe how you clean up some of the accounting messiness created when you enter information into these lists.

The Magic and Mystery of Items

The first QuickBooks list you need to finish setting up is the *Item list* – the list of stuff you buy and sell. Before you start adding to your Item list, however, you need to know that QuickBooks isn't very smart about its view of what you buy and sell. It thinks that anything you stick on a sales invoice or a purchase order is something you're selling.

If you sell colourful coffee mugs, for example, you probably figure (and correctly so) that you need to add descriptions of each of these items to the Item list. However, if you add delivery charges to an invoice, QuickBooks thinks that you're adding another mug. And if you add a discount to an invoice, well, guess what? QuickBooks again thinks that you're adding another mug.

This wacky definition of items is confusing at first. But just remember one thing, and you'll be okay: you aren't the one who's stupid; QuickBooks is. No, we are not saying that QuickBooks is a bad program. It's a wonderful accounting program and a great tool. What we are saying is that QuickBooks is only a dumb computer program; it isn't an artificial-intelligence program. It doesn't pick up on the little subtleties of business – such as the fact that even though you charge customers for delivery, you aren't really in the shipping business.

Each entry on the invoice or purchase order – the mugs that you sell, the subtotal, the discount, the delivery charges, and the VAT – is an *item*. Yes, we know this setup is weird, but getting used to the wackiness now makes the discussions that follow much easier to understand.

If you want to see a sample invoice, take a peek at Figure 3-1. Just so you're not confused, to make more room for the invoice window, we removed the QuickBooks Open Windows list that typically appears along the left edge of the QuickBooks window.

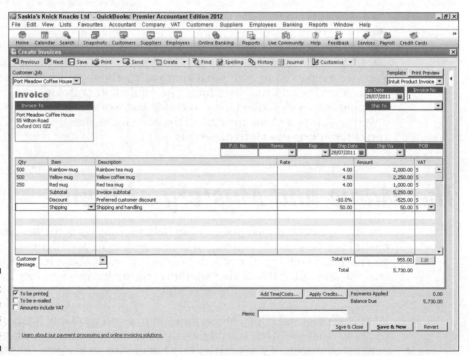

Figure 3-1:
A sample QuickBooks invoice.

Do you see those first three items: Rainbow tea mug, Yellow mug, and Red mug? You can see the sense of calling them *items,* right? These mugs are things that you sell.

But then suppose that you give frequent buyers of your merchandise a 10 percent discount. To include this discount in your accounting, you need to add a Subtotal item to tally the sale and a Discount item to calculate the discount. Figure 3-1 also shows this. See it? Kind of weird?

Then look at the Shipping and Handling item, which charges the customer £50 for delivery. Yes, that's right – another item. In sum, everything that appears on an invoice or a purchase order is an item that you need to describe in your Item list.

Just above the invoice total, if you look closely, you can see another item for including VAT on your invoices – and that's really an item, too.

We describe creating invoices in Chapter 4 and creating purchase orders in Chapter 7.

Adding items you might include on invoices

You may have added some items as part of the QuickBooks Setup process, but you'll want to know how to add any other needed items and how to add new items. To add invoice or purchase order items to the Item list, follow these steps:

1. **Choose Lists⇨Item List.**

   QuickBooks displays the Item List window, as shown in Figure 3-2.

2. **Click the Item button at the bottom of the Item List window and then choose New from the drop-down list.**

   When QuickBooks asks whether you want to set up multiple items, indicate "No way, mate" by clicking OK.

   If you reply, "Why yes, thank you very much" by clicking Take Me There, QuickBooks displays a worksheet (like the one used during the QuickBooks Setup process we describe in Chapter 2) that you can use to set up multiple items in one fell swoop. If you don't want QuickBooks to ask you this question every time you add a new item, just add a tick mark in the box next to Do Not Display This Message in the Future;

you can always recall the Multiple Item worksheet by clicking the Item button (at the bottom of the Item List), and selecting Add/Edit Multiple Items.

QuickBooks displays the New Item window, as shown in Figure 3-3.

Figure 3-2:
The QuickBooks Item List window.

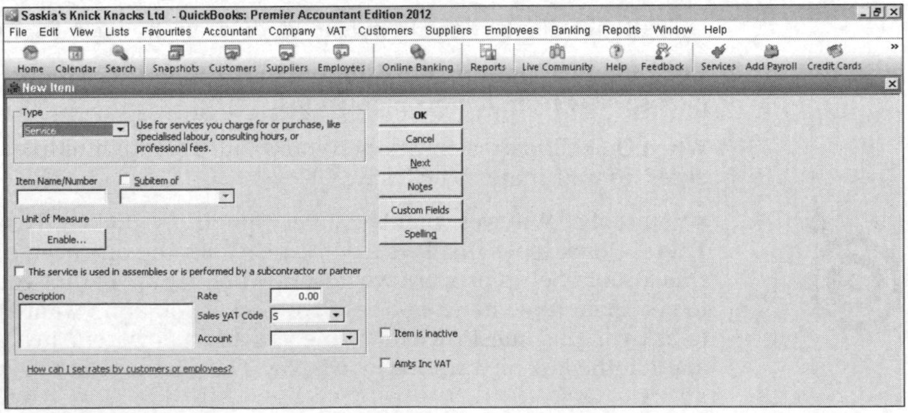

Figure 3-3:
The QuickBooks New Item window.

3. Categorise the item.

Select an item type from the Type drop-down list. The Item list that you see is dependent on the type of business you told QuickBooks you were in when you set up the program, so use the following as a sample – the type of items and the number of items that you need depend on the nature of your business, of course. Select one of the following item types by clicking the name in the list:

- *Service:* Select this type if you charge for a service – such as an hour of labour or a repair job.

- *Stock Part:* Select this type if what you sell is something that you buy from someone else, and you want to track your holdings of the item. If you sell thingamajigs that you purchase from the manufacturer Thingamajigs Limited, for example, you specify the item type as Stock Part. (For more information on using QuickBooks to track stock, see Chapter 7.)

- *Stock Assembly:* Select this type if what you sell is something that you make from other stock items. In other words, if you buy raw materials or other components and then assemble these things to create your finished product, the finished product is a Stock Assembly item.

- *Non-stock Part:* Select this type if what you sell is something that you don't want to track as stock. (You usually don't use this item type for products that you sell, by the way. Instead, you use it for items that you buy for the business and need to include on purchase orders, such as office supplies.)

- *Other Charge:* Select this item type for things such as delivery and handling charges that you include on invoices.

- *Subtotal:* This item type adds everything before you subtract any discount.

- *Group:* Use this item type to enter a bunch of items (which are already on the list) at one time. This item is a nice timesaver. For example, if you commonly sell sets of items, you don't have to specify those items individually every time you write an invoice.

- *Discount:* This item type calculates an amount to be subtracted from an item or the subtotal of multiple items.

- *Payment:* This option is wacky, but if your invoice sometimes includes an entry that reduces the invoice total – customer deposits at the time of sale, for example – select this item type. If this item type confuses you, just ignore it.

- *VAT Item:* This item is used by QuickBooks to account for VAT on invoices and purchases. We discuss VAT items in Chapter 11.

- *VAT Group:* This item type is used by QuickBooks to calculate and individually track two or more VAT items that apply to the same sale or purchase, as is the case for EC sales, purchases and so on. Again, flip to Chapter 11 for a discussion on VAT.

4. **Type an item number or name.**

   Press the Tab key or use your mouse to click the Item Name/Number text box below the Type drop-down list. Then type a short description of the item.

5. **(Optional) Make the item a subitem.**

   If you want to work with *subitems* – items that appear within other items – select the Subitem Of check box and use the corresponding drop-down list to specify the parent item to which a subitem belongs.

   If you set up a parent item for coffee mugs and subitems for red, yellow, and rainbow mugs, for example, you can produce reports that show parent items (such as mugs) and subitems (such as the differently coloured mugs). Subitems are just an extra complexity, so if you're new to this QuickBooks stuff, we suggest that you keep things simple by avoiding them.

6. **Describe the item in more detail.**

   Move the cursor to the Description text box and type a description. This description then appears on the invoice. Note that if you specified the item type as Stock Part in Step 3, you see two description text boxes (see Figure 3-4): Description on Purchase Transactions and Description on Sales Transactions. The purchase description appears on purchase orders and the sales description appears on sales invoices.

7. **If the item type is Service, Non-stock Part, or Other Charge, tell QuickBooks how much to charge for the item, whether the item is subject to VAT, and which income account to use for tracking the income you receive from selling the item.**

   - *For a Service type,* use the Rate text box to specify the price you charge for one unit of the service. If you charge by the hour, for example, the rate is the charge for an hour of service. If you charge for a job – such as a repair job or the completion of a specific task – the rate is the charge for the job or task.

   - *For a Non-stock Part type,* use the Price text box to specify the amount you charge for the item. (The Price text box replaces the Rate text box.)

   - *For an Other Charge type,* use the Amount or % text box, which replaces the Rate text box, to specify the amount you charge for the item. You can type an amount, such as **20** for £20.00, or you can type a percentage. If you type a percentage, QuickBooks calculates the Other Charge Amount as the percentage multiplied by the preceding item shown on the invoice. (You usually put in an Other Charge after using a Subtotal item – something we talk about in the "Creating other wacky items for invoices" section, later in this chapter.)

- *For all three types,* use the Sales VAT Code drop-down list to indicate the VAT rate applicable to the item. (*Note:* QuickBooks assumes that your business is VAT registered and turns on the VAT feature when it creates your company file. If your business is not VAT registered you can turn off the VAT feature by clicking Edit➪Preferences. Click the VAT icon in the list on the left, and in the Company Preferences tab select the No option in the Do You Charge VAT? area.)

If you tick the box next to This Item Is Used in Assemblies or Is Performed by a Subcontractor or Partner, QuickBooks lets you set both the purchase and sales information for the item. (You fill out the information the way you do for a stock part, described later in the chapter.) This is useful for example if you buy services from a subcontractor at a set cost and sell it on at a set price.

- *For all three types,* use the Account drop-down list to specify which income account you want to use to track the income you receive from the sale of this item.

8. **If the item type is Stock Part, tell QuickBooks how much to charge for the stock part, how much the stock part costs, and which income account to use for tracking the product sales income.**

For a Stock Part item type, QuickBooks displays the New Item window, as shown in Figure 3-4.

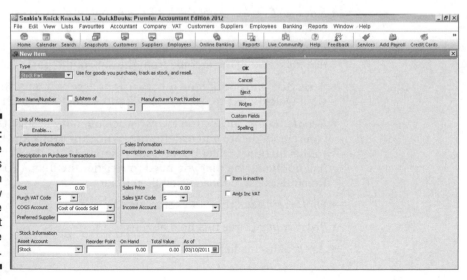

Figure 3-4: The QuickBooks New Item window with the Stock Part item type selected.

You use the extra fields that this special version of the window displays to record the following information:

- *Description on Purchase Transactions:* Describe the part. This description appears on the documents (such as purchase orders) that you use when you buy items for your stock.

- *Cost:* Specify the average cost per unit of the items that you currently have. This field acts as the default cost when you enter the item on a purchase transaction.

- *Purch VAT Code:* Select the appropriate default VAT code for purchase transactions.

- *COGS Account:* Specify the account that you want QuickBooks to use for tracking this item's cost when you sell it. (QuickBooks suggests the Cost of Goods Sold account. If you've created other accounts for your COGS, select the appropriate account.)

- *Preferred Supplier:* Specify your first choice when ordering the item for your business. (If the supplier isn't on your Supplier list, QuickBooks asks you to add it. If you say, "Yes, I do want to add it", QuickBooks displays the Add Supplier window, which you can then use to describe the supplier.)

- *Description on Sales Transactions:* Type a description of the item that you want to appear on documents, such as invoices and so on, that your customers see. (QuickBooks suggests the same description that you used in the Description on Purchase Transactions text box as a default, but you can change this.)

- *Sales Price:* Enter the amount that you charge for the item.

- *Sales VAT Code:* Select the VAT code that applies when you sell the item.

- *Income Account:* Specify the account that you want QuickBooks to use for tracking the income from the sale of the part.

- *Asset Account:* Specify the other current asset account that you want QuickBooks to use for tracking this Stock Part item's value.

- *Reorder Point:* Specify the lowest stock quantity of this item that can remain before you order more. When the stock level drops to this quantity, QuickBooks adds a Reminder to the Reminders list, notifying you that you need to reorder the item. (To see the Reminders list, choose Lists⇨Reminders.)

- *On Hand:* Leave this field set to zero.

- *Total Value:* Leave this field at zero.

- *As Of:* Skip this field.

- *If you are setting up a Stock Part type item for the first time as part of setting up QuickBooks, change the default settings for these fields as follows:* in the *On Hand* field enter the physical count of the item at the conversion date; skip the *Total Value* field (because QuickBooks calculates the value of this field by multiplying Cost by On Hand quantity); in the *As Of* field enter the conversion date.

9. **If the item type is Stock Assembly, tell QuickBooks which COGS and income account to use for tracking the item, how much to charge for the stock assembly, and how to build the item from other component stock items.**

   Note: The Stock Assembly item is available in QuickBooks Premier only.

   For a Stock Assembly item type, QuickBooks displays a special version of the New Item window. You use the extra fields that this window displays to record the following information:

   - *Cost:* Specify the total cost of the assembly unit, which may be total of the cost of the components in the Bill of Materials, or may include other costs not included in the Bill of Materials.

   - *COGS Account:* Specify the account that you want QuickBooks to use for tracking this item's cost when you sell it. (QuickBooks suggests the Cost of Goods Sold account. If you've created other accounts for your COGS, select the appropriate account.)

   - *Description:* Type a description of the item that you want to appear on documents that your customers see, such as invoices.

   - *Sales Price:* Enter the amount that you charge for the item.

   - *Sales VAT Code:* Select the VAT code that applies when you sell the item.

   - *Income Account:* Specify the account that you want QuickBooks to use for tracking the income from the sale of the part.

   - *Bill of Materials:* Use the Bill of Materials list to identify the component items and the quantities needed to make the stock assembly.

   - *Asset Account:* Specify the other current asset account that you want QuickBooks to use for tracking this stock item's value.

   - *Build Point:* Specify the lowest stock quantity of this item that can remain before you manufacture more. When the stock level drops to this quantity, QuickBooks adds a Reminder to the Reminders list, notifying you that you need to make more of the item.

   - *On Hand:* Leave this field set to zero.

   - *Total Value:* Leave this field at zero.

   - *As Of:* Skip this field.

- *If you are setting up a Stock Assembly type item for the first time as part of setting up QuickBooks, you need to fill in the following fields:* in the *On Hand* field enter the physical count of the assembly item at the conversion date; skip the *Total Value* field because QuickBooks calculates the value of this field by multiplying Cost by On Hand quantity; in the *As Of* field enter the conversion date.

10. **Click OK or Next when you're finished.**

    When you finish describing one item, click OK to add the item to the list and return to the Item List window. Click Next to add the item to the list and keep the New Item window onscreen so that you can add more items.

Creating other wacky items for invoices

In the preceding section we don't describe all the items that you can add. For example, you can create a *Subtotal item* to calculate the subtotal of the items you list on an invoice. You might want to create other wacky items for your invoices as well, such as payment and discounts. We describe these special types of items in the next few sections.

Creating Subtotal items to stick subtotals on invoices

You need to add a Subtotal item if you ever want to apply a discount to a series of items on an invoice. (We show a Subtotal item on the invoice shown in Figure 3-1.) To add a Subtotal item to your Item list, choose Lists⇨Item List, click the Item button, and select New from the drop-down list. This displays the New Item window – the same window we show several times earlier in this chapter. Specify the item type as Subtotal and then provide an item name (such as *Subtotal*).

Using multiple units of measurement

If you buy and sell stock items with the same measurement units – for example, say that you both *buy* and *sell* individual coffee mugs – you use a single unit of measure for your purchases and sales. Some businesses, however, use multiple units of measurement. For example, say that a business purchases boxes of coffee mugs, at 24 mugs to the box, but then sells those coffee mugs singly. In this case, purchases of an item would probably be counted in boxes (one measurement unit). Yet, sales of the item would probably be counted as individual mugs (another measurement unit). To deal with this complexity, where appropriate, the New Item dialog boxes include an Enable button under the Unit of Measure label (see Figures 3-3 or 3-4, for example). Click the Enable button and QuickBooks starts a little wizard that steps you through identifying the units of measure you need to use and how QuickBooks should convert from one unit of measure to another.

When you want to subtotal items on an invoice, all you do is stick this Subtotal item on the invoice after the items you want to subtotal. Keep in mind, though, that QuickBooks doesn't set up a subtotal feature automatically. You have to add a Subtotal item; otherwise, you can apply a Discount item that you create only to the single item that immediately precedes the discount. A *Discount item,* by the way, calculates a discount on an invoice.

Creating Group items to batch stuff you sell together

You can create an item that puts one line on an invoice that's actually a combination of several other items. To add a Group item, display the New Item window and specify the item type as Group. QuickBooks displays the New Item window, as shown in Figure 3-5.

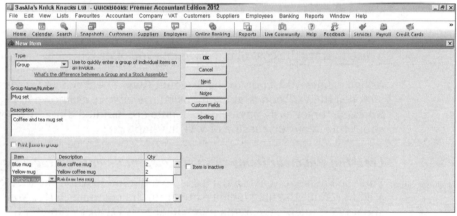

Figure 3-5: The QuickBooks New Item window with the Group item type selected.

For example, if you sell three items – say, blue mugs, yellow mugs, and red mugs – but sometimes sell the items together in a set, you can create an item that groups the three items. Note that when you create a group, you continue to track the stock of each group member individually; you don't track the stock of the group as a new item (the way that you do with Stock Assembly items).

In the New Item window, use the Item/Description/Qty list box to list each item included in the group. When you click an item line in the Item/Description/Qty list box, QuickBooks places a down arrow at the right end of the Item column. Click this arrow to open a drop-down list of items. (If the list is longer than can be shown, you can use the scroll bar on the right to move up and down the list.) If you select the Print Items in Group check box, QuickBooks lists all the items in the group on invoices. (In the case of the group shown, invoices list the individual blue, red, and yellow mugs instead of just listing the group name, such as *Mug Set.*)

Creating Discount items to add discounts to invoices

You can create an item that calculates a discount and sticks the discount on an invoice as another line item. (We show a Discount item on the invoice that appears in Figure 3-1.) To add a Discount item to the list, display the New Item window, specify the item type as Discount, and provide an item name or number and a description.

Use the Amount or % text box to specify how the discount is calculated. If the discount is a set amount (such as £50.00), type the amount. If the discount is calculated as a percentage, enter the percentage, including the percent symbol. When you enter a percentage, QuickBooks calculates the discount amount as the percentage multiplied by the immediately preceding item shown on the invoice. (If you want to apply the discount to a group of items, you need to use a Subtotal item and follow it with the discount, as Figure 3-1 shows.)

Use the Account drop-down list to specify the expense account that you want to use to track the cost of the discounts you offer.

Assign a Sales VAT code to the discount item. The Sales VAT code typically matches the VAT codes of the items on the invoice as shown in Figure 3-1. *Note:* customer early payment discounts are handled differently; we talk about this in our discussion of VAT in Chapter 11.

Creating Payment items to show down payments on invoices

You use Payment items to record a payment made when the invoice is created to reduce the final balance due from the customer later. *Note:* retainers and advance deposits are handled differently (refer to Chapter 5).

To add a Payment item to the list, display the New Item window, specify the item type as Payment, and provide an item name and a description. Use the Payment Method drop-down list to specify the method of payment. QuickBooks provides a starting list of several of the usual payment methods. You can easily add more payment types by choosing Add New from the drop-down list. When you choose this entry, QuickBooks displays the New Payment Method dialog box. In the dialog box's only text box, identify the payment method: cash, cheque, beads, shells, or some other what-have-you.

When you're finished, use the area in the lower-left corner of the New Item window to either group the payment with other undeposited funds or, if you use the drop-down list, deposit the payment to a specific account.

Inactivating list items

One of the neat features in QuickBooks is that it enables you to simplify your lists by hiding items that are no longer active, including those that you expect to be active again later. If you sell commemorative key chains only every five years, you can keep them from cluttering your Item list in the off years. You can also inactivate customers and suppliers from their respective lists.

To inactivate something from a list, all you have to do is open the list and double-click the item. When QuickBooks opens the item, employee, customer, or supplier that you want to inactivate,

select the Item Is Inactive check box. (The name of the check box changes, depending on what you're trying to inactivate.) Then click OK. QuickBooks hides this member from your list. The next time you display the list, the Include Inactive box appears.

To view and edit hidden members of your list, just click the Include Inactive box. Any inactive members show up with X icons beside them. If you want to reactivate a member, all you have to do is click the X icon, and the member is reactivated.

Editing items

If you make a mistake, you can change any piece of item information by displaying the Item List window and double-clicking the item. QuickBooks displays the Edit Item window, which you can use to make changes.

The Item List window provides another tool you can use to edit item information. If you click the Item button and choose the Add/Edit Multiple Items command, QuickBooks displays the Add/Edit Multiple List Entries window. This window provides a spreadsheet you can use to add or edit more than one item at a time. The method we describe in the previous paragraphs often works best because it allows you to collect more information – for example, information such as item descriptions. But if you need to enter or edit a large number of items, check out the Add/Edit Multiple Items command. Sometimes the command saves you time.

Read about inactivating items, employees, customers, and suppliers in the "Inactivating list items" sidebar.

Customers Are Your Business

Here's how you add customers to your Customer list:

1. **Choose Customers⇨Customer Centre.**

   The Customer Centre window appears.

2. **Click the New Customer & Job button and then click New Customer.**

   In the New Feature dialog box (where QuickBooks invites you to add multiple customers at once), click OK. (To stop QuickBooks from displaying this dialog box each time you add a new customer, tick the box next to Do Not Display This Message in the Future.) QuickBooks displays the Address Info tab of the New Customer window, as shown in Figure 3-6. Use this window to describe the customer in as much detail as possible.

   If you click the New Customer button and choose the Add Multiple Customer:Jobs command, QuickBooks displays a worksheet you can use to describe multiple customers at a time.

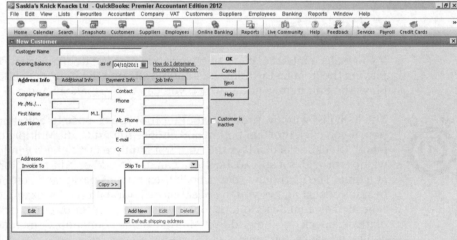

Figure 3-6: The New Customer window.

3. **Type the customer's name.**

   Enter the name of the customer as you want it to appear in the Customer list. You can list customers by company name or by the representative's last name.

4. **Enter the full company name as you want it to appear on an invoice or sales receipt.**

5. **(Optional) Enter the name of your contact, along with other pertinent information.**

   Move the cursor to the Mr./Ms. text box and type the appropriate title. Do the same with the First Name, M.I., and Last Name text boxes. (QuickBooks automatically fills in the names in the Contact text box as you type them. Nice touch, eh?)

   Go ahead and fill in the Phone, FAX, Alt. Phone, and E-mail text boxes while you're at it.

6. **(Really optional) Type the name of your alternative contact in the Alt. Contact text box.**

7. **Enter the billing address.**

   You can use the Bill To text box to provide the customer's billing address. QuickBooks copies the Company and Contact names to the first lines of the billing address, so you need enter only the address. To move from the end of one line to the start of the next, press Enter.

8. **Enter the shipping address.**

   You can use the Ship To field to provide the customer's shipping address. Click the Copy button to copy the billing address to the Ship To field. If the shipping address differs from the Bill To address, simply open the Ship To drop-down list, click Add New, and then enter the shipping address information the same way that you enter the Bill To address. You can add multiple shipping addresses. After you add a shipping address for a customer, you can select the shipping address from the Ship To drop-down list.

9. **(Optional) Click the Additional Info tab and record more data.**

   When you click this tab, QuickBooks displays the tab shown in Figure 3-7. You can use this tab to describe the customer in more detail. Among other things, you can define the customer terms and VAT details, both of which are important. Terms tell QuickBooks by which date the customer needs to pay an invoice. VAT details, such as the customer's country and VAT registration number, ensure that VAT is accounted for properly on VAT returns, especially for customers based in the EC. (For more information on EC customers have a look at Chapter 10.)

10. **(Optional) Click the Payment Info tab and record more data.**

    You can use the boxes on the Payment Info tab (see Figure 3-8) to record bits of customer information, such as the account number that should be included with any payments and the credit limit you are willing to grant the customer.

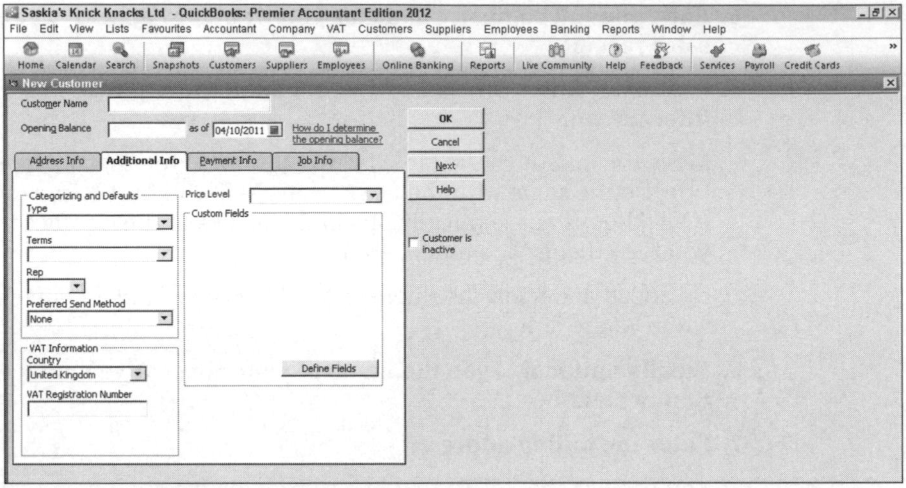

Figure 3-7:
Add more details on the Additional Info tab.

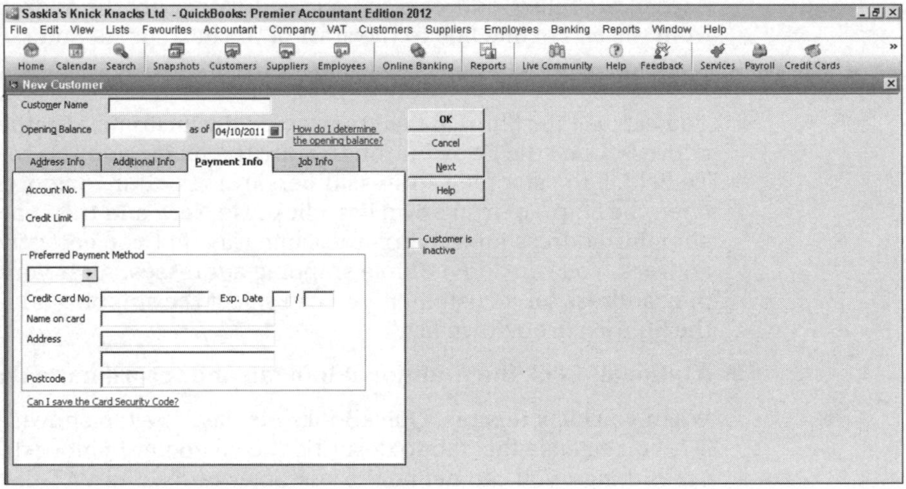

Figure 3-8:
The Payment Info tab.

11. **Specify the total of the customer's unpaid invoices at the QuickBooks conversion date by using the Opening Balance text box.**

Only use this box if you did not add customers and the total of their unpaid invoices at the conversion date, during the QuickBooks Setup process (as we recommended in Chapter 2). You can do so now.

Move the cursor to the Opening Balance text box and type the total amount owed by the customer on the conversion date.

Do not enter customer unpaid balances this way if you are reporting VAT on a cash basis. We describe the correct way of handling these later in this chapter.

12. **Enter the conversion date in the As Of text box.**

   Only enter the conversion date if you entered something in the Opening Balance text box, otherwise leave as is.

13. **(Optional) Click the Job Info tab to add specific job information.**

   Because you're creating a new customer account, not invoicing by jobs, I explain this step in the next section. If you're the "can't wait" type, feel free to take a look. You can add a specific job to the new customer's information.

14. **Save the customer information by clicking OK or Next.**

   When you finish describing a customer, you can save the info in one of two ways: click OK to add the customer to the list and return to the Customer Centre window, or click Next to add the customer to the list and keep the New Customer window onscreen so that you can add more customers.

If you want to change some bit of customer information, display the Customer Centre window, double-click the name of the customer record in which you want to change information, and then make changes in the Edit Customer window.

It's Just a Job

In QuickBooks, you can track invoices by customer or by customer and job. This may sound weird, but some businesses invoice customers (perhaps several times) for specific jobs.

Take the case of a construction subcontractor who does foundation work for a handful of builders. This construction subcontractor probably invoices his customers by job, and he invoices each customer several times for the same job. For example, he invoices Poverty Rock Builders for the foundation job at 11 Birch Street when he pours the footing and then again when he lays the block. At 28 Fairview, a foundation job takes more than one invoice, too.

To set up jobs for customers, you first need to describe the customers (as we explain in the preceding section). Then follow these steps:

1. **Choose Customers⇨Customer Centre.**

QuickBooks displays the Customer Centre window.

2. **Right-click the customer for whom you want to set up a job, choose Add Job from the contextual menu that appears and click the Add Job tab.**

QuickBooks displays the New Job window (shown in Figure 3-9). You use this window to describe the job. A great deal of the information in this window appears on the invoice.

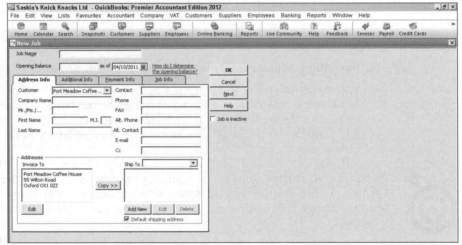

Figure 3-9:
The New
Job
window.

3. **Add the job name.**

The cursor is in the Job Name text box. Just type the name of the job or project.

4. **Identify the customer.**

On the off chance that you selected the wrong customer in Step 2, take a peek at the Customer drop-down list. Does it name the correct customer? If not, activate the drop-down list and select the correct customer.

5. **(Optional) Name your contact and fill in other relevant information.**

You can enter the name of your contact and alternative contact in the Mr./Ms., First Name, M.I., and Last Name text boxes. QuickBooks fills in the Contact text box for you. You probably don't need to be told this, but fill in the Phone and FAX text boxes just so that you have that information on hand. If you want to get really optional, fill in the Alt. Phone and Alt. Contact text boxes. Go ahead: take a walk on the wild side.

6. **Enter the job's billing address.**

   You can use the Invoice To text box to provide the customer's job billing address. Because the chances are good that the job billing address is the same as the customer billing address, QuickBooks copies the billing address from the Customer list. But if need be, make changes.

7. **Select the Ship To address.**

   You can use the Ship To text box to provide the job's shipping address. Click the Copy button if the shipping address is the same as the Bill To address.

8. **(Massively optional) Click the Additional Info tab and categorise the job.**

   You can use the Customer Type drop-down list to give the job type.

9. **Click the Payment Info tab and set the customer's credit limit (that is, if you've given the customer a credit limit).**

   You can set the customer's credit limit by using the Credit Limit box.

10. **(Optional) Click the Job Info tab and add specific job information.**

    Figure 3-10 shows the Job Info tab. You can use the Job Status drop-down list to choose None, Pending, Awarded, In Progress, Closed, or Not Awarded, whichever is most appropriate. The Start Date is (we know that this one is hard to believe) the day you start the job. As anyone knows, the Projected End and the End Date aren't necessarily the same. Don't fill in the End Date until the job is actually finished. The Job Description field can contain any helpful information you can fit on one line and the Job Type is an extra field you can use. (If you do use this field, you can add a new job type by choosing Add New from the Job Type list.)

11. **Save the job information by clicking OK or Next.**

    After you finish describing the job, you have two options: you can click OK to add the job to the list and return to the Customer Centre window, or you can click Next to add the job to the list and keep the New Job window onscreen so that you can add more jobs.

You can edit job information in the same way that you edit customer information. Display the Customer Centre window by choosing Customer⇨Customer Centre. When QuickBooks displays the window, double-click the job and make the changes in the Edit Job window that appears.

The little things do matter

If you aren't familiar with how payment terms work, you can get a bird's-eye view here. For the most part, payment terms just tell the customer how quickly you expect to be paid. For example, *Due on Receipt* means that you expect to be paid as soon as possible. If Net is followed by some number, as in Net 15 or Net 30, the number indicates the number of days after the invoice date within which the customer is supposed to pay. So Net 15 means that the customer is supposed to pay within 15 days of the invoice date.

Some payment terms, such as 2% 10 Net 30, include early payment discounts. In other words, the customer can deduct 2 percent from the bill if it's paid within 10 days. Either way, the customer must pay the bill within 30 days. For more information on how to make early payment discounts work for you, see Chapter 19.

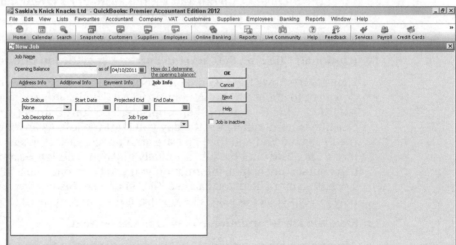

Figure 3-10:
The Job
Info tab.

To add a large number of customers or jobs to the Customers list at the same time, display the Customer Centre window, click the New Customer & Job button, and then choose the Add Multiple Customer:Jobs option. QuickBooks displays the Add/Edit Multiple List Entries worksheet, which lets you collect and edit all the same information that the regular customer and job windows do.

If you use the Add Multiple Customer:Jobs option described here you must make more columns visible in order to enter customer unpaid invoice balances. You do this by clicking the Customise Columns button, which loads a new window. In the Available Columns area on the left select Customer:Job Balance and click the Add button. Next, select Opening Balance as of Date and click the Add button. When you are finished click OK to return to the Add Multiple Customer:Jobs window where you can continue entering customer or job details.

Adding Suppliers to Your Supplier List

Adding suppliers to your Supplier list works the same basic way as adding customers to your Customer list. Here's how to get the job done:

1. **Choose Suppliers⇨Supplier Centre or click the Supplier Centre icon at the top of the screen.**

   QuickBooks displays the Supplier Centre window. Along with listing your suppliers, it lists the two suppliers QuickBooks automatically adds when it creates your company file: HMRC VAT (the VAT agency) and HM Revenue & Customs (for remitting payroll liabilities).

2. **Click the New Supplier button and then choose the New Supplier command from the menu that appears.**

   In the New Feature dialog box (where QuickBooks invites you to add multiple suppliers at one time), click OK. (To stop QuickBooks from displaying this dialog box each time you add a new supplier, tick the box next to Do Not Display This Message in the Future.)

   QuickBooks displays the Address Info tab of the New Supplier window, as shown in Figure 3-11. You use this window to describe your suppliers and all their little idiosyncrasies.

   If you click the New Supplier button and choose the Add Multiple Suppliers command, QuickBooks displays a worksheet you can use to describe multiple suppliers at a time.

3. **Enter the supplier name.**

   The cursor is already in the Supplier Name text box. All you have to do is type the supplier's name as you want it to appear in the Supplier list. If you want to list your suppliers by company name, enter the company name. To list them by the first or last name of the sales representative, enter one of these names. Just remember that the list is going to sort, alphabetically or numerically, by the information you enter in this field, not by the information below.

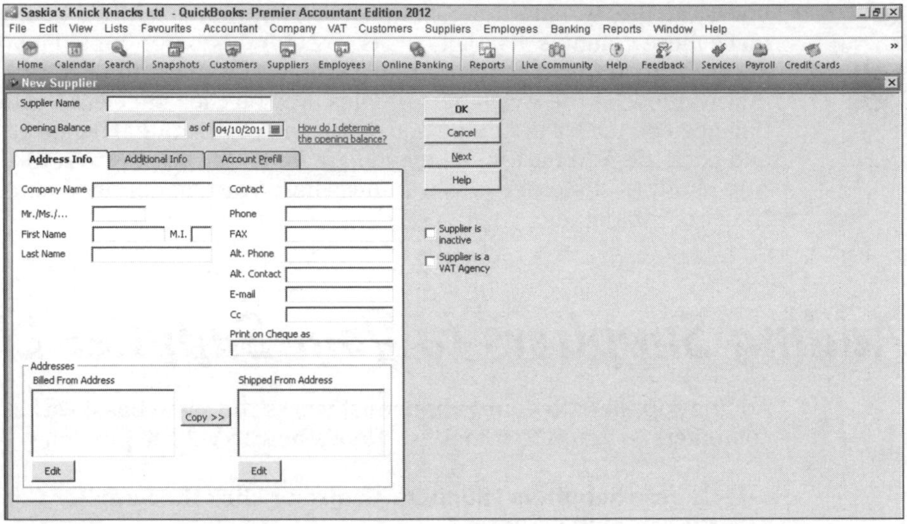

Figure 3-11:
The Address
Info tab of
the New
Supplier
window.

4. **(Optional) Enter the Company Name and the name of your contact.**

   Fill in the Company Name, Mr./Ms., First Name, M.I., and Last Name text boxes. QuickBooks fills in the Contact text box for you automatically.

5. **Enter the address to which you're supposed to send payment (or remittances).**

   You can use the Addresses text box to provide the supplier's address. QuickBooks copies the Company and Contact names to the first line of the address, so you need enter only the street address, city, county, and post code. To move from the end of one line to the start of the next, press Enter.

6. **(Optional) Enter the supplier's telephone and FAX numbers, and, if available, the e-mail address.**

   The window also has an Alt. Phone text box for a second telephone number. They thought of everything, didn't they?

7. **Verify the entry in the Print on Cheque As text box.**

   QuickBooks assumes that you want the company name to appear on any cheques you write to this supplier. If not, change the text box to whatever you feel is more appropriate.

8. **At this point, click the Additional Info tab.**

   The window you see onscreen hopefully bears an uncanny resemblance to Figure 3-12.

9. **(Optional) Enter your account number in the Account No. text box.**

   If the supplier has assigned account numbers or customer numbers to keep track of customers, type your account or customer number in the Account No. text box. You can probably get this piece of information from the supplier's last invoice.

   QuickBooks transfers the account number to the memo field of the payment cheque.

10. **(Optional) Categorise the supplier by selecting an option from the Type drop-down list.**

    See that Type drop-down list? We have never seen this used. Ever. If you want to be the first, have a go at it.

11. **Specify the payment terms that you're supposed to observe by selecting an option from the Terms drop-down list.**

    QuickBooks has already set up all the usual ones. (If you want to, you can choose Add New to set up additional payment terms.)

    If a supplier offers an early payment discount, it's usually too good a deal to pass up. Interested in more information about early payment discounts? Do you have an inquiring mind that needs to know? See Chapter 19 to find out about the advantages of early payment discounts.

12. **(Optional) Specify your credit limit, if the supplier has set one.**

    This procedure is obvious, right? You click in the Credit Limit text box and enter the number.

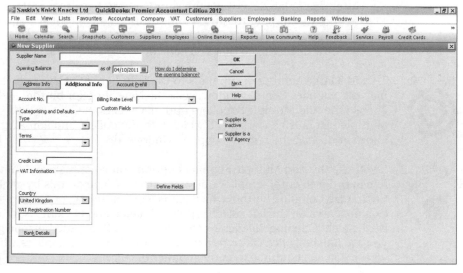

Figure 3-12: The Additional Info tab of the New Supplier window.

13. **(If applicable) Store the supplier's country and VAT registration number.**

    This one is obvious too, right? This information is particularly important if your supplier is based in the EC. We'll talk more about this in Chapter 10.

14. **Specify the total of the supplier's unpaid bills at the QuickBooks conversion date by using the Opening Balance text box.**

    Only use this box if you did not add suppliers and the total of their unpaid bills at the conversion date, during the QuickBooks Setup process

    Move the cursor to the Opening Balance text box and type the total amount you owed the supplier at the conversion date.

    Do not enter supplier unpaid balances this way if you are reporting VAT on a cash basis. We describe the correct way of handling these later in this chapter.

15. **Enter the conversion date in the As Of date field.**

    What you're doing here, by the way, is providing the date on which the value shown in the Opening Balance text box is correct. Leave as is if you did not enter anything in the Opening Balance text box.

    QuickBooks provides an Account Prefill tab on the New Supplier window. Use this tab to specify a set of expense accounts that QuickBooks will suggest any time you indicate you're writing a cheque, entering a bill, or entering a credit card charge for the supplier.

16. **Save the supplier information by clicking OK or Next.**

    After you finish describing the supplier, you have two options: click OK to add the supplier to the list and return to the Supplier Centre window, or click Next to add the supplier to the list and leave the New Supplier window onscreen so that you can add more suppliers.

To add a large number of suppliers to the Supplier list at the same time, display the Supplier Centre window, click the New Supplier button, and then choose the Add Multiple Suppliers option. QuickBooks displays the Add/Edit Multiple List Entries worksheet, which lets you collect and edit all the same information that the regular supplier windows do.

If you use the Add Multiple Suppliers option you must make columns visible in order to enter supplier opening balances. You do this by clicking the Customise Columns button, which loads a new window. In the Available Columns area on the left select Supplier Balance and click the Add button. Next, select Opening Balance As Of Date and click the Add button again. When you are finished click OK to return to the Add Multiple Suppliers window, where you can continue to enter supplier details.

The Other Lists

The preceding sections cover all the most important lists (with the exception of the Employee List, which is covered in Chapter 12). A few others we haven't talked about yet are Fixed Asset, Price Level, Billing Rate, VAT Code, Payroll Item, Classes, Other Names, Sales Rep, Customer Type, Supplier Type, Job Type, Terms, Customer Messages, Payment Method, Ship Via, Vehicle List, Templates, and Memorised Transactions. We don't give blow-by-blow descriptions of how you use these lists because you don't really need them. The other QuickBooks lists are generally more than adequate. You can usually use the standard lists as is without building other lists.

Just so we don't leave you stranded, however, we want to give you quick-and-dirty descriptions of these other lists and what they do. And by the way, we discuss the VAT Code list and Payroll Item list in Chapters 11 and 12, respectively.

To see some of these lists, choose the list from the Lists menu or choose Lists➪Customer & Supplier Profile Lists and choose the list from the submenu that QuickBooks displays.

The Fixed Asset list

If you buy *fixed assets* – things such as vehicles, various pieces of furniture, miscellaneous hunks of equipment, and so on – somebody is supposed to track this stuff in a list. Why? You need to have this information at your fingertips (or at your accountant's fingertips) to calculate depreciation. And if you later dispose of some item, you need this information to calculate the gain or loss on the sale of the item. For these reasons, QuickBooks includes a Fixed Asset list, used to describe and identify your fixed assets. But because the QuickBooks Fixed Asset list does not calculate the depreciation, it's not a list we get really excited about, or dwell on.

Note: We should tell you that your accountant most likely has such a list that he or she has been maintaining for you. So don't freak out because this is the first you've heard about this fixed assets business.

The Price Level list

You can use *price levels* in QuickBooks to set custom prices for different customers or jobs. This can be very useful if you offer one set of prices to a certain type of customer or job, and a different set of prices to another type of customer or job. The great thing about price levels is that once you define the price level, you can assign a price level to a customer (on the Additional Info tab of the customer or job record), and the next time your raise an invoice for that customer or job the custom price automatically appears on the invoice. Nice feature, don't you think? Think of it as a permanent mark-up or discount associated with that customer or job. (This may not make much sense until you see the Create Invoices window, which we describe in Chapter 4, but it's fairly straightforward.)

There are two types of price level you can define: a fixed percentage price level or a per-item price level. (*Note:* The per-item price level is only available in QuickBooks Premier.) With a fixed percentage, the prices of all the items are increased or decreased by, well, a fixed percentage. The per-item price level lets you define custom prices for each individual item.

To use this feature, choose Lists⇨Price Level List to display the Price Level List window, click the Price Level button, and choose New from the drop-down list. In the window that appears, you name the Price Level, choose a Price Level type and fill in the window. (Remember you only have more than one type available in QuickBooks Premier.)

The Billing Rate list

Note: Billing Rates are available only in QuickBooks Premier.

With *billing rates* you can charge your customers different prices for the same service, depending on who carried out the work. You would not want to charge your customer the same amount for artwork done by Linda, a senior graphic designer, as for work by John, a junior graphic designer, would you?

You can have a fixed hourly billing rate (so that all services performed by a person assigned this rate are billed out at this rate) or custom hourly rates for each service item.

Once defined, billing rates are assigned to an employee, a supplier, or a person on the Other Names list (discussed later in this chapter), and time worked is tracked in QuickBooks (discussed in Chapter 16), ready for invoicing the customer. Another handy feature, don't you think?

To use it, choose Lists⇨Billing Rate List to display the Billing Rate List window, click the Billing Rate Level button, choose New from the drop-down list, and then name the Billing Rate, choose a Billing Rate type and fill in the window.

The Class list

Classes enable you to classify transactions by department or location, for example, so that you can track trends and assess performance across parts of your business. Classes are cool (really cool), but they add another dimension to the accounting model that you use in QuickBooks, so we're not going to describe them here. We urge you – nay, implore you – to get comfortable with how the rest of QuickBooks works before you begin mucking about with classes. Here are just a handful of useful tidbits in case you want to use classes:

✔ You may need to turn on the QuickBooks Class Tracking feature. To do this, choose Edit⇨Preferences, click the Accounting icon, click the Company Preferences tab, and select the Use Class Tracking check box.

 Note: The Class box appears in data entry windows only after you turn on class tracking.

✔ To display the Class list, choose Lists⇨Class List.

✔ To add classes to the Class list, display the Class List window (choose Lists⇨Class List), right-click the window, choose New to display the New Class window, and then fill in the blanks.

✔ To tag transactions as falling into a particular class – invoices, bills, cheques, journal entries, and so on – select the appropriate class from the Class list box.

By the way, one other point: Before you go off and start using classes to complicate your accounting, make sure that you can't get what you want by beefing up your chart of accounts.

The Other Names list

QuickBooks provides a list of Other Names that works as a watered-down Supplier list. You can write cheques to people named on this Other Names list, but you can't do anything else. We find this list useful in instances where you don't need to capture a lot of supplier information – for example, when you need to make a cheque out to "Cash", Cash can be an entry in the Other Names list – or when you want to differentiate payments made to the same person or company – for example, when a shareholder is also an employee. This way you can write dividend cheques to the name listed in the Other Names list (which makes reporting on this easy) and reserve the Employee list for payroll activities.

To use this list, choose Lists⇨Other Names List to display the Other Names List window, click the Other Names button, choose New from the drop-down list, and then fill in the blanks in the New Name window.

The Sales Rep list

You can create a list of the sales representatives you work with and then indicate which sales representative sells to a customer or generates a sale. To do this, choose Lists⇨Customer & Supplier Profile Lists⇨Sales Rep. When you choose this command, QuickBooks displays the Sales Rep List window, which lists all the sales representatives. To add sales representatives, click the Sales Rep button, select New from the drop-down list, and then fill in the window that QuickBooks displays.

Customer, Supplier, and Job Types lists

You can create lists of customer types, supplier types, and job types and then use these lists to categorise customer, supplier, and job information. This is probably no surprise, but to do this, you need to use the appropriate command:

- ✔ Lists⇨Customer & Supplier Profile Lists⇨Customer Type List
- ✔ Lists⇨Customer & Supplier Profile Lists⇨Supplier Type List
- ✔ Lists⇨Customer & Supplier Profile Lists⇨Job Type List

When you choose one of these commands, QuickBooks displays the appropriate List window, which lists all the Customer types, Supplier types, or Job types. To add types, click the Type button, select New from the drop-down list, and then fill in the window that QuickBooks displays.

How you use any of these types of list depends on your business. In a situation in which you want to sort or segregate customers, suppliers, or jobs in some unusual way, use the Customer Type, Supplier Type, or Job Type list.

Over the last few years, we've used the Customer Type box to identify which marketing technique has brought us a client: yellow-pages advertising, professional referrals, client referrals, and so on. Because QuickBooks easily prints reports that summarise client sales by customer type, using the Customer Type field in this manner makes it easy to see how much income different marketing activities produce – and when there's a decent return on marketing spend.

The Terms list

QuickBooks maintains a Terms list, which you use to specify what payment terms are available. To add terms, choose Lists⇨Customer & Supplier Profile Lists⇨Terms List. When you choose this command, QuickBooks displays the Terms List window. To add more terms, click the Terms button, select New from the drop-down list, and then fill in the window that QuickBooks displays.

You use standard terms to indicate the number of days after the invoice date (or bill date) within which the customer is supposed to pay (or you are supposed to pay the supplier). Examples of this are Net 30, Due on Receipt, and so on. You use date-driven terms to specify the date each month that a customer is supposed to pay the invoices for the previous month or you are supposed to pay supplier bills for the previous month.

To set up a date-driven term, such as "14th of next month", you enter *14* in the Net Due Before field, and *14* in the Due the Next Month if Issued Within field and click OK.

The Customer Message list

This list is a minor player in the QuickBooks drama. You can stick messages at the bottom of invoices if you first type the message in the Customer Message list. QuickBooks provides a handful of boilerplate messages: "thank you", "happy holidays", and so on. You can add more messages by choosing Lists⇨Customer & Supplier Profile Lists⇨Customer Message List. When QuickBooks displays the Customer Message List window, click its Customer Message button and choose New. Then use the New Customer Message window that QuickBooks displays to create a new message.

The Payment Method list

Now this will be a big surprise. (Just kidding.) QuickBooks provides descriptions for the usual payment methods. But, of course, you can add to these by choosing Lists⇨Customer & Supplier Profile Lists⇨Payment Method. When you choose this command, QuickBooks displays a map of the lost city of Atlantis. Okay, not really. QuickBooks actually displays the Payment Method window. To add more methods, click the Payment Method button, select New from the drop-down list, and then fill in the window that QuickBooks displays.

The Ship Via list

QuickBooks provides descriptions for the usual shipping methods. These descriptions are probably entirely adequate. If you need to add more, however, you can do so by choosing Lists⇨Customer & Supplier Profile Lists⇨ Ship Via. When you choose this command, QuickBooks displays the Ship Via List window, which lists all the shipping methods that you or QuickBooks said are available. To add more methods, click the Shipping Method button, select New from the drop-down list, and then fill in the window that QuickBooks displays. Friends, it doesn't get much easier than this.

The Vehicle list

QuickBooks provides a Vehicle list that you can use to maintain a list of business vehicles. To see the Vehicle list, choose Lists⇨Customer & Supplier Profile Lists⇨Vehicle List. When you choose this command, QuickBooks displays the Vehicle List window, which lists all the vehicles that you previously said are available. To identify additional vehicles, click the Vehicle button, select New from the drop-down list and then fill in the window that QuickBooks displays.

To record vehicle mileage inside QuickBooks, choose Company⇨Enter Vehicle Mileage. Then use the window that QuickBooks displays to identify the vehicle, the trip length in miles, the trip date, and a bit of other trip-related information.

The Memorised Transaction list

The Memorised Transaction list isn't really a list. At least, it's not like the other lists that we describe in this chapter. The Memorised Transaction list is a list of accounting transactions – invoices, bills, cheques, purchase orders, and so on – that you've asked QuickBooks to memorise. To display the Memorised Transaction list, choose Lists⇨Memorised Transaction List.

You can have QuickBooks memorise transactions so that you can quickly record them later or even put them on a schedule for recurring usage. This feature can save you lots of time, especially for transactions you regularly make.

The Templates list

The templates list is a collection of forms that determine the appearance of your invoices, credit notes, purchase orders, and so on. We discuss how to customise templates in Chapter 4. To view the list, choose Lists➪Templates.

The Reminders list

Here's a list that isn't accessible from the Lists menu. QuickBooks keeps track of a bunch of stuff that it knows you need to monitor. If you choose Company➪Reminders, QuickBooks displays the Reminders window. Here, you see such entries as invoices and cheques that need to be printed, stock items you should probably reorder, and so on.

Organising Lists

To organise a list, you must be in single-user mode. (We describe multi-user mode in Appendix C.) Here are some ways that you can organise your list:

- ✔ **To move an item and all its subitems:** Click the diamond beside the item and then drag the item up or down the list to a new location.

- ✔ **To make a subitem its own item:** Click the diamond beside the item and then drag it to the left.

- ✔ **To make an item a subitem:** Move the item so that it's directly beneath the item you want it to fall under. Then click the diamond beside the item and drag it to the right.

- ✔ **To alphabetise a list:** Click the Name button at the top of the list window. QuickBooks alphabetises your list of customers, suppliers, accounts and so on in both "a to z" order and reverse "z to a" order.

You can't reorganise the Supplier list or the Employee list. These lists are always displayed in alphabetical order.

Printing Lists

You can print Customer, Supplier, and Employee lists by clicking the Print button at the top of the specific screen for the type of list you choose. The list is among the options available to print in a drop-down list.

You can print a regular list by displaying the list, clicking the button in the lower-left corner of the list window, and then choosing Print List. However, often the best way to print a list is to print a list report. You can create, customise, and print a list report by choosing Reports⇨List and then choosing the list that you want to print. You can also create one of a handful of list reports by clicking the Reports button in the list window and choosing a report from the pop-up menu. For more information on printing reports, see Chapter 15.

Click the Activities button in a list window to quickly access common activities associated with the items on that list. Or click Reports to quickly access common reports related to the items on the list.

Exporting List Items to Your Word Processor

If you use QuickBooks to store the names and addresses of your customers, suppliers, and employees, you can create a text file of the contact information for these people. You can then export this file to another application, such as a word processor, to create reports that use this information.

To export list information to a text file, click the button in the lower-left corner of the list window and choose Print List. When QuickBooks displays the Print dialog box, select the File option button, click Print, and then provide a file name when prompted.

The File menu Print Forms command also provides a Labels command for producing mailing labels for customers and suppliers. And before we forget, let us also mention that the last command of the Company menu – Prepare Letters with Envelopes – lets you prepare letters (and, duh, addressed envelopes) from the name and address information in the Customer, Supplier, and Employee lists.

Dealing with the Chart of Accounts List

After you get done setting up your Item, Customer, and Supplier lists, you still need to finalise one list: the Chart of Accounts. The Chart of Accounts just lists the accounts you and QuickBooks use to track income and expenses, assets, liabilities, and equity.

This is kind of a funny step, however, because a bunch of Chart of Accounts stuff is already set up. So what you're really doing here is just finalising the chart of accounts (and the trial balance in the process). Typically, this consists of: adjusting bank balances, describing customer balances, describing supplier balances, describing the VAT liability (or refund), and entering the rest of the trial balance. By the way, the trial balance is prepared on an *accrual basis* – if you have no idea what accrual-based accounting is (and want to know), have a look at Appendix B.

Adjusting bank balances

When you set up your bank accounts during the QuickBooks Setup process, QuickBooks asked you for the bank statement balance at the conversion date, which you faithfully entered. But what if you wrote a cheque or made a deposit prior to the conversion date, which has not appeared on the bank statement yet? In this section, we show you how to address these two situations so your trial balance figure matches the trial balance your accountant gave to you or that you pulled off your old accounting system.

For each cheque you wrote prior to the conversion date but which has not appeared on your bank statement at the conversion date, create a cheque as described in Chapter 8. Make sure that:

- ✔ You enter the original cheque date.

- ✔ On the Expenses tab, you select the Share Capital Account in the Account field.

- ✔ In the VAT Code column, you select the "O" VAT code. (If you are not registered for VAT you turn off the VAT feature by clicking Edit➪Preferences and choosing VAT in the list. In the My Company tab select No in the Do You Charge VAT? area. Click OK.) This adjustment is outside the scope of VAT (meaning that it should not appear on VAT reports you send to HMRC), and choosing the "O" VAT code lets QuickBooks know this is the case.

For each deposit you paid in prior to the conversion date but which hasn't appeared on your bank statement at the conversion date, create a deposit as described in Chapter 8. Ensure that:

- ✔ You enter the original cheque date.

- ✔ You leave the Payee field blank.

- ✔ In the account field, you select the Share Capital Account.

Your bank balances are sorted and you're ready to move to the next step. And don't worry, we describe later in the chapter how to clear the resultant balance in the Share Capital Account.

Describing customer balances

If you entered customer unpaid invoice totals when you set up customers (either in the QuickBooks Setup process or earlier in this chapter), you've already described your customer balances. You, my friend, can skip ahead to the next section, "Describing supplier balances". If your business is cash-based and you don't give customers invoices, you too can skip ahead.

If you didn't enter customer unpaid invoice totals because you prefer to enter each unpaid invoice individually so you can allocate customer payment against specific invoices, or because you are on the Cash VAT scheme and we advised you not to in Chapter 2, you need to supply that information now.

Follow these steps to enter individual unpaid customer invoices:

1. **Add an item to the Item List of the type Other Charge, Service, or Non-stock Part.**

   To do so, go to Lists⇨Items, click the Item button and select New from the drop-down list. For the item type select Service, Non-stock Part, or Other Charge (refer to Figure 3-3). You can choose any of these three types; it does not matter which.

2. **Name the item.**

   In the Item/Name field add something like Unpaid Bal. You use this name to recall the item on each unpaid customer invoice.

3. **Enter an item description.**

   In the Description field, enter a memo such as Customer Unpaid Balance.

4. **Skip the Rate, Price, or Amount field, and select a VAT Code.**

   What you select here depends on the way you report VAT. (If you are not VAT-registered turn off the VAT feature as described earlier.)

   • If you report VAT on an *accrual basis*, choose the "O" VAT code. You do not need to show the VAT on unpaid customer invoices; the VAT on these sales is included in the VAT liability (or refund) figure we describe later in the chapter.

• If you report VAT on a *cash basis*, enter the VAT code you used on the original invoice. That's so QuickBooks will know what VAT amount to report on the VAT return when the customer pays the invoice.

5. **Select the Uncategorized Income account in the Sales Account field.**

   This is the choice QuickBooks makes during the QuickBooks Setup process (or if you set up customers as discussed earlier in this chapter), so use this account to keep things tidy. Click OK to add the item.

6. **Individually enter each unpaid customer invoice at the conversion date, filling out each field on the invoice, as described in Chapter 4.**

   As you fill out the fields for each invoice make sure you:

   • Use the original invoice date.

   • Use the Opening Customer Balance item to summarise the total amount of the invoice.

   • Stick the total amount of the invoice in the Amount Column.

      If VAT is present on the invoice, tick the Amounts Include VAT box first, and then type the invoice total in the Amount column.

   If the Total shown on the QuickBooks invoice matches the total unpaid balance of the original invoice, you'll know the numbers are right.

   We have prepared an example of an unpaid customer invoice dated 22 June 2011 (this being the original invoice date), totalling £15,000 including £2500 VAT. Have a look at Figure 3-13 to see how the invoice is entered if you report VAT on an accrual basis. Look at Figure 13-14 to see how the same invoice is entered if you report VAT on a cash basis. Note the highlighted figures in the Amount and VAT code columns, and the Total VAT field (at the bottom of the invoice).

7. **Once you describe each unpaid customer invoice, inactivate the Customer Unpaid Balance item.**

   You don't need to use this item again and you don't want to accidentally use it in future. See the "Inactivating list items" sidebar in this chapter.

That wasn't too hard, right?

Describing supplier balances

If you entered supplier unpaid bill totals when you set up suppliers (either in the QuickBooks Setup process or earlier in this chapter), then you described your supplier balances. You can skip ahead to the next section "Entering your VAT liability or refund".

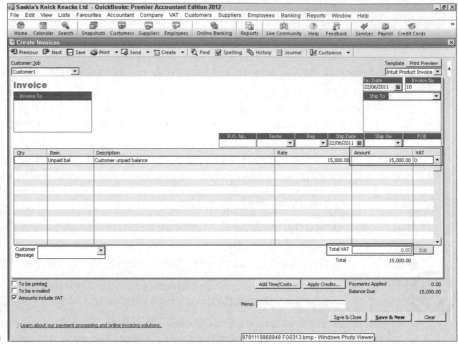

Figure 3-13: An example of an unpaid customer invoice if reporting VAT on an accrual basis.

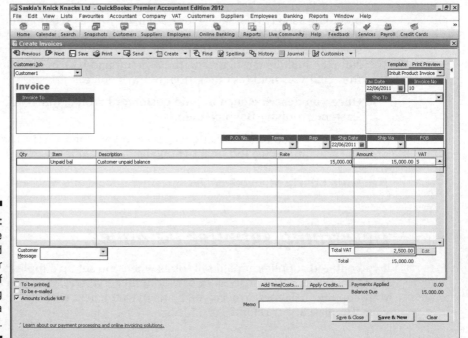

Figure 3-14: An example of an unpaid customer invoice if reporting VAT on a cash basis.

If you didn't enter supplier unpaid bill totals because you prefer to enter each unpaid bill individually in order to allocate your payment against specific bills or because you are on the Cash VAT scheme and we advised you not to in Chapter 2, you need to supply that information now.

We know that you won't be surprised to find out that you need to take a peek at Chapter 6 to see how to record a bill. Fill out each unpaid supplier bill as described in Chapter 6, ensuring that you:

✔ Use the **Uncategorized Expenses** account to summarise the total amount of the unpaid bill.

✔ Tick the **Amounts include VAT** box before you select a VAT code. (If you are not VAT registered turn off the VAT feature as described earlier.)

✔ Use the "O" VAT code (if you report VAT on an accrual basis) or the VAT code on the original bill (if you report VAT on a cash basis).

You entered the bill correctly if the Total shown on the QuickBooks bill matches the total unpaid balance of the original bill.

Entering your VAT liability or refund

If you are registered for VAT you now need to describe your VAT liability or refund balance. This is the VAT owed or due to be refunded at the conversion date.

It's *very* important that you enter the VAT liability or refund the way we describe in this section. We pretty much guarantee that you'll make a mess otherwise.

You enter your VAT liability or refund by telling QuickBooks the VAT figures at the conversion date for Boxes 1, 2 (if applicable) and 4 of your VAT return. You'll have to gather some information in order to do this. What information you gather depends on the way you report VAT.

If you report VAT on an *accrual basis*, gather documents whose *document date* falls between the date of your last VAT return and your conversion date. For example, if the date of your last VAT return was 31 May and your conversion date is 30 June, gather customer invoices and supplier bills dated from 1 to 30 June. If you report VAT on a *cash basis*, however, gather documents whose *payment date* falls between the date of your last VAT return and your conversion date. Using the same example, gather invoices paid by customers and bills you paid suppliers with a payment date between 1 and 30 June.

Also include documents that you didn't report, but should have reported, in a prior VAT return (for example, supplier bills you received late).

You may be able to gather this information from your old accounting system.

Remember, in QuickBooks you can report VAT using either the accrual or the cash basis method (see Chapter 11). If you're not sure which method you use, your accountant may be able to tell you. After you have these documents in hand, do the following to determine the amounts for:

- ✔ **Box 1 of your VAT return:** Add up the VAT on customer invoices.

- ✔ **Box 2 of your VAT return (if applicable):** Add up the VAT on bills for goods purchased from suppliers based in the EC.

- ✔ **Box 4 of your VAT return:** Tally the VAT of your supplier bills. If you entered an amount in Box 2 include that amount in Box 4 too.

By entering the Box 1, Box 2, and Box 4 figures of your VAT return at the conversion date, your trial balance figures are updated automatically.

Note: The steps to record your VAT return figures are the same whether you report VAT on an accrual or cash basis. (We discuss how to tell QuickBooks which VAT reporting method you use in Chapter 11.)

1. **From the Home screen, display the VAT Adjustment window, as shown in Figure 3-15.**

   Click the Manage VAT icon in the Suppliers area and then the Adjust VAT Owing button, or choose VAT➪Adjust VAT due.

2. **Set the Adjustment date to the conversion date.**

   Enter your conversion date in the Adjustment date field, and press the tab key *twice*. Remember to use a DD/MM/YYYY format.

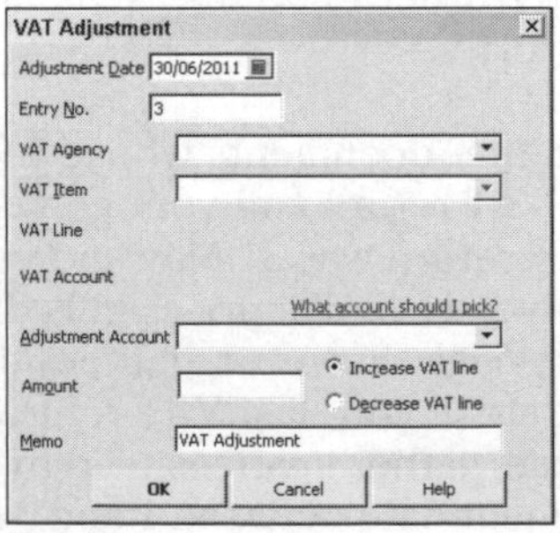

Figure 3-15:
The empty
VAT
Adjustment
window.

3. **Choose HMRC VAT as the VAT Agency.**

   The VAT agency is the body to which you remit VAT. Press the drop-down arrow to display a drop-down window and select HMRC VAT.

   HMRC VAT is one of the suppliers QuickBooks added automatically when you created your company file.

4. **Select a VAT item:**

   - **For Box 1 (VAT due on sales and other outputs):** Select Standard Sales.

   - **For Box 2 (VAT due on acquisitions from other EC Member States):** Select EC Purch Goods Standard.

   - **For Box 4 (VAT reclaimed on purchases):** Select Standard Purchases.

   Press the Tab key once. The VAT Line field then displays which Box (1, 2, or 4) of the VAT return your adjustment is about to affect. The VAT account field shows which VAT account (typically the VAT Liability account) is about to be updated.

   The process of adjusting VAT in QuickBooks only affects the figures in Boxes 1–4 of the VAT return. You need to tally the net figures in Boxes 6–9 (or you may be able to get them from your old accounting system) as you will need them when you file the VAT return online with HM Revenue & Customs.

5. **Select the Share Capital Account Adjustment Account.**

   Click the drop-down list next to Adjustment Account and scroll up in the list of accounts until you find the Share Capital Account listed with the other Equity accounts. Click it to select it.

6. **In the Amount field, enter the total amount you are adjusting. Leave the Increase VAT line selected.**

   Enter the total amount of the adjustment, without punctuation. Accept the selection QuickBooks makes for the Increase VAT line; this is the correct choice for each VAT adjustment entry you make.

   If you are owed a VAT refund, the figure in Box 4 will be greater than the sum of the figures in Boxes 1 and 2.

7. **(Optional) Add a memo in the Memo field.**

   If you want, enter a memo such as "VAT opening liability (or VAT opening refund)" so in future you will know why you made each adjustment.

Camouflaging some accounting weirdness

After you enter the bank account, stock, customer, supplier, and VAT liability (or refund) balances into QuickBooks, you need to enter the rest of the trial balance, which you do by taking two big steps. In the first step, you camouflage a couple of weird accounts, called *suspense accounts*. The second step, which we describe in the following section, is supplying the last few missing numbers.

Figure 3-16 shows trial balances after you enter the bank, stock, accounts receivable, accounts payable, and VAT liability (or refund) balances.

A VAT refund balance appears in the Debit column of the trial balance.

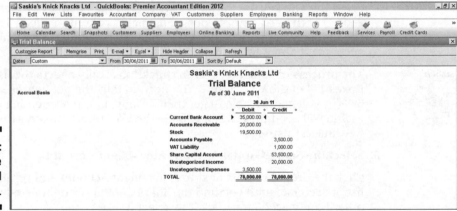

Figure 3-16:
A sample trial balance.

You can produce your own half-complete trial balance from inside QuickBooks by clicking the Report Centre icon and choosing Reports⇨ Accountant & Taxes⇨Trial Balance. QuickBooks displays the trial balance report in a document window.

If you need to do so, enter the conversion date in the As Of box by clicking in the To box and typing the conversion date in DD/MM/YYYY format. Figure 3-16, for example, shows the conversion date 30/06/2011 on the As Of line. You can set the From box to any value; the From and To range just needs to end with the conversion date. Make a note of the credit and debit balances shown for the Uncategorized Income and Uncategorized Expenses accounts. These are the suspense accounts that you are going to camouflage by reducing their balance to zero. Also, take a look at the Share Capital Account – you'll be working with this account too.

If you want, you can print the report by clicking the Print button; then, when QuickBooks displays the Print Report dialog box, click its Print button. Yes, you click *two* Print buttons.

After you have the conversion date balances for the Uncategorized Income and Uncategorized Expenses accounts, you're ready to make the necessary adjustments. To do so, follow these steps:

1. **From the Home screen, either click the Chart of Accounts icon in the Company area or choose Lists⇨Chart of Accounts to display the Chart of Accounts window, as shown in Figure 3-17.**

2. **Double-click the Share Capital Account in the Chart of Accounts list to display that account.**

   The Share Capital Account is an equity account and it's listed after the liability accounts. QuickBooks displays the *register* – just a list of transactions – for the Share Capital Account. Figure 3-18, coincidentally, shows this register.

3. **Select the next empty row of the register if it isn't already selected (although it probably is).**

   You can select a row by clicking it or you can use the up- or down-arrow key to move to the next empty row.

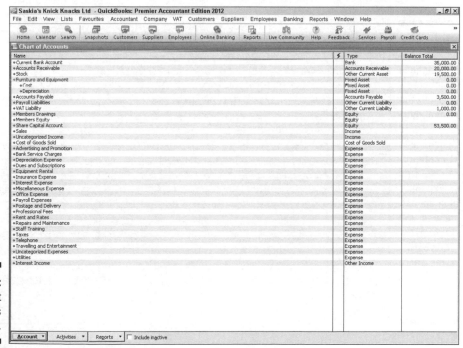

Figure 3-17:
The Chart of Accounts window.

4. **Type the conversion date in the Date field.**

   Move the cursor to the Date field (if it isn't already there) and type the date. Use the DD/MM/YYYY format. For example, you can type either **30062011** or **30/06/2011** to enter 30 June 2011.

5. **Type the Uncategorized Income account balance (from the trial balance report) in the Increase field.**

   In Figure 3-16, for example, the Uncategorized Income account balance is £20,000. In this case, click the Increase field and type **20000** in the field.

   You don't need to include the pound sign or the comma; QuickBooks adds the punctuation for you.

6. **Type** Uncategorized Income **(the account name) in the Account field.**

   Select the Account field, which is on the row under the word *Payee,* and begin typing **Uncategorized Income**, the account name. As soon as you type enough of the name for QuickBooks to figure out what you're typing, it fills in the rest of the name for you. When this happens, you can stop typing.

7. **Click the Record button to record the Uncategorized Income adjustment transaction.**

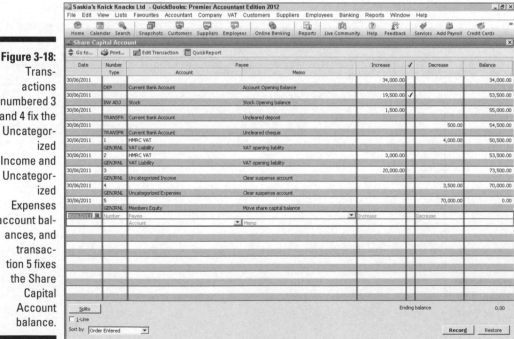

Figure 3-18:
Transactions numbered 3 and 4 fix the Uncategorized Income and Uncategorized Expenses account balances, and transaction 5 fixes the Share Capital Account balance.

8. **Again, select the next empty row of the register.**

   Click the row or use the up- or down-arrow key.

9. **Type the conversion date in the Date field.**

   Move the cursor to the Date field (if it isn't already there), and type the date. Again, you use the DD/MM/YYYY format.

10. **Type the Uncategorized Expenses account balance in the Decrease field.**

    In Figure 3-16, for example, the Uncategorized Expenses account balance is £3,500. In this case, you click the Decrease field and then type **3500**. We've said this before, but we'll say it again because you're just starting out: you don't need to include any punctuation, such as a pound sign or a comma.

11. **Type** Uncategorized Expenses **(the account name) in the Account field.**

    Select the Account field, which is on the second line of the register transaction, and begin typing **Uncategorized Expenses**, the account name. As soon as you type enough of the name for QuickBooks to figure out what you're typing, it fills in the rest of the name for you.

12. **Click the Record button to record the Uncategorized Expenses adjustment transaction.**

    Figure 3-18 shows the Share Capital Account register with transactions 3 and 4 making the correcting adjustment. See them?

13. **Again, select the next empty row of the register.**

    Click the row or use the up- or down-arrow key.

14. **Type the conversion date in the Date field.**

    Move the cursor to the Date field (if it isn't already there), and type the date in the DD/MM/YYYY format.

15. **Reduce the balance of the Share Capital Account to zero.**

    If the amount in the Balance column of the Share Capital Account is positive, click the Decrease field and type the amount in the Balance column. For example, if you see 70,000 in the Balance column of the Share Capital Account, type **70000** (without punctuation) in the Decrease column (for an example refer to Figure 3-18).

    If the amount in the Balance column of the Share Capital Account is negative, click the Increase field and type the amount in the Balance column. For example, if you see -70,000 in the Balance column of the Share Capital Account, type **70000** in the Increase column.

16. **Type the account name** Members Equity **(for Limited Companies),** Owners Equity **(for Sole Traders),** Retained Earnings **(for Partnerships), or** Unrestricted Net Assets **(for Non-Profits) in the Account field.**

Select the Account field (second line of the register transaction), and type the appropriate account name. Depending on the company type you specified in the QuickBooks Setup, QuickBooks adds either the Members Equity, Owners Equity, Retained Earnings or Unrestricted Net Assets account to the Chart of Accounts when it creates your company file. As soon as you type enough of the name for QuickBooks to figure out what you're typing, it fills in the rest of the name for you.

17. **Click the Record button to record the adjustment transaction.**

Acknowledge the message in the Retained Earnings message window by clicking OK.

You should see a zero balance in the Share Capital Account. If you do, you can close the Share Capital Account register at this point. You're finished with it. One way to close it is to click the Close button in the upper-right corner of the window.

You can check your work thus far – and checking it *is* a good idea – by producing another copy of the trial balance report. What you want to check are the Uncategorized Income, Uncategorized Expenses, and Share Capital Account balances. They should each be zero, as shown in Figure 3-19, and you should see a balance in the Members Equity, Owners Equity, Retained Earnings or Unrestricted Net Assets account.

You can produce a trial balance by choosing Reports⇨Accountant & Taxes⇨ Trial Balance. QuickBooks displays the trial balance report in a document window. If you need to enter the conversion date in the As Of line, click the box and type the conversion date in DD/MM/YYYY format.

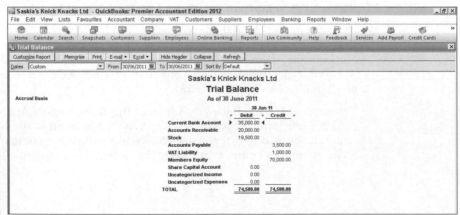

Figure 3-19: Another sample trial balance.

For accountants only

If you're reading this sidebar, we assume that you're an accountant who's been asked to help your client with the last piece of the QuickBooks conversion. Of course, you understand double-entry bookkeeping, and presumably you're familiar with the general mechanics involved in converting to new accounting systems. With those two caveats, you're ready to start.

First, your client has probably already installed QuickBooks and then, by running something called the QuickBooks Setup, partially set up a Chart of Accounts and loaded three master lists: the Item list, the Customer list, and the Supplier list. Probably your client has already described a number of account balances, such as bank, stock, accounts receivable (A/R) and accounts payable (A/P), and VAT liability (or refund). The result is a series of journal entries in QuickBooks which we describe in the following paragraphs. (By the way, Xs represent numbers, in case you're not familiar with this convention.)

For the conversion date bank account and stock balance (if either exists), QuickBooks shows the following entry:

	Debit	Credit
Bank Account	£X,XXX	
Stock Asset	£X,XXX	
Share Capital Account		£X,XXX

For the conversion date VAT liability balance (if it exists), QuickBooks shows this entry (in case of a VAT refund, the VAT Liability Account shows a debit and the Share Capital account shows a credit):

	Debit	Credit
VAT Liability Account		£X,XXX
Share Capital Account	£X,XXX	

For the conversion date A/R balance (if it exists), QuickBooks shows this:

	Debit	Credit
Accounts Receivable	£X,XXX	
Uncategorized Income		£X,XXX

For the conversion date A/P balance (if it exists), QuickBooks shows the following entry:

	Debit	Credit
Accounts Payable		£X,XXX
Uncategorized Expenses	£X,XXX	

To complete the picture, you need to do three housekeeping chores. First, you need to get rid of the credit to the Uncategorized Income account and the debit to the Uncategorized Expenses account – these are really just suspense accounts. Second, you need to reverse out the balance in the Share Capital Account and post it to the Profit and Loss Reserve Account. QuickBooks refers to this account as the Members Equity, Owners Equity, Retained Earnings or Unrestricted Net Asset account (depending on the legal format of the business). Third, you need to load the rest of the trial balance as described in the following section, "Supplying the missing numbers".

If the Uncategorized Income balance, the Uncategorized Expenses balance, and the Share Capital account balances don't show zero, you (with our help, of course) might have botched the adjustment. To fix the mistake, redisplay the Share Capital Account register (as noted earlier, you can double-click Share Capital Account in the Chart of Accounts list to display that account), select the adjustment transactions, and then check the account, amount, and field (Increase or Decrease). If one of the fields is wrong, select the field and replace its contents by typing over it.

Supplying the missing numbers

You're almost done. Really. Your last task is to enter the rest of the trial balance amounts into QuickBooks. To perform this task, you need to have a trial balance prepared as of the conversion date. If you followed the instructions in Chapter 2, you have one. Follow these steps:

1. **Choose either Company⇨Make Journal Entries or Accountant⇨Make Journal Entries.**

   QuickBooks displays the Make General Journal Entries window.

2. **Type the conversion date in the Date field.**

   Move the cursor to the Date field (if it isn't already there) and type the date. As you might know by now, you use the DD/MM/YYYY format.

3. **Type each trial balance account and balance that isn't already in the half-completed trial balance.**

   Okay. This step sounds confusing. But remember that you've already entered your bank, accounts receivable, stock, accounts payable, and VAT balances, and part of the Members Equity, Owners Equity, Retained Earnings or Unrestricted Net Assets account balance. Now you need to enter the rest of the trial balance – specifically, the year-to-date income and expense account balances and any missing assets, liabilities, or equity accounts.

   To enter each account and balance, use a row of the Make General Journal Entries window list box. Figure 3-20 shows how this window looks after you enter the rest of the trial balance into the list box rows.

   If you need an account that isn't already on your QuickBooks chart of accounts, that's no problem. Enter the account name you want into the Account column of the Make General Journal Entries window. When QuickBooks displays the pop-up window titled Account not found, click the Set Up button. QuickBooks then displays the Add New Account: Choose Account Type dialog box. Use it to identify the type of account you're setting up: Income, Expense, Fixed Asset, Bank, Loan, Credit, or Equity. Click Continue to display the Add New Account dialog box. Use it to create a longer description of the account (if you want) and to designate the account as a subaccount (if applicable) and then click Save & Close.

4. **Click the Save & New button to record the general journal entries that set up the rest of your trial balance.**

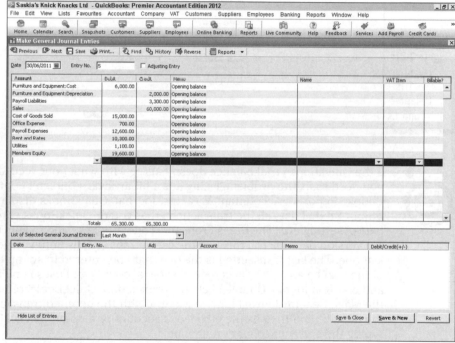

Figure 3-20: The completed Make General Journal Entries window.

Checking your work one more time

Double-checking your work is a good idea. Produce another copy of the trial balance report. Check that the QuickBooks trial balance is the one that you wanted to enter.

You can produce a trial balance by choosing Reports⇨Accountant & Taxes⇨ Trial Balance. Be sure to enter the conversion date in the As Of text box. If the QuickBooks trial balance report agrees with what your records show, you're finished (see Figure 3-21).

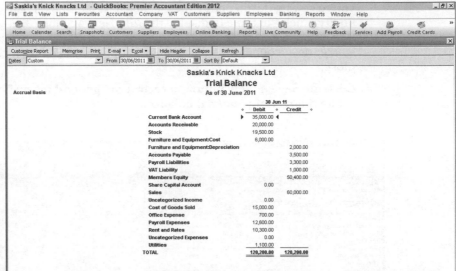

Figure 3-21:
The final
Trial
Balance
report.

TIP

If the QuickBooks trial balance doesn't agree with what your records show, you need to fix the problem. Fixing it is a bit awkward but isn't complicated. Choose Reports⇨Accountant & Taxes⇨Journal. QuickBooks displays a report or journal that lists all the transactions that you or QuickBooks entered as part of setting up. (The Dates From and To text boxes need to specify the conversion date.) Scroll through the list of transactions until you get to the last one. The last transaction is the one that you entered to set up the rest of the trial balance; it names recognisable accounts and uses familiar debit and credit amounts. Double-click this transaction. QuickBooks redisplays the Make General Journal Entries window with the botched transaction. Find the mistake and then fix the erroneous account or amount by clicking it and typing the correct account or amount.

Congratulations! You're done.

Part II
Daily Entry Tasks

The 5th Wave   By Rich Tennant

"It's really quite an entertaining piece of software. There's roller coaster action, suspense and drama, where skill and strategy are matched against winning and losing. And I thought managing our budget would be dull."

In this part . . .

Okay. You have QuickBooks set up, or maybe you were lucky enough to have someone else do all the dirty work. All that doesn't matter now, though, because this part is where you really get going. You need to start using QuickBooks to do a bunch of stuff on a regular, and maybe daily, basis. Invoice customers. Record customer payments. Pay bills. This part describes how you do all these things.

Chapter 4

Creating Invoices and Credit Notes

I n this chapter (you might be surprised to discover), we describe how to create and print invoices in QuickBooks as well as how to create and print credit notes.

You use the QuickBooks invoice form to invoice customers for the goods that you sell. You use its credit notes form to handle returns and cancelled orders for which you've received payment.

Making Sure That You're Ready to Invoice Customers

We know that you're probably all set to go. But first, you need to check a few things, okay? Good.

You should have installed QuickBooks already, of course. (We briefly describe how in Appendix A.) You should have set up a company and a Chart of Accounts in the QuickBooks Setup, as we describe in Chapter 2. You also should have entered all your lists and your starting trial balance (or talked your accountant into entering this for you), as we describe in Chapter 3. Unless you want to (or have to), enter each unpaid customer invoice separately (rather than as a lump sum). In that case, read the next section and then return to Chapter 3 to finish your work there.

Preparing an Invoice

Preparing an invoice with QuickBooks is a snap. If clicking buttons and fill-ing in text boxes are becoming old hat to you, skip the following play-by-play commentary and simply display the Create Invoices window – either by choosing Customers⇨Create Invoices or by clicking the Invoices icon on the Home page – and then fill in this window and click the Print button. If you want more help than a single sentence provides, keep reading for step-by-step instructions.

In the following steps, we describe how to create the most complicated and involved of all invoices: a *product invoice.* Some fields on the product invoice don't appear on the *service* or *professional invoice,* but don't worry whether your business is a service or professional one. Creating a service or profes-sional invoice works basically the same way as creating a product invoice – you just fill in fewer fields. And keep in mind that you start with Steps 1 and 2 no matter what type of invoice you create. Without further ado, here's how to create an invoice:

1. **Display the Create Invoices window by choosing Customers⇨Create Invoices.**

   The Create Invoices window appears, as shown in Figure 4-1.

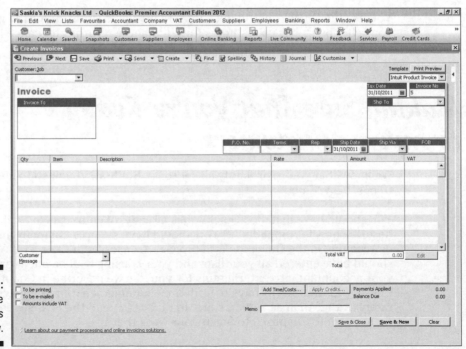

Figure 4-1:
The Create Invoices window.

2. **Select the template or invoice form that you want to use from the Template drop-down list located in the upper-right corner.**

   QuickBooks comes with predefined invoice form types, including Product, Professional, Service, and (depending on how you set up QuickBooks and which version of QuickBooks you're using) a handful of other specialised invoice templates as well. Which one appears by default depends on which one you told QuickBooks that you wanted to use in the QuickBooks Setup process. You can even create your own custom invoice template (or modify an existing one) by clicking the Customise button. We describe customising invoice forms in the "Customising Invoices and Credit Notes" section, later in this chapter.

3. **Identify the customer and, if necessary, the job by using the Customer:Job drop-down list.**

   Scroll through the Customer:Job drop-down list until you see the customer or job name that you need and then click it.

4. **(Optional) Assign a class to the invoice.**

   If you use classes (described in Chapter 3) to track expenses and income, activate the Class drop-down list and select an appropriate class for the invoice. To turn this handy way of categorising transactions on or off (which is overkill for some businesses), choose Edit➪Preferences, click Accounting on the left, click the Company Preferences tab, and then select or clear the Use Class Tracking check box. (Figure 4-1 doesn't show the Class box.)

5. **Give the invoice date.**

   Press Tab several times to move the cursor to the Tax Date text box. Then enter the correct date in DD/MM/YYYY format. You also can use the following secret codes to change the date:

   - *Press* + (the plus symbol) to move the date ahead one day.
   - *Press* – (the minus symbol) to move the date back one day.
   - *Press T* to change the date to today's date (as specified by the system time that your computer's internal clock provides).
   - *Press]* to move the date one week forward.
   - *Press [* to move the date one week backward.
   - *Press @* to move the date one month forward.
   - *Press ;* to move the date one month backward.
   - *Press M* to change the date to the first day of the month (because *M* is the first letter in the word *month*).
   - *Press H* to change the date to the last day of the month (because *H* is the last letter in the word *month*).

- *Press Y* to change the date to the first day of the year (because, as you no doubt can guess, *Y* is the first letter in the word *year*).

- *Press R* to change the date to the last day of the year (because *R* is the last letter in the word *year*).

You can also click the button on the right side of the Date field to display a small calendar. To select a date from the calendar, just click the date you want. Click the arrows in the top-left and top-right corners of the calendar to display the previous or next month.

6. (Optional) Enter an invoice number in the Invoice No text box.

QuickBooks suggests an invoice number by adding 1 to the last invoice number that you used. You can accept this number or, if you need to have it your way, you can tab to the Invoice No text box and change the number to whatever you want.

7. Fix the Invoice To address, if necessary.

QuickBooks grabs the invoicing address from the Customer:Jobs list. You can change the address for the invoice by replacing some portion of the usual invoice address. You can, for example, insert another line that says *Attention: William Bobbins,* if that's the name of the person to whom the invoice should go.

8. Fix the Ship To address, if necessary.

We feel like a broken record, but here's the deal: QuickBooks also grabs the shipping address from the Customer:Jobs list. So if the shipping address has something unusual about it for just this one invoice, you can change the address by replacing or adding information to the Ship To address block. Note that QuickBooks will keep track of each of the shipping addresses you use for a customer, so if you used a shipping address before, you may be able to select it from the Ship To drop-down list.

9. (Optional . . . sort of) Provide the purchase order number in the P.O. No text box.

If the customer issues purchase orders (POs), enter the number of the purchase order that authorises this purchase. (Just for the record, PO is pronounced *pee-oh,* not *poh* or *poo.*)

10. Specify the payment terms by selecting an option from the Terms drop-down list.

If you offer an early payment discount (and we hope you read the first couple of sections in Chapter 19 before you decide to offer these), there are specific VAT rules that apply, which at first sound kind of strange: whether or not your customer takes the discount, you account for the VAT on the invoice *as if* the customer does. The great thing is that

QuickBooks automatically adjusts the VAT on the invoice when you use terms which include early payments (for example, something like 2% 10 Net 30, which reads Net 30 days to pay but 2% discount if paid within 10 days). You can read about how Terms work in Chapter 3 or see how to add your own early payment discount term in Chapter 6. By the way, QuickBooks also tracks the date by which the customer needs to pay in order to get the discount – which is really helpful.

11. (Optional) Name the sales representative in the Rep field.

Rep doesn't stand for *Reputation,* so don't put three-letter editorial comments in here (although we can't imagine what you could do with three letters). If you want to track sales by sales representative, use the Rep drop-down list. Simply activate the list by clicking its arrow and then pick a name. Sales representatives can include employees, suppliers, and people you listed in the Other Names list (see Chapter 3). To quickly add a sales rep, select Add New and then use the handy dialog boxes that QuickBooks displays. To work with the Sales Rep list, choose Lists➪Customer & Supplier Profile Lists➪Sales Rep List.

12. Specify the shipping date if it's something other than the invoice date.

To specify the date, simply move the cursor to the Ship text box and then type the date in DD/MM/YYYY format. You can move the cursor by pressing Tab or by clicking the text box.

Oh – one other quick point: Remember all those secret codes that we talk about in Step 5 for changing the invoice date? They also work for changing the shipping date.

13. Specify the shipping method.

You can probably guess how you specify the shipping method, but parallel structure and compulsive personalities force us to continue. So to specify the shipping method, move the cursor to the Ship Via drop-down list and then select a shipping method from it.

By the way, you can add new shipping methods to the list by selecting Add New and then filling out the cute little dialog box that QuickBooks displays. Setting up new shipping methods is easy. Really easy.

14. Specify the FOB point by using the FOB text box.

FOB stands for *free-on-board.* The FOB point is more important than it first seems – at least in a business sense – because the FOB point determines when the transfer of ownership occurs, who pays for delivery, and who bears the risks of damage to the goods during shipping.

If a shipment is free-on-board at the *shipping* point, the ownership of the goods being sold transfers to the purchaser as soon as the goods leave the seller's shipping dock. (Remember that you're the seller.) In this case, the purchaser pays for delivery and bears the risk of shipping damage. You can specify the FOB shipping point either as FOB Shipping Point or by using the name of the city. If the shipping point is Oxford, for example, FOB Oxford is the same thing as FOB Shipping Point. Most goods are shipped as FOB Shipping Point, by the way.

If a shipment is free-on-board at the *destination* point, the ownership of the goods that are being sold transfers to the purchaser as soon as the goods arrive on the purchaser's shipping dock. The seller pays for the delivery and bears the risk of shipping damage. You can specify the FOB destination point either as FOB Destination Point or by using the name of the city. If the destination point is London, for example, FOB London is the same thing as FOB Destination Point.

15. Enter each item that you're selling.

Move the cursor to the first row of the Qty/Item/Description/Rate/Amount/VAT list box. Okay, we know that isn't a very good name for it, but you know what we mean, right? You need to start filling in the line items that go on the invoice. After you move the cursor to a row in the list box, QuickBooks turns the Item Code field into a drop-down list. Activate the Item Code drop-down list of the first empty row in the list box and then select the item.

When you select the item, QuickBooks fills in the Description, Rate, and VAT text boxes with whatever sales description, sales price, and VAT Code you've entered in the Item list. (You can edit the information for this particular invoice if you need to.) Enter the number of items sold in the Qty text box. (After you enter this number, QuickBooks calculates the amount by multiplying quantity by rate.) If you need other items on the invoice, use the remaining empty rows of the list box to enter each one.

You can put as many items on an invoice as you want. If you don't have enough room on a single page, QuickBooks adds as many pages as necessary to the invoice. Information about the invoice total, of course, goes only on the last page.

Click the Add Time/Costs button at the bottom of the form to display the Choose Billable Time and Costs dialog box. Use this dialog box to select costs that you've assigned to the customer or job, as described in more detail in Chapter 16. In brief, use the Items tab to select items purchased for the job, the Expenses tab to select reimbursable expenses and enter markup information, and the Time tab to select billable time recorded in the Weekly Timesheet or the Time/Enter Single Activity window.

16. Enter any special items that the invoice should include.

If you haven't worked much with QuickBooks items, you probably have no idea what we're talking about. (For more information about adding to and working with lists in QuickBooks, cruise through Chapter 3.)

To describe any of the special items, activate the Item Code drop-down list of the next empty row and then select the special item. After QuickBooks fills in the Description, Rate, and if applicable, VAT text boxes, edit this information (if necessary). Describe each of the other special items – subtotals, discounts, delivery, and so on – that you're itemising on the invoice by filling in the empty rows in the list box.

If you want to include a Discount item and have it apply to multiple items, you have two options. You can stick a Subtotal item on the invoice after the stock or other items that you want to discount, and then stick a Discount item directly after the Subtotal item. Or, you can use a Group item and then stick the Discount item after the last line of the group (which is really a subtotal line that QuickBooks adds to the invoice automatically). In either case QuickBooks calculates the discount as a percentage of the subtotal.

17. (Optional) Add a customer message.

Click in the Customer Message box, activate its drop-down list, and select a clever customer message. To add customer messages to the Customer Message list, choose Add New and then fill in the dialog box that QuickBooks displays.

18. Double check the VAT.

QuickBooks uses the VAT Codes you specified for each item as a default. If this isn't correct, move the cursor to the VAT column, activate the drop-down list, and select the correct VAT code. You'll see the Total VAT displayed at the bottom of the invoice.

If you offer an early payment discount, QuickBooks automatically adjusts the VAT in the Total VAT box to take into account the early payment discount. Remember, you need to account for the VAT *as if* the customer takes the discount (whether or not the customer does).

19. (Truly optional) Add a memo.

You can add a memo description to the invoice if you want to. This memo doesn't print on invoices – only on the Customer Statement. Memo descriptions give you a way of storing information related to an invoice with that invoice.

Figure 4-2 shows a completed Create Invoices window.

20. If you want to delay printing this invoice, clear the To Be Printed check box that's in the column in the lower-left area of the Create Invoices window.

We want to postpone talking about what selecting the To Be Printed check box does until we finish the discussion of invoice creation. We talk about printing invoices a little later in the chapter. We promise.

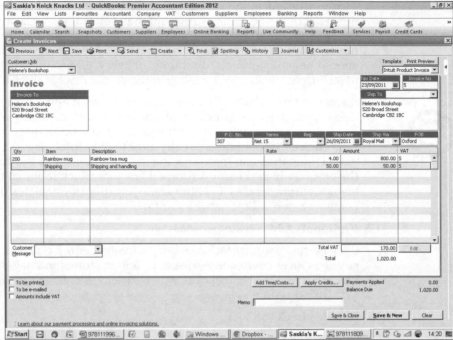

Figure 4-2:
A completed
Create
Invoices
window.

21. **Save the invoice by clicking the Save & New button or the Save & Close button.**

    QuickBooks saves the invoice that's onscreen. If you click Save & New, QuickBooks displays an empty Create Invoices window so that you can create another invoice.

    You can page back and forth through invoices that you created earlier by clicking the Next and Previous buttons.

    When you're done creating invoices, you can click the invoice form's Save & Close button. Or click the Close button, also known as the Close box, which is the little box marked with an X in the upper-right corner of the window.

Fixing Invoice Mistakes

Neither of the authors is a perfect person. You're not a perfect person. In fact nobody is; everyone makes mistakes. You don't need to get worked up over mistakes that you make while entering information in invoices, though, because in the following sections, we show you how to fix the most common mistakes that you might make on your invoices.

If the invoice is still displayed onscreen

If the invoice is still displayed onscreen (in other words, you have not yet saved it), you can just move the cursor to the box or button that's wrong and then fix the mistake. Because most of the bits of information that you enter in the Create Invoices window are short and sweet, you can easily replace the contents of some fields by typing over whatever's already there. To start all over again and clear all the information from the window, just click the Clear button. To save the invoice after you've made your changes, click the Save & New button.

If you need to insert or delete a line in the middle of the invoice, right-click to display a contextual menu and then choose Insert Line or Delete Line. Alternatively, press the Ctrl+Insert key to insert a line or the Delete key to delete a line. (For more QuickBooks keyboard shortcuts check out the online Cheat Sheet at www.dummies.com/cheatsheet/quickbooks2012uk.)

If the invoice isn't displayed onscreen

If the invoice isn't displayed onscreen and you haven't yet printed it, you can use the Next and Previous buttons to page through the invoices. When you get to the one with the error, simply fix the error as we describe in the preceding section. If you make an error fixing the invoice, you can click the Revert button to go back to the saved invoice. The Revert button replaces the Clear button when you're viewing an existing invoice – that is, an invoice that you've already saved.

If you printed the invoice, you also can make the sort of change that we describe in the preceding paragraphs. For example, you can page through the invoices until you find the one (now printed) that has the error. And you can correct the error and print the invoice again.

We don't recommend that you go this route, however, if you've already sent the invoice. You might want to consider fixing the invoice by issuing either a credit note (if the original invoice overcharged) or another invoice (if the original invoice undercharged). The reason why we suggest issuing a credit note (which we show you how to do in the appropriately titled section, "Preparing a Credit Note", later in this chapter) or another invoice is that life gets awfully messy if you and your customer have multiple copies of the same invoice floating around and causing confusion.

Deleting an invoice

We hesitate to mention this, but you can also delete invoices. Procedurally, deleting an invoice is easy. You just display the invoice in the Create Invoices window and choose Edit➪Delete Invoice. When QuickBooks asks you to confirm your deletion, click Yes. Read the following paragraph first, though, because you may not want to delete the invoice.

Even though deleting invoices is easy, it isn't something that you should do casually or for fun. Deleting an invoice is okay if you've just created it, only you have seen it, and you haven't yet printed it. In this case, no one needs to know that you've made a mistake. It's your secret. The rest of the time – even if you create an invoice that you don't want later – you should keep a copy of the invoice in the QuickBooks system. By doing so, you have a record that the invoice existed, which usually makes it easier to answer questions later.

"But how do I correct my books if I leave the bogus invoice?", you ask.

Good question. To correct your financial records for the invoice that you don't want to count any more, simply *void* the invoice. The invoice remains in the QuickBooks system, but QuickBooks doesn't count it because it loses its quantity, amount, and VAT information. Good news – voiding an invoice is as simple as deleting one. Just display the invoice in the Create Invoices window and then choose Edit➪Void Invoice.

Preparing a Credit Note

Credit notes can be a handy way to fix data-entry mistakes that you didn't find or correct earlier. A credit note is also a handy way to handle things like customer returns and refunds. If you've prepared an invoice or two in your time, you'll find that preparing a QuickBooks credit note is a lot easier than using old-fashioned methods.

The fastest way to issue a credit note is to find the invoice that you want to credit (by using the Previous and Next buttons in the Create Invoices window for example), and to click the Create button (located in the top row of icons in the window), then select Credit Note For This Window. QuickBooks opens the Create Credit Notes/Refunds window prefilled with the details of the invoice you want to credit. Check over the credit note and change the information as needed. Click Save & Close to save the credit note.

Sometimes, however, you need to create a credit note from scratch. In the following steps, we describe how to create the most complicated and involved kind of credit note: a *product credit note.* Creating a *service* or *professional credit note* works basically the same way, however. You just fill in fewer fields.

1. **Choose Customers⇨Create Credit Notes/Refunds or click the Refunds & Credits icon in the Customer section of the Home page to display the Create Credit Notes/Refunds window (as shown in Figure 4-3).**

2. **Identify the customer and, if necessary, the job in the Customer:Job drop-down list.**

   You can select the customer or job from the list by clicking it.

3. **(Optional) Specify a class for the credit note.**

   If you're using classes to categorise transactions, activate the Class drop-down list and choose the appropriate class for the credit note.

4. **Date the credit note.**

   Press Tab to move the cursor to the Tax Date text box. Then enter the correct date in DD/MM/YYYY format. You also can use the secret date-editing codes that we describe in the section "Preparing an Invoice," earlier in the chapter.

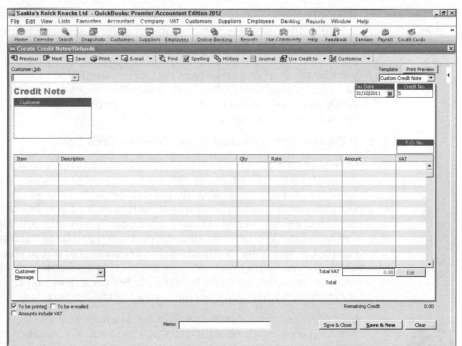

Figure 4-3:
The Create Credit Notes/ Refunds window.

5. **(Optional) Enter a credit note number.**

QuickBooks suggests a credit note number by adding 1 to the last *invoice* number you used. Yes, you read correctly. QuickBooks does not have a separate numbering system for invoices and credit notes. You can accept the number or tab to the Credit No. text box to change the number to whatever you want. For example you may want to prefix your credit notes with CN to easily identify them. (But beware that QuickBooks assumes that from now on you also want to prefix your invoices with CN, so you need to adjust the number of the first invoice you raise after you record a credit note.)

6. **Fix the Customer address, if necessary.**

QuickBooks grabs the invoicing address from the Customer list. You can change the address for the credit note by typing in the Customer text box. Typically, you should use the same address for the credit note that you use for the original invoice or invoices.

7. **(Optional . . . sort of) Provide the purchase order (PO) number.**

If the credit note adjusts the total remaining balance on a customer purchase order, you should probably enter the number of the purchase order into the P.O. No. text box.

Here's the logic of this suggestion, for those readers who care: if you invoice your customer £1000 against P.O. No. 1984, which authorises a £1000 purchase, you "used up" the entire purchase order – at least according to the customer's accounts payable clerk, who processes your invoices. If you make sure that a credit note for £1000 is identified as being related to P.O. No. 1984, however, you essentially free up the £1000 purchase balance, which might mean that you can use, or invoice, the purchase order again.

8. **If the customer returned items, describe each item.**

Move the cursor to the first row of the Item/Description/Qty/ Rate/ Amount/VAT text box. In the first empty row of the box, activate the Item drop-down list and then select the item. After you select it, QuickBooks fills in the Description, Rate, and VAT text boxes with whatever sales description, sales price, and VAT Code you entered in the Item list. (You can edit this information if you need to). Enter the number of items that the customer is returning (or not paying for) in the Qty text box. (After you enter this number, QuickBooks calculates the amount by multiplying Qty by Rate.) Enter each item that the customer is returning by filling in the empty rows of the list box.

In the case of stock items, QuickBooks assumes that the items you're showing on a credit note are returned to stock. You want to adjust your stock physical counts if unsold items are returned. But, if you charged your customer the wrong price for stock items, create a credit note (the fast way, described earlier) for the entire original invoice to cancel it out and return the items to stock, then do another invoice with the correct price on it and the items move out of stock again, this time at the correct price.

As with invoices, you can put as many items on a credit note as you want. If you don't have enough room on a single page, QuickBooks keeps adding pages to the credit note until you're finished. The total information, of course, goes on the last page.

9. **Describe any special items that the credit note should include.**

If you want to issue a credit note for other items that appear on the original invoice – delivery, discounts, other charges, and so on – add descriptions of each item to the Item list.

To add descriptions of these items, activate the Item drop-down list of the next empty row and then select the special item. (You activate the list by clicking the field once to turn it into a drop-down list and then by clicking the field's down arrow to access the list box.) After QuickBooks fills in the Description, Rate and VAT text boxes, edit this information (if necessary). Enter each special item – subtotal, discount, delivery, and so on – that you're itemising on the credit note.

If you want to include a Discount item, you need to stick a Subtotal item on the credit note after the stock or other items that you've discounted. Then stick a Discount item directly after the Subtotal item. In this way, QuickBooks calculates the discount as a percentage of the subtotal.

10. **(Optional) Add a customer message.**

Activate the Customer Message list and select a clever customer message.

11. **Double check the VAT.**

QuickBooks uses the VAT Codes you specified for each item as a default. If the code isn't correct, move the cursor to the VAT column and click to activate the list box, then select the correct VAT Code. You'll see the Total VAT displayed at the bottom of the invoice.

12. **(Optional, but a really good idea. . . .) Add a memo.**

You can use the Memo text box to add a memo description to the credit note. For example, you might use this description to explain your reasons for issuing the credit note and to cross-reference the original invoice or invoices. Note that the Memo field prints on the Customer Statement, so make sure your memo is polite. Figure 4-4 shows a completed Create Credit Notes/Refunds window.

13. **If you want to delay printing this credit note, clear the To Be Printed check box.**

We postpone talking about what selecting the To Be Printed check box does until we finish the discussion of credit note creation. Coverage of printing invoices and credit notes comes up in a later section.

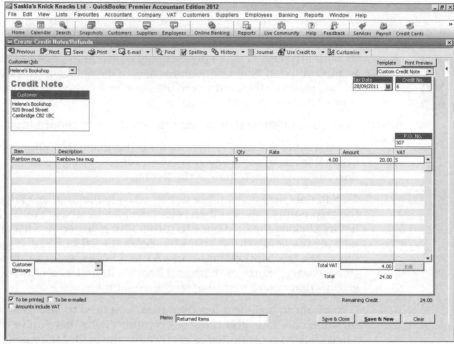

Figure 4-4:
A completed
Create
Credit
Notes/
Refunds
window.

14. **Save the credit note.**

To save a completed credit note, click either the Save & New or Save
& Close button. QuickBooks then displays a dialog box that asks what
you want to do with the credit note: retain as an available credit, give a
refund, or apply to an invoice. Make your choice by clicking the button
that corresponds to what you want to do. If you choose Apply to an
Invoice, QuickBooks asks for some additional information. QuickBooks
then saves the credit note that's onscreen and, if you clicked Save &
New, displays an empty Create Credit Notes/Refunds window so that
you can create another credit note. (Note that you can page back and
forth through credit notes that you created earlier by clicking the Next
and the Previous buttons.) When you're done creating credit notes, you
can click the credit note form's Close button.

If you indicate that you want to print a refund cheque, QuickBooks displays
the Write Cheques window and automatically fills out the cheque, linking it to
the credit note.

Fixing Credit Note Mistakes

Sure, we can repeat the same information that we gave you in the section "Fixing Invoice Mistakes", earlier in this chapter, and leave you with a strange feeling of *déjà vu*. But we won't.

Here's everything you need to know about fixing credit note mistakes: you can fix credit note mistakes the same way that you fix invoice mistakes. If you need more help, refer to the earlier section "Fixing Invoice Mistakes".

History Lessons

Would you mind doing us a small favour? Take another peek at the images shown in Figures 4-1 and 4-4, and then look at the Create Invoices window shown in Figure 4-5. See the difference? That panel of customer history information?

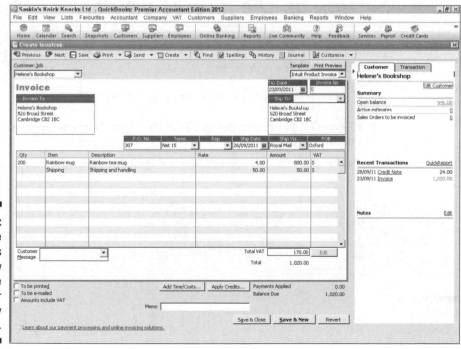

Figure 4-5: The Create Invoices window with the customer history information.

QuickBooks lets you view historical information about a customer from the Create Invoices window, the Create Credit Notes/Refunds window, and most other customer information windows, too. To see historical information about a customer on a window, click the little tab that appears in the upper-right corner of the window just to the right of the Print Preview button. Note that you can click links in the historical information panel to drill down and get more information about, for example, a listed transaction. To hide the historical information, click the little tab again.

Printing Invoices and Credit Notes

We assume that you've already set up your printer. If you've ever printed anything, your printer is already set up. Really. We also assume that if you're going to print on blank letterhead you have letterhead lying around. If you decide to use preprinted forms, we assume that you've ordered those forms and received them.

Setting up the invoice printer

You need to set up the invoice printer only once, but you need to specify a handful of general invoice-printing rules. These rules also apply to credit notes and purchase orders, by the way.

To set up your printer for invoice printing, follow these steps:

1. **Choose File⇨Printer Setup. From the Form Name drop-down list, choose Invoice.**

   QuickBooks displays the Printer Setup dialog box, as shown in Figure 4-6.

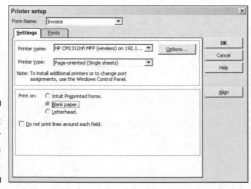

Figure 4-6:
The Printer
Setup
dialog box.

2. **Select the printer that you want to use to print invoices.**

   Activate the Printer Name drop-down list to see the installed printers. Select the one that you want to use for printing invoices, credit notes, and purchase orders.

3. **(Optional) Select the printer type.**

   The Printer Type drop-down list describes the kind of paper that your printer uses. Accept the Page-oriented selection, meaning single sheets (as opposed to Continuous, where you have a ream with perforated edges).

4. **Select the type of invoice form.**

   Select the option button that describes the type of form that you want to print on: Intuit Preprinted Forms, Blank Paper, or Letterhead. Then select the Do Not Print Lines around Each Field check box if you don't like the nice little boxes that QuickBooks creates to separate each field.

   For more on these types of form, read the sidebar, "What am I printing on?"

5. **(Optional, but a really good idea . . .) Print a test invoice on real invoice paper.**

   Click the Align button. When QuickBooks displays the Align Printer dialog box, choose the type of invoice that you want to print from the list and then click OK. When QuickBooks displays the Fine Alignment dialog box, as shown in Figure 4-7, click the Print Sample button to tell QuickBooks to print a dummy invoice on whatever paper you've loaded in the invoice printer.

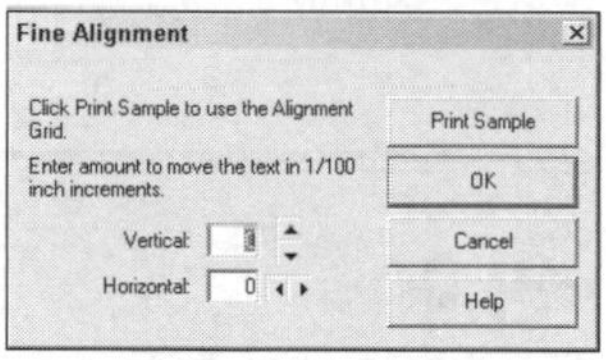

Figure 4-7:
The Fine Alignment dialog box.

The dummy invoice that QuickBooks prints gives you a chance to see what your invoices will look like. The invoice also has a set of alignment gridlines that prints over the Invoice To text box. You can use these gridlines if you need to fine-align your printer.

6. **Fix any form-alignment problems.**

   If you see any alignment problems after you complete Step 5, you need to fix them. To fix any big alignment problems – like stuff printing in the wrong place – you need to adjust how the paper feeds into the printer.

When you finally get the paper loaded as best you can, be sure to note exactly how you have it loaded. You need to have the printer and paper set up the same way every time you print.

For minor (but nonetheless annoying) alignment problems, use the Fine Alignment dialog box's Vertical and Horizontal boxes to adjust the form's alignment. Then print another sample invoice. Go ahead and experiment a bit. You need to fine-tune the printing of the invoice form only once. Click OK in the Fine Alignment dialog box when you finish, and QuickBooks redisplays the Printer Setup dialog box.

Clicking the Options button in the Printer Setup dialog box (refer to Figure 4-6) opens the selected printer's Windows printer setup information, where you can do such things as specify quality settings or print order. Because this information relates to Windows and not to QuickBooks, we are not going to explain it. If you're the curious type or accidentally click it and then have questions about what you see, refer either to your Windows user's guide or the printer's user's guide.

7. **Save your printer settings stuff.**

   After you finish fiddling with all the Printer Setup dialog box settings, click OK to save your changes.

   If you always want to use some particular settings to print a particular form (maybe you always print two copies of an invoice, for example), see the "Customising Invoices and Credit Notes" section, later in this chapter.

You can print invoices and credit notes one at a time or in a batch. How you print them makes no difference to QuickBooks. Pick whatever way seems to fit your style the best. The following sections show you how.

What am I printing on?

Sometimes people get confused about the difference between preprinted forms, letterhead, and plain paper. Here's the scoop: *preprinted forms* have your company name, perhaps your logo, and a bunch of other boxes and lines (often in another colour of ink) already printed on them. Preprinted forms are often multipart forms.

Letterhead is what you usually use for letters that you write. It has your company name and address on it, for example, but nothing else. To save you from having to purchase preprinted forms, QuickBooks enables you to use letterhead to create invoices and forms. (To make the letterhead look a little more bookkeeper-ish, QuickBooks draws lines and boxes on the letterhead so that it looks sort of like a preprinted invoice.)

Plain paper is, well, plain paper. Nothing is printed on it. So QuickBooks needs to print everything — your company name, all the invoice stuff, and (optionally) lines and boxes.

Printing invoices and credit notes as you create them

If you want to print invoices and credit notes as you create them, follow these steps:

1. **Click the Print button after you create the invoice or credit note.**

   After you fill in the boxes in the Create Invoices window (refer to Figure 4-2) or the Create Credit Notes/Refunds window (refer to Figure 4-4), click the Print button. QuickBooks, ever the faithful servant, displays either the Print One Invoice dialog box (as shown in Figure 4-8) or the Print One Credit Note/Refund dialog box (which looks almost like the Print One Invoice dialog box).

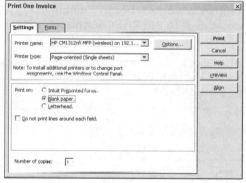

Figure 4-8:
The Print One Invoice dialog box.

2. **(Optional) Select the type of invoice or credit note form.**

   If you're using a different type of invoice or credit note form than you've described for the invoice printer setup, select the type of form that you want to print from the Print On radio button choices. You can select Intuit Preprinted Forms, Blank Paper, or Letterhead.

   You shouldn't have to worry about printing test invoice or credit note forms or fiddling with form alignment problems if you addressed these issues when you set up the invoice printer, so we're not going to talk about the Align button here. If you want to do this kind of stuff and you need help, refer to the preceding section, "Setting up the invoice printer", in which we describe how to print test forms and fix form-alignment problems.

3. **Print the form.**

   Click the Print button to send the form to the printer. QuickBooks prints the form.

4. **Review the invoice or credit note and reprint the form, if necessary.**

   Review the invoice or credit note to see whether QuickBooks printed it correctly. If the form looks wrong, fix whatever caused the problem (perhaps you printed it on the wrong paper, for example) and reprint the form by clicking the Print button again.

Printing invoices in a batch

If you want to print invoices in a batch, you need to mark the To Be Printed check box that appears in the lower-left corner of the Create Invoices window. This check mark tells QuickBooks to put a copy of the invoice on an invoices-to-be-printed list.

When you later want to print the invoices-to-be-printed list, follow these steps:

1. **Display the Create Invoices window (choose Customers➪Create Invoices), click the arrow next to the Print button, and choose Print Batch from the drop-down list.**

   QuickBooks displays the Select Invoices to Print dialog box, as shown in Figure 4-9. This box lists all the invoices that you marked as To Be Printed that you haven't yet printed.

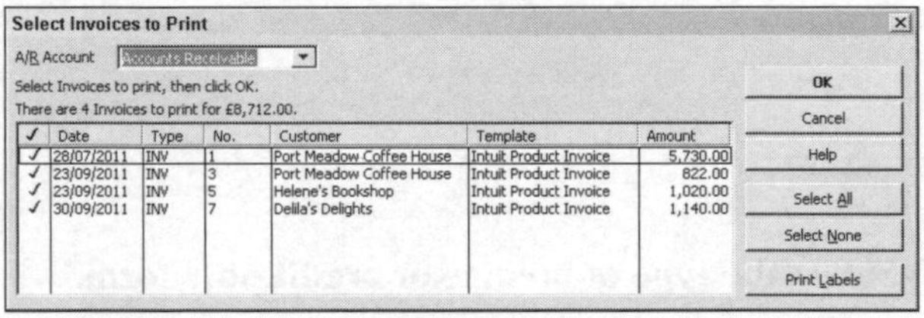

Figure 4-9: The Select Invoices to Print dialog box.

2. **Select the invoices that you want to print.**

   Initially, QuickBooks marks all the invoices with a check mark, indicating that they'll be printed. You can select and deselect individual invoices on the list by clicking them. You also can click the Select All button (to mark all the invoices) or the Select None button (to deselect all the invoices).

3. **Click OK.**

   After you correctly mark all the invoices you want to print – and none of the ones you don't want to print – click OK. QuickBooks displays the Print Invoices dialog box (this is identical to the dialog shown in Figure 4-8, aside from the title).

4. **(Optional) Select the type of invoice form.**

   If you use a different type of invoice form than you described during the invoice setup, select the type of form that you want to print on by using the Print On options. You can choose Intuit Preprinted Forms, Blank Paper, or Letterhead.

   For more on these types of forms, read the sidebar, "What am I printing on?" elsewhere in this chapter.

5. **Print the forms.**

   Click the Print button to send the selected invoice forms to the printer. QuickBooks prints the forms and then displays a message box that asks whether the forms printed correctly.

6. **Review the invoice forms and reprint them if necessary.**

   Review the invoices to see whether QuickBooks printed them all correctly. If all the forms look okay, click OK in the message box. If one or more forms don't look okay, enter the invoice number of the first incorrect form in the message box. Then fix whatever problem fouled up the form (perhaps you printed it on the wrong paper, for example) and reprint the bad form(s) by clicking the Print button again. (The Print button is in the Print Invoices dialog box.)

Printing credit notes in a batch

If you want to print credit notes in a batch, you need to select the To Be Printed check box that appears in the lower-left corner of the Create Credit Notes/Refunds window. Selecting this box tells QuickBooks to put a copy of the credit note on a credit-note-to-be-printed list.

Printing credit notes in a batch works similarly to printing invoices in a batch. Because I describe how to print invoices in a batch in the preceding section, here I speed through a description of printing credit notes in a batch. If you get lost or have questions, refer to the preceding section.

When you're ready to print the credit notes that are on the to-be-printed list, follow these steps:

1. **Display the Create Credit Notes/Refunds window (refer to Figure 4-4), click the down arrow next to the Print button, and choose Print Batch from the drop-down list.**

   QuickBooks displays the Select Credit Notes to Print dialog box.

2. **Select the credit notes that you want to print.**

3. **Click OK to display the Print Credit Notes dialog box.**

4. **Use the Print Credit Notes dialog box to describe how you want your credit notes to be printed.**

5. **Click the Print button to send the selected credit notes to the printer.**

   QuickBooks prints the credit notes.

Sending Invoices and Credit Notes via E-Mail

If you have e-mail already set up on your computer you can e-mail invoices rather than print them.

To set up an e-mail provider:

1. **Click Edit⇨Preferences and select Send Forms in the list of icons on the left.**

   Click the My Preferences tab (see Figure 4-10).

2. **Click the Add button to configure a new e-mail client.**

   In the Add Email Info window, fill in the e-mail settings:

   • Enter an Email Id (that's your login ID)

   • Select the Email Provider (for example Yahoo!)

   • If you select Gmail, Yahoo!, or Hotmail/Live, QuickBooks configures the SMTP Server details area. If you select Others you need to give the Server Name, Port Number, and whether SSL (encryption) applies. (If you need help with this please contact your e-mail service provider.)

   Click OK to save your new configuration. You can configure multiple e-mail clients by repeating this step. QuickBooks saves the first e-mail configuration as the default client, but when you configure a second client QuickBooks asks you whether you want to set the new client as the default. Make your selection.

   Note: if you want QuickBooks to configure Microsoft Outlook or Mozilla Thunderbird as clients, you need to have them installed.

3. **Click OK to save the new e-mail client settings and exit the Preferences window.**

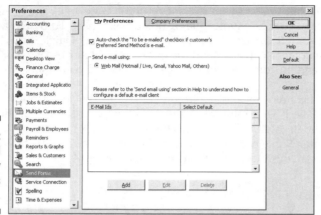

Figure 4-10:
The Send
Forms My
Preferences
dialog box.

To e-mail an invoice or credit note, click the Send button, which appears at
the top of the Create Invoices window. (The button shows a picture of a little
envelope with a green arrow.) QuickBooks displays the Send Invoice dialog
box, as shown in Figure 4-11.

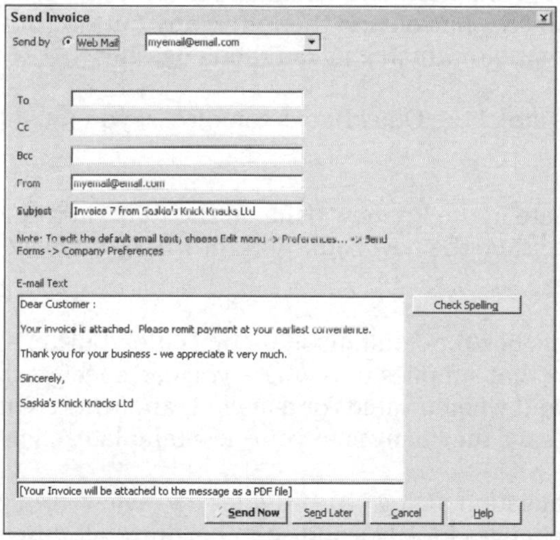

Figure 4-11:
The Send
Invoice dia-
log box.

Enter the e-mail address of the business to which you want to send an
invoice or credit note, edit the message as appropriate (make sure to click
that Check Spelling button), and then click the Send Now button.

If you want to wait to send your invoice or credit note, click the Send Later button while in the Send Invoice dialog box or select the To Be E-Mailed check box in the lower-left corner of the invoice window, and QuickBooks batches your e-mail invoices. You can send the entire batch later by clicking the arrow next to the Send button and choosing the Send Batch command.

You can also fax invoices and credit notes from inside QuickBooks if you have a modem installed. To do this, click the Print button at the top of the Create Invoices or the Create Credit Notes/Refunds window, choose your fax/modem from the Printer Name drop-down list, and then use the wizard that appears to send the fax via your modem. (Phone charges may apply.)

Customising Invoices and Credit Notes

With QuickBooks, you can easily customise the invoice and credit note templates, or create new invoices and credit notes based on one of the existing QuickBooks templates. All you have to do is open the form that you want to customise and click the Customise button.

When QuickBooks displays the Basic Customisation window (Figure 4-12), click the Manage Templates button and then the Copy button (bottom left) to create a copy of the template which you can then customise.

Note: you cannot edit one of the QuickBooks templates; you must first make a copy of it.

Name your new template in the Preview pane on the right, in the Template Name field. Click OK to save the new name and return to the Basic Customisation window.

To customise the form, click the Additional Customisation button. QuickBooks displays the dialog box that supplies tabs where you can specify which fields appear on the screen and when printed (or e-mailed) and where you can rename field titles. To save the changes to your new template, click OK.

The Additional Customisation dialog box provides a Preview area you can use to see what your changes look like and a Cancel button if things get terribly out of hand. Furthermore, the Additional Customisation dialog box also provides a Layout Designer button, which you can click to open the Layout Designer window, as shown in Figure 4-13. In this window, you can become a true layout artist and observe how the overall look of your invoice changes when you move fields around the page using your mouse.

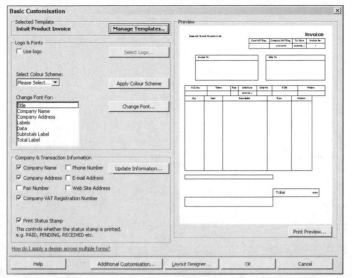

Figure 4-12:
The Basic
Customisa-
tion
window.

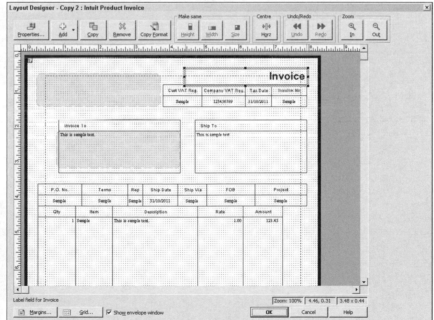

Figure 4-13:
Use the
Layout
Designer to
customise
an invoice.

Chapter 5

Collecting Your Just Rewards

*Y*ou need to record the amounts that customers pay you when they hand over cash, at the time of a sale or after you have invoiced them. In this chapter, we describe how to record these receipts and explain how to make bank deposits, track the amounts that customers owe and pay, and assess finance charges.

If you've been using QuickBooks to prepare customer invoices, you're ready to begin recording receipts. You'll have no problem. If you haven't been invoicing customers, you need to make sure that you have a couple things ready to go before you can record cash sales.

First, you need to make sure that your lists are up-to-date. (We describe updating these lists in Chapter 3.) And second, if you want to print sales receipts, you need to have your printer set up to print them. You do so by choosing File⇨Printer Setup and then selecting Sales Receipt from the Form Name drop-down list. Setting up your printer to print sales receipts works just like setting it up to print invoices and credit notes (as we describe in Chapter 4).

Recording a Sales Receipt

You record a *sales receipt* when a customer pays you in full for goods or services at the point of sale. Sales receipts work similarly to regular sales (for which you first invoice a customer and then later receive payment on the invoice). In fact, the big difference between the two types of sales is that sales receipts are recorded in a way that changes your cash balance rather than your accounts receivable balance.

In the following steps, we describe how to record sales receipts for products, which are the most complicated type of cash sale. Recording sales receipts for services works basically the same way, however. You simply fill in fewer fields.

1. **Choose Customers⇨Enter Sales Receipt.**

   Or, on the Home screen, click the Create Sales Receipts icon. Or, in the Customer Centre, choose the customer from the list and then choose New Transactions⇨Sales Receipts. The Enter Sales Receipts window appears, as shown in Figure 5-1.

   Your Enter Sales Receipts window may not look exactly like mine because QuickBooks customises (and you can customise) its forms to fit your particular type of business.

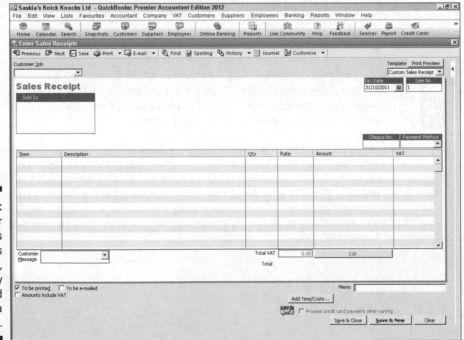

Figure 5-1: The Enter Sales Receipts window, strangely empty and perhaps a bit lonely.

Customising sales receipt forms works in a similar way to customising invoices and credit notes, as we describe in Chapter 4. If your Enter Sales Receipts window includes more fields than we describe here, you can also turn to that chapter for help on how to fill out the additional fields or turn them off.

2. **Identify the customer and, if necessary, the job.**

   Activate the Customer:Job drop-down list by clicking the down arrow to the right of the box. Scroll through the Customer:Job list until you see the customer or job name that you want and then click it. Note that unlike with invoices, the Customer:Job field isn't required for cash sales.

3. **(Optional) Specify a class for the sales receipt.**

   If you're using classes to categorise transactions, activate the Class drop-down list and select the appropriate class for the sales receipt. (We don't show the Class list box in Figure 5-1, so don't look for it there.)

4. **Date the sales receipt.**

   Press Tab to move the cursor to the Date text box. Then type the correct date in DD/MM/YYYY format. You can change the date by using any of the date-editing codes. (You can find these codes in Chapter 4 and on the online Cheat Sheet for this book at www.dummies.com/cheatsheet/quickbooks2012uk.)

5. **(Optional) Enter a sale number.**

   QuickBooks suggests a cash sale number by adding 1 to the last cash sale number you used. Use this number or tab to the Sale No. text box and change the number to whatever you want.

6. **Fix the Sold To address, if necessary.**

   QuickBooks grabs the address from the customer's record in the Customer list and uses it as the Sold To address. You can change the address for the cash sale, however, by replacing the appropriate part of the usual address.

7. **Record the cheque number.**

   Enter the customer's cheque number in the Cheque No. text box. If the customer is paying with cold hard cash, or by debit or credit card, you can leave the Cheque No. text box empty.

8. **Specify the payment method.**

   To specify the payment method, activate the Payment Method drop-down list and select something from it: Cash, Cheque, Visa, MasterCard, or whatever. If you don't see the payment method that you want to use, you can add the method to the Payment Method list. Choose Add New to display the New Payment Method dialog box. Enter a description of the payment method in the text box and click OK.

9. **Describe each item that you're selling.**

Move the cursor to the first row of the Item/Description/Qty/Rate/Amount/VAT list box. When you do this, QuickBooks turns the Item field into a drop-down list. Activate the Item drop-down list of the first empty row in the list box and then select the item. QuickBooks fills in the Description, Rate, and VAT text boxes with whatever sales description, sales price and VAT code you entered in the Item list. (You can edit this information if you want, but that probably isn't necessary.) Enter the number of items sold in the Qty text box. Describe each of the other items you're selling by filling in the next empty rows of the list box.

If you add a stock item to an invoice, QuickBooks adds a small button to the Quantity field when the cursor rests on it. If you click the button, QuickBooks displays a window that describes the on-hand quantities of the stock item. (***Note***: this handy little feature is only in QuickBooks Premier.)

If you've already read the chapter on invoicing customers (Chapter 4), what we're about to tell you will seem very familiar: you can put as many items on a sales receipt as you want. If you don't have enough room on a single page, QuickBooks adds as many pages as you need to the receipt. The sales receipt total, of course, goes on the last page.

10. **Describe any special items that the sales receipt should include.**

If you didn't set up the Item list in QuickBooks, you have no idea what we're talking about. Here's the scoop: QuickBooks thinks that anything that you stick on a receipt (or an invoice, for that matter) is something that you're selling. If you sell blue, yellow, and red thingamajigs, you obviously need to add each of these items to the Item list. But if you add delivery charges to your receipt, QuickBooks thinks that these charges are just another thingamajig and requires you to enter another item in the list. The same is true for a volume discount that you want to stick on the receipt. (For more information about working with your Item list and adding new items, refer to Chapter 3.)

To include one of these special items, move the cursor to the next empty row in the Item box, activate the drop-down list by clicking the arrow on the right side of the box, and then select the special item. After QuickBooks fills in the Description, Rate, and VAT text boxes, you might need to edit this information. Enter each special item – subtotals, discounts, delivery, and so on – that you're itemising on the receipt by filling in the next empty rows of the list box.

If you want to include a discount item (so that all the listed items are discounted), you need to stick a subtotal item on the receipt after the stock items or other items you want to discount. Then stick the discount item directly after the subtotal item. In this way, QuickBooks calculates the discount as a percentage of the subtotal.

11. **(Optional) Add a customer message.**

    Click in the Customer Message box, activate its drop-down list, and choose a clever customer message. To add customer messages to the customer message list, select Add New. When QuickBooks displays the New Customer Message box, fill it in and then click OK.

12. **(Truly optional and probably unnecessary for cash sales) Add a memo in the Memo text box.**

    You can include a memo description with the cash sale information. This memo isn't for your customer. It doesn't even print on the cash receipt, should you decide to print one. The memo is for your eyes only. Memo descriptions give you a way to store information that's related to a sale with the sales receipt information.

13. **Decide whether you're going to print the receipt.**

    If you aren't going to print the receipt, make sure that the To Be Printed check box is empty – if not, click it to remove the check.

    Figure 5-2 shows a completed Enter Sales Receipts window.

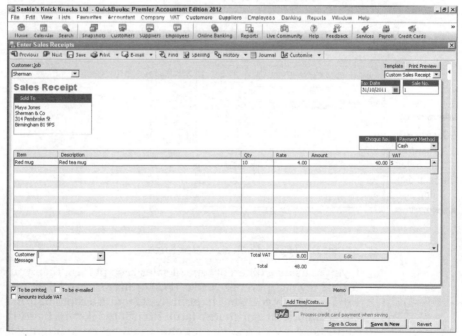

Figure 5-2:
The completed Enter Sales Receipts window.

14. **Save the sales receipt.**

To save a completed sales receipt, click either the Save & Close button or the Save & New button. QuickBooks saves the sales receipt that's onscreen and then, if you clicked Save & New, displays an empty Enter Sales Receipts window so that you can create another sales receipt. (Note that you can page back and forth through receipts that you created earlier, by clicking the Next and Previous buttons. You can also display and remove historical information for the selected customer by clicking the little white arrow to the right of the Print Preview button in the upper right-hand corner of the screen.) When you're done creating sales receipts, you can click the Enter Sales Receipts window's Close button.

Printing a Sales Receipt

To print a single sales receipt as you're recording the information, click the Print button in the Enter Sales Receipts window. The Print One Sales Receipt dialog box appears, as shown in Figure 5-3. The following steps tell you how to complete this dialog box:

Figure 5-3:
The Print One Sales Receipt dialog box.

1. **Select the type of sales receipt form.**

If you're using a different type of sales receipt form than you described for the invoice/purchase order (PO) printer setup, select the type of form on which you want to print by selecting a radio button in the Print On section. You can choose Intuit Preprinted Forms, Blank Paper, or Letterhead. (See Chapter 4 for more on these printer options.)

You shouldn't have to worry about printing test receipts or fiddling with form alignment problems if you addressed these issues during the invoice/PO printer setup, so we're not going to talk about the Align button here. If you want to print a test receipt or need to change the alignment, read Chapter 4 for how to proceed.

2. **Print the form.**

   Click the Print button to send the form to the printer. QuickBooks prints the sales receipt.

3. **Review the sales receipt and reprint the form, if necessary.**

   Review the sales receipt to see whether QuickBooks printed it correctly. If the form doesn't look okay, fix whatever problem fouled up the printing; perhaps you forgot to include the company name and address, for example. Then reprint the form by clicking the Print button (in the Enter Sales Receipts window) again, selecting the form on which you want to print (again), and then clicking the Print button in the Print One Sales Receipt dialog box (you got it – again).

To print a batch of receipts, make sure that you select the To Be Printed check box on each receipt that you want to print and then display the Enter Sales Receipts window, click the arrow beside the Print button, and choose Print Batch from the drop-down list. QuickBooks displays the Select Receipts to Print dialog box, which enables you to choose which receipts to print. Select the desired receipts by putting a check mark in the first column and then click OK. The Print Sales Receipts dialog box appears. This dialog box resembles the Print One Sales Receipt dialog box in just about every way, and the instructions work in exactly the same manner. For help with this dialog box, refer to the sections on printing invoices and credit notes in batches in Chapter 4.

Special Tips for Retailers

Are you a retailer? If so, you're probably saying, "Hey guys, what you just described is way too much work to do every time someone walks into the store and buys some £3 item."

You know what? You're right. So here's what retailers do to record their sales. Retailers record the day's sales by using one, two, or three sales receipt transactions. Retailers don't record each individual sales receipt transaction.

Say that some coffee mug retailer sold 2500 red coffee mugs in a day for £3.50 (net) each. In that case, at the end of the day, the retailer needs to record total sales of £8750 plus £1750 in VAT (at 20%). The *daily* sales (£10,500) would be recorded using a sales receipt transaction like the one shown earlier in Figure 5-2.

Pretty straightforward, right? And that's not too much work, all things considered.

Let us share a handful of other tips for recording retail sales:

- **You probably want to record a sales receipt transaction for each bank deposit you make.** In this manner, you can indicate that a particular sales receipt transaction (really a batch of sales) is deposited at one time into your bank account – which makes reconciling your bank account relatively easy.

- **You probably want to separate cash sales from credit card sales because often credit card sales are handled differently.** Your credit card processing company, for example, might hold on to credit card sales for a few days, or it might deduct a fee before depositing the money into your bank account (described in Chapter 9). You want to record a separate sales receipt transaction for each deposit that you make (or some other company makes) into the bank account – again, to make reconciling the bank account easier.

- If you don't use the Item list to monitor your stock (because you have too many items to store in the QuickBooks Item list or it's not feasible because you're a food retailer, for example), use items that are designated as non-stock parts. For example, you might use non-stock part items, such as *daily cash sales, daily debit card sales,* and *daily Visa/MC sales* if you make three deposits every day for cash and cheque sales, for debit card sales, and for Visa and MasterCard sales. If you don't track stock using QuickBooks items, your accountant handles the stock and cost of goods sold calculations on your financial year end returns. He or she probably also records a journal entry transaction to get your account balances correct as of the end of your financial year.

Correcting Sales Receipt Mistakes

If you make a mistake in entering a sales receipt (cash sale), don't worry. Here's a list of common problems and how to fix them:

- **If the sales receipt is still displayed onscreen:** If the sales receipt is still onscreen, you can move the cursor to the box or button that's incorrect and then fix the mistake. Most of the bits of information that you enter in the Enter Sales Receipts window are fairly short or are entries that you've selected from a list. You can usually replace the contents of some field by typing over whatever's already there or by making a couple of quick clicks. If you really messed up and want to start over from scratch, you can click the Clear button. To save a receipt after you've entered it correctly, click either the Save & Close button or the Save & New button.

If you need to insert a line in the middle of a sales receipt, right-click where you want to insert the line and choose Insert Line from the shortcut menu. To delete a line, right-click it and then choose Delete Line from the shortcut menu.

✔ **If the sales receipt isn't displayed onscreen:** If the sales receipt isn't onscreen, and you haven't yet printed it, you can use the Next and Previous buttons to page through the sales receipts. When you get to the one with the error, fix the error as we describe in the preceding bullet. If you make a mistake while editing a receipt, you can click the Revert button to go back to the saved receipt and not save your changes. Note that Clear toggles to Revert after you edit a transaction.

Even if you printed the customer's receipt, you can make the sort of change that we just described. For example, you can page through the sales receipts by using the Next and Previous buttons until you find the receipt (now printed) with the error. And you can correct the error and print the receipt again. We're not so sure that you want to go this route, however. Things will be much cleaner if you void the cash sale by displaying the sales receipt and choosing Edit➪Void Sales Receipt. Then enter a new, correct cash sales transaction.

✔ **If you don't want the sales receipt:** You usually won't want to delete sales receipts, but you can delete them. (You'll almost always be in much better shape if you just void the sales receipt.) To delete the receipt, display it in the Enter Sales Receipts window (choose Customers➪Enter Sales Receipt and then page through the sales receipts by using the Next and Previous buttons until you see the cash sale that you want to delete) and then choose Edit➪Delete Sales Receipt. When QuickBooks asks you to confirm the deletion, click Yes.

If you want to see a list of all your cash sales, choose Edit➪Find, and the Simple Find screen appears. Select Transaction Type➪Sales Receipt and then click Find. Select the receipt you want to see from the list that appears. If you're already viewing a sales receipt, choose Edit➪Find Sales Receipts. Another screen pops up and asks for details of the sales receipt that you're looking for. Click the Find button on that screen and QuickBooks gives you a list of your cash sales for the criteria you selected.

Recording Customer Payments

If your customers don't always pay you upfront for their purchases, you need to record another type of payment: the payments that customers make to pay off or pay down what you've invoiced them. To record the payments, of course, you first need to record invoices for the customer. If you issue credit notes that customers can use to reduce the amounts they owe, you also first need to record credit notes for each customer. (Check out Chapter 4 to find out how to create and record these items.) The rest is easy.

To access a wealth of customer information all on one page, click the Customer Centre icon at the top of the screen or choose Customers➪Customer Centre.

The Customer Centre appears, listing outstanding balances for all customers and detailed information for the customer selected in the Customers & Jobs list.

To display the Receive Payments window, click the Receive Payments icon on the Home screen or click the Customer Centre icon and select the customer you need. Click New Transactions and Receive Payments or choose Customers⇨Receive Payments from the top menus. Then describe the customer payment and the invoices paid. If you want the gory details, read through the following steps:

1. **Choose Customers⇨Receive Payments.**

   The Receive Payments window appears.

2. **Identify the customer and, if necessary, the job.**

   Activate the Received From drop-down list and select the customer (and job, if necessary) by clicking its name. QuickBooks lists the open, or unpaid, invoices for the customer in the list box at the bottom of the window, as shown in Figure 5-4.

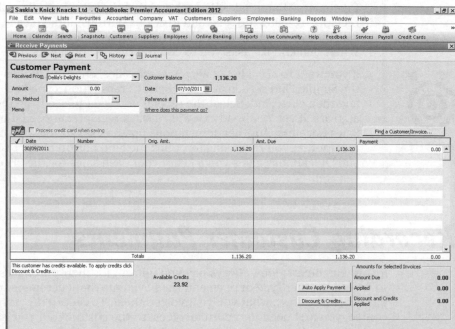

Figure 5-4:
The Receive Payments window with a customer selected.

3. **Specify the payment date.**

   Press Tab to move the cursor to the Date text box (the one right above the Reference # text box), and type the correct date in DD/MM/YYYY format. To edit the date, you can use the secret date-editing codes that we describe in Chapter 4 and on the online Cheat Sheet for this book at www.dummies.com/cheatsheet/quickbooks2012uk.

4. **Enter the amount of the payment.**

   Move the cursor to the Amount field and type the customer payment amount. *Note:* If the customer is paying with a credit card and your merchant bank deducts a fee from the individual payments, record the full amount of the payment on this payment screen and the merchant fee separately as we describe in Chapter 9.

5. **(Optional) Specify the payment method.**

   Activate the Pmt. Method drop-down list and choose the payment method.

6. **(Optional) Enter the cheque number.**

   You can guess how this works, right? You move the cursor to the Reference # field. Then you type the cheque number from the customer's cheque. Do you need to complete this step? Nope. But this bit of information might be useful if you or the customer later ends up with questions about which cheques paid for which invoices. So it's a good idea to enter the cheque number.

7. **(Optional) Add a Memo description.**

   Use the Memo description for storing some bit of information that will help you in some way. Note that this field prints on the Customer Statement.

8. **Identify which open invoices the customer is paying.**

   By default, QuickBooks automatically applies the payment to the open invoices, starting with the oldest open invoice. You can change this by entering amounts in the Payment column. Simply click the open invoice's payment amount and enter the correct amount.

   You can leave a portion of the payment unapplied, if you want to. QuickBooks then asks what you want to do with the overpayment: you can leave the amount on account to be applied or refund the amount to the customer or client. By the way, if you record an underpayment, QuickBooks asks whether you want to just leave the unpaid amount sitting there or, instead, you want to write off the remaining balance.

   If you want to apply the customer payment to the oldest open invoices, click the Auto Apply Payment button. If you want to unapply payments that you have already applied to open invoices, click the Clear Selections button. Clear Selections and Auto Apply Payment are the same button. QuickBooks changes the name of the button, depending on whether you have already applied payments.

9. **If the customer has any outstanding credits, decide whether to apply them in this payment.**

   In a little white box in the lower left of the screen QuickBooks tells you if the customer has credits by displaying the message "This customer has credits available. To apply credits click Discount & Credits" (see Figure 5-4). QuickBooks totals the amounts of any of the customer's existing credits. They can be anything from an overpayment on a previous invoice to a return credit or anything else.

If you want to apply a credit note to a specific open invoice, select the invoice and then click the Discounts & Credits button. When QuickBooks displays the Credits tab of the Discount and Credits dialog box, as shown in Figure 5-5, click the credit note that you want to apply and then click Done.

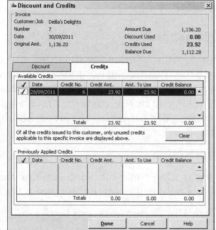

Figure 5-5:
The Credits tab of the Discount and Credits dialog box.

10. **Apply the early payment discount, if necessary.**

If you offer payment terms that include an early payment discount, QuickBooks shows the date by which the customer needs to pay to be eligible for the discount, in the Disc. Date column (not shown in Figure 5-4). *Note*: QuickBooks only displays the Disc. Date column if there are no credit notes available for this customer.

To apply the early payment discount, select the open invoice to which the discount applies, and then click the Discount & Credits button. With little or no hesitation, the Discount tab of the Discount and Credits dialog box appears, as shown in Figure 5-6. QuickBooks displays the suggested discount amount, which you can change if you want, in the Amount of Discount text box. Specify the expense account that you want to use to track discounts by activating the Discount Account drop-down list and selecting one of the accounts. (You may want to set up a special expense account called something like *Discount Expense*.) You also need to specify a VAT Code for this discount, but note that QuickBooks only uses this to know in which box of the VAT Return (Box 6 or Box 8) to report the net discount. Remember, the VAT has already been accounted for correctly on the invoice.

If the customer is paying multiple invoices, you need to apply the early payment discount to each invoice.

When you're finished, click Done to return to the Receive Payments window. (For more information on the costs and benefits of early payment discounts, see Chapter 19.)

11. **Record the customer payment information.**

   After you identify which invoices the customer is paying, you're ready to record the customer payment information.

QuickBooks displays a white box in the lower left of the Receive Payments window if the customer underpaid or overpaid (not shown in Figure 5-4). Here you see the amount of the under- or overpayment and you can tell QuickBooks what to do with the difference.

To save the customer payment information shown on screen, click either the Save & New button or the Save & Close button. If you click Save & New, QuickBooks displays an empty Receive Payments window so that you can enter another payment.

You can return to customer payments you recorded earlier by clicking the Previous button.

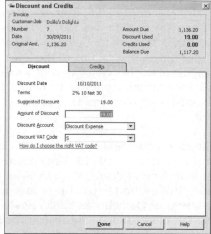

Figure 5-6:
The Discount tab of the Discount and Credits dialog box.

Correcting Mistakes in Customer Payments Entries

You can correct mistakes that you make in entering customer payments in basically the same way that you correct mistakes that you make in entering cash sales.

First, you display the window you used to enter the transaction. In the case of customer payments, click the Customer Centre icon and select the customer you need. You see a list of that customer's transactions on the right side. Double-click the payment transaction you want to change and the original payments screen appears. And then you make your changes. Then you click Save & Close. Pretty straightforward, right?

If you have already recorded a deposit that includes the payment you want to alter, you need to void or delete the deposit before you can edit, void, or delete the payment.

Making Bank Deposits

Whenever you record a cash sale or a customer payment on an invoice, QuickBooks adds the cash to its list of undeposited funds. These undeposited funds could be a bunch of cheques that you haven't yet deposited, or they could consist of *coinage* (currency and coins) or even credit card payments, if you accept those.

You can also tell QuickBooks to give you the choice of indicating that a particular payment or sales receipt is deposited directly into a specified account. To tell QuickBooks to give you this choice, choose Edit➪Preferences, scroll down to the Payments icon, click the Company Preferences tab, and then deselect the Use Undeposited Funds as a Default Deposit to Account option. After you make this change, QuickBooks adds buttons and a box to the lower-left corner of the Enter Sales Receipt and middle of the Receive Payment windows so that you can indicate into which bank account the money is deposited. Specifying a bank account is very handy if a customer pays you via electronic bank transfer, for example.

If you lump several customer cheques (or several days' worth of cash sales) and pay them into the bank together, specify the Undeposited Funds account in the Enter Sales Receipt or Receive Payment window, and use the Make Deposit window described in this section to pay the money into the QuickBooks bank register. That way your QuickBooks bank register will only show one deposit entry which will be easy to reconcile against the bank statement (we discuss bank reconciliations in Chapter 8).Once you take the money out from under your mattress and deposit it in the bank, follow these steps:

1. **Choose Banking➪Make Deposits.**

   Alternatively, select Record Deposits on the Home screen in the Banking section.

   The Payments to Deposit dialog box appears, as shown in Figure 5-7. This dialog box initially lists all the payments, regardless of the payment method. You can, however, use the View Payment Method Type drop-down list to indicate that you want to see payments only of a particular type – such as credit card payments. (This feature can be pretty handy because it lets you batch all your credit card transactions together.)

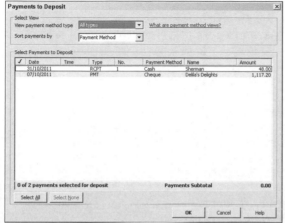

Figure 5-7:
The
Payments
to Deposit
dialog box.

2. **Select the payments that you want to deposit.**

Click a payment or cash receipt to place a check mark in front of it, marking it for deposit. If you want to deselect a payment, click it again. To deselect all the payments, click the Select None button. To select all the payments, click the Select All button. If you have lots of payments to look through, you can also filter the list by clicking View Payment Method Type at the top and display only the Cash or Credit Cards to select among. If you're recording credit card payments deposited, you don't need to sort through the cheque payments. They aren't gone; they just don't appear until you select that type of payment or All.

3. **Click OK.**

After you indicate which payments you want to deposit, click OK. QuickBooks displays the Make Deposits window, as shown in Figure 5-8.

If you need to redisplay the Payments to Deposit dialog box – maybe you made a mistake or something and now you need to go back to fix it – click the Payments button at the top of the Make Deposits screen. Note, though, that QuickBooks won't display the Payments to Deposit dialog box unless the undeposited funds list still has undeposited payments in it.

4. **Tell QuickBooks into which bank account you want to deposit the money.**

Activate the Deposit To drop-down list and choose the bank account in which you want to place the funds.

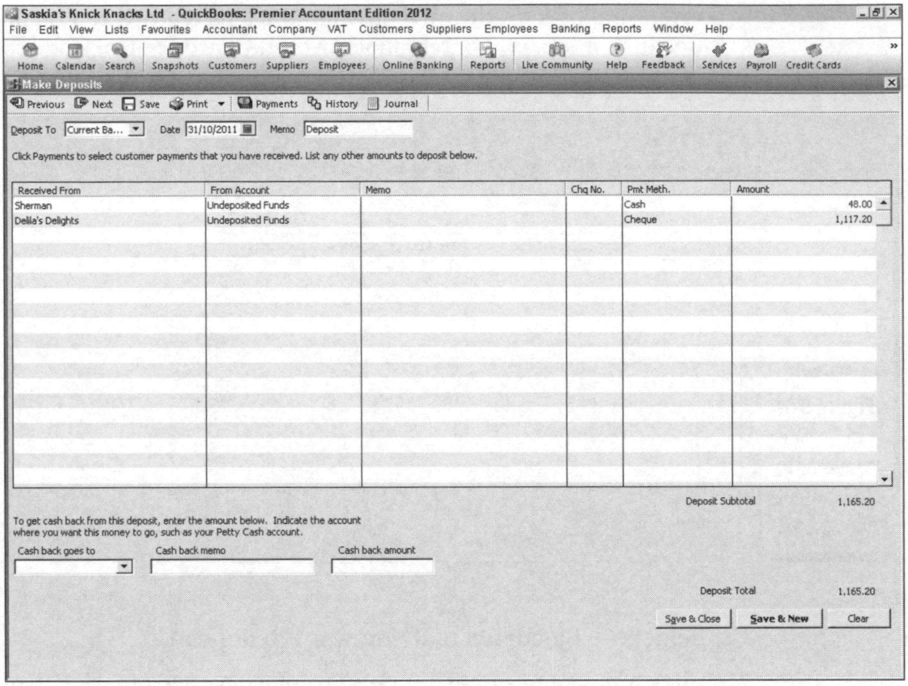

Figure 5-8:
The Make
Deposits
window.

5. Specify the deposit date.

Press Tab to move the cursor to the Date text box and then type the correct date in DD/MM/YYYY format. Use the secret date-editing codes if you need to edit the date. (Get these codes from Chapter 4 or from the online Cheat Sheet at www.dummies.com/cheatsheet/quickbooks 2012uk if you don't know them.)

6. (Optional) Add a Memo description if you want to.

If you really want to, you can enter the deposit folio number here. Most people leave this field alone though.

7. Specify the cash-back amount.

If you want cash back from the deposit, activate the Cash Back Goes To drop-down list and choose a cash account, such as Petty Cash. Then enter a memo in the Cash Back Memo text box and the amount of cash back you're taking in the Cash Back Amount text box.

8. Record the deposit by clicking the Save & Close button or the Save & New button.

If you click Save & New, QuickBooks displays a new blank Make Deposits window.

If you sometimes take cash from the till or from the day's collections to spend on business supplies or for COD (collect on delivery) payments, you need to record those expenses in the Petty Cash bank account, using the Write Cheque window, as we describe in Chapter 8. That way you account correctly for the VAT on the expense. (Note that there is no place on the Make Deposit window to show VAT amounts.)

Improving Your Cash Inflow

We're not going to provide a lengthy discussion of how to go about collecting cash from your customers. We do, however, want to quickly tell you about a couple of other details. You need to know how to monitor what your customers owe you and how to assess finance charges. Don't worry, though. We'll explain these two things as briefly as we can.

Tracking what your customers owe

You can track what a customer owes in a couple of ways. Probably the simplest method is to display the Customer Centre by choosing Customer⇨ Customer Centre. Next, select the customer from the Customers & Jobs list (which appears along the left edge of the window). QuickBooks whips up a page that lists transactions for the customer. It also shows the customer's contact information. Figure 5-9 shows the Customer Centre information for a customer.

You also should be aware that QuickBooks provides several nifty accounts receivable (A/R) reports. You get to these reports by clicking the Report Centre icon and choosing Customers & Receivables. Or you can choose Reports⇨Customers & Receivables. QuickBooks then displays a submenu of about half a dozen reports that describe how much money customers owe you. Some reports, for example, organise open invoices into different groups based on how old the invoices are. (These reports are called *aged debtor reports.*) Some reports summarise only invoices or payments. And some reports show each customer's open, or unpaid, balance. There's even a nifty report called Average Days to Pay Summary that shows you the bad payers.

In Chapter 15, we describe, in general terms, how you go about producing and printing QuickBooks reports. So read Chapter 15 if you have questions. You can't hurt anything or foul up your financial records just by printing reports. So go ahead and play around.

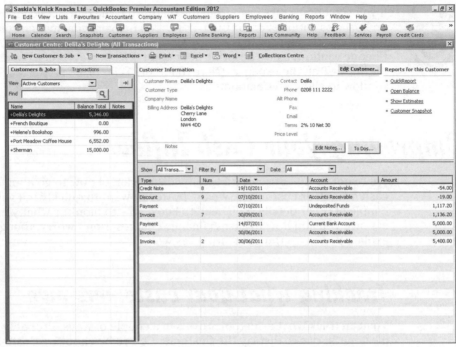

Figure 5-9:
The
Customer
Centre.

You can print a statement to send to a customer by choosing Customers⇨
Create Statements. Use the Create Statements dialog box to describe which
customers you want to print statements for and the date ranges you want the
statements to show, and then click Print or E-Mail to print or e-mail the statements. Statements are a handy way to remind forgetful customers or clients
about overdue amounts. You don't, by the way, need to send statements to
everybody for every month. You can send out statements only to customers
or clients with overdue accounts.

Assessing finance charges

We were not exactly sure where to stick this discussion of finance charges.
Because finance charges seem to relate to collecting the cash your customers owe, we figured that this is a good place to talk about assessing finance
charges.

QuickBooks assesses finance charges on unpaid open invoices without considering any unapplied payments. Accordingly, you'll want to make sure that
you apply any payments and credit notes to open invoices before assessing
finance charges.

Using QuickBooks to write a letter

You can seamlessly integrate your QuickBooks data to create collection letters in Microsoft Word. You can also use the QuickBooks business letter templates to speed the process of writing business letters. To have QuickBooks help you write a letter, choose Company➪Prepare Letters with Envelopes. Then choose the submenu command for the type of letter you want to create or edit. Or from the Customer Centre, click the Word icon and choose the letter from the menu there.

If you're creating a collection letter, you can specify which customers and jobs you want QuickBooks to search for money owed to you. You can tell QuickBooks whether you want to create a separate letter for each customer who owes you money or each job on which you're owed money. You can also specify the limit for how overdue an invoice must be to warrant a collection letter. After you set the parameters and click Next, QuickBooks searches for overdue invoices that fit your criteria.

If you're creating a type of letter other than a collection letter, QuickBooks offers many choices based on whether you're sending the letter to a customer, a supplier, an employee, or someone else. For example, you can create credit approval, credit denial, or credit request letters. You can create birthday or apology letters. And you can create faxes or bounced cheque letters, just to name a few.

After you specify the information about the type of letter that you want to create, QuickBooks asks you a few questions about how you want to sign the letter. Then it creates the letter and displays it in Microsoft Word so that you can edit the letter as necessary and then print or save it.

To assess finance charges, follow these steps:

1. **Choose Edit➪Preferences, click the Finance Charge icon in the list on the left, and then click the Company Preferences tab.**

   To be able to assess finance charges, you first need to set them up.

   Only the QuickBooks administrator can change the company finance charge settings and he or she can do so only in single-user mode.

   QuickBooks displays the Preferences dialog box, as shown in Figure 5-10. (If you've assessed finance charges before, QuickBooks displays the Assess Finance Charges window. You can display the Preferences dialog box and check or edit your finance charge settings by clicking the Settings button in the Assess Finance Charges window.)

2. **Enter the annual interest rate that you want to use to calculate finance charges.**

   Move the cursor to the Annual Interest Rate (%) text box and enter the annual interest rate.

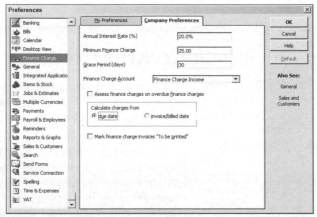

Figure 5-10:
The
Preferences
dialog box
for finance
charges.

3. **(Optional) Enter the minimum finance charge – if one exists.**

   Move the cursor to the Minimum Finance Charge text box and enter the minimum charge. If you always charge at least $25.00 on an overdue invoice, for example, type **25**.

4. **Enter the number of days of grace that you give.**

   Days of Grace. That sounds kind of like an artsy movie or a serious novel, doesn't it? Basically, this number is how many days' slack you're willing to give people. If you type **30** in the Grace Period (Days) text box, QuickBooks doesn't start assessing finance charges until 30 days after the invoice is overdue.

5. **Specify which account you want to use to track the finance charges.**

   Activate the Finance Charge Account drop-down list and select an Income or Other Income type account.

6. **Indicate whether you want to charge finance charges on finance charges.**

   Does this statement make sense? If you charge somebody a finance charge, and he or she doesn't pay the finance charge, eventually it becomes overdue, too. So then what do you do the next time you assess finance charges? Do you calculate a finance charge on the finance charge? If you want to do this select the Assess Finance Charges on Overdue Finance Charges check box.

7. **Tell QuickBooks whether it should calculate finance charges from the due date or the invoice date.**

   Select either the Due Date or Invoice/Billed Date option button. As you might guess, you calculate bigger finance charges if you start accruing interest on the invoice date.

8. **Tell QuickBooks whether it should print finance charge invoices.**

   Select the check box for Mark Finance Charge Invoices "To Be Printed" if you want to print invoices later for the finance charges that you calculate.

9. **Click OK.**

   After you use the Preferences dialog box to tell QuickBooks how the finance charges should be calculated, click OK.

10. **Choose Customers➪Assess Finance Charges.**

    Alternatively, click the Finance Charges icon on the Home screen. The Assess Finance Charges window appears, as shown in Figure 5-11. This window shows all the finance charges that QuickBooks has calculated, organised by customer.

    If there are any credit notes or payments not yet allocated to a customer, the Customer Has Unapplied Payments window pops up. It also tells you that QuickBooks marked such customers with an asterisk (*) in the Assess Finance Charges Window.

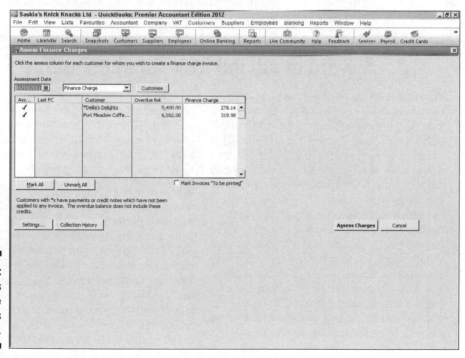

Figure 5-11: The Assess Finance Charges window.

11. **Give the finance charge assessment date.**

    Move the cursor to the Assessment Date text box and enter the date when you're assessing the finance charges, which is probably the current date. (This date is also the invoice date that will be used on the finance charge invoices, if you create them.)

12. **Confirm which customers you want to be assessed finance charges.**

    QuickBooks initially marks all the finance charges, which means that it sets up a new invoice for each finance charge. (QuickBooks marks finance charges with a little check mark.) If you want to unmark (or, later, mark) a finance charge, click it. To unmark all the charges, click the Unmark All button. To mark all the charges, click the Mark All button.

    You can produce a collection report for any of the customers or jobs listed in the Assess Finance Charges window by selecting the customer name and then clicking the Collection History button.

13. **Click the Assess Charges button.**

    When the Assess Finance Charges window correctly describes the finance charges that you want to assess, click Assess Charges. You're finished with the finance charge calculations and assessments.

TIP

A word of advice from an accountant

While we're on the subject of tracking what your customers owe you, let us share a thought about collecting this money. You should have firm collection procedures that you follow faithfully. For example, as soon as an invoice is a week or so overdue, it's very reasonable to place a friendly telephone call to the customer's accounts payable department to verify whether the customer has received the invoice and is in the process of paying. You have no reason to be embarrassed because some customer is late paying you! What's more, you may find out something surprising and essential to your collection process. You may discover, for example, that the customer didn't receive the invoice. Or you may find out that something was wrong with the gizmo you sold or the service you provided.

As soon as an invoice is a month or so overdue, you need to crank up the pressure. A firm letter asking that the customer call you to explain the overdue amount is very reasonable – especially if the customer assured you only a few weeks ago that payment was forthcoming.

When an invoice is a couple of months overdue, you need to get pretty serious. You'll probably want to stop selling the customer anything more because it's unclear whether you'll be paid. And you may want to start a formal collection process. You may also want to consider assigning credit limits to your customers (on the Additional Info tab of the customer record), so that QuickBooks warns you if you try to create an invoice that will exceed the customer's credit limit. This prevents you from shipping goods down a black hole.

We don't describe how to print invoices that contain finance charges because we already slogged through invoice printing in painstaking detail in Chapter 4. If you have questions about how to print the invoices, you might want to visit that chapter.

Dealing with customer deposits

While we're on the subject of improving your cash flow, let us briefly mention one other powerful cash flow technique – and discuss the bookkeeping required for that technique.

One easy way to improve your cash flow is to accept or require upfront deposits or retainers from clients or customers before you do the actual work. In other words, before you begin work or order stock or do whatever is the first step in your business for completing a sale, you collect cold, hard cash.

Unfortunately, these *customer deposits,* as they're called, create a bit of bookkeeping trouble. The question becomes, basically, how do you record a cheque or cash deposit for stuff that you haven't yet done or sold? You have two basic options:

- ✔ **The Easy Way:** You can just record a sales receipt for the service or product. (See "Recording a Sales Receipt" at the beginning of this chapter.) In this way, you count the cash coming into your business, recognise the income, and account for the VAT. Note, too, that if the deposit is nonrefundable – and, for cash-flow purposes, the deposit should be nonrefundable – you should count the income when you receive the deposit if you report VAT on a cash basis.

- ✔ **The Precise Way:** You can recognise the deposit as a new liability. You do this by creating a journal entry that records the increase in your cash account and that records the increase in your Customer Deposits current liability account. (For help on entering journal entries, refer to Chapter 18.) If the deposit is refundable and you report VAT on a cash basis, or if you report VAT on an accrual basis, you probably should use this method. But you don't account for the VAT on the journal. When your sale is completed and invoiced later (and this is where you stick the full VAT amount), use the Customer Deposit item as a minus amount on the sales invoice to move the amount from the liability account and apply it to the invoice balance due.

Chapter 6

Paying the Bills

In This Chapter

▶ Using the Write Cheques window to pay bills

▶ Using the accounts payable method to pay bills

▶ Deleting and editing bill payments

▶ Handling early payment discounts

▶ Reminding yourself to pay bills

*Q*uickBooks gives you two ways to pay and record your bills. And you have many options when it comes to deciding when to pay your bills, how to pay your bills, and how to record your bills for the purposes of tracking stock and expenses.

In this chapter, we explain how to record and pay supplier bills.

Pay Now or Pay Later?

When it comes to paying bills, you have a fundamental choice to make. You can either record and pay your bills simultaneously or you can record your bills as they come in and then pay them when they're due. The first method is easiest, as you might guess, because you do everything at once. The second method, called the *accounts payable method,* gives you more accurate financial records and makes for more precise management of your cash and outstanding bills.

If you have a small business with few overheads, you may just as well record and pay bills simultaneously. If you need precise measurement of your expenses and bills, though – if you want to use what's termed *accrual-basis accounting* – you should use the accounts payable method of paying bills. Using the accounts payable method with QuickBooks isn't as difficult as it may seem at first.

And now you're ready to begin. In the next section, we describe how to pay bills by writing cheques. A little later in the chapter, in the "Recording Your Bills the Accounts Payable Way" section, you find out how to pay bills by using the accounts payable method.

Recording Your Bills by Writing Cheques

When you record bills by writing cheques, you're doing *cash-basis accounting*. In a nutshell, this means that you account for bills as expenses when you write the cheque to pay the bill.

We talk a little bit about cash-basis accounting in Appendix B, but we'll tell you here that a trade-off is implicit in the choice to use cash-basis accounting. If you use cash-basis accounting, you greatly simplify your bookkeeping, but you lose precision in your measurement of your expenses. And you don't keep track of your unpaid bills inside QuickBooks. They just stack up in a pile next to your desk.

As long as you understand this trade-off and are comfortable with it, you're ready to begin using this method, which you do by following the steps we provide in the paragraphs that follow.

Writing a cheque

To use the Write Cheques window to write cheques, follow these steps:

1. **Choose Banking⇨Write Cheques.**

   Alternatively, click the Write Cheques icon in the Banking section of the Home screen. The Write Cheques window appears, as shown in Figure 6-1. Notice that this window has three parts:

   - *The cheque part on the top,* which you no doubt recognise from having written thousands of cheques in the past.

   - *The buttons* at the top and bottom.

   - *The Expenses and Items tabs* in the lower half of the window. This part is for recording what the cheque is for, as we explain from Step 8 onward.

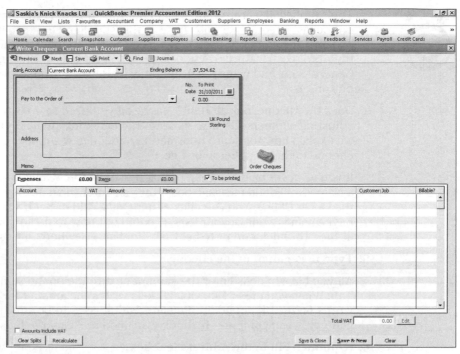

Figure 6-1:
The Write
Cheques
window.

2. **Click the Bank Account drop-down list and choose the account from which you want to write this cheque.**

This step is very important if you have more than one account. Make sure that you choose the correct account; otherwise, your account balances in QuickBooks will be incorrect.

3. **Specify the cheque date.**

Click in the Date field and type the cheque date. Remember that you can enter today's date by pressing the T key. You can also click the button to the right of the Date box to get a pop-up calendar. To select a date from the pop-up calendar, click the calendar day that you want to use.

4. **Fill in the Pay to the Order Of line.**

If you've written a cheque to this person or party before, the AutoFill feature fills in the name of the payee in the Pay to the Order Of line for you after you start typing the name. (AutoFill does this by comparing what you type with names shown in the Customer, Supplier, Employee, and Other Names lists.) AutoFill also puts the payee's address in the Address text box.

The AutoRecall feature can even fill out the entire cheque for you, based on the last cheque that you wrote to this supplier. Or, it can just pre-fill expense accounts you used in the past for this supplier. (You can enable the AutoRecall feature by choosing Edit⇨Preferences, clicking the General icon, and using the Automatically Recall Information box and buttons.)

Does the cheque look all right? Maybe all you need to do is tab around, adjusting numbers. Otherwise, read the remaining steps. (In these steps, we explain how to record information about a new supplier and pay a cheque to that supplier in one go.)

If you've never paid anything to this person before, QuickBooks displays a Name Not Found message box after you enter the name on the Pay to the Order Of line. You can click either Quick Add or Set Up to add the payee name to one of your lists. (To find out how to do so, have a look at the "To Quick Add or to Set Up?" sidebar, elsewhere in this chapter.)

5. Type the amount of the cheque.

All you have to do is enter the amount next to the pound sign and press Tab. When you press Tab, QuickBooks writes the amount for you in words on the UK Pound Sterling line. Isn't it good to be alive in the 21st century, when computer technology can do these marvellous things?

6. (Optional) Fill in the Address text box.

You need to fill in this field only if the address isn't there already and if you intend to post the cheque in a window envelope.

7. (Optional) Fill in the Memo line.

You can put a message to the payee on the Memo line – such as, *Quit bleeding me dry*. But you usually put your account number on the Memo line so that the payee can record it.

If you try to click the Save & New button and close the dialog box now, QuickBooks tells you that you can't and tries to bite your leg off. Why? Because you can't write a cheque unless you fill out the Expenses and Items tabs. You use these tabs to describe what the cheque pays.

8. Move the cursor down to the Account column of the Expenses tab and then enter an expense account name.

Chances are that you want to enter the name of an account that's already on the Chart of Accounts. If that's the case, move the cursor to a field in the Account column; QuickBooks turns the field into a drop-down list. Click the down arrow to see a list of all your accounts. You'll probably have to scroll down the list to get to the expense accounts. Click the one that this cheque applies to – perhaps it's Rent. If you need to create a new expense account category for this cheque, choose Add New from the top of the list to see the New Account dialog box. Fill in the information and then click OK.

What if the money that you're paying with this cheque can be distributed across two, three, or four expense accounts? Simply click below the account that you just entered. The down arrow shoots down next to the cursor. Click the down arrow and enter another expense account, and another, and another, if you need to.

9. **Select a VAT code in the VAT column.**

   This is straightforward stuff – look at your bill and choose a VAT Code in QuickBooks that corresponds to the VAT rate on the bill. Click your mouse in the VAT column of the first account row and when the drop-down list appears, select a VAT Code. (You can expand the drop-down list window by dragging its bottom right corner to the right to make it bigger. You can then view the descriptions and rates of all the VAT Codes so you can be sure you are choosing the right one.)

   You need to select a VAT Code for each account line. If the expense is outside the scope of VAT, select the "O" VAT code. (An "O" VAT Code tells QuickBooks to exclude that account line from VAT reports.)

   Let's say you're writing a cheque to the mobile phone company, and you can see that there are two different VAT rates on the bill – 0% and 20%. Well, although the whole cheque can be categorised as a telephone expense, you should enter the portion of the telephone expense that's zero rated VAT on a separate line from the portion that is standard (20%) rated VAT. That way your VAT reports will be correct.

   One handy little trick for the efficient (or lazy?) among you is to associate default VAT Codes with expense accounts. That way, each time you recall the account on a cheque or bill, QuickBooks populates the VAT column with the default VAT Code you specified (which you can change if need be on the cheque or bill). You can set default VAT Codes when you add a new expense account by selecting an entry in the VAT Code box, before you save the new account. To add default VAT Codes to existing expense accounts, find the expense account in the Chart of Accounts (Lists➪Chart of Accounts), right-click and select Edit Account. Make your selection in the VAT Code box and click Save & Close.

10. **Tab over to the Amount column, if necessary, and change the numbers.**

    QuickBooks calculates and sticks the Net Amount of the bill in the Amount column if you are only using one expense account and the "S" (Standard 20%) VAT Code.

    If you're distributing this cheque across more than one account or multiple VAT Codes, make sure that the numbers in the Amount column correctly distribute the cheque. Figure 6-2 shows a completed cheque.

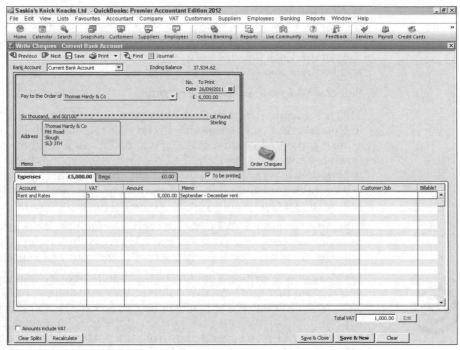

Figure 6-2:
A completed
cheque.

11. **(Optional) Enter words of explanation or encouragement in the Memo column.**

    Some day, you may have to go back to this cheque and try to figure out what these expenses mean. The Memo column may be your only clue. Enter some wise words here such as *August rent, copier repair,* or *company party.*

12. **(Optional) Assign the expense to the Customer:Job column.**

    If you plan to be reimbursed for these expenses, or if you just want to track your expenses by job, enter the name of the customer who is going to reimburse you. Click the down arrow to find the customer. Enter an amount for each customer or job, if necessary.

13. **(Optional) Assign the expense to a class (if you have told QuickBooks you want to use classes).**

    You also can track expenses by class by making entries in the Class column. Notice the usual down arrow, which you click to see a list of classes. You won't see the Class column, however, unless you told QuickBooks that you wanted to use classes (as described in Chapter 3).

    To tell QuickBooks to use classes, choose Edit⟹Preferences. When QuickBooks displays the Preferences dialog box, click the Accounting icon, click the Company Preferences tab, and then check the Use Class Tracking box.

To Quick Add or to Set Up?

If you click Quick Add in the Name Not Found message box, you see a Select Name Type message box asking whether the payee is a Supplier, a Customer, an Employee, or Other. Most likely, the payee is a supplier, in which case you click Supplier (but you can, of course, click one of the other three options). The address information that you write on the cheque goes in the Supplier list – or Customer, Employee, or Other Names list, depending on what you clicked. (Read through Chapter 3 if you're in the dark about adding to your lists.) With Quick Add, QuickBooks requires you to collect only a minimal amount of information.

Selecting the Set Up option in the Name Not Found message box allows you to enter all the details relevant to the payee, including address, terms, VAT details, credit limit, and so forth. When you select this option, you also see the Select Name Type box. Click Supplier, Customer, Employee, or Other. Click OK, and then you see the New *Whatever* window (as we discuss in Chapter 3) if you've already added suppliers, customers, or employees to your lists.

14. **Use the Items tab to record what you're purchasing.**

    You may be purchasing stock items, or you may already have filled out a purchase order for the items for which you're paying (by the way, we talk about purchase orders in Chapter 7). If either of these cases is so, click the Items tab. If you don't have a purchase order for the items, go on to Step 15. If you do have a purchase order for the items, click the Select PO button to see a list of purchases on order with this supplier. Check those for which you're paying, and click OK.

    QuickBooks doesn't show its purchase order (PO) feature unless you turn it on. If you think you want to use it, choose Edit⇨Preferences. When QuickBooks displays the Preferences dialog box, click the Items & Stock button, click the Company Preferences tab, and then select the Stock and Purchase Orders Are Active check box.

15. **Move the cursor to the Item column and enter a name for the item.**

    Notice the down arrow in this column. Click the arrow to see the Items list. Does the item that you're paying for appear on this list? If so, click it. If not, choose Add New from the top of the list and fill out the New Item window. (Read about this in Chapter 3.)

16. **Fill in the rest of the rows of items on the Items tab.**

    You can enter all the items that you're purchasing on this tab. Make sure that the Items tab accurately shows the items that you're purchasing: their cost, quantity, and VAT Codes.

17. **When you finish adding items, you may want to use one of the following options that appear in the Write Cheques window:**

    • The Print button sends the cheque in the Write Cheques window to the printer. This option doesn't print all the cheques that you have written and marked to be printed, however. (We explain how to print more than one cheque at a time in Appendix D.)

    • The Clear Splits button deletes any individual amounts that you entered for separate expenses or items in the Expenses and Items tabs. Then QuickBooks enters the total amount of the cheque in the Amount column on the Expenses tab.

    • The Recalculate button totals the items and expenses in the window and puts the total on both the numeric and text amount lines of the cheque, overwriting any amount that was already there.

    • The To Be Printed check box designates the cheque for printing. Select this check box if you want to print the cheque with QuickBooks by using your printer and preprinted cheque forms. Clear this check box if you're recording a handwritten cheque and enter the cheque number in the No. field instead.

18. **Double check the Total VAT on the cheque.**

    The amount in the Total VAT box (at the bottom right of the window) needs to match the VAT on the supplier invoice. If you are wildly out, check the amounts in the Amount column; you made a mistake somewhere in there. If you are out by just a penny or two, it may be a rounding difference between your supplier and QuickBooks. Edit the Total VAT amount to match the supplier's invoice. To do so, simply enter the new amount in the Total VAT box.

    If there are multiple VAT Codes in use, click the Edit button next to the Total VAT field and make your adjustments there. Click OK when finished to return to the Write Cheques window.

19. **Click the Save & New button or the Save & Close button to finish writing the cheque.**

    Click Save & Close to tell QuickBooks that you want to save the cheque and close the cheque form. Click Save & New to tell QuickBooks that you want to save the cheque and then display another blank cheque form. If you don't want to save the cheque, close the dialog box and then click No when QuickBooks asks whether you want to save the cheque.

    You can also use the Next and Previous buttons to move to previously written cheques or to a blank cheque form. If you write cheque number 101, for example, clicking Next takes you to cheque 102 so that you can write that one. (Clicking Previous moves you to cheque 100, in case you need to edit a cheque that you've written earlier.)

Well, that's over with. For a minute there, we thought that it would never end.

Changing a cheque that you've written

What if you need to change a cheque after you've already entered it? Perhaps you made a terrible mistake, such as recording a £52.50 cheque as £25.20. Can you fix it? Sure. If the cheque is still onscreen, just make your change there.

If it's not onscreen, you need to find the cheque first. One way to find it is to open the Write Cheques window again (Banking➪Write Cheques) and use the Previous or Next button to move through the cheques (remember, they're in date order) until you find the one you want. You can also search for the cheque as we describe in the "Using the Find dialog box" sidebar later in this chapter.

After you have located and opened the cheque so it's onscreen, make your changes. When you finish, click Save & Close.

Recording Your Bills the Accounts Payable Way

The accounts payable (A/P) way of paying bills involves two steps. The first is a trifle on the difficult side but the second step is as easy as pie. First, you record your bills. If you read the preceding section in this chapter on writing cheques, you're already familiar with using the Expenses tab and the Items tab to record bills. You need to fill out those tabs for the A/P method as well if you want to distribute a bill to accounts, customers, jobs, classes, and items. If you read the first part of this chapter, some of what follows will be old hat.

After you record your bills, you can go on to the second step: telling QuickBooks which bills to pay. Then QuickBooks writes the cheques. You print them. You post them.

To make the A/P method work, you have to record your bills as they come in. That doesn't mean that you have to pay them right away. By recording your bills, you can keep track of how much money you owe and how much money your business really has. QuickBooks reminds you when your bills are due so that you don't have to worry about forgetting to pay a bill.

When you record bills the accounts payable way, you're using accrual-basis accounting. We explain accrual-basis accounting in Appendix B.

Recording a bill

To record a bill through the Enter Bills window, follow these steps:

1. **Choose Suppliers➪Enter Bills.**

   Alternatively, click the Enter Bills icon in the Suppliers area on the Home page. Figure 6-3 shows the Enter Bills window. You no doubt notice that the top half of this window looks a great deal like a cheque, and that's because much of the information that you put here ends up on the cheque that you write to pay your bill. (If you see the word *Credits* at the top of the form rather than *Bills,* select the Bill radio button in the top-left corner.)

   You also use this screen to enter credit notes from suppliers, largely as described next. The main difference is that a credit note does not have a due date so the Terms and Bill Due fields are not present on a credit note, so you skip Step 3.)

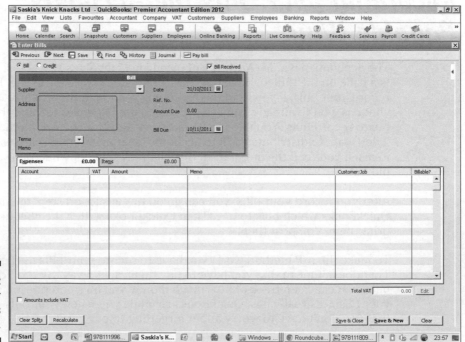

Figure 6-3:
The Enter
Bills
window.

2. Select the name of the supplier.

If you want to pay this bill to a supplier who's already on the Supplier list, click the down arrow at the end of the Supplier line and choose the supplier. (Then QuickBooks automatically fills the Enter Bills window with as much information as it knows.) If this supplier is new, QuickBooks asks you to Quick Add or Set Up some information about the supplier: the address, credit limit, payment terms, and so on. You provide this information in the New Supplier window. If you aren't familiar with this window, make a brief visit to Chapter 3.

If you have one or more unfilled purchase orders with the supplier that you select, QuickBooks asks you whether you want to receive against a purchase order. Click Yes if you do or No if you don't. If you choose to receive against a purchase order, QuickBooks displays the Open Purchase Orders dialog box, as shown in Figure 6-4. It lists the open purchase orders you've recorded. When you select one or more purchase orders to receive against, QuickBooks fills in the items and amounts from these orders for you, which you can modify as necessary. When you finish with the Purchase Orders dialog box, click OK to get back to the Enter Bills window.

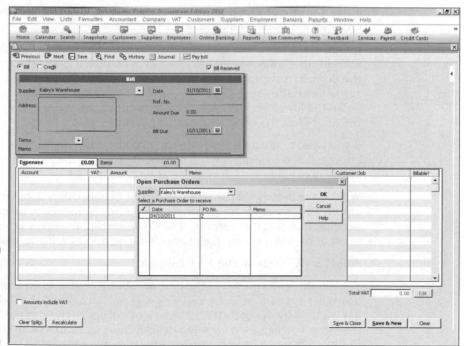

Figure 6-4:
Paying a bill against a purchase order.

Hey, you know what? We don't talk about purchase orders until Chapter 7. But here's the abbreviated version: to create a *purchase order,* which is a record of items you order from a supplier, choose Suppliers⇨Create Purchase Orders. When QuickBooks displays the Create Purchase Orders window, describe your order. You print and edit purchase orders, by the way, in the same manner as you print invoices and credit notes.

3. **Select the payment terms that describe when the bill is due.**

   On the Terms line (Figure 6-3), open the drop-down list and choose the payment terms (if the information isn't already there from when you set up the supplier).

4. **Enter the supplier's reference number.**

   Enter the supplier's reference number for the bill – this is the purchase invoice number – the reference number prints on the voucher that's part of the printed cheque.

5. **(Optional) Enter a memo to describe the bill.**

   You can enter a note in the Memo text box. The note that you enter appears on the A/P register.

6. **Move the cursor down to the Account column of the Expenses tab and enter an expense account name.**

   Chances are good that you want to enter the name of an expense account that's already on the chart of accounts. If that's the case, click the down arrow to see a list of all your accounts. You probably have to scroll down the list to get to the expense accounts. (A fast way to move down the list is to start typing the account name; you go straight down the list.) Click the account that this bill represents.

   If you need to create a new expense account category for this bill, choose Add New from the top of the list. You see the New Account dialog box. Fill in the information and click OK.

   What if the money that you're paying out because of this bill can be split among two, three, or four expense accounts? Simply click below the account that you just entered. The down arrow appears. Click it to enter another expense account, and another, and another, if you need to.

7. **Select a VAT code in the VAT column.**

   Click in the VAT column of the first account row and when the drop-down list appears, select a VAT Code. (You can expand the drop-down list window by dragging its bottom right corner to the right to make it bigger. You can then view the descriptions and rates of all the VAT Codes so you can be sure you are choosing the right one.)

You need to select a VAT Code for each account line. If the expense is outside the scope of VAT, select the "O" VAT code. (An "O" VAT Code tells QuickBooks to exclude that account line from VAT reports.)

If the entire bill can be categorised to one expense account but you see two different VAT rates on the supplier's invoice, use a separate account line for each VAT rate.

If you want to, you can associate default VAT Codes with expense accounts so each time you recall the account on a cheque or bill, QuickBooks populates the VAT column with the default VAT Code you specified (which you can change if need be on the cheque or bill). You can set default VAT Codes when you add a new expense account by selecting an entry in the VAT Code box, before you save the new account. To add default VAT Codes to existing expense accounts, find the expense account in the Chart of Accounts (Lists➪Chart of Accounts), right-click and select Edit Account. Make your selection in the VAT Code box and click Save & Close.

8. Tab over to the Amount column, if necessary, and change the numbers.

QuickBooks calculates and sticks the Net Amount of the bill in the Amount column if you are only using one expense account and the "S" (Standard 20%) VAT Code.

If you're splitting this bill among several accounts or VAT codes, make sure that the numbers in the Amount column add to the total Net Amount of the bill.

9. (Optional) Enter words of explanation or wisdom in the Memo column.

10. (Optional) Assign the expense to a Customer:Job.

If you plan to be reimbursed for these expenses, or if you just want to track your expenses by customer or job, enter the customer name in Customer:Job column. You can use the down arrow to find customers and then select them. To tell QuickBooks to pass the charges on to the customer when you raise the invoice, place a tick mark in the Billable? column. If only part of the bill is reimbursable (or attributable to a job), separate the reimbursable from the non-reimbursable amounts on different account lines.

11. (Optional) Assign the expense to a class (if you have told QuickBooks you want to use classes).

You also can track expenses by class by making entries in the Class column. Notice the usual down arrow, and click it to see a list of classes. (You don't see a Class column unless you told QuickBooks that you want to use classes, which we describe in Chapter 3.)

If you want to have QuickBooks track expenses by class, choose Edit➪Preferences. When QuickBooks displays the Preferences dialog box, click the Accounting icon, click the Company Preferences tab, and then select the Use Class Tracking check box.

If you want, click the Recalculate button to total the expenses. *Note:* doing so overwrites your entry in the Amount Due field at the top of the bill.

12. Use the Items tab to record the various items that the bill represents.

Click the Items tab. Enter the items you purchased and the prices you paid for them.

If you realise after partially completing the bill that the bill is against a purchase order, click the Select PO button, which appears on the Items tab of the Enter Bills window.

From the Supplier drop-down list, choose the name of the supplier who sent you the bill. In the list of open purchase orders, click in the column on the left to put a check mark next to the purchase order (or orders) which you want to add to the bill. Easy enough? Click OK when you're done; QuickBooks fills out the Items tab for you automatically.

13. Move to the Item column and enter a name for the item.

Notice the down arrow in this column. Click it to see the Item list. Does the item you need appear on this list? If so, click that item. If not, choose Add New from the top of the list and fill out the New Item window. (See Chapter 3.)

14. Fill in the rest of the rows of items on the Items tab.

You can enter all the items you're purchasing here. Make sure that the Items tab accurately shows the items that you're purchasing, their costs, quantities, and VAT Codes. If you want to, click the Recalculate button to total the items. (Remember, this overwrites the entry in the Amount Due field in the top part of the bill.)

15. Double check the Total VAT on the bill.

The amount in the Total VAT box (bottom right of the window) needs to match the VAT on the supplier invoice. If you are wildly out, check the amounts in the Amount column, you made a mistake somewhere in there. If you are out by just a penny or two, it may be a rounding difference between your supplier and QuickBooks. Edit the Total VAT amount to match the supplier's invoice. To do so, simply enter the correct amount in the Total VAT box.

If there are multiple VAT Codes in use, click the Edit button next to the Total VAT field and make your adjustments there. Click OK when finished to return to the Enter Bills window.

16. **Save the bill.**

Click Save & New to save your record of the bill and then enter another bill. Or click Save & Close to record your bill but not enter another bill.

QuickBooks lets you see historical information about a supplier in the Enter Bills window and many other "supplier information" windows. To add historical supplier information to a window, click the little white tab that appears in the upper-right corner of the window (if you mouse over it, you'll see "Show History"). You click links in the Show History panel to drill down and get even more information about, for example, a listed transaction.

Entering a bill with an early payment discount

Perhaps you are among the fortunate ones who are offered early payment discounts by your suppliers – in which case you can read more about the benefits of this in Chapter 19. Entering a bill with early payment discount terms is pretty much the same thing as entering a bill without a discount, but there are a few twists in the plot you need to know about. The biggest one is that you account for the VAT on the bill as if you took the discount, regardless of whether you actually take the discount. Kind of weird, right?

The good news is that QuickBooks does the hardest parts for you. So here's how to enter a bill with an early payment discount:

1. **In the Enter Bills window, fill in the Supplier name, bill Date, Reference No, and Amount Due fields as described in the preceding section.**

2. **In the Terms field select an existing early payment discount term or add your own.**

Out of the box, QuickBooks comes with two common early payment discount terms: 1% 10 Net 30, and 2% 10 Net 30. In English, this means the bill is due 30 days from the bill date, but if you pay within 10 days of the bill date you get a 1% (or 2%) discount. You can edit one of these terms to suit your needs, or create a new payment term.

For the fun of it, let's add the new term 1% 7 Net 28 (see Figure 6-5). Click the drop-down arrow next to Terms and select Add New. In the New Terms dialog box that appears, accept the Standard selection and add the following terms:

- Enter **28** in the Net Due in *x* Days field

- Type **1.0%** in the Discount Percentage Is field

- Add **7** in the Discount If Paid Within field

- Click OK to save the new term and add it to the bill.

Figure 6-5:
The New
Terms
dialog box
with the
1% 7 Net 28
term.

3. **Fill in the Expenses tab or Items tab.**

Choose the expense accounts or items that you need to add to the bill. QuickBooks automatically adjusts the VAT in the Total VAT box to take into account the early payment discount. Remember, you need to account for the VAT *as if* you took the discount (whether you take it or not).

We show an example of a bill with early payment discount in Figure 6-6. For the sake of illustration, we used easy-to-work-with numbers. The Net amount of the Cost of Goods purchased is £1000 and 20% VAT on this is £200. But notice that QuickBooks shows £198 in the Total VAT field. That's because the discounted Net amount is £990, and 20% VAT on £990 is indeed £198. Note also that the Amount Due field shows a total of £1198.00.

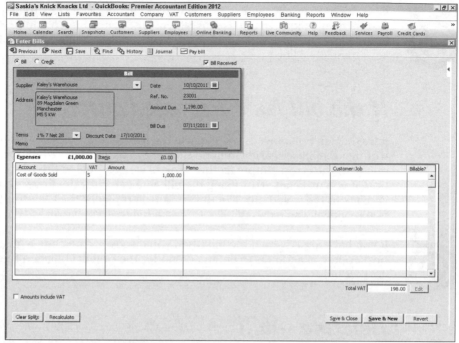

Figure 6-6:
A completed
Enter Bills
window
showing
an early
payment
discount.

4. **Click Save & New or Save & Close to record the bill.**

Fixing Bill Mistakes

It's inevitable that at some point you'll make a mistake on a bill. But don't worry, these are easy to fix in QuickBooks.

If the bill is still displayed onscreen

If the bill is still displayed onscreen, you can just move the cursor to the box or button that's wrong and then fix the mistake. Because most of the bits of information that you enter in the Enter Bills window are short and sweet, you can easily replace the contents of some fields by typing over whatever's already there. To start all over again, just click the Clear button. To save the bill after you've made your changes, click the Save & New button.

If you need to insert a line in the middle of the bill, right-click to display a contextual menu and then choose Insert Line or Delete Line. (If you prefer keyboard shortcuts, press the Ctrl+Insert keys to insert a line and Ctrl+Delete keys to delete a line.)

If the bill isn't displayed onscreen

If the bill isn't displayed, you can use the Next and Previous buttons to page through the bills, bearing in mind they are in date order. When you get to the one with the error, simply fix the error as we describe in the preceding section. If you make an error fixing the bill, you can click the Revert button to go back to the saved bill. The Revert button replaces the Clear button when you're viewing an existing bill – that is, a bill that you've already saved.

If you have already paid the bill when you discover you made a mistake, the best course of action is to enter a credit for the original bill, and then enter the correct bill.

Deleting a bill

Suppose that you accidentally enter the same bill twice or enter a bill that was really meant for the business next door. (Just because you're tracking bills by computer doesn't mean that you don't have to look at things carefully any more.)

There are a number of ways to find a bill, like using the Previous and Next buttons in the Enter Bills window, or doing a search for the bill as we describe in the sidebar called "Using the Find dialog box", later in this chapter. After you locate the bill, follow these steps to delete it:

1. **Select the bill that you want to delete by clicking anywhere in the bill.**

2. **Choose Edit⇨Delete Bill.**

   QuickBooks confirms that you really, truly want to delete the transaction. If you click OK, it dutifully deletes the bill.

If you entered a bill twice and paid one of the bills, make sure you delete the bill which has not been paid. It's easy to see whether a bill has been paid: it will have a big "Paid" stamp across it.

Using the Find dialog box

When you can't remember the information that you need to find a particular entry or transaction, you can search for it by using the Find dialog box. For example, if you can't recall when you entered the bill, choose Edit⇨Find to open the Find dialog box. Choose a *filter* (the category to search by). The box to the right changes to include drop-down lists or text boxes that you can use to specify what you want to search for.

Choose as many filters as you like, but be careful to enter information accurately, or QuickBooks will look for the wrong information. Also, try to strike a balance, choosing only as many filters as you really need to find your information. The more filters you choose, the more searching QuickBooks does, and the longer the search takes.

After you finish choosing filters, click the Find button, and the transactions that match all your filters appear in the list at the bottom of the window. Click the transaction that you want to examine more closely and then click Go To. QuickBooks opens the appropriate window and takes you right to the transaction. Very snazzy, indeed.

Consider crediting the bill if you have already accounted for the VAT in another VAT period, or voiding it so that you can keep a record of the bill and add a memo to remind yourself why you had to void it. To void a bill, find the bill as described previously and click Edit⇨Void Bill. QuickBooks removes the amount, VAT (and, for items, quantity) information.

Remind Me to Pay That Bill, Will You?

You could tie a string around your finger, but the best way to make sure that you pay your bills on time is to have QuickBooks remind you. In fact, you can make the Reminders message box the first thing that you see when you start QuickBooks.

To adjust the QuickBooks reminder options, you must be logged on as the administrator in single-user mode. Then choose Edit⇨Preferences. When QuickBooks displays the Preferences dialog box, click the Reminders icon from the list on the left. Click the My Preferences tab and tick the box next to Show Reminders List when Opening a Company File. This is a personal preference that applies only to you. To set companywide preferences that apply to everyone using the file, click the Company Preferences tab to access the dialog box shown in Figure 6-7, with the Reminders item on the list.

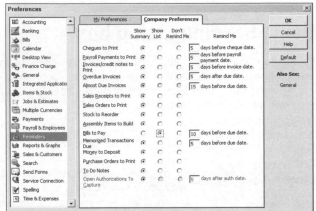

Figure 6-7:
The
Company
Preferences
dialog box.

Make sure that the Show Summary or Show List option button is selected and then give yourself several days' notice before you need to pay bills by typing a number (10 is the default and usually works well) in the Days Before Due Date text box, in the Remind Me column.

If you select the Show Summary option (the first button to the right of the option), you get a summary of the bills that you owe each time you start QuickBooks. If you select Show List (the second button to the right of the option), you get the details about each bill.

Be sure to review the Reminders window when you start QuickBooks or open a new company file. The window lists reminders (such as forms you need to print and payments you need to transmit) and tells you which unpaid bills you're supposed to pay. You can see this list by choosing Company⇨Reminders.

Paying Your Bills

If you've done everything right and recorded your bills correctly, paying bills is easy. Just follow these steps:

1. **Choose Suppliers⇨Pay Bills.**

   Alternatively, click the Pay Bills icon located on the Home page. You see the Pay Bills window, as shown in Figure 6-8.

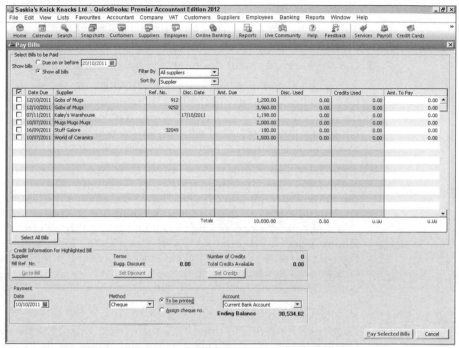

Figure 6-8:
The Pay
Bills
window.

2. **Set a cutoff date for showing bills.**

   In the Show Bills Due On or Before date field, tell QuickBooks which
   bills to show by entering a date. If you want to see all the bills, select the
   Show All Bills radio button.

3. **Use the Sort By drop-down list to tell QuickBooks how to sort the bills.**

   You can arrange bills by due date with the oldest bills listed first,
   arrange them alphabetically by supplier, or arrange them from largest to
   smallest. If you sort by discount date you can see the oldest early payment discounts first.

4. **Identify which bills to pay.**

   If you want to pay all the bills in the dialog box, click the Select All Bills
   button. If you want to clear all the bills you marked, click the Clear
   Selections button. If you want to pick and choose, click to the left of
   the bill's due date to pay the bill. A check mark appears where you
   click. Note that after you apply a payment, the Clear Selections button
   replaces the Select All Bills button.

5. **Change the Amt. to Pay figure if you want to pay only part of a bill.**

   That's right – you can pay only part of a bill by changing the number in the Amt. to Pay column.

6. **Get the early payment discount rate on your bills, if any.**

   You may be eligible for an early payment discount on some bills, and if so you'll see an entry in the Disc. Date column showing the date you need to pay by to receive the discount. To find out how much of a discount you get, select a bill with an early payment discount date and look at the Sugg. Discount amount (above the Set Discount button).

   To take the discount if you are within the discount date terms (shown in the Disc. Date column), click the Set Discount button. In the Discount tab of the Discount and Credits dialog box, change the Discount Amount if necessary and use the Discount Account box to specify which account should be used for recording the money saved through the discount. Finally, select a Discount VAT Code (such as "S", for example). *Note*: the sole purpose of the VAT Code in this context is simply to tell QuickBooks in which Box on the VAT Return (7 or 9) to show the discount. There is no further `VAT charged or discounted.

7. **Get a list of credit notes that you can apply to the payment.**

   Click the Set Credits button to see the Credits tab of the Discount and Credits dialog box. If you want to use one of the credits listed to reduce the amount of the bill, click it and then click Done.

8. **Select a payment date, method, and bank account.**

   Use the Payment area's Date field to specify the payment date of the bill(s). By default, this field shows today's date. If you want another date on the payment cheque(s) – for example, if you're postdating the cheque(s) – change this date. (See the online Cheat Sheet at www. dummies.com/cheatsheet/quickbooks2012uk for some secret date-editing codes.)

   Use the Method drop-down list to select the payment method you want to use (Cheque, Online Banking or Credit Card), and the Account drop-down list to select the bank account from which payment will be made.

9. **If you plan to print the cheque, select the To Be Printed option button.**

   Many businesses use QuickBooks to keep track of cheques, but instead of printing the cheques, they have employees write them by hand. If your business uses this method, select the Assign Cheque Number radio button. Then, when QuickBooks asks how it should number the cheque, either give the number by typing it into the appropriate box or tell QuickBooks to automatically number the cheque.

10. **Click the Pay Selected Bills button to pay the bills and close the Pay Bills window.**

    QuickBooks notes in the Accounts Payable register that you paid these bills; then it goes into the Bank register and "writes" the cheque or cheques. Figure 6-9 shows you what a paid bill looks like in the Bank register. Note BILLPMT in the Type column.

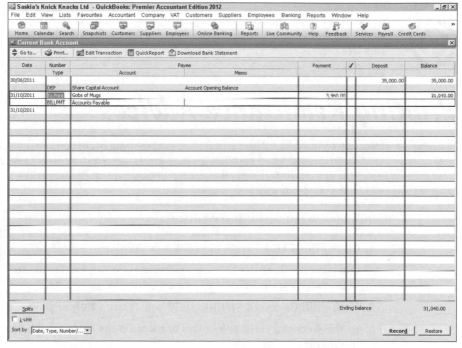

Figure 6-9: How a paid bill looks in the Bank register. Oooh. Cool.

QuickBooks shows the original bill amount as the amount that's paid, not the original bill amount minus the early payment discount. It needs to use this method to completely pay off the bill.

But don't kid yourself – these bills aren't really paid yet. Sure, they're paid in the mind of QuickBooks, but the mind of QuickBooks extends only as far as the metal (or trendy plastic) box that holds your computer. You still have to write or print the cheques and deliver them to the payees.

If you're going to write the cheques by hand, enter the cheque numbers from your chequebook into the QuickBooks register Number column. You want these numbers to jibe, not jive. (We know: a pun is the lowest form of humour.) If you plan to print the cheques, see Appendix D.

And another thing: If you enter a bill, you absolutely must use the Pay Bills command to record the payment that pays off the bill. If you don't do this, the unpaid bill just sits there forever, lonely and forlorn.

You can see if you have any straggler bills by looking at the Unpaid Bills report, which you can access from Reports⇨Suppliers and Payables⇨Unpaid Bills Details.

Printing Remittance Advices

If you pay your bill by electronic banking or handwritten cheques, you may want to print and send remittance advices to let your suppliers know which bills you are paying. (Printed cheques include a remittance advice so you don't have to print any if you use those.)

Here's how to print remittance advices:

1. **Click File⇨Print Forms⇨Remittance Advice.**

    QuickBooks displays the Select Remittance Advice Forms to Print dialog window (Figure 6-10).

2. **In the Bill Payment Method field select the Cheque payment method.**

3. **In the Account field select the bank account from which you made the payments.**

4. **Enter a date range (or a single date) in the Dated and Thru fields, and press the Tab key.**

    QuickBooks displays a list of remittance advices which fit your criteria. If you expect to see entries but none are displayed, check your settings.

5. **Click to remove the check marks next to the remittance advices that you don't want to print and then click OK.**

    All the remittance advices are selected at first, which is fine if you want to print them all. If not, click the check marks next to the remittance advices that you don't want to print so that QuickBooks removes the check marks. If you want to print only a few of the remittance advices, click the Select None button and then click next to the remittance advices that you want to print so that QuickBooks places a check mark in the column.

When only the remittance advices that you want to print have check marks, click OK to continue. QuickBooks displays the Print Remittance Advice Forms dialog box.

6. **Either click Print to accept the default settings, or make changes in the dialog box and then click Print.**

   If appropriate, change the printer name. QuickBooks prints the remittance advices.

Figure 6-10:
The Select
Remittance
Advice
Forms
to Print
window.

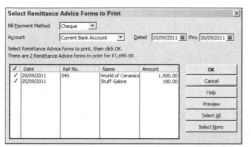

If the remittance advices are missing your business details in the top right corner, you need to enter these in QuickBooks by clicking Company⇨Company Information. To do so, log in to QuickBooks as the administrator, in single user mode (see Appendix C). If the Paid To and Account No. fields are empty, however, you need to enter this information in the supplier record (see Chapter 3).

A Quick Word on the Supplier Centre Window

We end this chapter by briefly talking about the Supplier Centre. This is where QuickBooks provides an overview of a particular supplier, including all the transactions (purchase orders, bills, credit notes, payments) associated with that supplier. While this doesn't provide you with new information, it does give you a slick way to view all the information you have regarding a particular supplier. (It's also a good way to find a transaction for that supplier.)

To get to the Supplier Centre choose Suppliers⇨Supplier Centre or click the Supplier Centre icon. You determine which supplier's information appears in the Supplier Centre window by selecting the supplier from the list that appears at the left edge of the window.

Chapter 7

Stock Magic

· ·

In This Chapter

▶ Using the Item list to track stock

▶ Keeping stock as you purchase and sell items

▶ Using purchase orders to help track stock

▶ Adjusting stock records to reflect what's really in stock

▶ Taking the lazy person's approach to stock

· ·

*F*or small and growing businesses, stock is one of the toughest assets to manage. First, of course, you need to physically care for stuff. Second, you have to make sure that you don't run out of some item or have too much of some other item.

QuickBooks (fortunately) provides elegant sophistication in its stock management features, making stock management easy. With a little jiggering, you can probably get it to work in any simple case – and even in many more complex cases.

If you want to make stock accounting really easy and don't care about a bit of imprecision, take a peek at the last section of this chapter, "The Lazy Person's Approach to Stock".

Setting up Stock Items

Before you can track your stock, you need to do two things. First, you need to tell QuickBooks that you want to track stock. To do this, choose Edit➪Preferences. When QuickBooks displays the Preferences dialog box, click the Items & Stock icon in the list on the left. Your screen should look remarkably similar to the one in Figure 7-1. (You might have to click the Company Preferences tab first.) Make sure that the Stock and Purchase Orders Are Active check box is marked and that one of the Warn If Not Enough Stock to Sell radio buttons is marked.

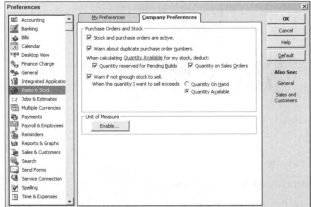

Figure 7-1:
The
Preferences
dialog box
for Items
and Stock.

Here's the second thing that you need to do: Create an *Item list.* This list is a description of all items that you might conceivably put on an invoice. In other words, all items that you order and sell belong on the Item list.

You should have set up your initial Item list during the QuickBooks Setup process, as we describe in Chapter 2. If you need to add an item to your list, choose Lists⇨Item List. Then click the Item button, choose New from the drop-down list, and fill in the New Item window. If you want the blow-by-blow, go to Chapter 3 and get it straight from the horse's mouth.

After you turn on the stock stuff and set up (or update) your Item list, you can track your stock.

When You Buy Stuff

As you unload items from a truck, receive them in the mail, or buy them from a street seller, you have to record the items so that QuickBooks can track your stock. How you record the items and pay for them depends on whether you pay cash, receive a bill along with the items, or receive the items without a bill (in which case, you pay for the items later).

And you may have filled out a purchase order (PO) for the items that you're receiving. If that's the case, receiving the items gets a little easier. If you receive items for which you have already filled out a PO, see the section, "How Purchase Orders Work", later in this chapter. We strongly recommend filling out a PO when you order items that you're going to receive and pay for later.

Recording items that you pay for upfront

Okay, you just bought three porcelain chickens in the bazaar at Marrakech, and now you want to add them to your stock and record the purchase. How do you record stock you paid for over the counter? By using the Write Cheques window, of course – the same way you record any other bills you pay for upfront. Just make sure that you fill out the Items column as we describe in Chapter 6.

Recording items that don't come with a bill

What happens if the items come before the invoice? Lucky you – you have the stuff and you don't have to pay for it yet. However, you do have to record the stock you just received so that you know you have it on hand. You can't do that in the Write Cheques window because you won't be writing a cheque to pay for the stuff – at least not for a while. How do you record items that you receive before paying for them? Read on:

1. **Either Choose Suppliers⬦Receive Items or click the Receive Stock icon on the Home screen, and select the option to Receive Stock without a bill.**

   You see the Create Item Receipts window, as shown in Figure 7-2. This window is similar to the Enter Bills window that we describe in Chapter 6, but it reads Item Receipt Only. (You see the Enter Bills window again when you receive the bill for the items.)

2. **Fill in the top part of the window.**

   If you want to record items from a supplier who's already on the Supplier list, click the down arrow and then choose the supplier. If the supplier is a new supplier, choose Add New from the drop-down list and then, in the New Supplier dialog box that appears, click Set Up to set up information about the supplier: the address, the credit limit, payment terms, and so on. When you're done with the New Supplier dialog box, click Save & Close.

   A tidy way to keep track of the orders is to enter the PO number in the Ref. No. field of the Item Receipt. That way when you get the bill you'll quickly be able to see to which order it relates.

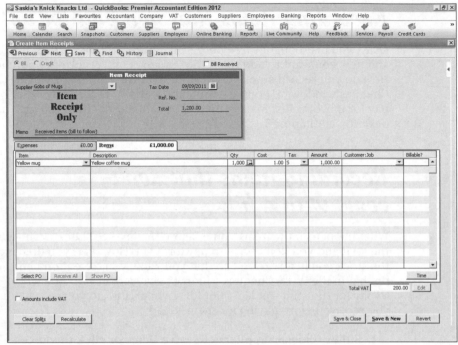

Figure 7-2:
The Create
Item
Receipts
window.

3. Click the Items tab.

You need to click the Items tab only if it isn't already displayed. It probably is.

4. Move to the Item column and type a name for the item.

Notice the down arrow in the Item column. Click it to see the Item list. Does the item that you're paying for appear on this list? If so, click it. If not, enter a new item name. You see the Item Not Found message box. Click Set Up, fill out the New Item dialog box and then click Save & Close. (See Chapter 3 for help with describing new items.)

You may just as well go down the packing slip or delivery note, entering the items on the Items tab. Make sure that the Items tab accurately shows what's on the packing slip. And put a brief description of the items in the Memo field (where it says Received Items (bill to follow) in Figure 7-2) because that description might prove useful later when you want to match up your item receipt with the bill. When you finish, the Create Item Receipts window should look something like what you see in Figure 7-2.

5. **Provide quantity and cost.**

   - *Qty column:* Describe the quantity you received.

   - *Cost column:* Describe the item unit cost. If the item unit cost you enter represents a change, QuickBooks asks if you want to update its standard item cost (as stored on the Items list) and whether you want to update your standard price for the item.

   - *Tax column:* QuickBooks calls up the Tax (that is, the VAT Code) you specified on the stock item record. You'll double check this against the bill when you receive it.

6. **Click the Save & New button or the Save & Close button to record the items that you just received.**

   The items are officially part of your stock. The item receipt has been entered on the Accounts Payable register. Not only that, but you're all set for when the bill comes.

Paying for items when you get the bill

The items arrive and you fill out an item receipt. Three weeks pass. What's this in your post? Why, it's the bill, of course! Now you have to enter a bill for the items that you received three weeks ago. This job is easy:

1. **Choose Suppliers⇨Enter Bill for Received Items.**

   Or, from the Home screen, click the Enter Bills against Stock icon. If you're on the Supplier Centre, click New Transactions and then Enter Bill for Received Items. The Select Item Receipt dialog box appears, as shown in Figure 7-3.

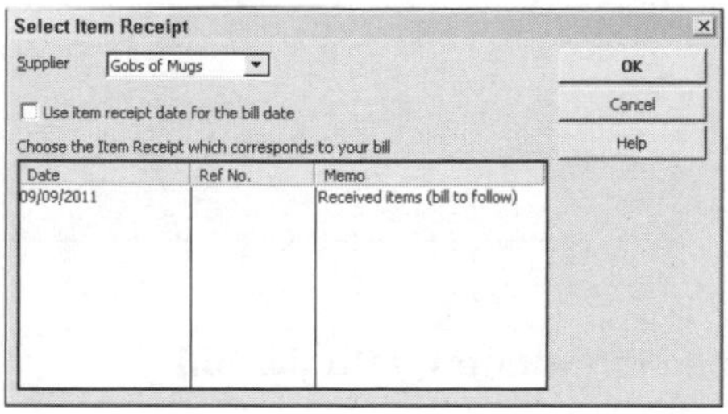

Figure 7-3: The Select Item Receipt dialog box.

2. **Click the Supplier drop-down list and choose the name of the supplier who sent you the bill.**

   You see one or more item receipts in the box, with the date you put on the receipt, its reference number (which will be the PO number if you followed our earlier Tip), and the memo that you wrote on the receipt.

3. **Select the item receipt for which you want to enter a bill and then click OK.**

   The Enter Bills window appears, as shown in Figure 7-4. Does this information look familiar? It should – it's the same information that you put in the Create Item Receipts window, only now you're working with a bill, not a receipt.

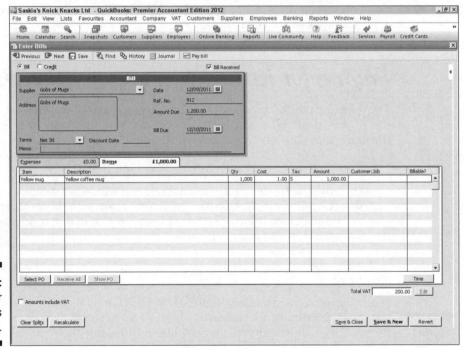

Figure 7-4:
The Enter Bills window.

4. **Compare the Items tab in the window with the bill.**

   Are you paying for what you received earlier? Carriage charges may have been added to your bill. You can add this either to the Expenses tab or the Items tab (if you set up Carriage as an Item). You may also need to adjust the quantity, cost of the items or the VAT code (in the Tax column), because you may have been guessing when you recorded receiving the items. If so, add to and adjust the bill information by using the Items tab. (You can click the Recalculate button to add the new items.)

Did you enter the bill reference number? (That's the supplier's purchase invoice number.) If not, do so. How many days do you have to pay this bill? Is it due now? Take a look at the Terms line to see what this supplier's payment terms are. Change the payment terms if they're incorrect by selecting a different entry from the drop-down list. Remember: you want to pay your bills at the best possible time, but for you to do so, the terms in the Enter Bills window must match the supplier's payment terms.

5. **Click Save & New or Save & Close to record the bill.**

   Of course, you still need to pay the supplier's bill. Fair enough. Take a look at Chapter 6 if you need help.

Recording items and paying the bill all at once

Suppose that you receive the bill when you receive the goods. The items are unloaded from the elephant's back, and the elephant driver takes a bow and hands you the bill. Here are the steps you follow:

1. **Choose Suppliers➪Receive Items and Enter Bill.**

   Or, from the Home screen, click Receive Stock and then select the Receive Stock with Bill option there. Or, from the Supplier Centre, click New Transactions and then Enter Bill for Received Items. You see the Enter Bills window (refer to Figure 7-4). If you've been reading this chapter from its beginning, you're familiar with this window, and you know exactly what it is and what it does. If you parachuted into this page by way of the index, you need to know, for stock purposes, how to record the items you're paying for.

2. **Fill out the top part of the window.**

   This stuff is pretty basic. Choose a supplier from the drop-down list and make sure that the supplier's terms for paying this bill are shown correctly. If this supplier is new, choose Add New. QuickBooks asks you to fill in an information dialog box about the supplier. Do it. Make sure that you fill out the Bill Due line correctly.

3. **Click the Items tab and list all the items that you're paying for.**

   To see the Item list, move the cursor to the Item column and click the down arrow that appears. Make sure that the quantity, cost, and Tax (meaning VAT code) of the items are listed correctly on the Items tab.

4. **Click Save & New or Save & Close.**

   QuickBooks adds the items you listed to the Item list and makes them an official part of your stock.

When You Sell Stuff

In Chapter 4, we tell you how to list items on an invoice. Maybe you noticed the similarities between the Items tab in the Enter Bills window and the Quantity/Item/Description/Rate/Amount/VAT box of an invoice. QuickBooks uses both for keeping stock.

When you sell stuff, QuickBooks automatically adjusts your stock. In other words, if you buy 400 porcelain chickens and sell 350 of them, you have only 50 on hand. QuickBooks updates records for this change. Isn't this great? No more lying awake at night, wondering whether you have enough chickens or wombats or whatever. The same thing happens when you make cash sales. When you list the items on the sales receipt, QuickBooks assumes that they're leaving your hands and subtracts them from your stock.

One moral of this story is "Keep a good, descriptive Item list". And the other moral is "Enter items carefully on the Items tab of cheques and bills and in the Item/Description/Quantity/Rate/Amount/VAT box of sales receipts and invoices".

How Purchase Orders Work

If you have to order stuff for your business, consider using POs. Create a QuickBooks PO even if you order goods by phone, by telegraph, or over the Internet – that is, whenever you don't request goods in writing. Filling out a PO enables you to determine what items you have on order and when the items will arrive. All you'll have to do is ask QuickBooks, "What's on order and when's it coming?" Never again will you have to rack your brain to remember whether you've ordered those thingamajigs and watchamacallits.

And when the delivery or bill arrives, you'll already have the details itemised on the PO form. Guess what? Having written all the items on your PO, you don't have to fill out an Items tab on your cheque when you pay the bill. Or, if you're paying bills with the accounts payable method, you don't have to fill out the Items tab in the Enter Bills window. (Look at Chapter 6 if you don't know what we're talking about here.) When the items arrive, all you have to do is let QuickBooks know; the items are immediately added to your stock list.

Use POs for items that you order – that is, for items that you'll receive and pay for in the future. If you buy items over the counter or receive items that you didn't order, you obviously don't need a PO. What you need to do is pay the bill and stock the items that you just bought, as we explain in the first half of this chapter.

Customising a purchase order form

QuickBooks allows you to customise your purchase order form by editing the Custom Purchase Order template. To customise this template, choose Suppliers⇨Create Purchase Orders, and click the Customise button. When QuickBooks displays the Basic Customisation window, click the Manage Templates button to rename the template. You do so in the Preview pane on the right, in the Template Name field. Click OK to save the new name and return to the Basic Customisation window. To customise the form, click the Additional Customisation button. QuickBooks displays the dialog box that supplies tabs where you can specify which fields appear on screen and when the form is printed (or e-mailed) and where you can rename field titles. To save your new template, click OK.

The Additional Customisation dialog box provides a Preview area you can use to see what your changes look like and a Cancel button if things get terribly out of hand. Furthermore, the Additional Customisation dialog box also provides a Layout Designer button, which you can click to open the Layout Designer window. The Layout Designer window allows you to become a true layout artist and make all sorts of changes to the overall look of your purchase order simply by moving fields around the page with your mouse.

Filling out a purchase order

Perhaps you're running low on gizmos, or watchamacallits, or some other item on your Item list, and you're ready to reorder these things – whatever they are. Follow these steps to fill out a PO:

1. **Choose Suppliers⇨Create Purchase Orders.**

   You could also click the Purchase Orders icon on the Home screen, or click the New Transactions area of the Supplier Centre and then select Purchase Orders. You see the Create Purchase Orders window, which is similar to what's shown in Figure 7-5. Note that the exact details of this window depend on how you customise your PO form.

2. **Choose a supplier from the Supplier drop-down list.**

   Click the down arrow to see a list of your suppliers. Click a supplier to see its name and address in the Supplier box. If you can't find the name of the supplier on your list, click Add New from the list and then fill in the information about the supplier in the resulting New Supplier dialog box. Click Save & Close when you're done with the dialog box.

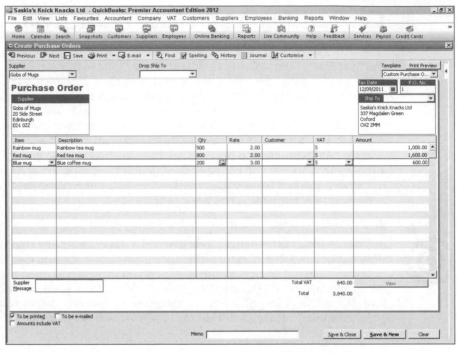

Figure 7-5:
The Create
Purchase
Orders
window.

3. **If you track your stock by class, select a class from the Class drop-down list.**

   The Create Purchase Orders window may not have a Class drop-down list. If it doesn't and you want it to have one, you have to set up QuickBooks to track expenses by Class (as we describe in Chapter 3).

4. **(Optional) Select a Rep, an Expected Date, and a FOB (which we describe in Chapter 4) if you're using them on your PO.**

   You may have to fill in other fields before you get to the item-by-item descriptions at the bottom. Again, these fields may not appear if you haven't indicated that you want them on your form.

5. **Move to the Item column and start entering the items you're ordering.**

   Entering the items is the most important part of creating a PO. When you move into the Item column, it turns into a drop-down list. Click its down arrow to see the Item list. You may need to scroll to the item that you want to enter. A fast way to scroll to the item is to type the first few letters of the item name. If you type the name of an item that isn't on the Item list, QuickBooks asks whether you want to set up this item. If so, click Set Up and then fill in the New Item dialog box.

Enter as many items as you want in the Item column. QuickBooks fills in an item description for you, but you can edit whatever it puts into the Description column, if need be. In the Qty column, indicate how many of each item you need. QuickBooks recalls the item's VAT code, which you can change once you get the bill, if need be.

6. **If you want to, fill in the Supplier Message field – but definitely fill in the Memo field.**

   The Supplier Message field is where you put a message to the party receiving your order. You could write, "Get me this stuff pronto!"

   No matter what you do, be sure to fill in the Memo field. What you write in this field appears in the Open Purchase Orders dialog box, and this info is the surest way for you to identify what this PO is for. Write something meaningful that you can understand two weeks, three weeks, or a month from now, when you pay for the items that you're ordering.

   At the bottom of the Create Purchase Orders window is the To Be Printed check box, which tells you whether you printed this PO. If you want to print the PO, make sure that this check box is selected. After you print the PO, the check disappears from the box.

7. **Click Print to print the PO.**

   If this PO is one of many that you've been filling out and you want to print several at once, click the arrow beside the Print button and choose Print Batch from the drop-down list. Before you print the PO, however, you may want to click the down arrow beside the Print button and choose Preview to see what the PO will look like when you print it. QuickBooks shows you an onscreen replica of the PO. We hope it looks okay.

   You use the History button after you receive the items you've so carefully listed on the PO. After you receive the items and record their receipt, clicking this button tells QuickBooks to give you the entire history of an item – when you ordered it and when you received it.

   As for the other buttons at the top, we think that you know what those are.

8. **Click Save & New or Save & Close to record the PO.**

   QuickBooks saves the PO and displays a new, blank PO window in which you can enter another order.

Checking up on purchase orders

You record the POs. A couple weeks go by, and you ask yourself, "Did I order those watchamacallits?" Choose Reports➪Purchases➪Open Purchase Orders to see a report that lists outstanding POs. Or click the Reports Centre, select Purchases in the left column, click the List view button in the top-right corner to get a list of purchasing reports, and then click the Open Purchase Orders report. Alternatively, you can use the Report Centre carousel to "page" through the reports in a category: To use the carousel, select Purchases in the left column, click the Carousel view button (next to the List view button), and then click the stack-of-reports image that appears to the left or the right of the picture of the selected report.

Receiving purchase order items

After your watchamacallits and gizmos have arrived by camel train, you need to record the receipt of the items and add them to your Item list.

The first two things to do are to note whether the stuff came with a bill and then decide how you want to pay for it. These decisions are the same ones that you have to make if you receive goods without having first filled out a PO.

You record PO items that you receive in the same way you record other items you receive:

- ✔ If you pay for PO items with a cheque, use the Write Checks window.

- ✔ If you receive the PO items without a bill, use the Create Item Receipts window.

- ✔ If you receive the PO items with a bill, use the Enter Bills window.

Regardless of the window you're using, when you select the supplier who sold you the PO items, QuickBooks alerts you that open POs exist for the supplier and asks you whether you want to receive against a PO. Of course you do. (*Receive against* simply means to compare what you ordered with what you received.) When you click Yes, QuickBooks displays the Open Purchase Orders dialog box, as shown in Figure 7-6. Select the PO(s) that you're receiving against and then click OK. QuickBooks fills out the Items tab to show all the stuff you ordered. If what QuickBooks shows isn't what you received, you may have to make adjustments.

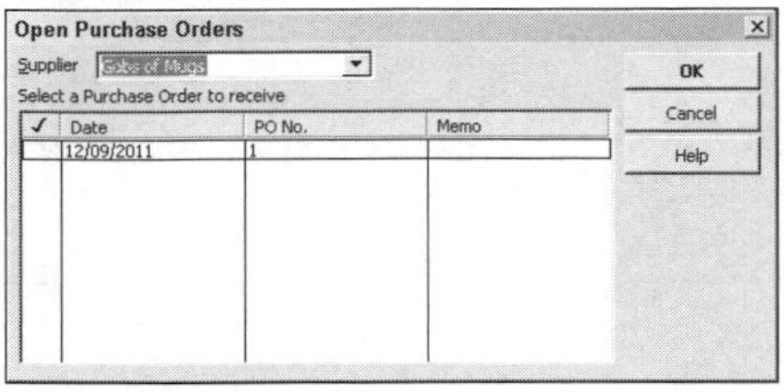

Figure 7-6:
The Open
Purchase
Orders dia-
log box.

Assembling a Product

QuickBooks Premier includes a cool tool for accounting for the manufacture of items. Suppose that Saskia's Knick Knacks Ltd, the example business we use in this book, mostly just buys and resells coffee mugs and other knick knacks. But also suppose that, once a year, Saskia's Knick Knacks Ltd assembles a romantic collection of red coffee mugs into a boxed St Valentine's Day gift set. In this case, QuickBooks can record the assembly of a boxed gift set that combines, for example, six red coffee mugs, a cardboard box clad in shiny red foil, and some red tissue paper.

Identifying the components

Each component that makes up the assembly – in this example, the St Valentine's Day boxed gift set – needs to be an item on your Item list. Chapter 3 describes how to add items to the Item list, so we don't repeat that information here. The weird thing about assembly items, however, is that the New Item window identifies the parts that make up the assembly. For example, the St Valentine's Day boxed gift set assembly includes these items: six red tea mugs, a cardboard gift box, and some tissue paper that loved ones can use when they become emotionally overwhelmed by the generosity of this thoughtful gift. These items get listed as the pieces that make up the boxed gift set.

Building the assembly

To build an assembly, choose Suppliers⇔Stock Activities⇔Build Assemblies. QuickBooks displays the Build Assemblies window, as shown in Figure 7-7. All you do is choose the item that you want to build from the Assembly Item drop-down list and then the quantity that you (or some hapless co-worker) entered in the Quantity to Build text box (in the lower-right corner). Then you click either the Build & Close button or the Build & New button. (Click Build & New if you want to record the assembly of some other items.)

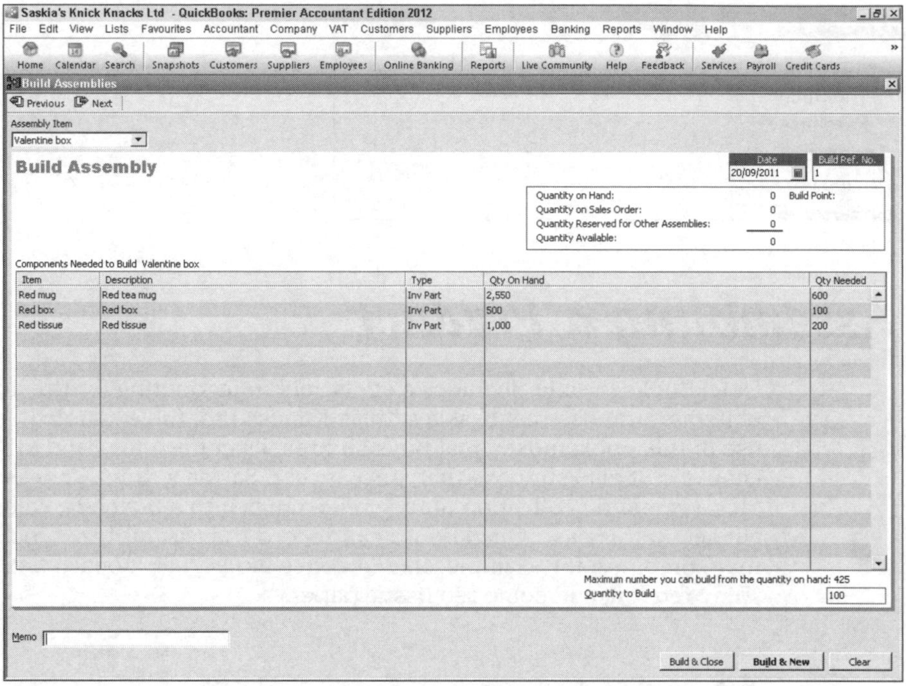

Figure 7-7:
The Build
Assemblies
window.

While we're on the subject, here's a handful of observations about the Build Assemblies window and the Build Assemblies command:

- ✓ In the top-right portion of the window, QuickBooks shows the quantities of the assembly that you have on hand and for which customers have placed orders. That's pretty useful information to have, so, hey – remember that it's there.

- ✓ The main part of the Build Assemblies window shows you what goes into your product. Not that you care, but this is called a *bill of materials*.

- ✓ At the bottom of the bill of materials list, QuickBooks shows you the maximum number of assemblies you can make, given your current stock holdings.

- ✓ When you build an item, QuickBooks adjusts the stock item counts. For example, in the case of boxed gift sets – each with six red tea mugs, two pieces of wrapping tissue, and a cardboard box – QuickBooks reduces the item counts of red tea mugs, wrapping tissue, and boxes, and increases the item counts of the boxed gift sets when you record building the assembly.

- ✓ Some of the components used in an assembly may not be stock items. When you use non-stock parts in an assembly, QuickBooks doesn't care about the item counts.

Time for a Reality Check

QuickBooks does a pretty good job of tracking stock, but you're still going to have to make that complete annual check of what you have in stock. What we're saying here is that you're going to have to go over everything and count it by hand. Sorry. You just can't avoid that chore.

QuickBooks will produce a handy physical stock worksheet that you and your minions can use to count stock. To produce this report, choose Suppliers⇨Stock Activities⇨Stock Take Worksheet. Then, after QuickBooks produces an onscreen version of this worksheet report, click the Print button to print hard copies of the worksheet. You can use the printed worksheet to record actual physical counts of the stock items you hold.

After you make your count, what happens if your stock figures differ from those QuickBooks has? First, you have to decide who's right: you or QuickBooks. You're right, probably. Products get dropped. They break. And that means that you have to adjust the QuickBooks stock numbers.

Choose Suppliers⇨Stock Activities⇨Adjust Quantity/Value on Hand. Or click the Adjust Quantity on Hand icon in the Company section of the Home screen. The Adjust Quantity/Value on Hand window appears, as shown in Figure 7-8.

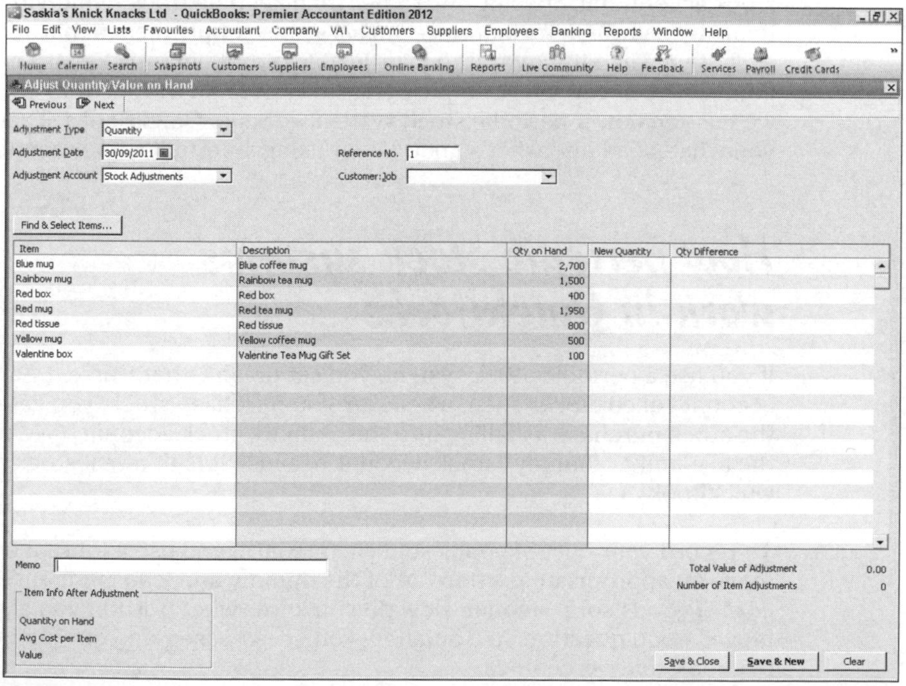

Figure 7-8: The Adjust Quantity/Value on Hand window.

Item	Description	Qty on Hand	New Quantity	Qty Difference
Blue mug	Blue coffee mug	2,700		
Rainbow mug	Rainbow tea mug	1,500		
Red box	Red box	400		
Red mug	Red tea mug	1,950		
Red tissue	Red tissue	800		
Yellow mug	Yellow coffee mug	500		
Valentine box	Valentine Tea Mug Gift Set	100		

The first thing to do is choose an account for storing your stock adjustments from the Adjustment Account drop-down list. You also can select a class from the Class drop-down list, if you turned on Class tracking as described in Chapter 3.

For what it's worth, some accountants like to use a "Stock Adjustments" expense account to provide a way to see the total stock adjustments over the year.

Go down the Item column, selecting items from the Item list whose counts you need to update. When you select an item, QuickBooks shows the item count that it thinks is correct in the Quantity on Hand column. If this count is wrong, enter the correct count in the New Quantity column. Click Save & Close when you're done.

The Lazy Person's Approach to Stock

The stock accounting approach that we describe in the previous sections is the textbook approach. What's more, the approach is a really good one because it lets you accurately calculate your cost of goods sold and accurately estimate the value of the stock you're holding.

You should know, however, that you can also use a simpler approach to stock accounting. Specifically, rather than keeping track of individual stock items by using a *perpetual stock system* – this simply means that you track each item when it moves into your business and out into a customer's car or minivan – you can use a simple periodic system. In the sections that follow, we tell you how a periodic stock system works in QuickBooks. Then we tell you what's bad and what's good about using a periodic stock system.

How periodic stock systems work in QuickBooks

If you use a periodic stock system, you set up an Other Current Asset type account called *Stock*. Then, whenever you purchase stock, you categorise the stock purchase as falling into this dummy stock account. (We're calling the account a "dummy" stock account because it isn't a real stock account to QuickBooks.)

To record your cost of goods sold each month, you use a journal entry to move an appropriate portion out of the dummy stock account and into your cost of goods sold account. How do you know what portion you should move? Good question. In a nutshell, you guess based on your historical cost of goods sold percentage.

Here's an example of how this works: Suppose that since time immemorial, your cost of goods sold has run 45 percent of your sales income, and that last month, you sold £10,000 of stuff. In this case, you'd figure that 45 percent of £10,000 (£4500) equals the cost of the stock that you sold. Accordingly, you'd move £4500 out of the fake stock account and into cost of goods sold.

Predictably, this rough-and-ready approach means that your stock and cost of goods sold numbers are going to be wrong. So, at the end of the year, you still perform a physical stock count to figure out exactly what you truly hold in stock. At that point, you adjust the stock and cost of goods sold balances so that they match what your physical stock shows.

For example, it may be that over the course of the year, your rough 45 percent number has meant that you moved £5000 too much from stock to cost of goods sold. In this case, you'd move £5000 out of cost of goods sold and back to stock.

Or you may find that you moved £5000 too little from stock to cost of goods sold. To fix that problem, you move £5000 from stock to cost of goods sold.

A final quick point about using a periodic stock: As we note in this little discussion, you don't use stock items if you're using a periodic stock. So what you put on invoices or sales receipts is just a generic, non-stock part item.

The good and bad of a periodic stock system

A periodic stock system is good for some types of businesses. For example, if you have too many items to track with the QuickBooks Item list, the approach that we describe here can be a lifesaver.

However, periodic stock systems create some problems. Here are what we think are the four biggest and baddest problems:

✔ You won't really know which items are selling well and which aren't because you won't be tracking sales by stock items. This means that you can't stock more of the hot-selling stuff and less of stuff that's not selling. (You also won't know an item's profitability so you can't tell how profitable your hot-selling stuff is.)

✔ You won't know what you really hold in your stock except when you take that year-end physical stock. (You won't know the worth of the stock you're holding nor will you know which item quantities you're holding.)

✔ Because you won't make item-level adjustments based on your physical stock, you won't know which items are prone to shrinkage from problems such as theft, breakage, and spoilage.

✔ You'll need to make the journal entries that record the money moving out of stock and into cost of goods sold. These journal entries aren't terribly difficult, but they can be a little bit tricky to figure out the first few times.

You'll need to decide whether you want or need to go with a simpler periodic stock system in spite of the problems such a system presents. The one final thought that we'll leave you with is this: many small businesses – especially small retailers – successfully use periodic stock systems.

Chapter 8

Working with Your Banking Register

In This Chapter

▶ Some special circumstances for writing cheques

▶ Recording deposits and transfers

▶ Voiding and deleting transactions

▶ Handling bounced cheques

▶ Searching for transactions

---

*T*he finances and cash flows of a business revolve around the bank account. Which means this chapter is mighty important. Here, you're going to see how to do a number of everyday tasks that affect your bank account: writing certain types of cheque, making deposits, and handling bank transfers. Along the way, you also find out about some neat tools that QuickBooks provides for making these tasks easier, faster, and more precise.

When Only a Cheque Will Do

This chapter is all about transactions that affect your bank account, and the one thing that you do most often that affects your bank account is to write a cheque. In Chapter 6 we discuss, blow by blow, how to use the Write Cheques method to enter and pay your bills in one fell swoop, so we won't repeat it here. But even if you typically use the accounts payable method (also described in Chapter 6) to handle supplier bills and payments, there are times when only the Write Cheques window will do. It may be because you don't have a bill from a supplier or it's not the kind of transaction where a bill makes sense.

You find the Write Cheques window in QuickBooks by clicking Banking⇨Write Cheques.

Here are some examples of instances where only the Write Cheques window will do:

✔ You walk into a shop and see an item you must have (er, for the business, of course). You pay with your debit card and walk out happily with your new purchase (and a receipt). You enter this into QuickBooks in the Write Cheques window, exactly as described in Chapter 6, but instead of a cheque number you enter something such as DebitCard.

✔ You use cold hard cash to pay for an expense out of the petty cash tin (see the sidebar later in this chapter on "Paying for items with cash").

✔ You pay your business insurance premium by direct debit every year and you don't get a bill, just a reminder that it's due. In the Write Cheques window, you use an expense account such as Insurance and the "E" VAT Code (see Figure 8-1) – this is one of the few instances where you get to use the Exempt VAT Code. Enter something such as DD or DirectDebit for the cheque number.

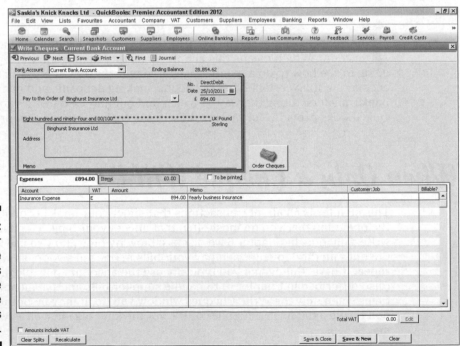

Figure 8-1:
Paying your insurance premiums from the Write Cheques window.

✔ You need to record your bank's services charges. In the Write Cheques window, select the Bank Charges expense account and the "E" VAT Code (yippee, another Exempt VAT code).

✔ You log in to your online banking facility and pay your corporation tax (for limited companies). In the Write Cheques window, you use the Corporation Tax expense account and select the "O" VAT Code. Paying your corporation tax is outside the scope of VAT (thankfully!).

✔ You write a cheque which draws funds out of the business, say for dividends or owner's drawings (see Chapter 18).

✔ You make your monthly bank loan payment (see Chapter 18).

You get the idea, right?

There are a whole bunch of situations when you want to use the Write Cheques window to let QuickBooks know about some expense, purchase, or payment, and it doesn't make sense to use the accounts payable method to do so. By the way, we talk about how you enter some of these transactions in Chapter 18.

By now you have probably figured out that the Write Cheques window in QuickBooks is not only used for a physical cheque. You can record debit card payments, online banking payments, cash point withdrawals, and petty cash expenses in the same way that you record a physical cheque that you write. What differs is the reference in the Cheque No. field of the Write Cheques window. Here you can enter things such as DebitCard, BACS, CASH, DirectDebit, and so on.

Paying for items with cash

To track petty cash purchases, you need a petty cash account. You can set up a petty cash account (which works just like a bank account) by following the steps in "Setting up a second bank account", later in this chapter. To record purchases that you make from the money in that coffee tin beside your desk, use the petty cash register. You can record cash purchases just like you record cheques. (Of course, you don't need to worry about using the correct cheque numbers when you record cash purchases; you can just use the numbers 1, 2, 3, and so on.) To record cash withdrawals to be used for petty cash in the business, just record the withdrawal as a transfer to your petty cash account, as we describe later in the chapter.

Depositing Money into a Bank Account

You can't write cheques unless you deposit some money in your bank account. You didn't know that? Well, the next time you're taking your exercise in the prison yard, give it some serious thought.

From time to time, you must deposit money in your bank account and record those deposits in the QuickBooks bank register, using the Make Deposits window.

Depositing money from customers

Have you been recording customer payments as they come in? (You do so by choosing Customers⇨Receive Payments or Customers⇨Enter Sales Receipt, as we describe in Chapter 5; by selecting the Create Sales Receipts or Receive Payments icon on the Home screen; or by clicking the Customer Centre and selecting New Transactions, Sales Receipts, or Receive Payments.) If you've recorded customer payments and told QuickBooks to group them with your other undeposited funds, QuickBooks places these payments in your Undeposited Funds account. You transfer the undeposited funds to your bank account, as we describe in detail in Chapter 5.

Depositing other money

It's quite likely that not all of the money you'll receive in your business will be from customers. You may, for example, receive bank interest on your current or savings accounts on a regular basis (yeah, right), or get a bank loan at some point. Maybe your favourite Auntie decides to give you a gift of £100 to help you with your business. For whatever reason, at one point or another, you will need to use the Make Deposits window for deposits other than customer payments or receipts. In Figure 8-2, we show an example of a completed Make Deposits window for a £10,000 loan.

Here's what you do:

1. **Choose Banking⇨Make Deposits.**

   You can also click the Record Deposits icon in the Banking section of the Home screen. You now see the Make Deposits window as shown in Figure 8-2.

   Note: If you have undeposited funds from customers, you see the Payments to Deposit dialog box first, which lists the cheques you've received but haven't paid into your bank account yet. Because you are not recording customer receipts or payments right now, click the

Cancel button in the Payments to Deposit dialog box. (Don't worry, the payments you just ignored remain queued in the Payments to Deposit window until you decide to action them.)

Do not use the Make Deposits window if you need to record a deposit where VAT is involved. That's because there is no field in the Make Deposits window to specify VAT. Avoid this route even for a deposit that's zero rated VAT (or VAT exempt) because such a receipt still needs to be reported in Box 6 (Net Sales) on the VAT 100 Return. Use a sales receipt and the appropriate VAT Code instead.

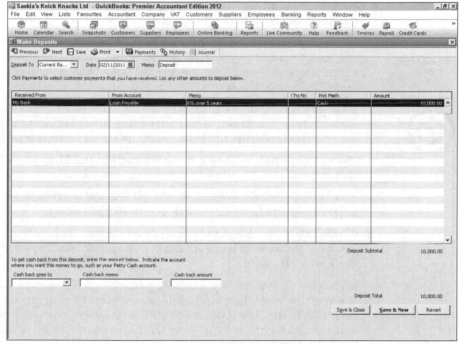

Figure 8-2:
The Make Deposits window showing a loan deposit.

2. **Select the bank account to receive the deposit, and choose the deposit date.**

   Select the account from the Deposit To drop-down list at the top of the window. And while you're at it, make sure that the Date field shows the correct date for the deposit. If you're depositing a bank loan, for example, enter the date you received the funds into your bank account.

3. **In the Received From field, find the name of the person or business who gave you the money.**

   Click your mouse in the Received From field and start typing the name of the person or business paying you the money. If QuickBooks recognises the name, it will autofill it. If it does not recognise the name, you see the Name Not Found dialog box when you tab to the next field. Click either Quick Add or Set Up to add the new name, and in the next dialog box specify whether the new name is a supplier, customer, employee, or other name. Click OK and then fill in the details. Click OK again to save your new name and return to the Make Deposits window.

4. **In the From Account field, select an account to specify what the money is for.**

   Click the down arrow in the From Account field and choose an account from the Chart of Accounts list to describe what the money is for. For example, if you are recording the receipt of a bank loan, find and select the liability account where you track the loan. If you have not set up such an account, select Add New (you see this option when you click the down arrow in the From Account field).

   In the Add New Account: Choose Type dialog box, select the type of account you need to set up. In the second Add New window, enter a name for the account. Click OK to save your changes and return to the Make Deposits window.

   If you are setting up a bank loan account, choose an Other Current Liability type of account; if you are setting up an account to record interest you received from the bank, select an Other Income type account.

5. **(Sort of optional) Write a note to yourself in the Memo box to describe this deposit.**

   You should probably write a memo in case you need to know what this deposit is years from now, when you're old and dotty.

6. **(Optional) If you are paying in a cheque, enter its number in the Chq No. field (otherwise leave it blank) and specify the Payment Method in the Pmt Meth. field.**

   If you don't see a suitable Payment Method when you click the drop down arrow in the Pmt Meth. field, you can add a new one. Select Add New and, in the New Payment Method dialog box, name the new method and select a Payment Type. Click OK to save your addition and return to the Make Deposits window.

7. **Enter the amount of the deposit in the Amount column.**

   Finally, the good part! You know what to do.

8. **Click the Save & Close button at the bottom of the Make Deposits window.**

   The deposit is recorded in QuickBooks. It appears in your register next to the letters DEP (see Figure 8-3).

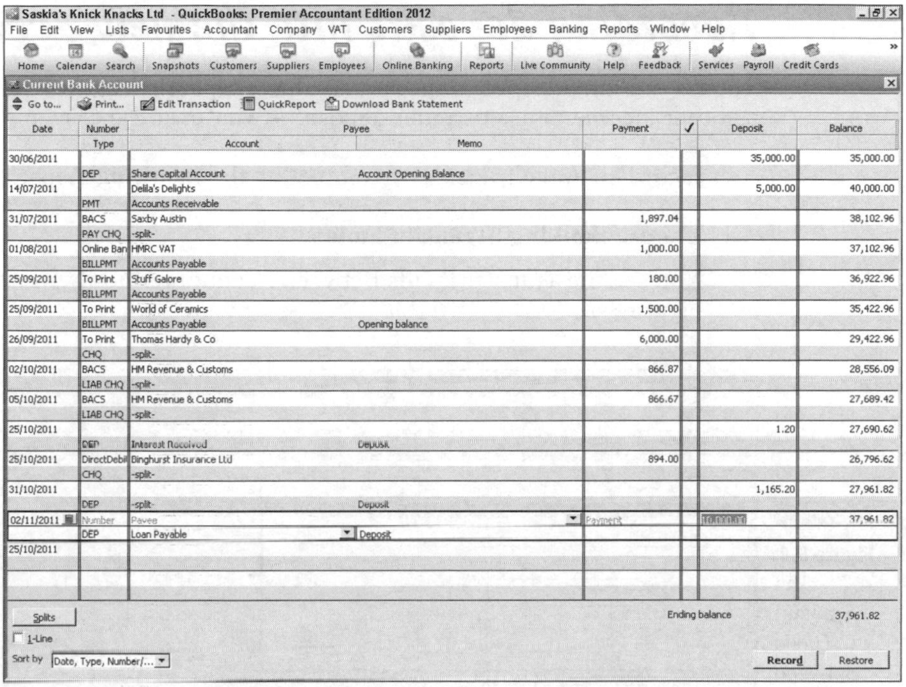

Figure 8-3:
The Bank
Register
showing
the new
deposit.

Transferring Money Between Accounts

Account transfers occur when you move money from one account to another – for example, from your savings account to your current account. QuickBooks makes quick work of account transfers as long as you've already set up both accounts.

Setting up a second bank account

Open the Chart of Accounts by choosing Lists➪Chart of Accounts, or just click the Chart of Accounts icon on the Home screen in the Company section. Click the Account button (bottom left of the window) and choose New. When QuickBooks displays the Add New Account: Choose Account Type dialog box, click the Bank radio button and then the Continue button. In the second Add New Account dialog box, enter the name of the account and (if you want) a description of the account, the bank account number, sort code, and other information you want to store.

Recording deposits into the new account

You record initial deposits the way we describe earlier in this chapter (either as other income or as customer deposits – whatever the case may be).

You record an initial transfer by completing the following steps:

1. **Choose Banking⇨Transfer Funds.**

   You see the Transfer Funds Between Accounts window, as shown in Figure 8-4.

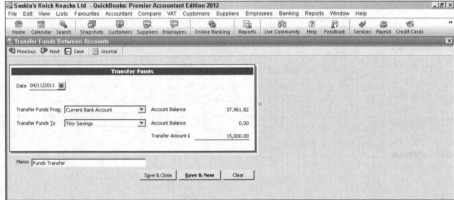

Figure 8-4:
The Transfer Funds Between Accounts window.

2. **Select the bank account from which you're going to transfer the money.**

   From the Transfer Funds From drop-down list at the top of the window, choose the account.

3. **Select the bank account to which you want to transfer the money.**

   From the Transfer Funds To drop-down list, select the account that receives the funds.

4. **Enter the amount that you want to transfer and, optionally, fill in the Memo box.**

   Provide the transfer amount for the obvious reason: QuickBooks can't read your mind.

5. **Click the Save & New button or the Save & Close button.**

   QuickBooks records the transfer, which you can confirm by opening your register. You see that the transfer has the letters TRANSFR in the Type column and the name of the account to which you transferred the money in the Account column. The amount that you transferred shows in the Payment column (because you transferred the funds out of this account). Figure 8-5 shows a £15,000 transfer from a bank account called Current Bank Account to a savings account called Tiny Savings. You can tell this transaction is a transfer because the other account name shows up in the Account box.

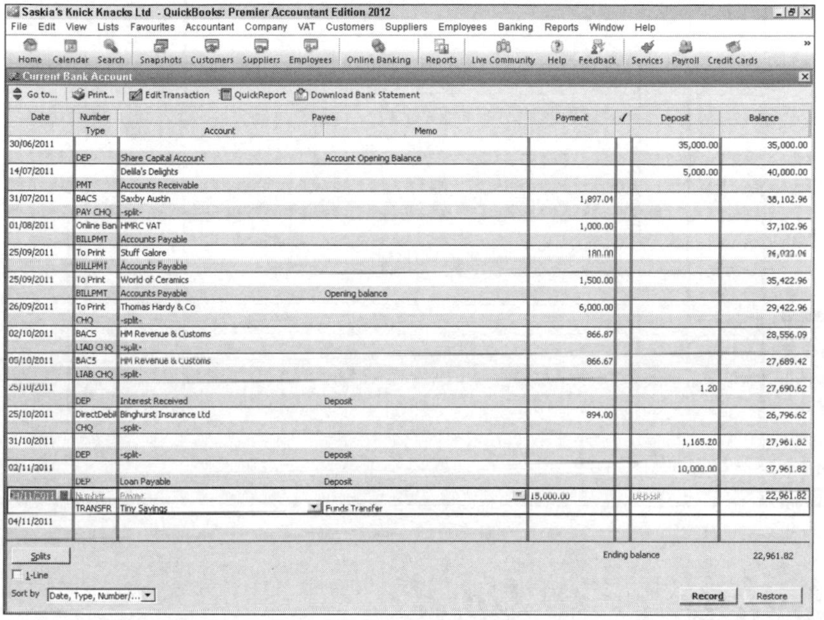

Figure 8-5: A transfer transaction in the register.

About the other half of the transfer

Here's the cool thing about transfer transactions: QuickBooks automatically records the other half of the transfer for you. Figure 8-6 shows the other half of the transfer from Figure 8-5. This register is for a savings account called Tiny Savings. The £15,000 transfer from your bank account actually made it into your savings account. The transfer once again shows up as a TRANSFR.

Changing a transfer that you've already entered

Changing a transfer that you already entered is very simple. First, you find the transfer in the bank account register (either bank register will do, but it makes sense to pick the register with fewer transactions), and then you right-click and select Edit Transfer. Make your changes in the Transfer Funds between Accounts window, and then click Save & New or Save & Close. You return to the register, where your deposit is adjusted accordingly.

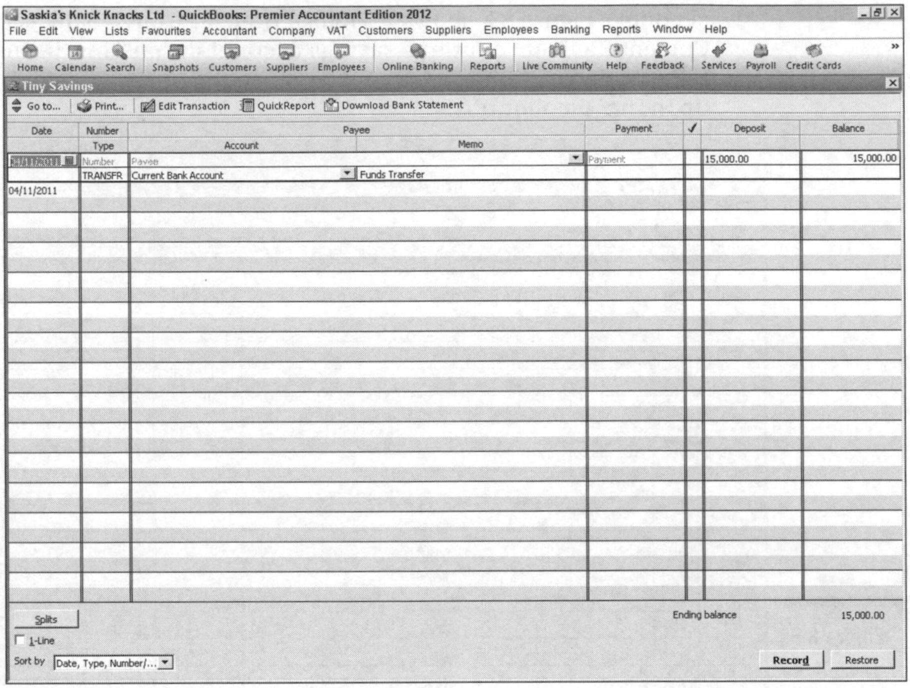

Figure 8-6:
The other
half of the
transfer
transaction.

To Delete or to Void?

What happens if you put a transaction – a deposit, cheque, or transfer payment – in a register and later decide that it shouldn't be there? You have two ways of handling this situation. If you want to keep a record of the transaction but render it meaningless, or null, you void the transaction. But if you want to obliterate the transaction from the face of the Earth as though it never happened, you delete it.

Decide whether you want to void or delete the transaction and then follow these steps:

1. **Find the transaction in the bank account register by clicking Current Account Register on the Home screen (or by clicking Banking⇨Use Register), selecting the desired bank account and scrolling through the register until you find the transaction.**

   In the upcoming section, "The Big Register Phenomenon", we tell you some quick ways to find transactions.

2. **Choose either Edit⇨Delete Cheque or Edit⇨Void Cheque and then click the Record button.**

There; the deed is done. Figure 8-7 shows a bank register window with a voided cheque. The voided transaction is the one selected. Notice the word VOID in the Memo column. If this cheque had been deleted, it wouldn't even show up in the register.

An alternative method is to select the cheque in the register and then right-click and choose Void Cheque.

Figure 8-7: The register shows a voided cheque.

Saskia's Knick Knacks Ltd - QuickBooks: Premier Accountant Edition 2012

File Edit View Lists Favourites Accountant Company VAT Customers Suppliers Employees Banking Reports Window Help

Home Calendar Search Snapshots Customers Suppliers Employees Online Banking Reports Live Community Help Feedback Services Payroll Credit Cards

Current Bank Account

Go to... Print... Edit Transaction QuickReport Download Bank Statement

Date	Number	Payee		Payment	✓	Deposit	Balance
	Type	Account	Memo				
30/06/2011						35,000.00	35,000.00
	DEP	Share Capital Account	Account Opening Balance				
14/07/2011		Della's Delights				5,000.00	40,000.00
	PMT	Accounts Receivable					
31/07/2011	BACS	Saxby Austin		1,897.04			38,102.96
	PAY CHQ	-split-					
01/08/2011	Online Ban	HMRC VAT		1,000.00			37,102.96
	BILLPMT	Accounts Payable					
25/09/2011	To Print	Stuff Galore		180.00			36,922.96
	BILLPMT	Accounts Payable					
25/09/2011	To Print	World of Ceramics		1,500.00			35,422.96
	BILLPMT	Accounts Payable	Opening balance				
26/09/2011	To Print	Thomas Hardy & Co		6,000.00			29,422.96
	CHQ	-split-					
02/10/2011	BACS	HM Revenue & Customs		866.87			28,556.09
	LIAB CHQ	-split-					
05/10/2011	BACS	HM Revenue & Customs		866.67			27,689.42
	LIAB CHQ	-split-					
25/10/2011						1.20	27,690.62
	DEP	Interest Received	Deposit				
25/10/2011	DirectDebi	Binghurst Insurance Ltd		0.00	✓		27,690.62
	CHQ	-split-	VOID:				
31/10/2011						1,165.20	28,855.82
	DEP	-split-	Deposit				
02/11/2011						10,000.00	30,055.82
	DEP	Loan Payable	Deposit				
04/11/2011				15,000.00			23,855.82
	TRANSFER	Tiny Savings	Funds Transfer				
04/11/2011							

Splits

☐ 1-Line

Sort by Date, Type, Number/...

Ending balance   23,855.82

Record   Restore

The Edit menu changes depending on what kind of transaction shows or is selected in the open window (that is, Void Bill Pmt – Cheque, Void Deposit, Void Transfer, and so on).

Do not void cheques from a previous financial year. If you do, you'll adjust the previous year's figures, and you don't want to do this because you can no longer prepare profit and loss statements and balance sheets that correspond to your year-end financial statements. If you do have a cheque that should be voided – say, it's outstanding and has never been banked or was a mistake in the first place – record a journal entry in the current year that undoes the effect of the cheque. Normally, the entry is a debit to the Bank account and a credit to whichever account the cheque originally affected, in the amount of the cheque.

Handling Bounced Cheques from Customers

We've had clients in the past who wanted to know how to handle customer cheques that bounce. Here's how we suggest handling this situation:

1. **Record the service charge that the bank charges you for handling the returned cheque, just like any other bank service charge.**

   You can record the bank service fee as though it's a cheque that you just wrote (and use the "E" VAT Code). Remember, anything coming out of your bank account is entered like a cheque.

2. **Record the bounced cheque as a decrease to your bank account balance.**

   In the Write Cheques window, enter the following information (see Figure 8-8):

   - Choose the customer's name in the Payee field.

   - Enter something such as ReturnedChq in the No. field.

   - Enter the date the cheque bounced in the Date field.

   - On the Expenses tab, in the Account column, select the Accounts Receivable account.

   - In the VAT column, select the "O" VAT Code (this is outside the scope of VAT).

   - In the Memo field, add a memo if you want to.

   - In the Customer:Job field enter the customer's name again (QuickBooks will not let you save the cheque without this).

   The effect of this cheque is to show the customer's unpaid balance in the Accounts Receivable register again. This means that you can use the Receive Payments window to record the new payment from the customer, if you are fortunate enough to be able to collect it.

3. **Try to collect the cheque again.**

   Ask the customer to pay again, preferably by bank transfer this time. You might also try to assess the customer for a bounced cheque fee. (See Chapter 4 for information on invoicing customers.) If the customer does pay, record the payment as you normally would, using Customers⇨Receive Payments.

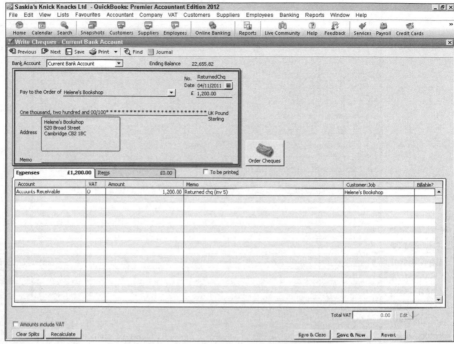

Figure 8-8:
An example
of how to
record a
bounced
customer
payment.

The Big Register Phenomenon

If you start entering cheques, deposits, and transfers into your registers, you soon find yourself with registers that contain hundreds, or even thousands, of transactions. There are some things that you can do to help you deal with . . . (drum roll, please) . . . the big register phenomenon.

Packing more into the register

Usually, QuickBooks displays two rows of information about each transaction you enter. If you want to pack more transactions into the visible portion of the register, select the 1-Line check box at the bottom of the register window. When you select this check box, QuickBooks uses a single-line format to display all the information in the register except the Memo field. (See Figure 8-9.)

Moving through a big register

You can use the Page Up and Page Down keys to move up and down through your register a screenful of transactions at a time. Some people call this activity *scrolling*. You can call it whatever you want.

Saskia's Knick Knacks Ltd - QuickBooks: Premier Accountant Edition 2012						

File Edit View Lists Favourites Accountant Company VAT Customers Suppliers Employees Banking Reports Window Help

Home Calendar Search   Snapshots Customers Suppliers Employees   Online Banking   Reports Live Community   Help Feedback   Services Payroll Credit Cards

Current Bank Account

Go to...   Print...   Edit Transaction   QuickReport   Download Bank Statement

Date	Number	Payee	Account	Payment	✓	Deposit	Balance
30/06/2011			Share Capital Account			35,000.00	35,000.00
14/07/2011		Delila's Delights	Accounts Receivable			5,000.00	40,000.00
31/07/2011	BACS	Saxby Austin	-split-	1,897.04			38,102.96
01/08/2011	Online Ban	HMRC VAT	Accounts Payable	1,000.00			37,102.96
25/09/2011	To Print	Stuff Galore	Accounts Payable	180.00			36,922.96
25/09/2011	To Print	World of Ceramics	Accounts Payable	1,500.00			35,422.96
26/09/2011	To Print	Thomas Hardy & Co	-split-	6,000.00			29,422.96
02/10/2011	BACS	HM Revenue & Customs	-split-	866.87			28,556.09
05/10/2011	BACS	HM Revenue & Customs	-split-	866.67			27,689.42
25/10/2011			Interest Received			1.20	27,690.62
25/10/2011	DirectDebit	Binghurst Insurance Ltd	-split-	0.00	✓		27,690.62
31/10/2011			-split-			1,165.20	28,855.82
02/11/2011			Loan Payable			10,000.00	38,855.82
04/11/2011	ReturnedC	Helene's Bookshop	Accounts Receivable	1,200.00			37,655.82
04/11/2011			Tiny Savings	15,000.00			22,655.82
04/11/2011	Number	Payee	Account	Payment		Deposit	

Splits

Ending balance   22,655.82

☑ 1-Line

Sort by Date, Type, Number/...

Record   Restore

Figure 8-9:
The register
window
when using
1-Line
display.

You can also use the Home key to move through the register. Press the Home key once to move to the front of the field you're currently in; press it twice to move to the first field of the transaction you're on (the Date field); or press it three times to move to the first transaction in the register.

The End key works in a similar fashion. Bet you can guess how this works. Press the End key once to move to the end of the field you're in, press it twice to move to the last field of the transaction you're on (the Memo field), or press it three times to move to the last transaction in the register.

Of course, you can use the vertical scroll bar along the right edge of the register, too. (You only see the vertical scroll bar if there are more transactions in the register than can fit one your computer screen.) Click the arrows at either end of the vertical scroll bar to select the next or previous transaction. Click either above or below the square scroll box to page back and forth through the register. Or, if you have no qualms about dragging the mouse around, you can drag the scroll box up and down the scroll bar.

QuickBooks lets you sort your register in different ways, which makes scrolling through and finding transactions much easier. To sort your register the way you prefer, choose an option from the Sort By drop-down list in the lower-left corner of the register window.

Finding that transaction

Want to find that one cheque, deposit, or transfer? No problem. We discuss this technique elsewhere in the book, but it's appropriate here, too. The Edit menu's Find command provides a handy way for doing just such a thing. Here's what you do:

1. **Choose Edit⇨Find.**

   This command displays the Simple tab of the Find window. The Simple tab enables you to search for transactions by using the transaction type, customer or job name, date, number, or amount.

2. **Switch to an advanced search by clicking the Advanced tab.**

   QuickBooks, with restrained but obvious enthusiasm, displays the Advanced tab of the Find window (see Figure 8-10). You use this window to describe – in as much detail as possible – the transaction that you want to find.

3. **Choose a filter that describes the information that you already have.**

   In the figure, the Name filter is chosen. When you click different filters, the Find window changes.

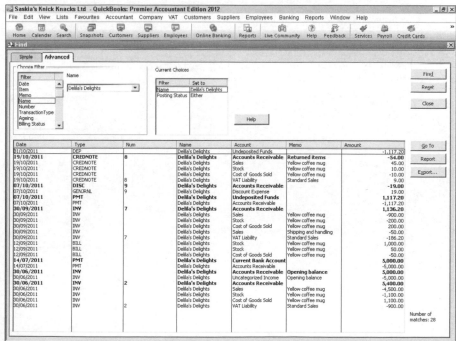

Figure 8-10:
The Advanced tab of the Find window.

4. **Describe the filter that identifies the transaction that you want to locate.**

   In the upper-left box, which is set to Name in Figure 8-10, choose the filter that describes the subject of your search from the drop-down list. In the case of an account-based filter, for example, you can select to look at all accounts, just income accounts, just expense accounts, and so on. Other filters provide different boxes for setting the filter.

   By the way, the case of the text doesn't matter. If you type **rainy**, for example, QuickBooks finds *RAINY* as well as *Rainy*.

5. **Repeat Steps 3 and 4 as necessary.**

   Yes, you can filter through as many fields as you want. In fact, you can filter so much that nothing matches your specification.

6. **Click Find to let the search begin.**

   Click the Find button to begin looking. If QuickBooks finds transactions that match the one you described, QuickBooks lists them in the bottom half of the window.

Chapter 9

Paying with Plastic

· ·

In This Chapter

▶ Setting up credit card accounts

▶ Entering credit card charges

▶ Changing charges that you've entered already

▶ Reconciling credit card statements

▶ Paying the monthly bill

▶ Handling debit cards

▶ Handling customer credit cards

· ·

*Y*ou can use QuickBooks to track your business credit cards in much the same way that you use it to keep your cheque book. The process is almost the same but with a few wrinkles.

By the way, although this chapter is really about your spending money on your credit cards, at the very end of the chapter, we talk about how to handle the tricky problem of your customers paying with credit cards.

Tracking Business Credit Cards

If you want to track credit card spending and balances with QuickBooks, you need to set up a credit card account – if you didn't already do so when you loaded your trial balance, which you can read about in Chapter 3. (In comparison, you use bank accounts to track the money that flows into and out of a current, savings, or petty cash account.)

To set up a credit card account, you follow roughly the same steps that you use to set up a bank account:

1. **Choose Lists⇨Chart of Accounts or click the Chart of Accounts icon on the Home screen to display the Chart of Accounts window.**

2. **Click the Account button in the lower-left corner of the Chart of Accounts window and then choose New.**

   QuickBooks displays the first Add New Account window, which simply displays a list of option buttons corresponding to the different types of accounts QuickBooks allows.

3. **Select the Credit Card option.**

   Selecting Credit Card tells QuickBooks that you want to set up a credit card account. Click Continue. QuickBooks displays the second Add New Account window, as shown in Figure 9-1.

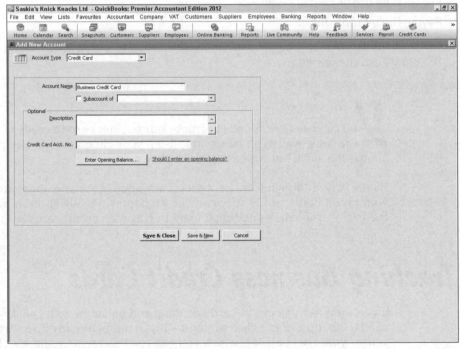

Figure 9-1:
The second
Add New
Account
window.

4. **Type a name for the account in the Account Name text box.**

5. **(Optional) Type the card number in the Credit Card Acct. No. text box.**

   If you're creating a general Credit Card account for more than one card, leave the Credit Card Acct. No. text box empty.

   While you're at it, you can describe the card, too. You might want to type **Exorbitant!** in the Description text box, depending on your card's interest rate.

6. Click the Save & Close button.

QuickBooks redisplays the Chart of Accounts window. Now, the window lists an additional account: the credit card account that you just created.

Entering Credit Card Transactions

To tell QuickBooks that you want to enter credit card charges, you can click the Enter Credit Card Charges icon in the Banking area of the Home screen, or you can select Banking⇨Enter Credit Card Charges.

Recording a credit card charge

Recording a credit card charge is similar to recording a cheque or bank account withdrawal. For the sake of illustration, suppose that you take a new customer out to your favourite gastro-pub and charge £40.00 to your card. Here's how you record this charge:

1. Choose Banking⇨Enter Credit Card Charges.

The Enter Credit Card Charges window appears, as shown in Figure 9-2.

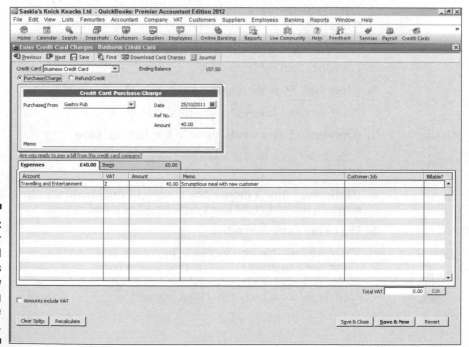

Figure 9-2: The Enter Credit Card Charges window showing a sample entry.

2. **From the Credit Card drop-down list, select the credit card that you charged the expense against.**

   If you have just one Credit Card account, QuickBooks selects it for you.

3. **In the Purchased From field, record the name of the business that you paid with a credit card.**

   In the Purchased From line, start typing the supplier's name until QuickBooks recognises and fills in the rest of the name.

   If QuickBooks does not have that name in the Supplier List, you'll find that you end up typing the entire name and when you move away from this field the Name Not Found pop-up appears. Click the Quick Add button, select the Supplier radio button and click OK. QuickBooks adds the name to the Supplier List and returns you to the Enter Credit Card charges window.

4. **Select the appropriate radio button to indicate whether the transaction is a purchase or a refund.**

   Accept the Purchase/Charge radio button selection if you want to record a purchase (which is what you do most of the time and what this example shows you). Select the Refund/Credit radio button if you want to record a credit on your account (if you returned something, for example).

5. **Enter the charge date in the Date field.**

   Move the cursor to the Date line (if the cursor isn't already there), and type the date, using the DD/MM/YYYY format. If you're entering this charge two or three days after the fact, don't enter today's date. Enter the date when the charge was made. Using that date makes reconciling your records with your credit card company's records easier when you get your monthly statement.

6. **(Optional) Type the charge amount in the Amount field.**

   In the Amount line, enter the total charge.

7. **(Optional) Enter a reference in the Ref No. field.**

   If the sales receipt you have for the purchase shows a reference number enter it here.

8. **(Optional) Enter a memo description in the Memo text box. This memo appears in the Credit Card register (described later).**

9. **Fill in the Expenses tab.**

   We're hoping that you've read Chapters 6 and 8 so that you know all about the Expenses tab – and that you're thoroughly bored by the topic. However, if you opened the book right to this page, you use the Expenses tab to record business expenses.

a. Move to the Account column of the Expenses tab, click the down arrow, and choose an Expense account from the list (most likely, Travel and Entertainment). If you enter a name here that QuickBooks doesn't already know, it asks you to set up an expense account.

b. Select a VAT Code for the purchase.

If you have set up VAT Code defaults for expense accounts as described in Chapter 8, QuickBooks displays the default VAT Code for you. Change the VAT Code as appropriate.

c. Accept or edit the amount that QuickBooks prefills in the Amount column. QuickBooks automatically fills in the Amount column with the Net amount when you enter a sum in the Amount field, and calculates the Total VAT, which it shows at the bottom right of the window.

d. Type something in the Memo column (this memo appears in expense account reports) and assign this expense to a Customer:Job and Class if you want to. (You need to turn on class tracking if you want to assign the expense to a class, as we described in Chapter 3.)

10. **Fill in the Items tab.**

Because this charge is for a meal, you don't itemise the charge. However, if you were charging stock items you'd fill in the Items tab.

If you have a purchase order (PO) on file with the supplier that you entered in the Purchased From line, QuickBooks tells you so. Click the Select PO button to see a list of your outstanding purchase orders with the supplier. If you don't know how to handle purchase orders, see Chapter 7.

11. **Record the charge by clicking the Save & New button or the Save & Close button.**

The charge is recorded in the Credit Card register.

Figure 9-3 shows what the Credit Card register looks like after a handful of charges. To get to the Credit Card register, choose Lists➪Chart of Accounts to display the Chart of Accounts window. Double-click the credit card account whose register you want to view. It looks a lot like a Bank register, doesn't it? It also has the same functionality as the Bank register. The Credit Card register lists each credit card charge, refund and payment. When you record a charge, QuickBooks updates the credit card balance.

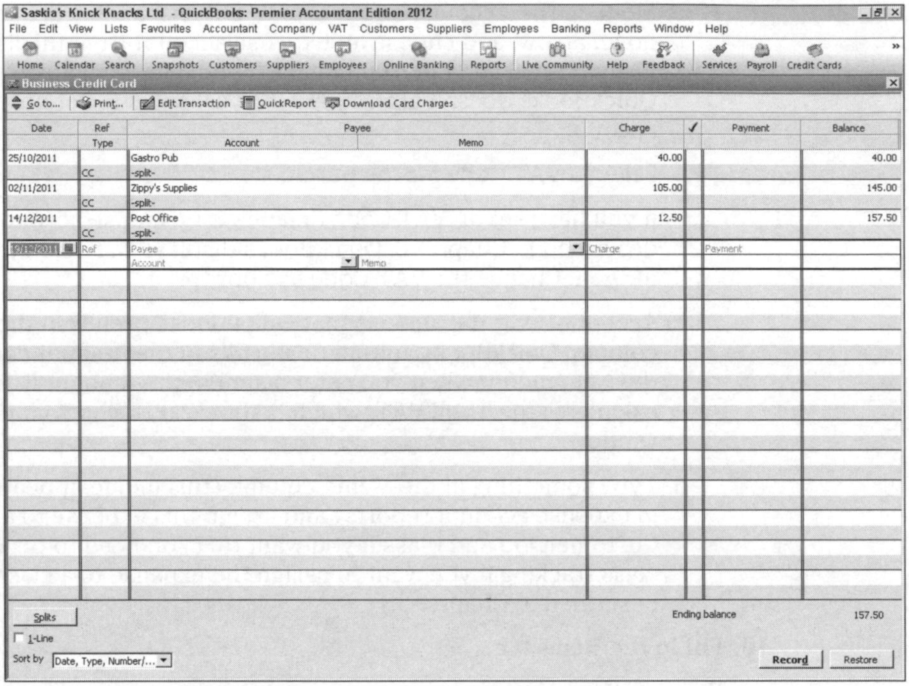

Figure 9-3:
The Credit
Card
Register
window
with some
transac-
tions.

Changing charges that you've already entered

Perhaps you record a credit card charge and then realise that you recorded it incorrectly. Or perhaps you shouldn't have recorded it at all because you didn't pay for the business lunch. (Someone else paid for it after one of those friendly arguments over who should pay the bill. You know the type of argument: "No, I insist." "On the contrary, I insist." You get the picture.)

You have to go into the Credit Card register and either edit or delete the charge by following these steps:

1. **Choose Lists⇨Chart of Accounts to display the Chart of Accounts window. Double-click the credit card account where the faulty charge is.**

   Like magic, the Credit Card register appears onscreen.

2. **Select the credit card transaction that you want to delete or change.**

   That's easy. Just move the cursor to the transaction.

3. **Void, delete, or edit the transaction:**

  - *To void the credit card transaction:* Choose Edit⇨Void Credit Card Charge and then click OK.

  - *To delete the transaction:* Choose Edit⇨Delete Credit Card Charge. QuickBooks displays a message box that asks whether you really want to delete the transaction. Click OK.

  - *To edit the transaction:* Click the Edit Transaction button at the top of the window. You return to the Enter Credit Card Charges window. Make your changes there and then click Save & New or Save & Close. You also can make changes inside the Credit Card register and then click Record when you're done.

Reconciling Your Credit Card Statement and Paying the Card

You *reconcile,* or balance, a credit card account the same way you balance a bank account. (For help with this task, see Chapter 14.) After you successfully get the account to balance and click Reconcile Now, QuickBooks displays the Make Payment dialog box, asking how you want to pay the bill. You can either pay by cheque or enter a bill to be paid later. We recommend you choose cheque – it's one quick step. When you opt to pay by writing a cheque, you go straight to the Write Cheques window and the Expenses tab is all filled out for you. Fill in the name of the card issuer, the date, and so on. Click Save & New or Save & Close when you're done. The payment is recorded in both the Bank account register and the Credit Card register because you charge the credit card liability account with the cheque total.

The enter bill option is the accounts payable method. In that case you go to the Enter Bills window. Fill everything out just as you would if you were in the Write Checks window. When you click Save & New, the transaction is recorded in the Accounts Payable register and the Credit Card register. Don't forget to record the bill payment later.

See Chapter 8 if you need to know more about either the Write Cheques or the Enter Bills window.

So What about Debit Cards?

Debit cards, when you get right down to it, aren't really credit cards at all. Using a debit card is akin to writing a cheque – rather than withdrawing money by writing a cheque, however, you withdraw money by using a debit card.

Although a debit card transaction looks (at least to your friends and the merchants you shop with) like a credit card transaction, you should treat a debit card transaction like you treat a cheque. In a nutshell, here's what you need to do:

- When you charge something to a debit card, record the transaction just like you record a regular cheque. You may want to enter the transaction number in the Memo line so that you can keep track of the transaction.

- When you withdraw cash by using a debit card, record the transaction as a regular withdrawal (or transfer to a petty cash account) as if you went to the bank with a withdrawal slip.

- When you make a deposit through a cash machine by using a debit card, record the transaction just like you record a regular deposit.

What about Customers Who Pay by Credit Cards?

We want to talk about how to handle customer credit card payments before closing our discussion about how to work with credit cards.

Okay, if you don't already know this, although your customers probably love to pay you with credit cards, customer credit cards create a headache for you. The reason is that your merchant bank or credit card processor aggregates customer credit card charges and then – maybe on a daily basis or maybe every few days – deposits a big wad of cash into your bank account. The cash represents the sum of the recent credit card charges minus a (hopefully modest) fee.

You can use the following method to record these transactions whether you invoice your customers or use sales receipts:

1. **Create another bank account (as discussed in Chapter 8) to track the customer credit card payments and call it something like Customer Card Payments.**

2. **When your customer pays you, deposit the money into the Customer Card Payments account (just a dummy bank account, really).**

   You do this either using the Receive Payments window to record individual invoices being paid, or using a Sales Receipt to record the day's credit card receipts (as described in Chapter 5).

3. **When the merchant bank or credit card processor transfers money into your real bank account, you do the same, using the Transfer Money window in QuickBooks, as described in Chapter 8.**

4. **When the merchant bank or credit card processor charges you a service fee (which they'll describe on the statement they send you), use the Write Cheques window in QuickBooks to record it.**

   Make sure that you specify the Customer Card Payments account as the Bank Account and that you account for any VAT on the service fee correctly.

When you receive a statement from the merchant, use this to reconcile the Customer Card Payments account to ensure that the customer card receipts you record in QuickBooks match what the merchant shows on the statement, and follow up on any differences with the merchant. (For help with reconciling a bank account see Chapter 8.)

It may not be the most elegant way to do this, but it works and keeps things clear on your end.

Chapter 10

Working with Multicurrency

You won't be surprised to hear that QuickBooks makes it very easy to track what you sell and buy in a foreign currency. You can assign a currency to a customer and raise an invoice that shows the prices of your items in a foreign currency. When your customer pays, you can record the payment in the foreign currency and deposit the money into a foreign bank account. The same goes for purchases made in a foreign currency – you can show the value of the bill in a foreign currency and pay your supplier from a foreign bank account, in the currency of the bill. In this chapter, we show you how.

Getting Ready to Use Multicurrency

We need to tell you something very important about the Multicurrency feature in QuickBooks. Are you ready? Okay, here it is. Once you turn it on, it cannot be turned off.

Because it's so important, we'll say it again: you cannot turn off the multicurrency feature once it is turned on.

Before you turn on the feature please do yourself a big favour and back up your company file, as described in Chapter 17. QuickBooks recommends this, and so do we. That way if you want to just play about with the feature but are not serious about using it (or you decide it's not for you), you can restore (also described in Chapter 17) your file to the pre-Multicurrency version.

No doubt you know this, but we'll mention it nonetheless. If you restore your file to an earlier version, you'll lose all the work you did since you backed up. This is good news if you were just playing about, but not so good if you were entering transactions you intended to keep.

Turning on the feature

To turn on the multicurrency feature, select Edit➪Preferences and select Multiple Currencies from the list on the left. In the Company Preferences tab, click the radio button for Yes, I Use More than One Currency. The Tracking Multiple Currencies window is displayed. It urges you to back up your file and tells you that once the feature is turned on you cannot turn it off. This is the point of no return (not really, because *you* backed up your file so you can restore that backup in case you change your mind later). Click Yes to the question "Are you ready to turn on multicurrency in this file?"

QuickBooks returns you to the Company Preferences window. Note that the *home currency* field (the currency you use on financial reports) is now active and is set to British Pound Sterling (GBP). We're going to assume in this chapter that your home currency is indeed the British Pound Sterling and we'll refer to it as just "the pound" or GBP.

At this stage you can change the home currency to something other than the pound, but once you save your changes and turn on Multicurrency you cannot edit the home currency.

Changing the home currency from the pound will disable the payroll feature.

When you click OK to save your changes, QuickBooks warns that it will close your company file and reopen the file with the changes. When QuickBooks reopens your company file, the multicurrency feature is turned on.

Understanding exchange rates

Let's first take a minute to talk about exchange rates. An *exchange rate* is simply the rate that one currency can be exchanged for another. For example, if the euro exchange rate for the pound is 0.8713 this means that 1 euro can be exchanged for 0.8713 pounds.

In QuickBooks, exchange rates are always shown as the number of home currency units (for example, £0.8713) it takes to equal 1 foreign currency unit (for example, €1).

If you find this exchange rate business confusing, you're not alone. That's why QuickBooks provides a handy currency calculator to help you figure out the relationships between different currencies (see Figure 10-1). To access the QuickBooks currency calculator, select Company⇨Manage Currency⇨ Currency Calculator (or use the keyboard keys combination of Ctrl+Alt+C).

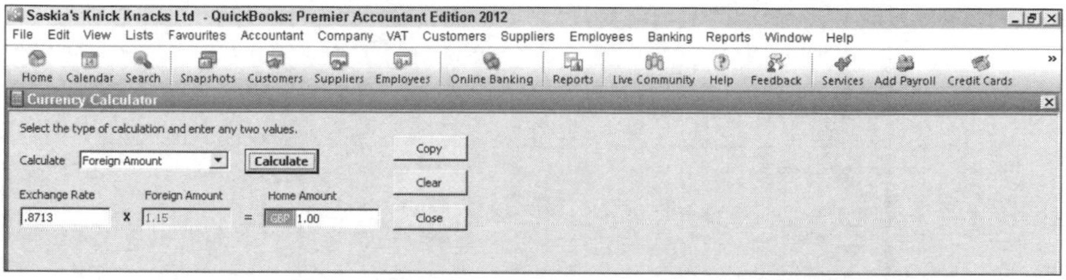

Figure 10-1:
The
Currency
Calculator.

To use the calculator, you first click the down arrow to the right of the Calculate field and specify what it is that you want to calculate: Home Amount, Foreign Amount, or Exchange Rate. You then enter values in the white boxes and QuickBooks calculates the value in the yellow box. For example, to calculate what £1 is worth in euros at an exchange rate of 0.8713, select Foreign Amount in the Calculate field, then type 0.8713 in the Exchange Rate field, and accept 1.00 in the Home Amount field. Once you click the Calculate button, QuickBooks displays 1.15 in the Foreign Amount field. This means that at an exchange rate of 0.8713, £1 is worth €1.15. Nifty, isn't it?

Activating currencies in the Currency List

The Currency List is where you maintain your exchange rate currencies in QuickBooks. It displays the name of each currency you intend to use, its three letter abbreviation code, and the exchange rate of each currency in relation to the pound as of a particular date (see Figure 10-2).

You can find the Currency List by selecting Company⇨Manage Currency⇨ Currency List (alternatively click List⇨>Currency List). By the way, these menus are only present after you turn on Multicurrency in QuickBooks.

Out of the box, QuickBooks comes with an impressive list of currencies, most of which are inactive (an inactive currency is designated by an X next to it). To activate a particular currency move your cursor to the left of the currency, and when the cursor changes to an X, click the mouse to remove the X. Likewise, you can inactivate a currency you don't need by placing your cursor to the left of the currency and when the cursor changes to an X, click to apply the X to that currency.

To view only the active currencies deselect the box next to Include Inactive (at the bottom of the list).

Figure 10-2 shows a list of active currencies.

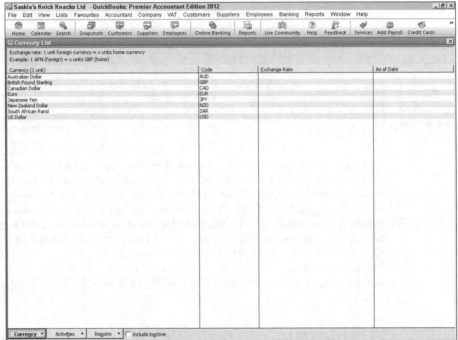

Figure 10-2:
The
Currency
List showing
active
currencies.

Updating currencies

You can update foreign currencies in QuickBooks in one of two ways: by entering your own exchange rates or by downloading the latest exchange rates for free within QuickBooks. The method you choose depends on your circumstances. You may decide, for example, to use a particular exchange rate (not the market rate) for one or all of your foreign currencies, in which case you'll manually update the exchange rates in the Currency List. Alternatively, you can ask QuickBooks to download the latest market value currency exchange rates for you. How frequently you update your currencies is up to you.

✔ **To manually update a currency:** In the Currency List, double-click the name of the currency you intend to update. The Edit Currency window appears, as shown in Figure 10-3. In this window, you can change the number format of the currency by clicking the Change Format button.

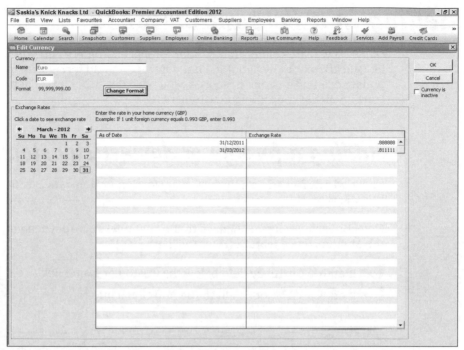

Figure 10-3:
The Edit
Currency
window.

Select in the mini calendar the date on which the new exchange rate will take effect. QuickBooks adds that date to the As Of Date field in the white text box. Next, enter the exchange rate in pounds in the Exchange Rate field. For example, if 1 euro is £0.87, enter 0.87. When you are finished, click OK to save your changes.

✔ **To download the latest currencies:** You need to be connected to the Internet. In the Currency List (Figure 10-2), click the Activities button and select Download Latest Exchange Rates. (Alternatively, select Company➪Manage Currency➪Download Latest Exchange Rates.) QuickBooks retrieves the exchange rate for each *active* currency in your Currency List and populates the Exchange Rate field with the latest exchange rate, and the As Of Date field with the update date. To return to the Currency List, click OK in the Download Exchange Rate confirmation window, which QuickBooks displays if the update was successful.

QuickBooks logs every update to each currency in the Currency List, giving you a history of exchange rates used. Cool, isn't it? For example, Figure 10-3 shows two different exchange rates, one as of 31 December 2011, the other as of 31 March 2012.

Selling in a Foreign Currency

Okay, so you are selling stuff to your foreign customers and you want to let QuickBooks know about it. First you need to add foreign customers, or update existing customer records, which we describe next. Then you can start invoicing your foreign customers.

Adding a foreign or domestic customer

Guess what? You add a new customer (foreign or domestic) as we describe in Chapter 3.

QuickBooks makes two changes to the customer record when you turn on the Multicurrency feature (refer to Figure 10-4):

✔ It adds a Currency field below the Customer Name field.

✔ It adds a VAT Code field to the Additional Info tab.

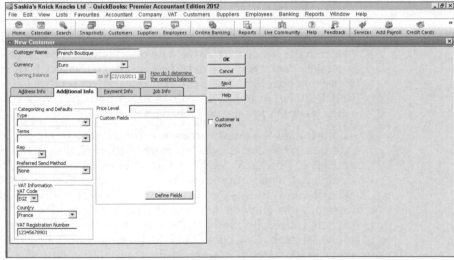

Figure 10-4:
The New Customer window with Multicurrency turned on.

When you add a new customer, QuickBooks automatically populates the Currency field with British Pound Sterling. For domestic customers, you accept the QuickBooks selection; for foreign customers, you specify the appropriate currency in the Currency field. To do this, simply click the down arrow in the Currency field and select the desired currency from the list of active currencies.

If you don't see the currency you need in the Currency field it means that the currency is inactive. In the Currency field, select View More Currencies. When QuickBooks displays the full list of currencies, find and select the desired currency. A pop-up window tells you that this currency is inactive. Click the Make It Active button to activate the currency in the Currency List. Don't forget to set the exchange rate for that currency (in the Currency List), as we describe earlier in this chapter.

The second change that QuickBooks makes to the customer record once you turn on the Multicurrency feature is to add the VAT Code field to the customer record. Here's how you fill out the VAT Information area in the Additional Info tab (see Figure 10-4):

1. **Select your customer's country.**

   Click the down arrow beside the Country field and select the country.

2. **Enter your customer's VAT Registration Number (if the customer is VAT registered).**

   This field is particularly important if your customer is based in the European Community (EC). What you need to enter here is the *international trade* tax ID that your customer was assigned by the tax authorities in their country. So if the customer is French, enter their TVA tax ID, if the customer is Spanish enter their IVA tax ID, and so on.

   You can validate the VAT number given to you by an EC customer using the VIES VAT number validation tool on the European Commission website, found at `http://ec.europa.eu/taxation_customs/vies/vieshome.do?selectedLanguage=EN`.

   Your customer may, however, be a private person or a business without a VAT registration number, in which case you leave the VAT registration field blank.

   If the customer is based in the EC, QuickBooks won't let you save the record without a VAT Registration Number even if the customer is not VAT registered (or won't give you a VAT registration number). In that case, enter a zero in the VAT Registration Number field (but make sure you deal with the VAT appropriately as described next).

3. **Select a VAT Code using the following guidelines:**

   For domestic customers and EC customers who are not registered for VAT (or EC customers for whom you cannot obtain a VAT registration number):

   - **Select S (Standard Rated VAT) if you charge VAT at the standard rate on all goods or services you sell.**

   - **Select Z (Zero Rated VAT) if you charge VAT at the zero rate on all goods or services you sell.**

- **Leave this field blank if you charge different rates of VAT to your customers** (for example S or Z depending on the item). When you save and close this record, QuickBooks will add a default VAT Code. To tell QuickBooks to leave the field blank, go to Edit⇨Preferences and select VAT in the list on the left. On the Company Preferences tab, in the Customer & Supplier Default VAT Codes area, remove the VAT Code from the Domestic Customer field. Save your change by clicking OK and return to the customer record to continue.

For VAT-registered EC customers:

- **Select EGZ (EC Goods Zero Rated VAT) if you sell mainly goods.**

- **Select ESZ (EC Services Zero Rated VAT) if you sell mainly services.**

For all other foreign customers (non-EC, such as US, Australian, South African and so on) select **Z (Zero-Rated VAT)**.

Here comes our disclaimer: the VAT Codes guideline is just that, a guideline. So do the smart thing and seek advice from the helpful staff on the HMRC helpline for your specific circumstances, or if you are at all unsure about what to enter in the VAT Information area or which VAT code to use for a particular transaction. VAT is a complex area and not what this book is about. Thank goodness.

When you are finished entering information in the customer record, click the OK button to save your changes.

Let's say you have a large international customer with offices in several different countries and you need to invoice in different currencies. The best way to do this is to set up a customer record for each location. For example, add a customer record for the Italian office, another record for the Canadian office, and so on.

One other thing: when you add a foreign currency customer, QuickBooks adds an Accounts Receivable account for that currency in the Chart of Accounts. For example, if you add a customer whose currency is euros, QuickBooks adds Accounts Receivable – EUR to the Chart of Accounts. All sales transactions in the foreign currency can be viewed in this register.

Updating existing customers

If you have customers in your Customer:Jobs list when you turn on the Multicurrency feature, QuickBooks assigns British Pound Sterling to each customer, and displays the three letter abbreviation (GBP) next to the customer name in the Customer:Jobs list. This is because QuickBooks treats existing customers as domestic ones. And if you have already sold any thingamabobs or services to an existing customer, you won't be able to edit that customer's currency. This makes sense – you don't want to mess up your records by changing the currency of existing transactions, right?

QuickBooks also assigns the 'S' VAT Code to each existing customer. Now this might be just the ticket for you if you charge VAT at the standard rate on everything you sell to domestic customers.

But in case it's not, you may want to change or remove the VAT Code of each existing customer. (If you don't make any changes, each time you raise an invoice QuickBooks will apply the Customer VAT Code to all the items on the invoice and ignore the VAT Code of each item. Sorry.)

You edit the VAT Code field in the Additional Info tab, in the VAT Information area as described earlier (see Figure 10-4).

What about jobs?

When you add a new job to a customer, the job simply inherits the customer's currency and VAT details, so you add a new job exactly as we describe in Chapter 3.

Preparing an invoice

Now we're getting to the good part: invoicing your foreign customer.

We bet you're really surprised to read that you invoice a foreign customer in pretty much the same way that we describe in Chapter 4. Right?

So what *is* different? Well, take a look at Figure 10-5. After you identify the foreign customer and press Tab to move to the next field, QuickBooks performs several tasks:

- It recalls the correct foreign currency Accounts Receivable account (in this case Accounts Receivable – EUR).

- It applies the foreign currency of the customer to the invoice (for example, EUR) and shows the invoice Total, Payments Applied, and Balance Due in the foreign currency. QuickBooks also displays the invoice Total and Balance Due in pounds. (See Figure 10-5.)

✔ It adds the Exchange Rate information field to the invoice. You can edit the entry in the exchange rate field by typing a new number if necessary.

The exchange rate in QuickBooks is always shown as the number of GBP units it takes to equal 1 foreign currency unit.

QuickBooks applies the currency exchange rate you specified in the Currency List, for the invoice date. If you didn't specify an exchange rate at all, or the rate you specified is not valid for the invoice date, QuickBooks displays a pop-up window to let you know this. You can ignore the message and simply adjust the exchange rate on the invoice, or, before you save the invoice, you can update the currency in the Currency List as we described earlier, and QuickBooks will apply the new rate to the invoice.

✔ It adds the Customer VAT Code (you know, the VAT Code you specified when you added the customer to the Customer:Jobs list as described earlier) to the invoice (for example, EGZ). QuickBooks applies this code to *every item* on the invoice, overriding the item's own VAT code. You can see this in the VAT column of Figure 10-5. If you didn't specify a VAT Code when you set up the customer, QuickBooks uses the VAT code of the items on the invoice.

If you modify the entry in the Customer VAT Code field, QuickBooks changes the VAT codes of all the items on the invoice.

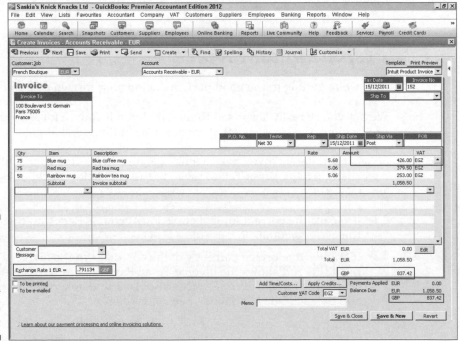

Figure 10-5:
A completed Create Invoices window for a foreign customer.

Before you save the invoice make sure the VAT codes in the VAT column are correct for *each item*. For example, goods and ancillary services – services associated with providing those goods – sold to a VAT-registered EC customer use a different VAT code (EGZ) from services (ESZ). Not to sound like a broken record, but VAT rules relating to EC and foreign trade are complex, so don't be afraid to ask HMRC for guidance.

To change the VAT code of an item on the invoice, click in the VAT column of the item line you need to change. When the down arrow appears, select the correct VAT code.

One final thing: if you sell to a VAT-registered EC business, your invoice must show your customer's VAT registration number. You may need to adjust your invoice template (as we describe in Chapter 4) to include your customer's VAT registration number.

Preparing a credit note

We'll make this short and sweet: you prepare a credit note as described in Chapter 4.

What's more, the changes we described in the preceding section for multicurrency invoices also apply to multicurrency credit notes.

Enough said.

Getting paid

One thing you probably want to do (if you haven't done so already) is to tell QuickBooks to give you the choice to specify into which bank account to deposit customer payments. Unless, of course, you are fine with all customer payments going to the Undeposited Funds account from where they can be deposited to a bank account in a separate step in QuickBooks.

We describe how to set the option to specify the bank account in Chapter 5 but, briefly, choose Edit⇨Preferences and click on the Payments icon in the list, and then click the Company Preferences tab. Deselect the Use Undeposited Funds as a Default Deposit to Account option. QuickBooks will close all open windows and reopen them with this new setting. After you make this change, QuickBooks adds a Deposit To field on the Receive Payments window (shown in Figure 10-6) so you can choose into which bank account the money is deposited.

If your customer pays you via electronic banking payments, you definitely want the option to choose a bank account on the Receive Payment window.

When your foreign customer pays you, you fill out the Receive Payments window pretty much as we describe in Chapter 5. There are, however, a few differences you should be aware of (see Figure 10-6).

After you identify the foreign customer and press Tab to move to the next field, QuickBooks:

- ✔ Recalls the correct foreign currency Accounts Receivable account.

- ✔ Applies the foreign currency of the customer to the payment.

- ✔ Uses the last transaction date to auto-populate the Date field.

- ✔ Adds the Exchange Rate field to the payment window, and populates this field using the exchange rate specified in the Currency List for the date in the Date field. You can, of course, edit the exchange rate if necessary.

   If you change the date in the Date field and the exchange rate on the new date is different from the exchange rate QuickBooks displayed for the original date, QuickBooks displays the Exchange Rates pop-up message. It tells you that you have changed the date and that you have a different exchange rate, and the new rate and home currency amounts will be updated in the transaction. Click OK to acknowledge the message and return to the Receive Payments window.

- ✔ Shows the Amount Due, Applied, and Discounts and Credits Applied in the foreign currency, and the Amount Received in the home currency.

In QuickBooks, you may deposit the customer payment to either a UK bank account or to a foreign currency bank account. To add a new foreign currency (or UK) bank account, in the Deposit To field, select Add New. In the Add New Account window, name the bank account and select the currency in the Currency field (fill in the Description and Bank Acct. No. fields if you really want to). Click Save & Close to return to the Receive Payments window.

One other thing: if you decide to use Undeposited Funds as the Deposit To account, you need to deposit the customer payment into a Bank account. We describe how you do this in Chapter 5.

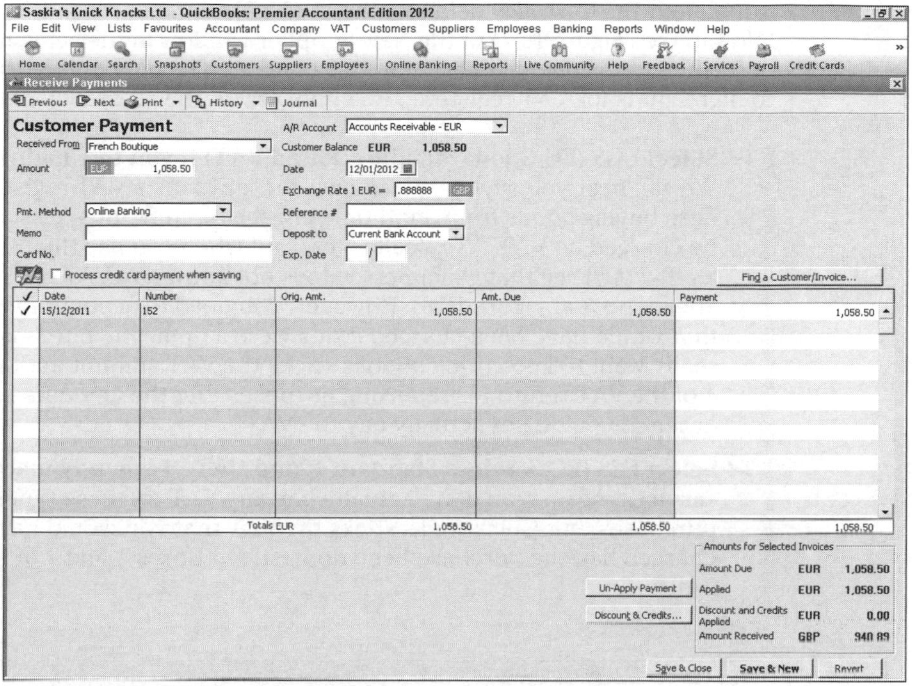

Figure 10-6:
A completed
Receive
Payments
window for
a foreign
customer.

Buying in a Foreign Currency

In this section, we talk about the things you need to know to buy in a foreign currency. If you read the earlier section "Selling in a Foreign Currency", most of what follows will be old hat. And since you already know most things, we'll only point out the bits you don't.

Adding a foreign or domestic currency supplier

You add a foreign or domestic currency supplier as we describe in Chapter 3. But you must include some additional information.

The two new fields that you need to fill out are the same two new fields that we described for multicurrency customers in the earlier section "Adding a foreign or domestic customer", namely, the Currency field and the VAT Code field.

You fill out the Currency field and the VAT Information area in the Additional Info tab (see Figure 10-7) of the New Supplier window in the same manner we described for a customer earlier in this chapter. The only difference we need to highlight is for VAT-registered EC suppliers. In the VAT Code field:

✔ **Select EGS (EC Goods Standard Rated VAT) if you buy mainly goods.** We can hear you saying: "Hang on a sec, guys. As a VAT-registered business buying goods from another VAT-registered EC business, shouldn't I be charged no VAT?" Typically, yes. And when you use this VAT code on a bill, you'll see that QuickBooks does not show any VAT on the bill (go ahead, peek at Figure 10-8). However, you need to account for the VAT that would have been charged if this were a domestic purchase. If you really want to know, QuickBooks sticks the VAT amount in Boxes 2 and 4 of the VAT return for reporting purposes, but the amounts cancel each other so you do not actually pay the VAT.

✔ **Select ESS (EC Services Standard Rated VAT) if you buy mainly services.** Again, you don't actually pay any VAT on these types of purchases, but QuickBooks sticks the VAT that you would have been charged had the purchase been domestic in Boxes 1 and 4 of the VAT return.

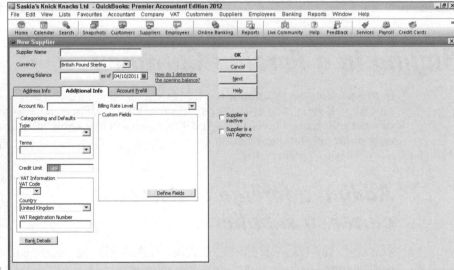

Figure 10-7: The New Supplier window with Multi-currency turned on.

You fill out the rest of the fields in the New Supplier window in the same way as we describe in Chapter 3.

And by the way, QuickBooks adds an Accounts Payable account in the Chart of Accounts for each supplier currency. For example, if you add a supplier whose currency is US Dollars, QuickBooks adds Accounts Payable – USD to the Chart of Accounts. All purchase transactions in the foreign currency can be viewed in this register.

Voilà.

Updating existing suppliers

You know what to do. Really. You do exactly the same thing for existing suppliers that you did for existing customers, described earlier in this chapter.

QuickBooks assigns the 'S' VAT Code to each existing supplier. If this is right for you, because you are charged VAT at the standard rate on everything you buy, skip to the next section. Otherwise consider updating the VAT Code field of existing suppliers.

You make these changes in the Additional Info tab, in the VAT Information area (see Figure 10-7).

Entering a bill

Not to bore you, but entering a supplier bill or credit when the Multicurrency feature is turned on is very similar to entering a bill or credit without the Multicurrency feature. We describe how you do this in Chapter 6.

The Enter Bills window is slightly different with the Multicurrency feature turned on. You see this best after you select a foreign currency supplier, and press Tab to move to the next field (see Figure 10-8). The changes QuickBooks makes are to:

- ✔ Recall the correct foreign currency Accounts Payable account.
- ✔ Apply the foreign currency of the supplier to the bill or credit.
- ✔ Show the Amount Due field in both the foreign and home currency.
- ✔ Display the foreign currency in the Amount column of the Expenses and Items tab.
- ✔ Display the Total VAT field in the foreign currency.
- ✔ Add the Supplier VAT Code field at the bottom of the window.

The Supplier VAT Code overrides the VAT code of items (in the Items tab) and accounts (in the Expenses tab). If you change the Supplier VAT Code on the bill or credit, the new Supplier VAT Code applies to all items and accounts.

✔ Add the Exchange Rate field to the Enter Bills window and populate it with the exchange rate that applies as of the date in the Date field.

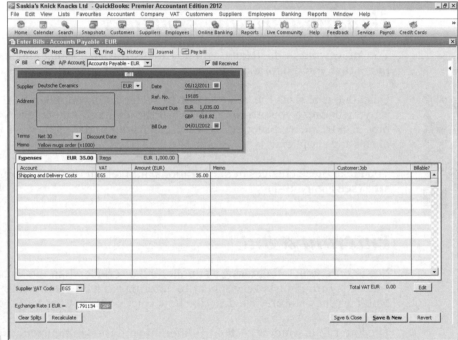

Figure 10-8:
The Expenses tab of the Enter Bills window with Multi-currency turned on.

Paying your bills

When it's time to pay your suppliers, select Suppliers⇨Pay Bills (or, from the Home Page, click the Pay Bills icon). In the Pay Bills window, click the down arrow in the A/P Account field and select the Accounts Payable foreign currency account of the bills you want to pay. For example, select Accounts Payable – EUR. QuickBooks then displays the bills in this currency (see Figure 10-9).

Each currency has its own Accounts Payable account in which QuickBooks tracks all the purchase transactions in that currency.

This window should look very familiar to you. And we bet we don't even need to tell you that you fill in the fields in the same manner as we discuss in Chapter 6.

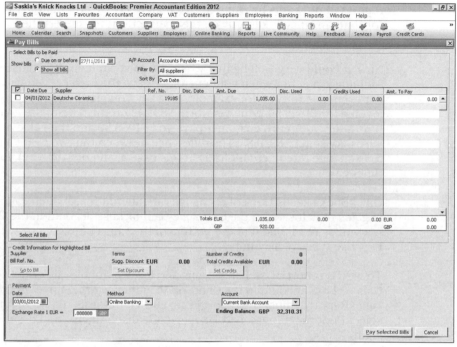

Figure 10-9:
The Pay
Bills win-
dow with
Multi-
currency
turned on.

The only differences are that you get to set the exchange rate of the bill payments in the Exchange Rate field at the bottom of the window, and the amounts you are paying are shown in the foreign currency. QuickBooks also displays the GBP currency values at the bottom of the Amt. Due and Amt. To Pay columns.

You can make a payment from a UK bank account or a bank account in the foreign currency.

By the way, you cannot pay a euro bill, for example, from a different currency bank account, such as a US dollar bank account. We've been asked by clients in the past if you can do that, so we thought we'd mention it.

Did I Gain or Lose?

QuickBooks always reports the value of your foreign currency transactions in GBP on financial statements, such as the Profit & Loss and Balance Sheet reports. It does this by using the exchange rates you set in the Currency List (or that you specify directly on the transaction) to convert the foreign currency into the GBP equivalent.

Now, it could very well be that when you raise an invoice you use one exchange rate, but when your customer pays the invoice, you use a different exchange rate. So for example, let's say you give your euro customer an invoice for €1058.50, which is worth £837.42 on the date of the invoice. Some time later, your euro customer pays you €1058.50 and the value of those euros goes up to £940.89. The difference between the two GBP values, due to exchange rate fluctuations, is in this case a gain of £103.47 in your favour. (Lucky you.)

QuickBooks keeps track of exchange rate fluctuations, which can result in gains *or* in losses, in the Exchange Gain or Loss account in the Chart of Accounts. You'll find it at the bottom of the Chart of Accounts, with Other Expense types of accounts.

To view a report of exchange gains and losses, double-click the Exchange Gain or Loss account in the Chart of Accounts to bring up an Account QuickReport. Adjust the report From and To dates as required. Alternatively, select Reports➪Company & Financial➪Realised Gains and Losses (see Figure 10-10).

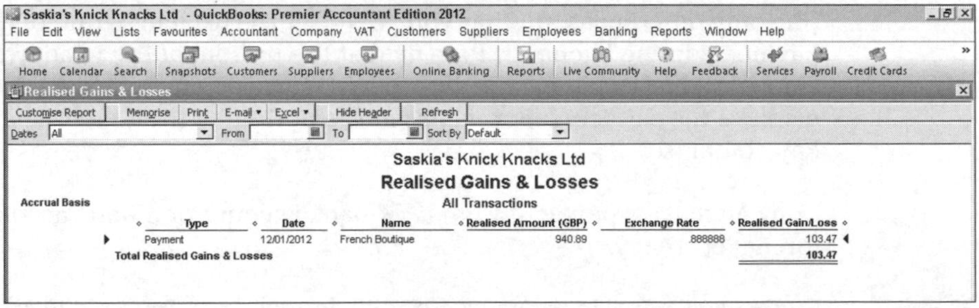

Figure 10-10:
The Realised
Gains and
Losses
Report
window.

You only see gains (or losses) on paid foreign currency transactions. In other words, a gain (or a loss) only happens after a customer pays an invoice or you pay a supplier. This is called a *realised* gain or loss because the exchange rate fluctuations are known (or realised) once the invoice is paid.

You can, however, also view a report of *unrealised* gains or losses on unpaid foreign currency transactions. An unrealised gain or loss is simply a forecast because the final exchange rate is unknown until the transaction is paid. The gains or losses on unpaid foreign currency invoices and unpaid foreign currency bills are calculated as of a certain date, using a particular set of exchange rates. You get to this report by selecting Reports⇨Company & Financial⇨Unrealised Gains and Losses. In the Enter Exchange Rates window, QuickBooks asks you to enter the report date and then displays the exchange rate as of that date for each currency with open transactions. You can of course edit the exchange rates before you click the Continue button to view the report. You can change the way you view the information in the Unrealised Gains & Losses report by changing the selection in the Total By field, at the top left of the report.

Making a home currency adjustment

The last thing we need to tell you about is the *home currency adjustment*. A home currency adjustment is a calculation of unrealised gains and losses that is posted to the books as an adjustment. Its purpose is to state the GBP value of your foreign balances at the end of a reporting period (such as a month, a quarter, or a financial year), using the exchange rate on the last day of the period.

The home currency adjustment affects the GBP value of your balance sheet accounts but not the foreign balance amount. So the customer still owes the same amount in the foreign currency, it's just that the value of the transactions in GBP changes.

To make the adjustment:

1. **Select Company⇨Manage Currency⇨Home Currency Adjustment to display the Home Currency Adjustment window (Figure 10-11).**
2. **Enter the Date of the adjustment.**

3. **Choose the Currency you want to adjust.**

4. **Adjust the value in the Exchange Rate field if necessary.**

   QuickBooks displays the currency exchange rate in the Exchange Rate field, as of the adjustment date. (If you didn't specify an exchange rate in the Currency List as of the adjustment date, QuickBooks enters 1 in the Exchange Rate field.) To edit the exchange rate, simply type another value.

5. **Click the Calculate Adjustment button.**

   QuickBooks then displays all unpaid customer invoices and supplier bills.

6. **Select the transactions you want to adjust.**

   You can select an individual transaction by clicking the mouse to the left of each transaction so that a check mark appears. To select all transactions, click the Select All button.

7. **(Optional) Enter a memo.**

   If you want to, type a memo to remind you later why you are making this adjustment.

8. **Click Save & Close to finish, or Save & New to save this adjustment and enter another.**

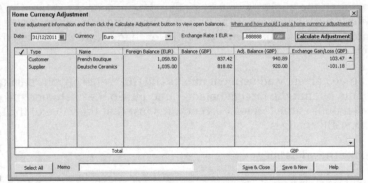

Figure 10-11:
The Home
Currency
Adjustment
window.

You adjust one currency at a time using the Home Currency Adjustment window.

To sum up, a home currency adjustment gives you an idea of what your exposure to currency fluctuations is at any given point in time. Now that you know about it, you may decide that you don't want to bother with home currency adjustments. But, in case you want to make the adjustment, you know how to.

Editing a home currency adjustment

If you make a mistake, you can edit a home currency adjustment. To do so, navigate to the Exchange Gain or Loss account in the Chart of Accounts, and call up the Account QuickReport as we described earlier. Adjust the From and To dates as required. The home currency adjustment appears as a journal entry in the list of transactions. Find and double-click the transaction you want to change and make the desired changes. When you are finished, click the Save & Close button.

Part III
Stuff You Do from Time to Time

The 5th Wave   By Rich Tennant

I don't know-My spreadsheet tells me we should base our overhead budget on sales figures rather than fixed, my plot chart indicates we should escalate our marketing thrust, and my psychoanalysis program tells me I depend too much on outside input and should trust my instincts more.

In this part . . .

After you start using QuickBooks, you need to complete some tasks at the end of every week, month, quarter, or year. This part describes these tasks: managing VAT, payroll, and budgeting. Fortunately, QuickBooks can really help you to get the job done.

Chapter 11

Managing VAT

QuickBooks makes a tedious part of being in business – managing VAT – easy and (almost) painless. And that's how it should be.

In this chapter, we explain how QuickBooks manages VAT. We show you how to generate VAT reports and submit VAT returns, and talk about how to pay your VAT liability or record a VAT refund. We end the chapter by looking at some special VAT circumstances.

What we don't talk about in this chapter is the VAT rules. These can be quite complex and the best advice we can give you is to seek advice from HMRC or your accountant for your own specific circumstances.

We also make the assumption that you are registered to submit your VAT online, which most businesses need to do nowadays.

VAT Schemes in QuickBooks

Although you probably already know this, we thought we'd mention, that there are a number of VAT schemes for which you can register with HMRC, in addition to the standard scheme, which is accrual-based VAT reporting. Some of the schemes have specific thresholds, or apply to specific industries. For more information on this you can visit the HMRC website at www.hmrc. gov.uk/vat/start/schemes/basics.htm.

We tell you this because the important thing for you to know is that you can use QuickBooks to report VAT either on an accrual basis or a cash basis. If you want know more, have a look at the sidebar in this chapter where we describe the differences in these schemes.

QuickBooks can also report your VAT figures for different intervals, including monthly, quarterly, or annually. In this chapter, we assume that you are sending in quarterly returns as this is the most common scenario.

Adjusting Your VAT Settings

QuickBooks automatically turns on the VAT feature when you create your company file, and you learn in Chapter 2 that QuickBooks also adds HMRC VAT to the Supplier list during the QuickBooks Setup process.

Now, HMRC VAT is no ordinary supplier (in reality it's not a supplier at all, but never mind). To see what's different about this supplier, open the supplier record by clicking the Suppliers icon on the Home Page (or choosing Suppliers⇨Supplier Centre) and then double-clicking HMRC VAT in the Supplier List.

Notice that in addition to the three tabs normally present on a supplier record there is a fourth tab, called VAT Agency Info (see Figure 11-1). This tab is included because QuickBooks puts a check mark next to Supplier Is a VAT Agency, and this option is what makes HMRC VAT a "special" supplier.

On the VAT Agency Info tab you get to describe a whole bunch of important VAT settings. For example, you can select the:

- *VAT Return type:* in this case VAT 100 (UK).

- *VAT Reporting Period:* how often you submit your VAT.

- *Period Ending:* that's the ending month in the reporting period (for example, if your quarters run January to March, March to June and so on, choose Mar/June/Sep/Dec).

- *Account to Track VAT on Purchases and Sales:* VAT Liability account is a good choice. (Don't change this unless you really know what you're doing.)

- *Method for reporting VAT:* accrual or cash basis VAT (for more information, see the sidebar).

After you are finished adjusting the settings in this tab, click OK to save your work.

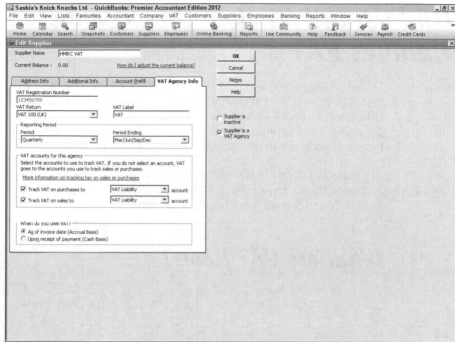

Figure 11-1:
The VAT
Agency Info
tab on the
HMRC VAT
supplier
record.

Cash and accrual VAT reporting

Be sure that you tell QuickBooks which way to report VAT – on a cash basis or an accrual basis – otherwise your VAT reports will be wrong. QuickBooks defaults to the accrual scheme so make sure you change this if you are on the cash-based scheme, otherwise it's a hair-pulling-out exercise that you may not live to tell about.

The difference between the two methods is the *timing* of when you have to pay or can reclaim the VAT. Using the accrual-based method, you become liable for the VAT on the customer invoice date and can reclaim VAT on the supplier bill date. For cash-based VAT reporting, you are liable for the VAT when your customer pays the invoice and can reclaim VAT when you pay your supplier's bill.

Let's say your VAT quarters are January–March, April–June and so on, and that you invoice your customer £1000 plus £200 VAT on 20 March. She pays you on 15 April. Accrual-based VAT reports show the £200 VAT in the January–March quarter. So even though your customer has not paid you, you have to pay over the VAT. In contrast, cash-based VAT reports show £200 VAT in the April–June quarter because your customer paid you in April. And if your customer only pays you half of the invoice (£600), you only need to pay half the VAT (£100).

You might think that it's a no brainer to sign up for cash-based VAT, but remember that you also get to reclaim VAT using the same rules. You reclaim VAT sooner with accrual-based VAT (based on bill date) than with cash-based VAT (based on the date you pay your supplier).

Understanding How QuickBooks Handles VAT

To get a sense of how QuickBooks handles VAT, you need to know about VAT Items and VAT Codes and how they work together. Out of the box QuickBooks comes with all the VAT Items and VAT Codes that you need to get going. For the most part they are just there, quietly doing their job in the background and you don't need to worry about them.

But if a new change in the VAT rate is introduced by the powers that be – and we've had a few of these VAT rate changes in recent years – you need to know what to do. We promise we'll be brief.

What are VAT Items?

We mention VAT Items in our discussion of items in Chapter 3, and at first glance they look kind of weird. But don't worry, they don't bite.

QuickBooks uses VAT Items for four things:

 ✔ To store the VAT rate (like 20%, 5%, or 0%).

 ✔ To link the VAT rate to the HMRC VAT tax agency.

 ✔ To know which boxes on the VAT return it should use to report the VAT it calculates for that item.

 ✔ To track the VAT to the VAT Liability account (not visible on the VAT Item itself, only in the Item List).

Figure 11-2 shows you what the Standard Sales VAT Item looks like. If you charge your customers VAT at 20% on a sale, QuickBooks uses the Standard Sales VAT item to report the VAT amount in Box 1 and the Net value of the sale in Box 6 of the VAT return.

There are many combinations of VAT rates and VAT return boxes possible, depending on whether you are making a domestic or foreign sale or domestic or foreign purchase, and that's why there are so many VAT Items in the Item List.

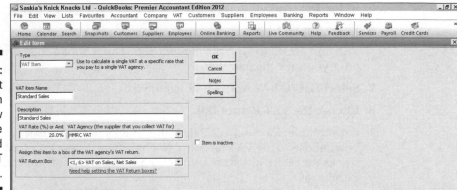

Figure 11-2:
The Edit
Item
window
with the
Standard
Sales VAT
Item.

Adding VAT Items

When there is a new VAT rate introduced, you need to create a new VAT Item. *Don't* be tempted to just edit the rate of an existing VAT item – you'll need the VAT Item for the old rate because there is always a transition period when you're still receiving bills and perhaps sending out invoices dated prior to the new VAT rate changeover date. You'll avoid any confusion if you keep the old and the new VAT rate VAT Items separate, and you'll be glad you did. (We're speaking from experience here.)

Whenever there is an imminent change in VAT legislation, Intuit (the makers of QuickBooks) publish guides to help you update your VAT settings correctly. Check the Intuit Community area of the QuickBooks website (`http://community.intuit.com/quickbooks/uk`) for this information. Intuit also periodically update QuickBooks, so ensure that you are up to date.

Add a new VAT item as follows:

1. **Choose Lists⇨Item List.**

   Or click the Items & Services icon on the Home screen to display the Item List window.

2. **Click the Item button in the lower-left corner of the Item List window and then choose New.**

3. **Select VAT Item from the drop-down list.**

4. **Name the VAT Item.**

   Each VAT item is associated with either a sale or a purchase, so specify this in the item name. Enter something like **Exorbitant VAT on Sales**, for example.

5. **In the Description field, write a longer description.**

6. **Enter the VAT Rate.**

   You don't need to type the percent sign; QuickBooks adds it for you after you save the new item.

7. **Select HMRC VAT as the VAT agency.**

8. **Choose the VAT Return Box.**

   For example, for a new VAT Item that tracks domestic sales VAT, you choose <1, 6> VAT on Sales, Net Sales; for a new VAT Item that tracks domestic purchases, you choose <4, 7> VAT on Purchases, Net Purchases.

9. **Click the Save & Close button.**

   When you're finished adding the new VAT Item, click OK to save the changes and return to the Item List, or Next to add another VAT Item.

Before we wrap up the discussion of VAT Items, we should mention that the Item List also contains VAT Groups (mentioned in Chapter 3). QuickBooks uses VAT Groups to calculate and individually track two or more VAT Items that apply to the same sale or purchase, as is the case for EC purchases of goods or services or EC sales of goods, or where Reverse Charge VAT rules apply. You normally don't need to set up new VAT Groups.

What about VAT Codes?

We talk a lot about VAT Codes in Chapter 10 and we mention VAT Codes throughout other chapters as well. We bet you can't wait to find out what VAT Codes actually do (in case you don't already know or haven't already guessed).

VAT Codes are what you use on a sale or purchase transaction to tell QuickBooks which VAT Items to apply to that sale or purchase. For example, when you use the "S" VAT Code on an invoice or sales receipt, QuickBooks knows to apply the Standard Sales VAT Item. And when you use the "S" VAT Code on a bill, cheque, or credit card transaction, QuickBooks knows to apply the Standard Purchase VAT Item.

QuickBooks knows all this because the VAT Code contains this information. For example, take a look at Figure 11-3, which shows the "S" VAT Code. In the Taxable Information area, the VAT Item for Purchases is Standard Purchases and the VAT Item for Sales is Standard Sales.

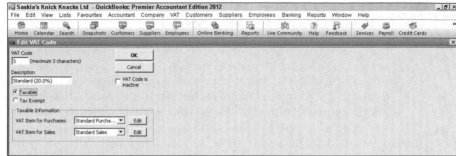

Figure 11-3:
The Edit
VAT Code
window for
the "S" VAT
Code.

Adding VAT Codes

To add a new VAT Code, you must first define the VAT Items as described in the preceding section. Then follow these steps:

1. **Choose Lists⇨VAT Code List.**

2. **Click the VAT Code button in the lower-left corner of the VAT Code List window and choose New.**

3. **Enter a VAT Code name (up to three characters).**

   You use this name to recall the VAT Code.

   If the first letter of the code is unique in your list there is less chance you will accidentally use the wrong VAT Code.

4. **Type a Description.**

   Enter a longer description for the VAT Code.

5. **Select the Taxable option.**

6. **Choose a VAT Item for Purchases.**

   Click the down arrow in this field and choose one of the VAT Items. You can click the Edit button to view the settings for that VAT Item and edit them if necessary.

7. **Choose a VAT Item for Sales.**

8. **Click the Save & Close button.**

Generating VAT Reports

QuickBooks has a bunch of reports to help you review and file your VAT returns. The VAT 100 report gives you a summary of the VAT return figures, the VAT Detail report shows you which transactions are included in the return (and which boxes on the return they report to), and the VAT Exception report shows you if you made any changes to prior VAT periods that are included in this VAT period.

When you generate your VAT reports, you should carefully review the figures to ensure that what you submit to HMRC is accurate and complete.

By the way, it's a good idea to print these reports for your records, save them to PDF format, or export to Excel, as we describe in Chapter 15. Although QuickBooks will save a copy of these reports in PDF format, you don't get to adjust the column widths of the saved reports, so some longer fields can get cut off in the PDF version.

The VAT 100 Report

To view the VAT 100 report simply click VAT⇨VAT 100 Report. QuickBooks displays the VAT Summary window (Figure 11-4) for the last VAT period, in this case a quarter.

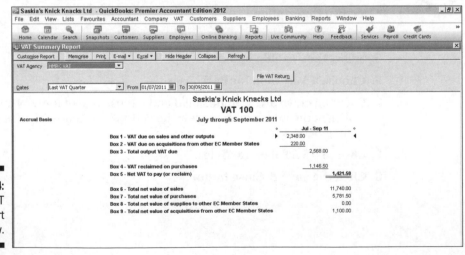

Figure 11-4: The VAT 100 report window.

The first time you bring up this report look at the left side of the window, where you will see either Accrual Basis or Cash Basis. This is the method that QuickBooks uses to prepare the report. Make sure this is set to correctly reflect your method.

If QuickBooks is using the wrong VAT reporting method, change the method (as we describe in the section "Adjusting Your VAT Settings") *before* you submit that first VAT return, otherwise the figures you report will be wrong. Changing the VAT reporting method alters the amounts in the report.

You can drill down on any of the figures in the report by placing your cursor above the figure you want to investigate. When you see what looks like a magnifying glass with the letter "z" inside it (Z stands for QuickZoom), double-click the mouse. QuickBooks then displays a list of the transactions that make up the summary figures.

The VAT Detail Report

A better way to view the figures in the return is in the VAT Detail Report, because it shows the transactions being reported for each box of the VAT Return, in one report.

To view the report, click VAT⇨VAT Detail Report. QuickBooks displays the VAT Detail Report window (Figure 11-5).

It may at first take a little practice to make sense of the data in the columns, because there are two types of information in the report. For Boxes 1, 2, and 4 of the VAT Return, the VAT Detail Report shows the *VAT amount of every transaction line*. For example, Figure 11-5 shows the VAT Item in the Item column, the percentage of VAT charged in the Rate column, and the VAT amount in the Amount column for every transaction line.

However, for Boxes 6, 7, 8, and 9, the VAT Detail Report shows the *Net summary of every transaction by VAT Code*. So QuickBooks shows the VAT code in the VAT Code column and the Net Amount in the Amount column (rather than in the Net Amount column – hopefully this is not too confusing now that you know about it). And in the Item column, where there are multiple items with the same VAT code in a transaction, QuickBooks displays -MULTIPLE-.

If there are transactions from an earlier VAT period included in the return, QuickBooks displays a starting amount in the Balance column of the relevant Boxes and adds a yellow warning sign icon next to the amounts. Double-clicking the warning sign (or the amount in the Balance column) takes you to the VAT Exception Report, discussed next.

Saskia's Knick Knacks Ltd

VAT Detail Report

Accrual Basis — As of 30 September 2011

Type	Date	Num	Source Name	Item	VAT Code	Rate	Net Amount	Amount	Balance
Box 1 VAT due on sales and other outputs									**900.00**
Invoice	28/07/2011	1	Port Meadow Coffee House	Standard Sales	S	20.0%	4,775.00	955.00	1,855.00
Invoice	23/09/2011	3	Port Meadow Coffee House	Standard Sales	S	20.0%	685.00	137.00	1,992.00
Invoice	23/09/2011	5	Helene's Bookshop	Standard Sales	S	20.0%	850.00	170.00	2,162.00
Credit Note	28/09/2011	6	Helene's Bookshop	Standard Sales	S	20.0%	-20.00	-4.00	2,158.00
Invoice	30/09/2011	7	Delila's Delights	Standard Sales	S	20.0%	950.00	190.00	2,348.00
VAT due on sales and other outputs								1,448.00	2,348.00
Box 2 VAT due on acquisitions from other EC Member States									**0.00**
Credit Card Charge	25/08/2011		Deutsche Ceramics	EC Purch Goods Standard	EGS	-20.0%	1,100.00	220.00	220.00
VAT due on acquisitions from other EC Member States								220.00	220.00
Box 4 VAT reclaimed on purchases									**0.00**
Credit Card Charge	10/08/2011		Zippy's Supplies	Standard Purchases	S	20.0%	100.00	20.00	20.00
Credit Card Charge	25/08/2011		Deutsche Ceramics	Standard Purchases	EGS	20.0%	1,100.00	220.00	240.00
Bill	06/09/2011	32049	Stuff Galore	Standard Purchases	S	20.0%	150.00	30.00	270.00
Bill	12/09/2011	912	Gobs of Mugs	Standard Purchases	S	20.0%	1,000.00	200.00	470.00
Bill	12/09/2011	9252	Gobs of Mugs	Standard Purchases	S	20.0%	3,300.00	660.00	1,130.00
Credit Card Charge	28/09/2011		Post Office	Standard Purchases	S	20.0%	82.50	16.50	1,146.50
VAT reclaimed on purchases								1,146.50	1,146.50
Box 6 Total net value of sales									**4,500.00**
Invoice	28/07/2011	1	Port Meadow Coffee House	-MULTIPLE-	S			4,775.00	9,275.00
Invoice	23/09/2011	3	Port Meadow Coffee House	-MULTIPLE-	S			685.00	9,960.00
Invoice	23/09/2011	5	Helene's Bookshop	-MULTIPLE-	S			850.00	10,810.00
Credit Note	28/09/2011	6	Helene's Bookshop	Rainbow mug	S			-20.00	10,790.00
Invoice	30/09/2011	7	Delila's Delights	-MULTIPLE-	S			950.00	11,740.00
Total net value of sales								7,240.00	11,740.00

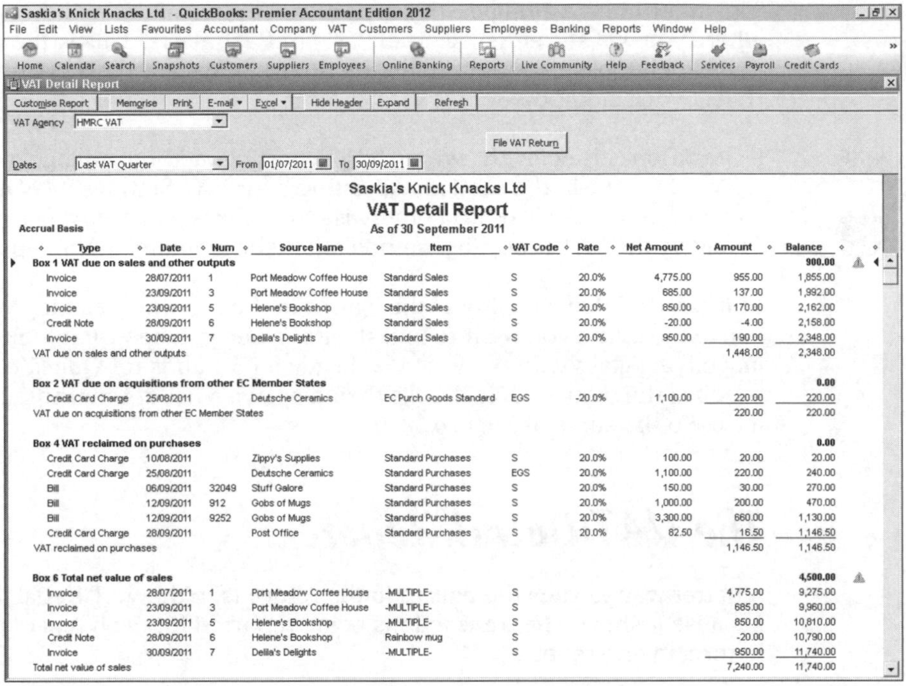

Figure 11-5: The VAT Detail Report window.

REMEMBER

You do not see a breakdown in the VAT Detail report for figures in Boxes 3 and 5 because these figures are calculated: the Box 3 figure is a sum of Box 1 and 2, and the Box 5 figure is Box 3 less Box 4.

The VAT Exception Report

The VAT Exception Report (see Figure 11-6) shows you transactions that should have been included in prior VAT Returns (but weren't for whatever reason) and are being included in the current VAT Return. So transactions you added, deleted or changed since you last filed your VAT Return in QuickBooks are in this report.

The information is displayed in a similar format to the VAT Detail Report, but you'll notice four new columns: Filed Date, Filed Amount, Current Amount, and Amount Difference. You can probably guess what QuickBooks sticks in each column, but for the sake of completeness we'll describe them.

A date in the Filed Date column shows in which prior VAT return the transaction was included; no date in the Filed Date column means the transaction has not been included in a return yet.

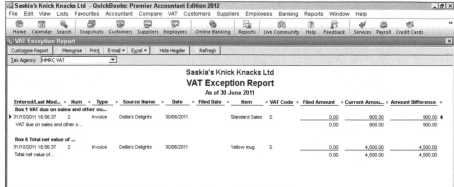

Figure 11-6:
The VAT
Exception
Report
window.

Any portion of the transaction that you included in a prior VAT return is shown in the Filed Amount column. The new transaction amount is in the Current Amount field and (you guessed it) the difference between the Filed Amount and Current Amount columns appears in the Amount Difference column.

Submitting Your VAT

After you have reviewed the figures in the VAT Return and before you submit them to HMRC, back up your file as we describe in Chapter 17. Once you submit your VAT Return, you cannot "unsubmit" it. We just happen to think (and you may think so too) that it's very wise to back up every time you are about to do something you can't undo.

When you are ready to submit the VAT return to HMRC, follow these steps:

1. **Choose VAT⊃File VAT.**

   The File VAT window is displayed (Figure 11-7).

2. **Select a VAT Agency.**

   If you have only HRMC VAT designated as a VAT Agency, QuickBooks selects HMRC VAT for you and shows the figures for the last VAT period.

   If you don't see any figures in the window it's because you specified multiple suppliers as VAT Agencies. You may have multiple VAT Agencies if you need to report to VAT to different bodies (for example Irish VAT and UK VAT). To select a VAT Agency, click the down arrow in the VAT Agency field and choose one from the list.

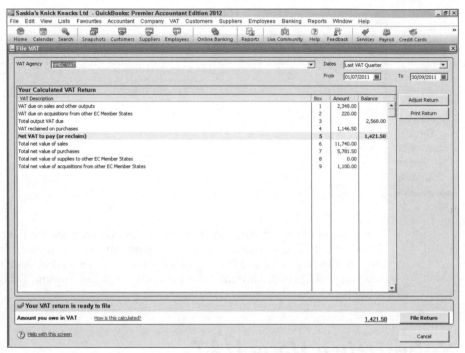

Figure 11-7:
The File VAT
window.

3. Amend the From and To Dates if necessary.

Check and amend as necessary the From and To dates. By default, QuickBooks shows figures for the last VAT period.

4. Click the File Return button.

When you are satisfied that you are filing the same figures as on the VAT 100 report, click the File Return button.

5. Select the method you are going to use to file the VAT return.

If you choose File Online, make sure you are connected to the Internet, and have your login details for the HMRC VAT Online service to hand. Click Continue:

   a. QuickBooks asks whether you want to print your VAT return (meaning the VAT 100 report). Make your selection.

   b. QuickBooks then displays the Online Filing Contact Information window where you enter your login details (User ID and Password) for the HMRC VAT Online service, and select your Agency Type (select Company if you are the business owner). Click OK.

   c. QuickBooks goes online and files the return. If the filing is successful, you'll see a success message.

If you choose Paper or Other Filing Method, QuickBooks will not communicate the figures to HMRC and you will need to log in to the HMRC VAT Online service on your own to file your return. Click Continue.

If you are filing your first VAT return in QuickBooks and the figures for the return are partly in QuickBooks and partly in another system, you need to choose the Paper or Other Filing Method. You fill in the actual return figures (including the correct Net amounts; the VAT adjustments you enter in Chapter 3 only include Box 1, 2, and 4 figures) directly on the HMRC VAT Online website.

6. **If you owe VAT, you'll see the Payment window.**

   In the Payment window, QuickBooks tells you the amount of VAT you need to pay, and that it will create an entry in the Accounts Payable account for this amount.

   Click either the Pay Now button or the Pay Later button to finish filing your VAT return.

7. **If you are getting a VAT refund, you'll see the Refund window.**

   In the Refund window, QuickBooks tells you the amount of VAT you are being refunded, and that it will create an entry in the Accounts Receivable account for this amount.

   Click either the Receive Now button or the Receive Later button to finish filing your VAT return.

8. **The QuickBooks Information window appears (see Figure 11-8).**

   This window tells you several things:

   - You finished processing your VAT return – congratulations!

   - QuickBooks has set a new closing date for your books (described later in this chapter) and that's the last date covered by the return.

   - Transactions dated prior to the closing date can only be modified by the QuickBooks Administrator.

   - You can view past VAT returns (or confirmations of submissions if you Filed Online) by clicking VAT⇨Prior VAT Returns.

   Click OK to close the window. Breathe a sigh of relief.

For the curious among you who are wondering what QuickBooks did during the VAT filing process, we'll tell you. QuickBooks marks the transactions included in the return as Filed and adds the last date of the return as the Filed Date. That's how QuickBooks knows not to include these transactions in future VAT returns. When you change a filed transaction, QuickBooks reports the changes to the transaction in the VAT Exception Report (as described earlier).

Oh, and by the way, QuickBooks also clears down the VAT 100 report figures for the period you just filed. If you don't believe us, go ahead, take a look.

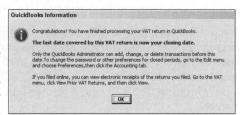

Figure 11-8:
The
QuickBooks
Information
window
confirming
that your
VAT
return is
processed.

Paying VAT or Getting a VAT Refund

After you file your VAT Return in QuickBooks, you need to pay the VAT or record a refund.

You pay the VAT as you pay any other supplier in QuickBooks, through the Pay Bills window. For a refresher on how to pay bills in QuickBooks, turn to Chapter 6. Remember, the supplier is HMRC VAT.

You record a VAT refund in the same way you record a customer payment, through the Receive Payments window. We describe how to do this in Chapter 5 and won't repeat it here. In this case, the customer is HMRC VAT – Receivable.

Closing the Books

As we mentioned earlier in this chapter, one of the things QuickBooks does when it processes a VAT Return is to add a closing date to your file, which is the last date covered by the return. Here we explain how this works.

Let's say you file your June–September 2011 VAT return. QuickBooks dutifully makes 30/09/2011 your new closing date. This means that only the QuickBooks administrator can add, edit, or delete a transaction dated prior to 30/09/2011. If you are logged in as the QuickBooks administrator, you will see a message like the one in Figure 11-9 when you attempt to add, delete, or modify a transaction dated prior to 30/09/2011. Simply click Yes to save the transaction or No if you change your mind.

Figure 11-9:
QuickBooks
alerts you
that the
entry you
are making
is prior to
the closing
date.

QuickBooks keeps track of changes made to the file after the last clos-
ing date in the Closing Date Exception Report (click Reports⇨Accountant
& Taxes⇨Closing Date Exception Report). QuickBooks also keeps both
summary and detail reports of voided or deleted transactions (click
Reports⇨Accountant & Taxes⇨Voided/Deleted Transactions Summary or
Voided/Deleted Transactions Detail).

Let's also say that when you set up your colleague, George, as a User with
certain (not full) access rights (see Appendix C), you did not give him access
to change transactions that are closed. When George attempts to make add,
delete, or edit a transaction dated prior to 30/09/2011, he cannot. He sees a
message that tells him he does not have the access rights.

You can change the closing date (but think carefully before you do this). You
can also add a password to the closing date, so that you are prompted for the
password each time QuickBooks needs to add, delete, or change a transaction dated prior to the closing date.

To change the closing date or add a password, make sure you are in single-
user mode (see Appendix C) and then log in as the QuickBooks Administrator
and click Company⇨Set Closing Date (or click Edit⇨Preferences⇨Accounting
and click the Company Preferences tab). In the window that appears, click
the Set Date/Password button. Click OK to save your settings.

Dealing with Special VAT Circumstances

We end this chapter by discussing three VAT circumstances which will not
apply to everyone: trading with businesses in the EC, generating an EC Sales
List, and adding fuel scale charges to a VAT return.

Trading with EC businesses

If you trade with EC businesses there are two things you need to do. One is to ensure that you record the VAT details of VAT-registered EC customers and/or suppliers in the Customer:Jobs list or the Supplier list. The other is to use EC VAT codes on sale or purchase transactions with EC businesses so that the VAT is reported correctly on the VAT return.

In Chapter 10 we discuss at length the VAT information you need to enter on the Additional Info tab of an EC customer or EC supplier record, so we won't repeat ourselves here.

The easiest way to ensure that you are using the correct EC VAT codes is to assign the EC VAT Codes directly to the customer or supplier records in QuickBooks. This way QuickBooks uses the EC VAT codes on the customer or supplier record on sale or purchase transactions, instead of the VAT code of items or accounts. To tell QuickBooks to give you the option to assign VAT codes to customers and suppliers, click Edit⇨Preferences and choose VAT from the list on the left. In the Company Preferences tab, in the Customer and Supplier VAT Codes area tick the boxes next to Use Customer VAT Codes and/or Use Supplier VAT Codes. Click OK to save your changes.

Remember to seek advice from HMRC or your accountant for your specific business circumstances. Another great resource is the QuickBooks help: simply go to Help⇨QuickBooks Help and click the Search tab, and then enter the help topic **VAT Codes For EC Businesses**.

Printing the EC Sales List

If you sell goods and related services to VAT-registered businesses in the EC, you need to submit an EC Sales List (ESL) known as the VAT 101 form to HMRC. HMRC will automatically send you the VAT 101 to complete if you show amounts in Box 8 of your VAT Return.

You need two bits of information to fill out a VAT 101 form. One is a list of customers to whom you sold goods (and related services) and the GBP value of those sales. You can get this list from the EC Sales List report in QuickBooks. Simply click VAT⇨EC Sales List and set the desired dates for the report in the From and To dates.

The other bit of information you need is the VAT registration details of each customer in the QuickBooks report. You can obtain that data from looking up the VAT details on the Additional Info tab of the customer record in the QuickBooks Customer:Jobs list.

You can find more information about sending in the ESL on the HRMC website at `www.hmrc.gov.uk/vat/managing/international/esl/reporting-esl.htm`.

Fuel scale charges

If you provide your employees with fuel for business and private use, and you reclaim the VAT on fuel, you need to account for fuel scale charges on your VAT returns.

The first thing you need to do is to create a VAT Item for the fuel scale charge. You do this as we described in the "Adding VAT Items" section earlier in the chapter. Set the VAT Rate to 0%, and in the VAT Return Box select ‹1, N› VAT on Sales, None. Call the VAT Item something such as **Fuel Scale**.

The second thing you need to do is to create a fuel scale charge expense account. We describe how to do this in Chapter 3. Go crazy and call it something such as **Fuel Scale Charges**.

Then, at the end of each VAT period you need to calculate the fuel scale charges, using the fuel scale charge table provided by HMRC (which you can find on the HMRC website as a PDF file). As the link for this table changes each year, we recommend you do a search for 'fuel scale charge' on the HMRC website at `www.hmrc.gov.uk`.

Once you know the fuel scale charge amount, you create a journal entry in QuickBooks at the end of each VAT period. You can see an example of a completed journal entry in Figure 11-10.

Figure 11-10: The Make General Journal Entries window showing a fuel scale charge entry.

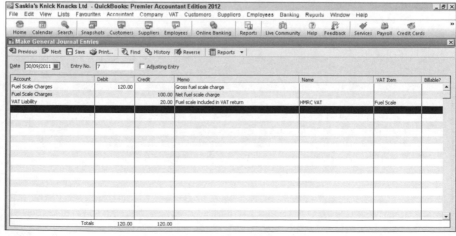

To make the journal entry, follow these steps:

1. **Choose Company⇨Make General Journal Entry.**

   The Make General Journal Entries window is displayed.

2. **In the date field, enter the last date of the VAT return period.**

   Move the mouse to the date field and type the last date of the VAT return using the DD/MM/YYYY format.

3. **In the first Account line select the Fuel Scale Charges account and enter the VAT inclusive (gross) amount in the *debit* column.**

   Remember to enter the Gross amount (Net plus VAT) of the fuel scale charge.

4. **In the second Account line select the Fuel Scale Charges account again, and enter the Net amount in the *credit* column.**

   This results in an overall debit (meaning charge) to the Fuel Scale Charges account that's equal to the VAT amount you are paying. In our example the overall effect in the Fuel Scale Charges account is a £20 charge.

5. **In the third Account line select the VAT Liability account, enter the VAT due (according to the HMRC table) in the *credit* column, and select the Fuel Scale VAT Item.**

6. **(Optional) Add memos to each line of the journal to specify what each line does (refer to Figure 11-10).**

7. **Click Save & Close to record the journal.**

Now when you look at the VAT Detail Report, you'll see the fuel scale charge journal entry in Box 1 of the VAT Return. Job done.

Chapter 12

Payroll

. . . .

In This Chapter

▶ Registering your business as an employer

▶ Adding employees to your list

▶ Preparing your QuickBooks to do payroll

▶ Paying your employees

▶ Making payroll liabilities payments

▶ Filing the Employer Annual Return

. . . .

Payroll is one of the major headaches of running a small business. Fortunately, QuickBooks helps in a big way. In this chapter, we explain how.

Registering as an Employer

Even before you set up QuickBooks for payroll, you need a few other items if you want to do payroll the right way (if you want to do payroll the wrong way, you're reading the wrong book):

✔ Obtain an employer's PAYE (pay as you earn) reference number.

✔ Register with the PAYE Online Service.

If you are already signed up as an employer, you can skip this section.

Getting your Employer PAYE Reference number

To register as an employer with HMRC, you need to call the New Employer Helpline (0845 60 70 143) and provide details over the phone. Alternatively, you can e-mail a registration form. The form you need to e-mail depends on your circumstances. The URL for the online forms is `www.hmrc.gov.uk/paye/intro/register-email.htm`.

You can register as an employer up to four weeks before your first pay day.

About two weeks after you register as an employer, you will receive your documentation. With the paperwork in hand, you need to update QuickBooks. Go to Company➪Company Information; in the Payroll Information section, enter the Employer PAYE Reference Number and the Tax Office Name. Also double-check in the Report Information area that the tax year begins in April and change it to April if it does not.

Signing up for the PAYE Online Service

As an employer, you need to file certain PAYE forms online, such as the Employer Annual Return (forms P35 and P14) and in-year starter and leaver forms (P46 and P45). You can't file online unless you enrol with the HMRC PAYE Online Service. The current URL to register is `https://online.hmrc.gov.uk/registration?`

The process is simple, but it takes between 5 and 10 days to complete. That's because once you register you are mailed an Activation Code (which is valid for 28 days) and it takes some time for this to arrive. You use this code to activate the service the first time you log on.

By the way, if you already use the HMRC Online Services for another service (such as filing VAT) you don't need to register again. Just log on to the HMRC site and in the Services You Can Add section find PAYE for Employers, click the Enrol for Service link and follow the instructions. In this case too, you will be mailed an Activation Code to activate the service.

Once you have an active PAYE Online Service you can file your payroll tax forms directly from within QuickBooks. We describe how you do this later in this chapter.

It's important to check the PAYE Online Service periodically for tax coding notices and messages from HMRC. These are not downloaded to QuickBooks.

A Word about Tax Forms

If you are new to payroll, you'll be glad to hear that you don't have to fill out and file a million tax forms each time you hire or release an employee. In fact, there are only two forms you need to know about: the P45 and the P46. These forms are used to notify HMRC when someone is hired or released. When you take on a new employee, you file an electronic version of the P45 or P46 form with HMRC (which form you file depends on circumstances). And when an employee leaves, you file an electronic version of the P45 with HMRC.

So how does this work? Well, let's say you've just hired Alice. When you get to the tax form part of your discussion with her, you need to ask her one question: Does she have a P45 form from her previous employer? The P45 is a summary of her earnings and income taxes withheld by her previous employer. It also shows the tax code used by her previous employer to calculate her income tax deductions. If Alice has a P45 form, she needs to give it to you. The P45 form comes in four parts, and you'll receive parts 2 and 3 (part 1a is a copy for the employee and part 1 was sent to the tax office by her previous employer). You'll use the information in part 2 to fill out a form in QuickBooks and QuickBooks will file an electronic version of part 3 of the P45 with HMRC. Isn't that nice?

But what if Alice has no P45 form? Maybe this is her first job this tax year, or it's her second job and she is still also employed by someone else, or she simply can't find her P45. In that case you need to hand her a P46 form to complete and return to you. Once again, you will use the answers she provides on the P46 to fill out a QuickBooks form so that you know which tax code to use for her income tax deductions. QuickBooks will also file the electronic equivalent of the P46 with HMRC. Very helpful, don't you think?

You'll probably want to have some P46 forms on hand to give to new employees. You can download them from www.hmrc.gov.uk/forms/p46.pdf.

When you release an employee, QuickBooks will prepare a P45 form that summarises the person's earnings and income taxes deducted while in your employ. With a few mouse clicks, QuickBooks will file Part 1 online with the tax office and print parts 1a, 2 and 3 for you to give to the person leaving. See the section "Releasing Employees" later in this chapter for more details. QuickBooks really takes the pain out of the whole tax form reporting requirement.

Adding Employees to Your Employee List

Okay, it's time to add some employees in QuickBooks. Describing employees is pretty easy using the following steps.

1. **Enter the employee's basic information.**

   On the Home Page click the Payroll Centre icon and click the Employees tab (or simply click the Employees icon at the top of the screen), then click the New Employee button that appears in the upper-left corner to have QuickBooks display the New Employee window, shown in Figure 12-1.

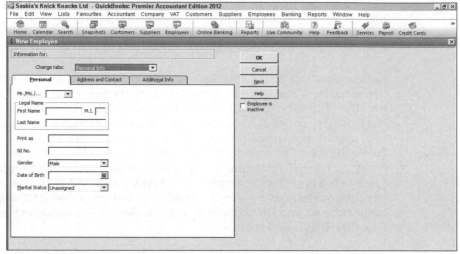

Figure 12-1:
The New
Employee
window.

The New Employee window is pretty straightforward. The first tab you
see is Personal Info. Just fill in the fields to describe the employee:

- The Personal subtab provides boxes for you to collect name,
  National Insurance (NI) number, date of birth (this is mandatory)
  and so on.

- The Address and Contact subtab stores just what it says it does.

- The Additional Info subtab enables you to create customisable
  fields in case you want to keep information that isn't covered by
  the QuickBooks' default fields – favourite colour, names of pets,
  and that type of thing.

To change to a new main tab, choose the new tab from the cleverly
named Change Tabs drop-down list.

2. Select the Payroll and Compensation Info tab.

You can use the Payroll Info subtab (see Figure 12-2) to describe
Earnings, such as yearly salary or hourly pay, Additions (tips, bonuses
and expenses reimbursements), Deductions (employee pension contributions and administrative fees), and Contributions (employer pension contributions). What you define here serves as a template for the
employee's payroll payment but you can change, add, or delete payroll
items when you create the payroll payment. If you don't see a payroll
item you need, it's easy to add your own (as described later in this
chapter). To tell QuickBooks to create payroll payments based on time
entries in QuickBooks, tick the related box.

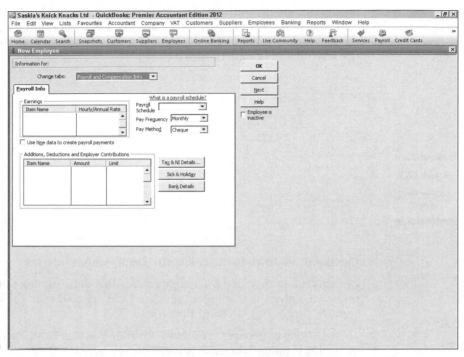

Figure 12-2:
The Payroll
Info subtab.

Choose a pay frequency for the employee in the Payroll Info subtab. Once you set up pay schedules (discussed in the "Schedule your payroll" section later in this chapter), QuickBooks will prompt you to assign employees automatically to the appropriate pay schedule. You'll be glad you've used pay schedules if you have a large number of employees.

3. Click the Tax & NI Details button.

The most important thing you do in the Payroll and Compensation Info tab is describe the employee tax and NI details. To do so, click the Tax & NI Details button, and in the Taxes pop-up window enter the relevant information (see Figure 12-3). See the "Getting Tax and NI Details Right" section for help in determining the correct tax and NI codes. Use the employee start date as the Effective From dates. Click OK and QuickBooks confirms that it will use these details for future payments.

Both the P45 and P46 have a Student Loan collections check box. Tick the corresponding box in the Taxes dialog if this is checked on the tax form.

If the employee is a company director tick the Is Director box in the Taxes dialog. QuickBooks then displays the Date Appointed field where you enter the date the director was appointed (which can be in the past). Select an NI contributions calculation method. The annual method means that the NI contributions allowance is taken upfront rather than spread evenly over the year. This can result in higher initial payroll payments. Click OK (and OK again to the QuickBooks message) to return to the Payroll and Compensation Info tab.

Figure 12-3:
The Taxes
window.

4. **Use the drop-down list to select the Employment Info tab.**

   Use this tab to describe the employment start date and tax form received. Enter the employee join date (and acknowledge the pop-up window by clicking OK) and then for

   - *Existing employees:* Tick the P45(3) or P46 Has Been Filed box – if this is indeed the case (otherwise see below).

   - *New employees:* Leave blank the P45(3) or P46 Has Been Filed box. Click the Enter P45/P46 Info button to display the P45/P46 Info form. Select the appropriate radio button and QuickBooks will display a screen version of the P45 part 2 or P46 form. Simply copy the information from the paper form into QuickBooks. Click OK to return to the Employee Info tab.

   After you finish describing an employee, click Next to save the employee details and add another employee, or click OK to add the employee to the Employee list and return to the Employee tab of the Payroll Centre.

   When you press Next or OK to save the employee details, QuickBooks may display the New Employee: Payroll Info (Other) dialog to prompt you to set up other details; if you are finished click the Leave As Is button. More pop-up messages will follow if you left the employee's join date, NI number, date of birth, or address blank. QuickBooks will display a separate pop-up window for each missing piece of information, asking you if you want to correct this before continuing. Click Yes to be returned to the tab where you can supply the missing information, or No to do so later. The exception to this is the join date, which must be entered for QuickBooks to save the employee details.

5. **Submit your new employee information to HMRC.**

   If you have just added a new employee, QuickBooks prompts you to submit your employee starter information to HMRC in the Employee

Reminder dialog window. Select Yes, Take Me to the Starter/Leaver Forms Centre. (You can always come back and do this later from Employees⇨ Payroll Forms⇨P45/P46 Starter/Leaver Forms.)

In the Starter/Leaver Forms Centre (see Figure 12-4) QuickBooks displays all the active employees in the left pane and highlights the employee whose forms you are about to submit. In the right pane, select the form you are filing (P45(3) For Starters or P46 For Starters) from the Select A Form drop-down list and keep an eye on the Status field that appears underneath.

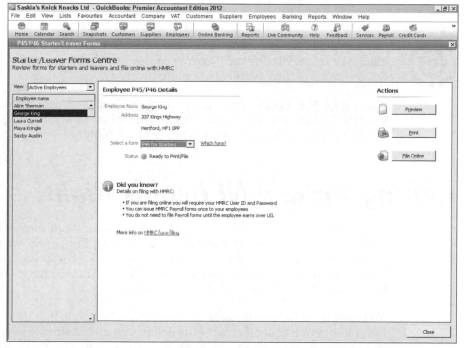

Figure 12-4:
The Starter/
Leaver
Forms
Centre
window.

If the status displays as Missing Information, click the link to supply the missing data. QuickBooks then displays the Payroll Forms Missing Information window, where you can review and fix the issues that are listed in the Type Of Issue column (left pane). For example, click the first issue in this column, and QuickBooks describes what you need to do to fix the problem in the right pane. Click the Fix The Issue button to supply the missing information, and then click OK to return to the Payroll Forms Missing Information window. When you have resolved all the problems listed in the Type of Issue column, QuickBooks displays this message in the right pane: "All issues for this employee have been fixed." Click the Close button to return to the P45/P46 Starter/Leaver Forms window.

If the Type of Issue in the Payroll Forms Missing Information window refers to the PAYE reference, add the missing information in the Company Information window as discussed in the "Getting your Employer PAYE Reference number" section.

When the Status field shows Ready to Print/File, click the File Online button and complete the Online Filing for P45/P46 Form (you'll need your login details for the HMRC PAYE Online Service). Click the File Online button at the bottom of the form to electronically send the form. You are connected to the Internet, right? QuickBooks goes online and communicates with the HMRC servers. A confirmation message appears once the form is filed successfully, and you will also be e-mailed a confirmation if you supplied an e-mail address when you signed up for the service.

You can double-check that you are using the correct tax code for the employee by previewing the P45 or P46 form you filed. Look at box 12 of the P45 or page 2 of the P46. Handy, wouldn't you say?

If you get a P6 tax code notice from HMRC (remember, these are delivered to your PAYE Online Service account), click the P6 button on the Employment Info tab of the employee's record and fill in the required fields.

Getting Tax and NI Details Right

You can find a lot of information on tax and NI codes, their meanings and how to apply them correctly on the HMRC website. But here's what you need to know for most situations. QuickBooks asks you for two pieces of information for each new employee: the tax code and the NI code. It uses these codes to calculate taxes due and NI contributions.

You need to know two things about tax codes. The first is that there are two tax codes most frequently used – the emergency and basic rate tax codes. The emergency tax code is a special code you can use until HMRC has sufficient information to send you the correct tax code for an employee. It is set each year by HMRC and is a number followed by the letter L. It indicates the tax free allowance for the year. For example, in the 2011–2012 tax year, the emergency tax code is 747L, which means that £7,475 is tax free. The basic tax rate, BR, deducts tax on earnings at the basic rate (20% in the 2011–2012 tax year). Note that while the numbers in the emergency code can change yearly (for example, it was 647L in 2009–2010), the letters BR always denote the basic rate, but the rate itself may change from year to year (for example, it was 22% in 2007–2008).

The other important thing to know about tax codes is that a tax code can be "cumulative" or "week 1/month 1". A cumulative tax code takes into account earnings and taxes paid from the beginning of the tax year to the current week (or month) to calculate tax due, whereas a week 1/month 1 tax code determines the tax due for each week (or month) individually.

Armed with this information, you can determine from Table 12-1 which tax code to use when an employee gives you a completed P46 form.

Table 12-1	Tax Codes to Match P46 Information	
Statement ticked	*Tax code to use*	*QuickBooks entry (for 2011–2012)*
Statement A	emergency cumulative	747L
Statement B	emergency month 1/week 1	747L X
Statement C	BR cumulative	BR
None	BR cumulative	BR

If your employee gives you a P45 (parts 2 and 3) and the leaving date in part 2, box 4 falls in the current tax year, simply take the tax code from part 2, box 6 and enter it into QuickBooks.

Now we have to tell you that, technically speaking, you can accept a P45 that's up to six tax years old. But in our opinion, if the P45 you receive is from a prior tax year, you and the employee are both better off going the P46 route. *You* are better off because you don't have another set of rules to remember. *The employee* is better off because his or her circumstances may have changed since the leaving date on the P45 and the questions asked on the P46 are more likely to capture present circumstances. So the chances are better that he or she will start off with a correct tax code.

Another thing you need to know is that HMRC expects you to check that the Total Tax in part 2, box 7 of the P45 is correct. Kind of crazy, right? Well, you can use the P45 checker on the free Employer CD-ROM provided by HMRC or you can search the Internet for a free P45 checker.

What about NI codes? Just use code A. For the three exceptions you are likely to encounter, QuickBooks will tell you if you got it wrong. In case you want to know, the exceptions are

- *Code C:* Employees over State pension age (depends on the year in which they were born).

- *Code D:* Employees who are members of a contracted-out salary related occupational pension scheme offered by the business. If you offer such a scheme you will have a registration certificate and an Employer Contracted Out Number. To tell QuickBooks that you are operating a contracted out scheme, enter your Employer Contracted Out Number in the Payroll Information area of the Company Information window, which you can access by clicking Company➪Company Information).

- *Code X:* Employees under the age of 16.

And this, in a nutshell, is all you need to know to handle most scenarios you will encounter.

Getting Ready to Do Payroll with QuickBooks

A quick word before we get started: we are making two assumptions. The first is that you already have a payroll subscription. You have a payroll subscription if you bought QuickBooks Pro + Payroll, QuickBooks Premier + Payroll or QuickBooks Premier Plus. If you did not buy one of these products and need to add a payroll subscription, call the friendly people at Intuit and they will put you on the monthly payment plan, which includes payroll.

The second assumption is that you have already made payments to your employees before your conversion date. If that's not the case, rejoice and skip the next section.

Getting year-to-date amounts

Before you can start making payroll payments in QuickBooks, for each employee you need to gather a summary of payments made (referred to as year-to-date or YTD figures) from the beginning of the tax year to your conversion date. The payroll tax year runs from 6 April to 5 April of the following year. For example, if your conversion date is 1 July, you need YTD figures for the period 6 April to the last payroll payment before, or on, 30 June. If the last payment you made to Saxby Austin was on 30 June, his YTD figures will show amounts from 6 April to 30 June. And if the last payment you made to Celine Huntsman was on 27 June, her YTD figures will show amounts from 6 April to 27 June.

If your conversion date is 1 July, your trial balance and opening figures are dated 30 June. For a refresher on this discussion see "The trial balance of the century" in Chapter 2.

The best place to get YTD information is from P11 working sheets. A P11 is specific to an employee. It simply lists each payroll payment and shows in detail the deductions made for income tax and national insurance. While you can obtain a lot of this information from historical payslips, the P11 displays extra information a payslip does not – things like the earnings thresholds for national insurance contributions. You will need this detail to correctly enter the YTD figures.

At a minimum there are eight figures that you need to know for each employee to set up YTD amounts:

✔ Gross pay

✔ Income tax withheld

✔ Employee NI contributions

✔ Employer NI contributions

✔ Details of four earnings thresholds as they apply to national insurance contributions

You can get the first four amounts from prior payslips, but you'll only find the last four figures on a P11.

In the unlikely event that you were using manual tax tables to calculate payroll payments (know that you are one in a million), you'll already have a P11 for each employee. A more likely scenario is that you used an external payroll service, in which case you can ask them for a printout of the P11s.

If you are the eager type who wants to skip all this YTD stuff and dive right in, here's a word of advice: don't. The YTD figures ensure that accurate year-to-date summaries appear on employee payslips, your payroll reports are correct and your end-of-year tax returns are accurate. Take the time to track down the P11 information and you won't be tearing your hair out when it's time to file your Employer Annual Return.

The good news is that the process of setting up payroll YTD figures – assuming that you have the information to hand and that you have only a handful of employees – shouldn't take much more than half an hour.

Stepping through the YTD wizard

It's easier to walk you through the YTD setup with an example in mind. Here's the scenario: your employee Saxby Austin is paid a monthly salary. Since the start of the payroll year on 6 April, he has received a total of £8,000 spread across three payments dated 30 April, 31 May, and 30 June. We'll use a QuickBooks conversion date of 1 July and the first payroll using QuickBooks will be on 31 July.

Figure 12-5 shows Saxby's P11 worksheet summary for income tax deductions. Each of the three payments is detailed in its own row. His gross pay of £8,000 is shown in column 3 and the total income tax withheld (£1,226) is shown in column 6.

Figure 12-6 shows Saxby's P11 worksheet summary for national insurance contributions, for the same three payments. Column 1f shows the total employee NI contributions (£743.28). To get the total employer NI contributions, subtract the total of column 1f from the total of column 1e. In our example that's £860.13.

Figure 12-5:
A sample P11 worksheet for income tax deductions.

Tax Period	Type	Pay in the period including statutory payments 2	Total pay to date 3	Total 'free pay' to date 4a	Total taxable pay to date 5	Total tax due to date 6	Total deducted or refunded in the period 7
1		2500.00	2500.00	623.26	1876.74	375.20	375.20
2		3000.00	5500.00	1246.52	4253.58	850.60	475.40
3		2500.00	8000.00	1869.78	6130.22	1226.00	375.40

We use the amounts in Figures 12-5 and 12-6 to walk you through the YTD wizard.

Before you launch the wizard you need to add all employees to whom you made payments between 6 April and your conversion date. After you have done this, follow these steps:

Figure 12-6:
A sample P11 worksheet for national insurance contributions.

Tax Period	Type	Earnings details				Contribution details	
		Earnings at the LEL (where earnings are equal to or exceed the LEL) 1a	Earnings above the LEL, up to and including the PT 1b	Earnings above the PT, up to and including the UAP 1c	Earnings above the UAP up to and including the UEL 1d	Total of employee's and employer's contributions 1e	Employee's contributions due on all earnings above the PT 1f
1		442	160.00	1898.00	0.00	491.47	227.76
2		442	160.00	2398.00	0.00	620.47	287.76
3		442	160.00	1898.00	0.00	491.47	227.76
Total		1326	480.00	6194.00	0.00	1603.41	743.28

1. **Choose Employees➪Payroll Setup➪Set Up YTD Amounts.**

   This launches the Set Up YTD Amounts wizard. Click Next.

2. **Type in your trial balance date.**

   In the When Should YTD Summaries Affect Accounts? window you are asked two questions. For both questions the date you need to enter is your trial balance date (in our example, that's 30 June). Click Next.

3. **Enter the date of your first payroll using QuickBooks.**

   Next you see the Earliest QuickBooks payroll date window. Here you enter the date you will be making your first payroll payments using QuickBooks. In our example, the date is 31 July. Click Next.

4. **Enter Employee Summary Information.**

   The Employee Summary Information window displays, listing your employees. Highlight the name of the first employee and click the Enter Summary button.

5. **Fill out the YTD adjustment form.**

   The YTD adjustment form displays. Figure 12-7 shows how we used the amounts from the P11 samples (refer to Figures 12-5 and 12-6) to complete a YTD adjustment form.

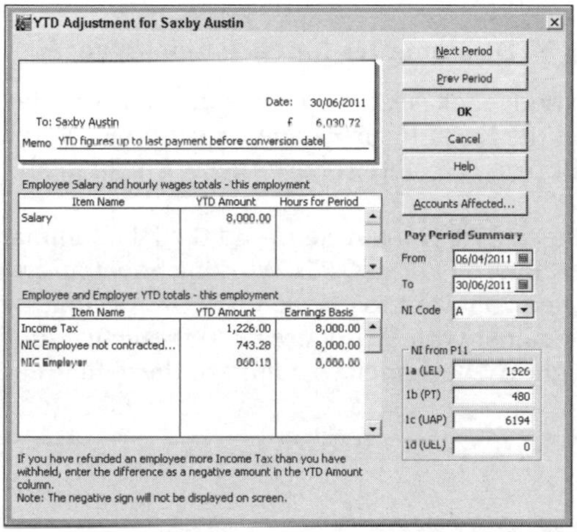

Figure 12-7: An example of a YTD adjustment.

Starting at the top, we added a handy memo in the Memo field. (*Note:* QuickBooks populates the Date with the date you enter in the Pay Period Summary area To field, and calculates the total amount based on the figures you enter in the middle and bottom white boxes.)

In the middle white box, we show his gross salary of £8,000.

In the bottom white box, we show the three taxes: income tax (£1,226); employee NI contribution (£743.28) and employer NI contribution (£860.13). The Earnings Basis is simply the gross salary. This may not always be the case, however. If there are payments made not subject to income tax or NI contributions (such as employee pension contributions), the earnings base would differ from the gross pay.

In QuickBooks the employee NI contribution is called NIC Employee Not Contracted-Out if you don't operate a contracted out occupational pension scheme, and NIC Employee Contracted-Out if you do.

The dates in the Pay Period Summary should be the start of the tax year to the last payment date prior to conversion. The NI code is "A" for most people (but see the discussion on this earlier in the chapter).

The amounts at the bottom right of the YTD adjustment form are taken from columns 1a–1d in the P11 worksheet (see Figure 12-6).

6. **Click the Accounts Affected button.**

   Select the radio button for Do Not Affect Accounts and click OK. It's very important that you do this. This choice means that the YTD adjustment will affect YTD figures on employee payslips, payroll liability reports, and Employer Annual return figures, but it will not change the figures on the trial balance you worked so hard to get right earlier, which is a very good thing! Once you have double-checked your entries and are satisfied they are correct, click the OK button to return to the Employee summary information window.

7. **Continue entering YTD summaries for each employee.**

   When you are finished, click Next. You can safely ignore the Create Payment button on the Enter Prior Payments window – you'll be using the normal QuickBooks payroll to record these. Click Finish.

If you want to double-check that you have entered the P11 summaries correctly, go to Employees➪Payroll Forms➪P11 Working Sheet and select the name of the first employee you want to check. Click OK. Compare the NIC Details form that loads against your P11 figures and then click the PAYE Details link at the top right of the screen to compare these figures. If all is well, congratulate yourself.

Housekeeping entry

When you add the employee YTD figures, QuickBooks thinks that all the payroll taxes withheld in the period covering 6 April and your conversion date still need to be paid to HMRC. You now need to make an adjustment to let QuickBooks know that this is not the case. You can get the figures for the adjustment by tallying up all the payroll liability payments you made to HMRC prior to your QuickBooks conversion date. Then follow these steps:

1. **Select Employees➪Payroll Taxes and Liabilities➪Adjust Payroll Liabilities.**

   The Liability Adjustment window displays. Enter your trial balance date in both the date and effective date fields. Leave the Company radio button selected and click in the first row under Item name. Using the drop-down box that appears, select the first payroll tax you need to adjust – income tax for example (see Figure 12-8). Continue entering adjustments as required. When you are finished, click the OK button.

2. **Click the Accounts Affected button.**

   Select the radio button for Do Not Affect Accounts and click OK. Once again, it's very important that you do this. Click the OK button to return to the Liability Adjustment window. Click OK to record your adjustment.

Double-check your work

Finally, you need to check that on the conversion date the payroll liabilities on the trial balance match the payroll liabilities on the P32 report. Huh? Okay, here's the deal. When you prepared your conversion date trial balance, you or your accountant entered an amount for the payroll liabilities owed. This was an accounting entry. In this chapter, you added payroll YTD figures and made a YTD adjustment; in both cases, you selected the option Do Not Affect Accounts. As a result, the YTD figures are sitting in a purely tax reporting side of QuickBooks and can be viewed via the Payroll Liabilities (P32) report. If the YTD figures are entered correctly, the payroll liability amounts on the trial balance will match those on the P32 report, at the conversion date.

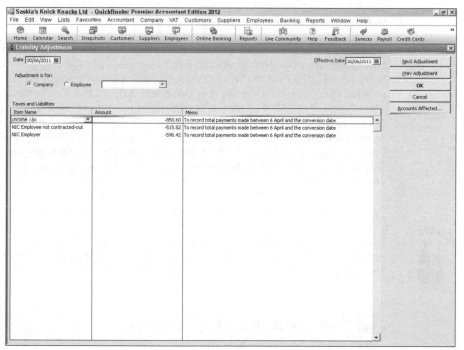

Figure 12-8:
Adjusting
payroll
liabilities.

To view the trial balance, select Reports⇨Accountant & Taxes⇨Trial Balance. Enter the correct trial balance date (one day prior to your conversion date). Find the Payroll Liabilities amount and make a note of it.

Now run the P32 Payroll Liabilities report by selecting Reports⇨Employees & Payroll⇨Payroll Liabilities (P32). This report shows what taxes QuickBooks thinks you need to remit to HMRC, based on the YTD summaries and YTD adjustment you made earlier in this chapter.

If you have followed our directions carefully, the two figures will match. If that's the case, buy yourself a beer. Or two.

Schedule your payroll

QuickBooks uses payroll schedules to group employees who are paid with the same pay frequency, for example monthly or weekly.

To do this, choose Employees⇨Payroll Setup⇨Add or Edit Payroll Schedules. When QuickBooks displays the Payroll Schedule List window, click the Payroll Schedule button and then click New. Describe the payroll you're scheduling. For example, if you're setting up a weekly payroll, name the payroll something like *Friday payroll*. Next, choose the appropriate frequency (weekly, fortnightly, four weekly, or monthly).

Add the end date of this pay cycle and the date of the first payment. These two dates are not necessarily the same: for example the pay period might run from Monday to Friday (Friday being the pay period end date) but employees receive their pay on Monday (the payment date). Click OK to save this schedule. If you entered a pay frequency in the employee record (described earlier in this chapter), QuickBooks displays the Assign Payroll Schedule dialog and asks you if you want to assign the payroll schedule to all employees with a matching pay frequency. Make your selection. (If you click No, QuickBooks displays the second Assign Payroll Schedule window, giving you a chance to change your mind.)

Repeat this process to set up additional payroll schedules if needed.

After you set up payroll schedules you can assign a schedule to new employees in the Payroll and Compensation Info tab of the employee record by selecting a schedule in the Payroll Schedule field.

Add or edit payroll items

QuickBooks uses different types of *payroll items* to track individual amounts on payroll payments and to calculate the year-to-date earnings and taxes for each employee. Out of the box QuickBooks comes with many common payroll items, though you may want to edit these or add your own.

You can view the Payroll Item list by clicking Home⇨Payroll Centre and selecting the Payroll Items link. QuickBooks organises payroll items in the list by type, such as salary, hourly pay, or payroll tax type.

It's easy to edit a payroll item: double-click the name of the payroll item you want to change, and QuickBooks launches the Edit Payroll Item wizard. You use the Next and Back buttons to navigate through the screens. Make your changes and click Finish to save your work and return to the Payroll Item list.

It's also straightforward to add a new payroll item. In the Payroll Item list, click the Payroll Item button and select New. QuickBooks displays the Add New Payroll Item wizard. First select the type of payroll item you want to add, and then step through the remaining screens of the wizard (which vary depending on type). Click Finish to add the new item and return to the Payroll Item list.

Paying Your Employees

After you set up your payroll schedule, you're ready to pay someone. This section is going to blow your mind, especially if you've been doing payroll manually. The process makes your decision to use QuickBooks to do your payroll worthwhile. Here's how:

1. **Start the payroll process by choosing Employees⇨Pay Employees⇨ Scheduled Payroll.**

   QuickBooks displays the Employee Centre: Payroll Centre window (see Figure 12-9). The Payroll Centre window identifies any payroll schedules you set up. Select the scheduled payroll you want to, well, do. Then click the Scheduled Payroll button. QuickBooks displays the Enter Payroll Information window (see Figure 12-10), which lists the employees who participate in the scheduled payroll. Initially, all the listed employees have a check mark beside their name, but you can click to remove a check mark and to remove an employee from the scheduled payroll.

2. **Create the payments.**

   Cast your eye over the top part of the screen to check that the three fields (Pay Period Ends, Payment Date, and Bank Account) show the expected information. If they don't, change as required. When the Enter Payroll Information window correctly lists which employees should be paid, click Continue. QuickBooks calculates employee gross wages, deductions, and net wages; the calculations appear in the Review and Create Payroll Payments window (not shown).

3. **(Optional) Review a payroll payment.**

   For most employees, this is an optional step. If the employee is a company director, there is a stop sign next to the name and you must review the first payment you make to verify that the desired NI contribution calculations method (annual or monthly) is used.

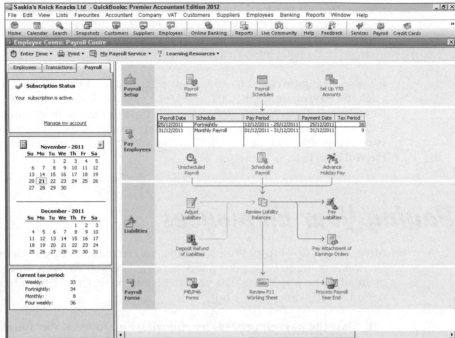

Figure 12-9:
The
Employee
Centre:
Payroll
Centre
window.

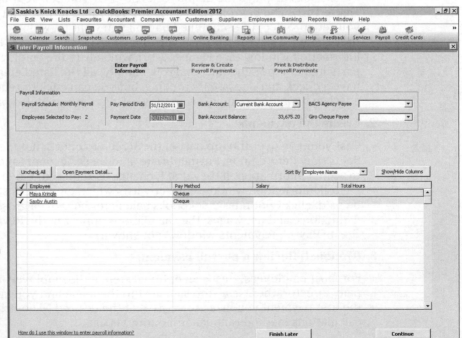

Figure 12-10:
The Enter
Payroll
Information
window.

You can preview any employee's payroll data by clicking his or her name in the Enter Payroll Information window or the Review and Create Payroll Payments window. When you click an employee's name, QuickBooks displays the Review Or Change Payroll Payment window for the employee (see Figure 12-11 for an example).

The main thing to pay attention to in this window is the Earnings text box. It shows what QuickBooks assumes you'll pay an employee based on the payroll items that you assigned when you set up the employee. For hourly paid employees, you fill in the number of hours the person worked and apply these hours to a customer or job, if necessary. If you opted to use time data for payroll payments (discussed earlier in this chapter), QuickBooks automatically populates the hours worked from time records you enter (see Chapter 16).

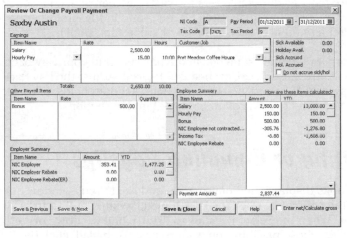

Figure 12-11:
The Review Or Change Payroll Payment window.

The Preview window also includes an Other Payroll Items input area which auto-populates with payroll items you defined when you set up the employee.

If information is inaccurate in the Earnings or Other Payroll Items areas, correct it by changing a rate or amount and deleting or adding a payroll item, as appropriate.

If you know the net rather than the gross payment amount, tick the box next to Enter Net/Calculate Gross. QuickBooks highlights the Payment Amount figure (above the tick box). Type the net figure in the highlighted area and press Tab for QuickBooks to calculate the gross amount and all the taxes. How cool is that?

QuickBooks calculates the employer taxes, the employee taxes and the amount of the net payment; this information appears in the Employee Summary area and the Employer Summary area of the Review or Change Payroll Payment window.

You might also note that QuickBooks keeps totals for both the current payment and the year to date.

4. **Print or assign cheque numbers to written cheques.**

   Before you finalise the pay cheques, you need to let QuickBooks know whether you are printing the cheques or handwriting them. Select the appropriate radio button (Print Pay Cheques from QuickBooks or Assign Cheque Numbers to Handwritten Cheques). If you direct QuickBooks to print the cheques, you print them in the same way that you print other, cheques, not for payroll. (Have a question about printing cheques? See Appendix D.) If you want to handwrite payroll cheques, give QuickBooks the first cheque number so it knows how to number the cheques that it records in your bank register. To generate the payments, click the Create Payments button.

If you are paying your employees by electronic banking, choose Assign Cheque Numbers to Handwritten Cheques and in the First Cheque Number field enter a reference, such as **BACS** or something similar.

If you forget to include someone in the pay run, find your way back to the Payroll Centre and select Unscheduled Payroll. Adjust the Pay Period Ends date, Payment Date and, if necessary, Bank Account fields and select the people you need to pay. Follow Steps 2–4 in this section.

Printing or E-mailing Payslips

QuickBooks displays the Confirmation and Next Steps window once you create the payments. Click the Print/Email Payslips button to print or e-mail payslips. When the Select Payslips to Print/Email window correctly lists the employees whose payslips you want to print or e-mail, click the Print or the Email button.

If you select Print, adjust the print settings, select the paper type (payslip forms or blank paper) and the payslip style (preview is a good idea to make sure you are choosing the desired layout) and click Print.

If you select Email, QuickBooks explains how payslip password protection works and warns you about e-mail security (click OK each time). In the Select Forms to Send window, you can edit the body of the e-mail before you click the Send Now button.

Note: you need to configure QuickBooks to use e-mail by going to Edit⇨ Preferences⇨Send Forms. On the My Preferences tab, configure a default mail client. Consult the QuickBooks help for more information.

Fixing payroll mistakes

In QuickBooks it's easy to fix a mistake after you run the payroll as long as it's the *last* payroll payment made to an employee. How you fix a mistake in the last payroll payment depends on the circumstances.

If you have not given the cheque to the employee or released the electronic bank payment, you can just edit the payment. To do so, select the employee in the Employee List (by clicking the Employees icon in the top row of icons and highlighting the employee name in the left pane). QuickBooks displays the employee's details in the top-right pane and a list of transactions for the employee in the bottom-right pane. Find the last payroll payment in the list of transactions and double-click on it to open it. QuickBooks displays the Payroll Payment window, which looks like a cheque. Click the Payment Details button to view the Review Payroll Payment window, where you make your changes. When you are finished, click OK to save your changes and return to the Payroll Payment window, and then click OK in this window to save your work and exit.

If you gave the cheque to the employee but you can get it back, you void the payment with the mistake (so that you have a record of the cheque number) and create a new payment with the correct details. To void the payment, find and open the last payroll payment, then click Edit➪Void Payroll Payment. Use an Unscheduled Payroll (described elsewhere in this chapter) to redo the payroll payment, and then print or write the new cheque.

If the employee paid the cheque into the bank or you already made the electronic bank payment, don't worry, all is not lost. If you overpaid the employee ask them to pay you back; if you underpaid the employee correct this on the next payroll payment.

While it's possible to edit a historical payment, you should only do this if you really know what you're doing because it can cause untold problems, including messing up your bank reconciliation and potentially affecting your payroll liability figures. Our best advice (and believe us when we say we're looking out for your best interests) is to seek the advice of your accountant or a QuickBooks Professional Advisor before you do this. To edit a historical payment, delete all subsequent payments, make your correction, and then re-enter each payment.

Releasing Employees

Releasing employees in QuickBooks is a breeze. You need to do three things.

1. **Let QuickBooks know the employee's leaving date.**

   That way when you process payroll in the future, you can't accidentally pay the former employee. After you have generated the final payroll payment, find the employee's record in the Employee Centre and in the Leaving Date field on the Employment Info tab enter the date of the last payroll payment. That's right: Use the date of the last payroll payment and not the actual date the person finished working for you. Click OK to save your changes.

2. **File the leaver form online with HMRC.**

   You do this in the Starter/Leaver Forms Centre; QuickBooks will offer to take you there when you exit the employee record. In the Starter/Leaver Forms Centre, select P45 for Leavers and continue the filing process as described earlier in this chapter.

3. **Print a copy of the P45 to give to your former employee.**

You can inactivate an employee from your Employee list if the list starts to get cluttered with names of employees who no longer work for you. (In Chapter 3 we describe how to inactivate names in lists.)

Paying Payroll Liabilities

Make no mistake: HMRC wants the income taxes, NI contributions, and student loan deductions that you withhold from an employee's pay. HMRC also wants the NI employer contributions you owe. So every month or quarter, you need to pay HMRC the amounts that you owe. You can opt to pay quarterly if your payroll liabilities are £1,500 a month or less by calling HMRC.

The tax month ends on the fifth day and payment needs to be received by HMRC by the 19th, or by the 22nd if paying electronically.

Determining the liability

QuickBooks makes it very easy to figure out how much you need to pay each month or quarter. It takes exactly three mouse clicks: Select Employees⇨ Payroll Taxes and Liabilities⇨Payroll Liabilities (P32). The report columns default to months, but you can change them to show quarters if necessary. To change from month to quarter use the drop-down arrow in the Columns field and select Quarter.

It's a good idea to print the P32 report each month for your records.

If you edit or delete an existing payroll payment or add a new payment after you pay your liabilities for a month or quarter, your payroll liabilities may change and you may have underpaid or overpaid. The best way to see if this is the case is to use the Payroll Liabilities Balances report. Go to Employees➪ Payroll Taxes and Liabilities➪Payroll Liabilities Balances. Change the Columns field to Total Only and adjust the From and To dates to the desired period. The report keeps track of liabilities incurred in the period and payments that relate to the period, even if the payment is made after the ending date of the report.

Paying the liability

Okay, so now you're ready to pay the payroll liabilities. Choose Employees➪ Payroll Taxes and Liabilities➪Pay Payroll Liabilities. A pop-up window prompts you to enter the date range for the liabilities.

Note: you cannot change the From date. It defaults to the beginning of the payroll tax year.

Enter the Through date with care because it tells QuickBooks to which period to assign the payment and it affects the Payroll Liabilities Balances report we mentioned earlier. Click OK.

When QuickBooks displays the Pay Liabilities window, choose the payroll items you want to pay, adjust the Bank Account and payment date, if necessary, and then click the Create button. QuickBooks creates the cheque and displays it for your review.

QuickBooks does not actually pay HMRC – but you already knew that. If paying by cheque, send in your cheque along with the P32 payment slip in your Liabilities Payment book (which you receive every year from HMRC). You can also pay online either from your bank account or through the HMRC website. By the way, if you pay online you need your Accounts Office Reference we mentioned earlier.

Do not use the Write Cheque window in QuickBooks to record your payroll liability payment. It creates a mess.

Receiving a refund

There may be instances (rare, but possible) when you are due a payroll liabilities refund. You record this deposit by clicking Employees➪Payroll Taxes and Liabilities➪Deposit Refund of Liabilities. Yep, you guessed it, do not use the Make Deposit window for this – it creates a mess.

Filing the Employer Annual Return

By 19 May following the close of the tax year on 5 April, you need to file online a bunch of forms collectively known as the Employer Annual Return. The return includes an annual summary of earnings, income tax, and employee and employer NI contributions for each employee who worked for you during the tax year. This summary is the P14 form. Then there is also the P35 form. The P35 summarises the information on the P14s, shows the total amount paid to HMRC and whether there is anything left to pay or due as a refund, and includes an employer's declaration.

Sound complicated? Well, we remember the days when this had to be done by hand. You can imagine how much fun it was to handwrite over 100 of these P14s and then summarise them on the P35, right? With that in mind, QuickBooks makes this process a pleasure. Okay, maybe that's overstating it, but QuickBooks certainly makes it painless with the Payroll Year End Wizard.

Using the Payroll Year End Wizard

To launch the wizard select Employees⇨Payroll Forms⇨Process Payroll Year End. All the employees who worked for you during the year, whether or not they are still with you, are listed in the Payroll Year End Process window (see Figure 12-12). To complete and file the annual return you simply work your way through the buttons on the right-hand side of the screen. The process involves the following steps: review each person's P14, print each P14, review the data on the P35, fill out the P35 checklist and declaration, print the P35 for your records, and then file the darn thing.

We won't bore you with a blow-by-blow of each mouse click; we know you can work your way through the wizard on your own. When you have worked your way through all the steps, the Test File Online and File Online buttons become active. QuickBooks wisely prevents you from accidentally sending the return until you have completed all the necessary steps.

When you review each P14, check for silly things such as gender being correct, addresses being complete, and so on. QuickBooks offers a lot of help with this when you add employees (see the "Adding Employees to Your Employee List" section), but it's a piece of software and sometimes only a human being can spot certain things that don't look right.

You only have one chance to file the return within QuickBooks. It's a good idea to make a backup of the file (described in Chapter 17) just in case you need to try again.

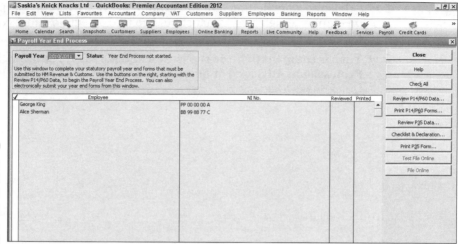

Figure 12-12:
The Payroll
Year End
Process
window.

Printing P60 forms

Another tax form? You got it. The P60 form is essentially the P14 form by another name. In case you have been wondering, that's why the buttons for reviewing and printing P14 forms in the Payroll Year End Process window say "P14/P60". You give a P60 form by 31 May to each person still employed with you at the close of the tax year.

HMRC publishes a handy guide to help you keep all the end-of-year filing deadlines straight. You can find it here: www.hmrc.gov.uk/paye/payroll/year-end/checklist.htm#1.

Getting Help with Payroll

While QuickBooks makes it easy to run your payroll, the legislation surrounding payroll can be terribly complex. Do yourself a favour and seek help when you get stuck. If you are like most people, you are busy running or working in a business and are not an expert in tax or employment law. So don't hesitate to ask for help. Places you can go include:

- ✔ **HMRC New Employer's Helpline:** For questions related to taxes (income tax deduction, NI contributions and tax treatment of benefits, pensions, and so on). (See www.hmrc.gov.uk/paye/index.htm.)

✔ **Advisory, Conciliation and Arbitration Service (ACAS):** For questions on employee rights and what should go into an employment contract. (See www.acas.org.uk.)

✔ **Your accountant (if he or she is QuickBooks savvy) or a QuickBooks Professional Advisor:** For questions on how to do something in QuickBooks. (See http://proadvisors.quickbooks.co.uk.)

Chapter 13

Building the Perfect Budget

In This Chapter

▶ Checking out powerful tips for business budgets

▶ Setting up and adjusting a budget

▶ Forecasting your profits and losses

▶ Projecting your cash flows

*W*e don't think that a budget amounts to financial handcuffs, and neither should you. After all, a *budget* is just a plan that outlines how you intend to generate sales, how you should spend your money and how you can best organise your firm's financial affairs.

Is This a Game You Want to Play?

If you created a good, workable chart of accounts (discussed in Chapter 3), you're halfway to a good, solid budget. (In fact, for 99 out of 100 businesses, the only step left is to specify how much you earn in each income account and how much you spend in each expense account.)

Does every business need a budget? No, of course not. Maybe you have a simple financial plan that you can monitor some other way. Maybe in your business, you make money so effortlessly that you don't need to plan your income and outgoings. Maybe Elvis Presley really is still alive and living somewhere in Alaska.

For everyone else, though, a budget improves your chances of getting your business wherever you want it to go financially. It gives you a way to "plan your work and work your plan". In fact, we'll stop calling it a "budget" because that word has such negative connotations. How about we call it *The Secret Plan?*

All Joking Aside: Some Basic Budgeting Tips

Before we walk you through the mechanics of outlining your Secret Plan, we want to give you a few tips. After that, we want to tell you a secret, a very special secret.

Here are five ways to increase the chances that your Secret Plan works:

- **Plan your income and expenses as a team, if that's possible.** For this sort of planning, two heads are invariably better than one. What's more, although we don't really want to get into marriage counselling or partnership counselling here, the budget of a business – oops, its Secret Plan – needs to reflect the priorities and feelings of everyone who has to live within the plan: partners, partners' spouses, key employees, and so on. So don't use a Secret Plan as a way to minimise what your partner spends on marketing or on telephone charges talking to pseudo-customers and relatives abroad. You need to resolve such issues before you finalise your Secret Plan.

- **Include some cushion in your plan.** In other words, don't budget to spend every last pound. If you plan from the start to spend every pound you make, you'll undoubtedly have to fight the mother of all financial battles – paying for unexpected expenses when you don't have any money. (You know the sort of things we mean: repair costs when the delivery truck breaks down; a new piece of essential equipment; an unexpected rise in the cost of materials; and so on.)

- **Regularly compare your actual income and expenses with your planned income and expenses.** This comparison is probably the most important part of budgeting and it's what QuickBooks can help you with the most. As long as you use QuickBooks to record what you receive and spend and to describe your budget, you can print reports that show what you planned and what actually occurred.

  If you find that you've budgeted £1000 per month for shipping costs, but you discover that you consistently spend twice that amount, you may need to shift some money from your monthly slush fund . . . unless you *like* coming in over budget on shipping charges.

- **Make adjustments as necessary.** When you encounter problems with your Secret Plan – and you will – you'll know that part of your plan isn't working. Then you can make adjustments (by spending a little less on calling relatives, for example).

> ✔ **A word to the wise: Don't gear up your business overhead or your personal living and lifestyle when you have a great year (or even a few great years) in the business.** When you have a good year or even a few good years, keep your overhead and expenses modest. Stash the extra cash. If you can, build up some financial wealth that's independent and apart from your business assets. For example, contribute to a pension plan.

A Budgeting Secret You Won't Learn at University

We also have a secret tip for you. (We're going to write very quietly now so that no one else hears. . . .)

Here's the secret tip: search on the Internet or go to the library and ask for references of business financial statistics. After you get these references, find a nice, quiet corner of the library and look up how other businesses like yours (that is, businesses that are the same size, sell the same stuff or services, and have the same gross and net profits) spend money. These references are really cool. You can look up, for example, what percentage of sales the average pub spends on beer and peanuts.

Plan to spend an hour or so at the library. Getting used to the way that these reports display information takes a while. The pubs page doesn't actually have a line for beer and peanuts, for example. Instead, you see some vague accounting term like *cost of goods sold.*

Make a few notes so that you can use the information you glean to better plan your own business financial affairs. If you spend about the same amount on beer and peanuts every year as the average pub, you're in good shape – well, unless you own a shoe store.

The point is that you can and should use this information to get a better handle on what businesses like yours earn and spend.

A final, tangential point: Have you ever heard businesspeople talk about *benchmarking?* The idea is that to compete in a market, you need to do at least as well as your competitors or similar firms in other markets. And one way to assess how you're doing compared with competitors is to compare financial ratios or benchmarks. For example, if you compare what you spend as a percentage of sales on advertising with what similar firms spend, you can often glean real insights into what you should do to improve your business. You'll discover, for example, where you're spending too much and where you're spending too little. You'll also sometimes see competitive advantages that you possess of which you were not aware earlier.

Setting Up a Secret Plan

Okay, enough background stuff. The time has come to set up your budget – er, your Secret Plan – in QuickBooks. Follow these steps:

1. **Choose Company➪Planning & Budgeting➪Set Up Budgets.**

   If you haven't yet set up a budget, QuickBooks displays the Create New Budget window, as shown in Figure 13-1. If you have already set up a budget, another window appears and you need to click the Create New Budget button to get to this window.

Figure 13-1:
The Create
New Budget
window.

2. **Select the year for which you want to budget.**

   Use the date field to specify the financial year. You use the arrows at the end of the field to adjust the year number incrementally.

3. **Select the type of budget that you want to create.**

   See those two option buttons on the Create New Budget window? They let you tell QuickBooks whether you want to create a budget of income and expense amounts (done with a *pro forma* profit and loss statement) or a budget of year-end asset, liability and owner's equity account balances (done with a *pro forma* balance sheet). Typically, you want to budget income and expense amounts.

   After you indicate the year for which you want to budget and whether you want to budget income statement amounts or balance sheet amounts, click Next.

4. **Provide any additional budgeting criteria and instructions.**

   QuickBooks asks next whether you want to budget using additional criteria, such as Customer:Job information or class information. (You only see the class option if you turned on Class tracking, as described in Chapter 3.) You answer this question by selecting the option button that corresponds to the budgeting criteria you want and then clicking Next. (If you're just starting out, don't worry about specifying additional criteria. Keep things simple.)

5. **Indicate whether you want to start from scratch and then click Next.**

   QuickBooks asks whether you want it to create a first cut at your budget by using last year's numbers or whether you just want to start from scratch. To answer this question, select the option button that corresponds to your choice. For example, to budget from scratch, select the Create Budget from Scratch radio button.

   QuickBooks displays the Set Up Budgets window (see Figure 13-2).

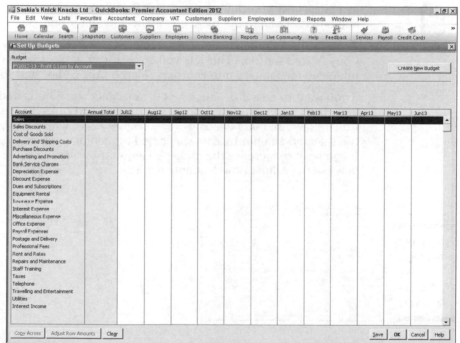

Figure 13-2: The Set Up Budgets window.

6. **Do your budget.**

   You use the Set Up Budgets window to identify the budgeted amounts that you plan for each account. Just click the monthly amount you want to budget and enter a value. If you say that you want to budget from scratch, by the way, QuickBooks shows a window with a bunch of empty columns (like the window in Figure 13-2). If you say that you want to base the coming year's budget on last year's real numbers, you see numbers in the columns.

If your Set Up Budgets window is too big for the monitor, QuickBooks shows only a few months of budgeted data at a time. Click the Show Next 6 Months button to move to the next part of the budget year. To move back to the first part of the year, click the Show Prev 6 Months button. (Only one of these Show buttons appears at a time.)

The Budget drop-down list at the top-left corner of the Set Up Budgets window lets you select the budget you want to work with. Why? You can work with several different versions of your budget (for example, a company-wide budget, or per customer, or by class). (To create a new budget, click the Create New Budget button, which steps you through the process described previously.)

For each financial year you can save only one of each type of budget. So in a given year you can have only one Profit and Loss by Account budget and one Profit and Loss by Account and Customer budget.

To copy the amount shown in the selected box across the row, click the Copy Across button. (This lets you copy, for example, the amount you budgeted for January into February, March, April, May, and so on.)

If you want to be a little fancier, you can select some budgeted amount and click the Adjust Row Amounts button. QuickBooks displays the Adjust Row Amounts dialog box (see Figure 13-3), which lets you adjust the selected amount by some specified percentage increase or decrease. If you want to increase the budgeted amount by, say, 25% per month, you use the Adjust Row Amounts window.

Figure 13-3: The Adjust Row Amounts dialog box.

7. Save your budgeting work.

After you enter your Secret Plan, click Save to save your work and leave the Set Up Budgets window open. Or click OK to save your work but close the Set Up Budgets window.

We should mention, too, that you can just click Cancel if you don't want to save your work (in case you've just been messing around).

To delete a budget, load the budget you want to delete and then press Edit➪Delete Budget.

Adjusting a Secret Plan

To later make additional changes to a budget, choose Company⇨Planning & Budgeting⇨Set Up Budgets. QuickBooks displays the Set Up Budgets window. Select the budget that you want to work with from the Budget drop-down list and then make your changes. All the same tools that you had for initially setting up your forecast (which we described in the preceding section) are available for editing your budget.

Forecasting Profits and Losses

If you're using the Premier flavour of QuickBooks you can also prepare a forecast of a year's profits (or losses). QuickBooks does this by calculating what your profit and loss statement will look like either based on the previous year's income and expenses or based on using actual numbers that you enter very similar to how you budget. (See the previous section's description of how to create a budget.)

To tell QuickBooks to forecast profits and losses, choose Company⇨Planning & Budgeting⇨Set Up Forecast. Then, when QuickBooks starts its clever little wizard, you follow the onscreen instructions. If you have questions, you can refer to the chapter's earlier discussion of setting up a budget.

Just a thought: you may want to use your budget to plan conservatively, and your forecast for an optimistic scenario.

Projecting Cash Flows

If you tell it to, QuickBooks attempts to project your business's cash flows for the next six weeks based on data such as due dates in accounts receivables and accounts payables. To tell QuickBooks to do this, choose Company⇨Planning & Budgeting⇨Cash Flow Projector, and then follow the onscreen instructions. (This cash flow projector essentially automates the same process that you'd step through on a scratch pad or the back of an envelope.)

Part IV
Housekeeping Chores

"You know kids – you can't buy them just <u>any</u> accounting software."

In this part . . .

We hope this doesn't surprise you, but your accounting system requires a bit of tender loving care. But don't worry, nothing unexpected. . . . You will want to know how to reconcile accounts (to keep your books squeaky clean), work with reports, handle job costing, and keep your files dust-free.

Chapter 14

The Balancing Act

*W*e want to start this chapter with an important point: balancing a bank account in QuickBooks is easy. No, we are not just trying to get you pumped up about an otherwise painfully boring topic. We don't think that balancing a bank account is any more exciting than you do.

Our point is simply this: because bank account balancing can be tedious and boring, use QuickBooks to reduce the drudgery.

Balancing a Bank Account

As we just mentioned, balancing a bank account is quite easy in QuickBooks. In fact, we'll go so far as to say that if you have any problems, they stem from . . . well, sloppy record-keeping that preceded your use of QuickBooks.

We get started by describing how you reconcile an account.

Giving QuickBooks information from the bank statement

In a *reconciliation,* as you probably know, you compare your records of a bank account with the bank's records of the same account. You should be able to explain any difference between the two accounts – usually by pointing to cheques you wrote which haven't yet cleared. (Sometimes deposits fall into the same category; you record a deposit, but the bank hasn't yet credited your account.)

The first step, then, is to supply QuickBooks with the bank's account information. You get this information from your monthly statement. Supply QuickBooks the figures it needs, as follows:

1. **Choose Banking⇨Reconcile or click the Reconcile icon on the Home screen.**

   QuickBooks displays the Begin Reconciliation dialog box, as shown in Figure 14-1.

Begin Reconciliation

Select an account to reconcile, and then enter the ending balance from your account statement.

| Account | Current Bank Account | last reconciled on 31/07/2011. |

Statement Date 31/08/2011

Beginning Balance 38,102.96   What if my beginning balance doesn't match my statement?

Ending Balance

Enter any service charge or interest earned.

| Service Charge | Date | Account |
| 0.00 | 31/12/2011 | |

| Interest Earned | Date | Account |
| 0.00 | 31/12/2011 | |

Locate Discrepancies   Undo Last Reconciliation   **Continue**   Cancel   Help

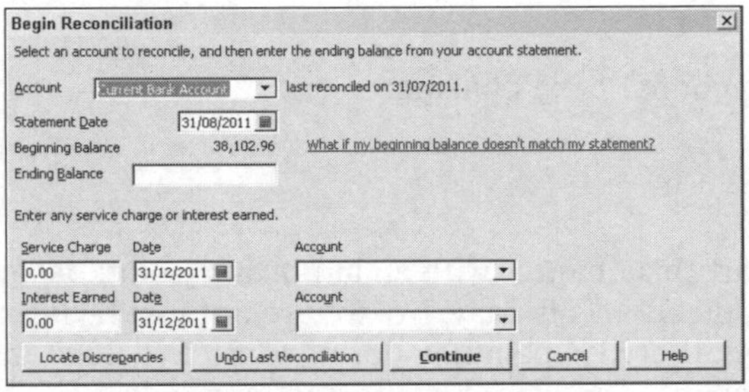

Figure 14-1:
The Begin Reconciliation dialog box.

2. **If the bank account shown isn't the one you want to reconcile, open the Account list and choose the correct account.**

   If you have several bank accounts, you may have to select which account you want to reconcile.

3. **Enter the bank statement date into the Statement Date text box.**

   You can adjust a date one day at a time by using the plus (+) and minus (–) keys. You can also click the Calendar button on the right side of the Statement Date text box to select a date from the calendar. See the online Cheat Sheet at www.dummies.com/cheatsheet/quickbooks 2012uk for a list of other date-editing tricks.

4. **Verify the bank statement opening balance.**

   QuickBooks displays an amount in the Beginning Balance text box, as shown in Figure 14-1.

   If the opening balance isn't correct, see the sidebar, "Why isn't my opening balance the same as the one in QuickBooks?" later in this chapter.

5. **Enter the ending balance from your bank statement into the Ending Balance text box.**

6. **Enter the bank's service charge.**

If the bank statement shows a service charge and you haven't already entered it (using the Write Cheques window), move the cursor to the Service Charge text box and type the amount. (For example, type 50 for a £50 service charge.)

7. **Enter a transaction date for the service charge transaction.**

   QuickBooks adds one month to the service charge date from the last time you reconciled. If this date isn't correct, type the correct one.

8. **Assign the bank's service charge to an account.**

   Enter the expense account to which you assign bank service charges in the first Account text box – the one beside the Date text box. Activate the drop-down list by clicking the down arrow and selecting the name of the account. We bet that you record these charges in the Bank Service Charges account that QuickBooks sets up by default.

   If you told QuickBooks that you also want to track income and expense amounts by using classes, QuickBooks adds Class boxes to the Begin Reconciliation dialog box so that you can collect this information.

9. **Enter the account's interest income.**

   If the account earned interest for the month and you haven't already entered this figure (using the Make Deposits window), type an amount in the Interest Earned text box.

10. **Enter a transaction date for the interest income transaction.**

    You already know how to enter dates. We won't bore you by explaining it again (but see Step 3 if you have trouble).

11. **Assign the interest to an account.**

    In the second Account text box, enter the account to which this account's interest should be assigned. Again, activate the drop-down list by clicking the down arrow and selecting the name of the account. We bet that you record this one under the Interest Income account.

12. **Click the Continue button.**

    QuickBooks displays the Reconcile window, as shown in Figure 14-2.

Marking cleared cheques and deposits

From the Reconcile window, shown in Figure 14-2, you tell QuickBooks which deposits and cheques have cleared at the bank, based on information on your bank statement.

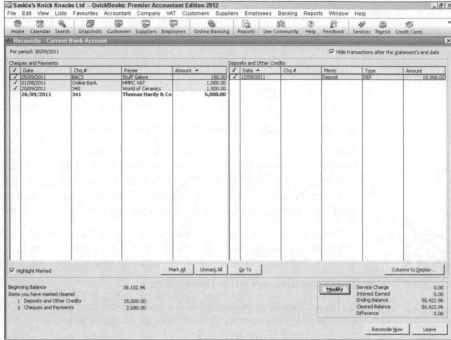

Figure 14-2:
The
Reconcile
window.

Let's take a minute to explain the Reconcile window. The left pane of the window shows money going out of the bank register (cheques and payments). The right pane shows money coming into the bank register (deposits and other credits).

The bottom right of the window is where all the action happens: here you see the ending balance you specified in the previous window, and as you reconcile your transactions in QuickBooks against the bank statement, the numbers in the Cleared Balance and Difference fields are updated. The end game, as you can no doubt guess, is for the amounts in the Ending Balance and Cleared Balance fields to match and for there to be a big fat zero in the Difference field.

With this in mind, here's what you do:

1. **Identify the first transaction that has cleared. Is it a payment or a deposit?**

   You know how to do this. Just leaf through the bank statement to find the first transaction listed, and see if it's a payment or a deposit.

2. **Mark the first cleared transaction as cleared.**

   If the transaction is a payment, scroll through the transactions listed in the Cheques and Payments section of the Reconcile window; find the first payment; and then click it.

   If the transaction is a deposit, scroll through the transactions listed in the Deposits and Other Credits section of the Reconcile window, find the deposit, and then click it.

   You also can highlight the payment or the deposit by using the Tab or arrow keys and then pressing the spacebar. QuickBooks places a check mark in front of the transaction to mark it as cleared and updates the cleared statement balance (that's the Cleared Balance amount).

3. **Record any cleared but missing transactions.**

   If you can't find a cheque or payment in QuickBooks, guess what? You haven't entered it in the register yet. Close or deactivate the Reconcile window by clicking the Leave button or by activating another window. Then enter the payment in the usual way. To return to the Reconcile window, reopen or reactivate it. When you return to the Reconcile window, the payment appears in the Cheques and Payments area.

   If you can't find a deposit in the Reconcile window, that's because you haven't entered it into the register yet. We can only guess why you haven't entered it. Maybe you just forgot. Again, close or deactivate the Reconcile window by clicking the Leave button. Now record the deposit in the usual way. To return to the Reconcile window, either reopen it or reactivate it. When you return to the Reconcile window, the deposit appears in the Deposits and Other Credits area.

4. **Repeat Steps 1–3 for all transactions listed on the bank statement.**

   Make sure that the dates match and that the amounts of the deposits are correct. If they're not, go back to the transactions and correct them. To get to a transaction, select it and click the Go To button. You see the window where the transaction was originally recorded (Write Cheques, Make Deposits, Sales Receipt and so on). Make the corrections there and then click Save & Close. You return to the Reconcile window.

QuickBooks enables you to sort the transactions listed on the Reconcile window by clicking the column headings in the Cheques and Payments section and in the Deposits and Other Credits section. You might want to experiment a bit with this handy feature. Sorting and re-sorting transactions – particularly in high-transaction volume bank accounts – often eases the work of reconciling a bank account.

5. **Mark the first cleared check as cleared.**

   Scroll through the transactions listed in the Checks and Payments section of the Reconcile window; find the first check; and then click it. You also can highlight it by pressing Tab and an arrow key. Then press the spacebar. QuickBooks inserts a check mark to label this transaction as cleared and updates the cleared statement balance.

6. **Record any missing but cleared checks.**

   If you can't find a check or withdrawal in QuickBooks, guess what? You haven't entered it in the register yet. Close or deactivate the Reconcile window by clicking its Leave button or by activating another window. Then display the register and enter the check or withdrawal. To return to the Reconcile window, reopen or reactivate it. Or you can just choose Banking⇨Write Checks, create the check right on top of the Reconcile window, and then click Save & Close to return to the Reconcile screen and carry on from where you left off.

7. **Repeat Steps 5 and 6 for all withdrawals listed on the bank statement.**

These steps don't take very long. Reconciling my account each month takes me about two minutes. And I'm not joking or exaggerating. By two minutes, I really mean two minutes.

QuickBooks also enables you to hide transactions dated after the statement date. To do so tick the check box (by clicking it with your mouse) in the top right corner of the Reconcile window next to Hide Transactions After the Statement's End Date. You'll come to love this little check box if you are catching up on bank reconciliations, or have loads of transactions in the current statement period which you don't want cluttering up your window.

Periodically check the bank statement balance against the Cleared Balance field in the Reconcile window. The two figures should match as you go along; if they don't, it flags you early on that you have messed up somewhere (for help see the section coming up on "Ten Things to Do if Your Account Doesn't Balance").

If the difference equals zero

After you mark all the cleared cheques and deposits, the difference between the Cleared Balance for the account and the bank statement's Ending Balance should equal zero. Notice that we said *should* – not *will*. Refer to Figure 14-2, which, fortunately, shows a Reconcile window in which everything is hunky-dory. If the difference is small, look for small differences between the amount of the cheques and deposits in the register and the actual cleared cheques and deposits on the bank statement. If you find a discrepancy with a particular transaction, just click the Go To button to open it and change the amount. Click Save & Close to go right back to the Reconcile window.

Why isn't my opening balance the same as the one in QuickBooks?

An opening balance that isn't the same as the one shown in the Opening Balance text box can mean a couple of things.

First, you may have mistakenly cleared a transaction the last time you reconciled. If you cleared a transaction last month that didn't go through until this month, your opening balance is wrong. Go back to the register and examine the transactions. Each one that's cleared has a check mark next to it in the narrow column between the Payment and Deposit columns. If one of the cheques that appears on this month's statement has a check mark, you made a mistake last month. From the register, click the check mark to remove it. You're asked to confirm your actions. The cheque now appears in the Reconcile window.

The other reason why the opening balance can be different is that a transaction that you cleared in the past got changed. If you deleted a transaction that occurred before this reconciliation period, for example, it threw off your balance. Why? Because the transaction that you deleted helped balance your account the last time around, but now that transaction has gone. To identify changed or deleted reconciled transactions, look at the Previous Reconciliation Discrepancy Report. You access it by clicking Reports⇨Banking⇨Reconciliation Discrepancy, and specifying the desired bank account in the Reconciliation Discrepancy Report pop-up window.

Whatever happens, don't fret. If you can't track down the faulty transaction, you can just have QuickBooks adjust the balance for you, which we explain elsewhere in this chapter. If you frequently find that your accounts don't balance, consider using the QuickBooks Audit Trail report, which lists changes to the QuickBooks data, when it's time to reconcile your accounts.

If the difference does equal zero, you're finished. Just click the Reconcile Now button. QuickBooks displays a congratulatory message box telling you that the reconciliation is complete. As a reward for being such a good boy or girl, the message box asks whether you want to print a free, all-expenses-paid Summary or Full reconciliation report. Click Summary or Full and then click OK if you want to print the report. Otherwise, just click OK.

Can't decide whether to print the reconciliation report? It's up to you, really. All that printing does is to prove that you reconciled the account. You probably *do* want to print the last bank reconciliation of your financial year to give to your accountant. If you have QuickBooks Premier you can always come back and print any bank reconciliation report later if necessary. If you have QuickBooks Pro, you can print the last bank reconciliation report. QuickBooks saves the reconciliation reports under Reports, Banking, Previous Reconciliation.

Now each deposit, withdrawal, and cheque that you just cleared is marked with a check mark in your register. If you don't believe us, open the register and find out.

If the difference doesn't equal zero

If the difference doesn't equal zero, you have a problem. If you click the Reconcile Now button, QuickBooks shows you the Reconcile Adjustment dialog box, as shown in Figure 14-3. This dialog box tells you how unbalanced your account is and asks whether you want to adjust your maladjusted account.

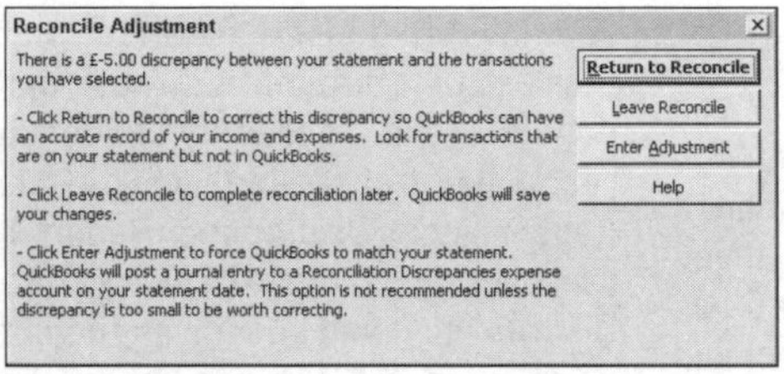

Figure 14-3:
The Reconcile Adjustment dialog box.

Reconcile Adjustment

There is a £-5.00 discrepancy between your statement and the transactions you have selected.

- Click Return to Reconcile to correct this discrepancy so QuickBooks can have an accurate record of your income and expenses. Look for transactions that are on your statement but not in QuickBooks.

- Click Leave Reconcile to complete reconciliation later. QuickBooks will save your changes.

- Click Enter Adjustment to force QuickBooks to match your statement. QuickBooks will post a journal entry to a Reconciliation Discrepancies expense account on your statement date. This option is not recommended unless the discrepancy is too small to be worth correcting.

Return to Reconcile

Leave Reconcile

Enter Adjustment

Help

Click the Return to Reconcile button if you want to go back to the Reconcile window and start the search for the missing or incorrectly entered transaction.

If you want to force the two amounts to agree, click OK. Forcing the two amounts to agree isn't a very good idea. To do so, QuickBooks adds a cleared transaction equal to the difference. (We talk about this transaction a little later in the chapter.)

We don't recommend making a bank account balance adjustment unless the difference is so small that it does not warrant the time spent tracking it down. The next section contains some ideas that can help you determine what the problem is. If you want to take a breather from the reconciliation (usually better than throwing the computer out the window), you can click the Leave button. When you are ready to return, you restart the reconciliation in the same way that you originate one.

Ten Things to Do if Your Bank Account Doesn't Balance

We want to give you some suggestions for reconciling an account when you're having problems. If you're sitting in front of your computer, wringing your hands, try the tips in this section:

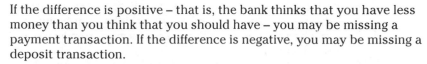

✔ **Make sure that you're working with the right account.** Sounds silly, doesn't it? If you have several bank accounts, however, ending up in the wrong account is easy. So go ahead and confirm, for example, that you're trying to reconcile your current account at Barclays by using the Barclays Current Account statement.

✔ **Look for transactions that the bank has recorded but you haven't.** Go through the bank statement to make sure that you have recorded every transaction that your bank has recorded. You can easily overlook cash-machine withdrawals, special fees, or service charges, automatic withdrawals, direct deposits, and so on.

If the difference is positive – that is, the bank thinks that you have less money than you think that you should have – you may be missing a payment transaction. If the difference is negative, you may be missing a deposit transaction.

✔ **Look for reversed transactions.** Here's a tricky one: if you accidentally enter a transaction backward – a deposit as a payment or a payment as a deposit – your account doesn't balance. And the error can be difficult to find. The Reconcile window shows all the correct transactions, but a transaction amount appears in the wrong pane. (The amount appears in the Deposits and Other Credits list when it belongs in the Cheque and Payments list, or vice versa.) The cheque that you wrote to Housewreckers Ltd for the demolition of your shed appears in the Deposits and Other Credits list, for example.

✔ **Look for a transaction that's equal to half the difference.** One handy way to find the transaction that you entered backward – if you have only one – is to look for a transaction that's equal to half the irreconcilable difference. If the difference is £200, for example, you may have entered a £100 deposit as a withdrawal or a £100 withdrawal as a deposit.

✔ **Look for a transaction that's equal to the difference.** While on the subject of explaining the difference by looking at individual transactions, here's an obvious point: if the difference between the bank's records and yours equals one of the transactions listed in your register, you may have incorrectly marked the transaction as cleared or incorrectly left the transaction unmarked (shown as uncleared). Hmmm. Maybe that was too obvious. Naaaah.

✔ **Check for transposed numbers.** Transposed numbers are flip-flopped digits. For example, you enter £45.89 as £48.59. These turkeys always cause headaches for accountants and bookkeepers. If you look at the numbers, detecting an error is often difficult because the digits are the same. For example, when you compare a check amount of £45.89 in your register with a check for £48.59 shown on your bank statement, both check amounts show the same digits: 4, 5, 8, and 9. They just show them in a different order.

Transposed numbers are tough to find, but here's a trick that you can try: Divide the difference shown in the Reconcile window by 9. If the result is an even number of pounds or pennies, chances are good that you have a transposed number somewhere.

✔ **Use the Locate Discrepancies button.** Would you mind, terribly, taking a peek back at Figure 14-1? The dialog box shown in that figure includes a Locate Discrepancies button, which you can click to display another dialog box that prints reports that may help you reconcile your account. In particular, the dialog box lets you view a report of changes made to previously cleared transactions (which definitely foul up your reconciliation). It also shows a report that lists transactions marked as cleared during previous reconciliations, which might be interesting because maybe you erroneously marked a transaction as cleared before it really was cleared.

✔ **Have someone else look over your work.** This idea may seem pretty obvious, but it's amazing how often a second pair of eyes can find something that you overlooked. Ask one of your co-workers or employees (preferably that one person who always seems to have way too much free time) to look over everything for you.

✔ **Be on the lookout for multiple errors.** If you find an error using this list and you still have a difference, start checking at the top of the list again. You may discover, for example, after you find a transposed number that you entered another transaction backward, or incorrectly cleared or uncleared a transaction.

✔ **Click the Unmark All button in the Reconcile window, and start again.** If all else fails, start the bank reconciliation again and check the amount of each transaction carefully as you tick it against the entries on the bank statement. Also keep an eye on the Cleared Balance field – the running balance amount on the bank statement should match the figure in the Cleared Balance field as you do the reconciliation.

Chapter 15

Reporting on the State of Affairs

• •

In This Chapter

▶ Exploring QuickBooks reports

▶ Printing reports

▶ QuickZooming report totals

▶ Editing and rearranging report information

▶ Customising reports

▶ Processing multiple reports

▶ Using QuickReports

▶ The Company Snapshot

• •

To find out whether your business is thriving or failing, you use the QuickBooks Snapshot and Reports features. The different kinds of reports in QuickBooks cover everything from cash flow to missing cheques, not to mention QuickReports. QuickReports are summary reports that you can get from the information on forms, account registers, or lists by merely clicking your mouse.

In this chapter, we tell you how to prepare reports, how to print them, and how to customise reports for your own needs.

What Kind of Reports Are There, Anyway?

If you run a small business, you don't need all the reports that QuickBooks offers, but many of these reports are extremely useful. Reports show you how healthy or unhealthy your business is, where your profits are, and where you're wasting time and squandering resources.

To make sense of what might otherwise become mass confusion, QuickBooks organises all its reports into categories. You can see all the categories by pulling down the Reports menu or by clicking the Report Centre icon. The names of the reports read a bit like BBC documentary names, don't they? "Tonight, Joob Taylor explores the mazelike government budget in Budget Reports." You select a report category to see a list of report names.

In Table 15-1, we describe reports by category and give a short description of the major reports in each category. To get a thorough description of a particular report, go to the Help feature. To find out what a standard profit and loss report does, for example, choose Help⇨QuickBooks Help and then click the Index tab. Type **financial statements** in the text box. (The Help information includes a wonderful discussion about how to understand the profit and loss and balance sheet financial statements.) Or, from the Reports Centre, select the type of report on the left; you see a list of the different reports available on the right side, with a description of the information contained in each one. To read the details about a topic, click that topic in the list.

Table 15-1	QuickBooks Report Categories
Report Category	*Description*
Company & Financial	These reports give you a bird's-eye view of your company's health and cash flow. They give you a snapshot of your assets, liabilities, and equity, showing income, expenses, and net profit or loss over time.
Customers & Receivables	These Accounts Receivable reports are great for finding out where you stand in regard to your customer invoices. You can list unpaid invoices and group them in various ways, including by customer, job, and aging status.
Sales	These reports show what you sold and who your customers are. You can see your sales by item, by customer, or by sales representative.
Jobs, Time & Mileage	These reports let you see job and item profitability, compare job estimates with actual costs, and view the time recorded on jobs and activities.
Suppliers & Payables	These Accounts Payable reports tell you everything you need to know about your unpaid bills. You can list bills in a variety of ways, including by supplier and by aging status.

Report Category	Description
VAT	These reports show you the VAT liability for a given period.
Purchases	If you enable the Items and Purchases option within QuickBooks (discussed in Chapter 7), these reports show from whom you bought, what you bought, and how much you paid. You can list purchases by item or by supplier. One handy report shows any outstanding purchase orders.
Stock	These reports help answer the ever-important question, "What items do I have in stock?" You can get an enormous amount of detail from these reports. For example, you can find out how many of an item you have on hand and how many you have on order. You can group stock items by supplier or by item.
Employees & Payroll	These reports, available if you signed up for QuickBooks payroll, offer ways to track payroll or check your payroll liability accounts. Believe us: these reports come in handy.
Banking	These reports list cheques and deposits, previous bank reconciliation details, and reconciliation discrepancies.
Accountant & Taxes	These reports include journal, general ledger and trial balance reports, as well as audit and closing date exception reports.
Budgets & Forecasts	These reports show you once and for all whether your budgeting skills are realistic. You can view budgets by job, by month, or by balance sheet account. Then you can compare the budgets with actual income and expense totals. (You need to have a budget already set up to use this report – something we discuss in Chapter 13.)
List	These reports let you see your lists in detail. For example, you can see the contacts, phone numbers, and addresses on your Customer, Supplier, Employee, or Other Names lists. You also can create a detailed report of your item prices.

If you're not sure which specific report you want, you can use the Report Centre. Just choose Reports➪Report Centre and choose a report category from the list on the left of the Report Centre window (see Figure 15-1). QuickBooks displays a picture of the most common reports within the category in the Report Centre window.

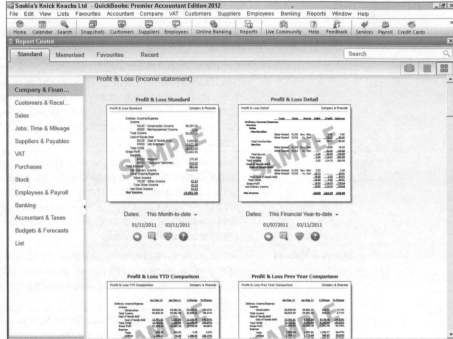

Figure 15-1:
The Report
Centre
window.

Creating and Printing a Report

After you decide what report you need, all you have to do is select it from the appropriate menu or from the Report Centre window. To create a standard profit and loss report, for example, choose Reports➪Company & Financial➪Profit & Loss Standard or select it from the Report Centre. Or, double-click the report image in the Report Centre window.

Depending on how much data QuickBooks has to process, you may see a Building Report box before the report appears onscreen in all its glory. Figure 15-2 shows a standard profit and loss report, also known as an *income statement.*

If you see a Customise Report dialog box instead of a report, you can tell QuickBooks to change this option. To do so, choose Edit➪Preferences and then click the Reports & Graphs icon in the list on the left. Click the My Preferences tab, if you have one and it isn't already selected. Remove the check mark from the Prompt Me to Modify Report Options Before Opening a Report check box.

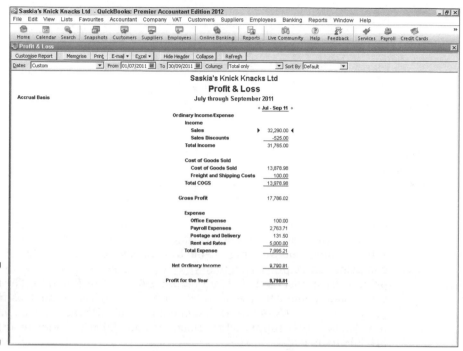

Figure 15-2:
A standard
profit and
loss report.

You can't see the entire onscreen version of a report unless your report is very small (or your screen is monstrously large). Use the Page Up and Page Down keys on your keyboard to scroll up and down, and use the Tab and Shift+Tab keys to move left and right. Or, if you're a mouse lover, you can use the scroll bar.

To print a report, click the Print button at the top of the report. QuickBooks displays the Print Reports dialog box, as shown in Figure 15-3. To accept the given specifications, which are almost always fine, click the Print button. You'll never guess what happens next: QuickBooks prints the report!

The first time you print a report, QuickBooks displays a Printing Features dialog box that explains a few things about the mechanics of choosing and printing reports.

Before we forget, we want to tell you that you can select the File radio button in the Print To panel to tell QuickBooks to save the report as a file instead of printing it. You can then choose the file format: ASCII Text File, Comma Delimited File, or Tab Delimited File. You can use either delimited-file format if you want to open the file later with a spreadsheet program, such as Microsoft Excel. After you click Print, use the Create Disk File dialog box to specify the filename and storage location.

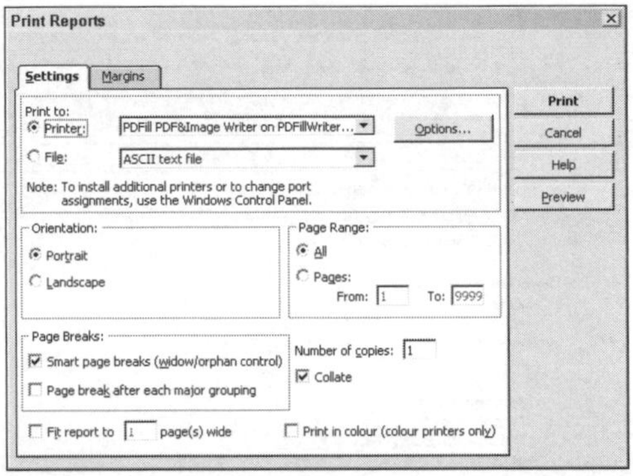

Print Reports ☒

| Settings | Margins |

Print to:
- ⦿ Printer: [PDFill PDF&Image Writer on PDFillWriter... ▾] [Options...]
- ○ File: [ASCII text file ▾]

Note: To install additional printers or to change port assignments, use the Windows Control Panel.

Orientation:
- ⦿ Portrait
- ○ Landscape

Page Range:
- ⦿ All
- ○ Pages:
  From: [1] To: [9999]

Page Breaks:
- ☑ Smart page breaks (widow/orphan control)
- ☐ Page break after each major grouping

Number of copies: [1]
☑ Collate

☐ Fit report to [1] page(s) wide   ☐ Print in colour (colour printers only)

[Print] [Cancel] [Help] [Preview]

Figure 15-3:
The Print
Reports
dialog box.

Another really popular option is to "print" your report to your desktop as a PDF file that can be attached to an e-mail and sent to anyone you choose. After sending, you can drag the file to your Recycle Bin. Anything that you can print can be processed this way and e-mailed. You need to have a PDF printer driver installed on your computer to use this function. These can be downloaded online for free if you don't have one already, such as from www. primopdf.com. (***Note:*** some documents in QuickBooks, such as Invoices, have an icon that supports PDF e-mailing and will automatically attach the PDF file to an e-mail.)

The Orientation settings tell QuickBooks how the report is supposed to appear on the paper. The Page Range settings specify the pages that you want to print. The Fit Report to *xx* Page(s) Wide check box enables you to shrink the report so that it fits on the number of pages you specify. The purpose of the Print in Colour (Colour Printers Only) check box is pretty self-evident.

QuickBooks includes two page-break options for creating easier-to-read reports:

✔ Select the first check box (Smart page breaks) to keep items that belong in the same group on the same page.

✔ Select the second check box to give each major group its own page.

You can preview the report by clicking the Preview button.

Editing and Rearranging Reports

You may have noticed that when QuickBooks displays the report document window, it also displays a row of buttons: Customise Report, Memorise, Print, E-Mail, Excel, and so on (refer to Figure 15-2). Below this toolbar are some drop-down lists that have to do with dates, a drop-down list called Columns, and a drop-down list called Sort By. (Not all these lists are available in every report document window. We don't know why, really. Maybe just to keep you on your toes.)

You don't need to worry about these buttons and lists. Read through the discussion that follows only if you're feeling comfortable, relaxed, and truly mellow, okay?

QuickZooming mysterious figures

If you don't understand where a number in a report comes from, point to it with the mouse. As you point to numbers, QuickBooks changes the mouse pointer to a magnifying glass marked with a Z. Double-click the mouse to have QuickBooks display a list of all the transactions that make up that number.

This feature, called *QuickZoom,* is extremely handy for understanding the figures that appear on reports. All you have to do is double-click any mysterious-looking figure in a report. QuickBooks immediately tells you exactly how it arrived at that figure.

Customising a report

When you click the Customise Report button, QuickBooks displays the Modify Report dialog box, as shown in Figure 15-4. From this dialog box, you can change the information displayed on a report and the way that information is arranged (by using the Display tab); the data used to generate the report (by using the Filters tab); the header and footer information (by using, predictably, the Header/Footer tab); and the typeface and size of print used for a report (by using the Fonts & Numbers tab).

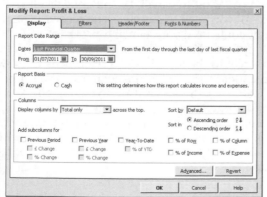

Figure 15-4: The Modify Report dialog box.

Memorising a report

If you do play around with the remaining buttons, you can save any custom report specifications that you create. Just click the Memorise button on the top toolbar. QuickBooks displays the Memorise Report dialog box (shown in Figure 15-5), which asks you to supply a name for the customised report and assign the memorised report to a report group. After you name and assign the customised report, QuickBooks lists it whenever you choose Reports➪Memorised Reports and then click the report group. You can also access Memorised Reports from the top of the Report Centre screen. Whenever you want to use your special report, all you need to do is choose it from the list and click the Report button.

Figure 15-5:
The
Memorise
Report
dialog box.

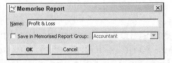

QuickBooks memorises the print orientation with the report, so if the print orientation isn't the way you want it for the report, you should first change it by choosing File➪Printer Setup. Select the orientation you want to memorise, click OK, and then memorise the report.

E-mailing a report

If you click the E-Mail button, QuickBooks displays a drop-down list of commands that lets you e-mail either an Excel workbook or a PDF version of the report to someone else. When you choose the command that corresponds to the report file format you want to e-mail, QuickBooks displays the Edit Email Information box. All you need to supply is the receiving person's e-mail address. If you have not configured your e-mail to work with QuickBooks yet, you see the Choose Your Email Method dialog box instead. Click the Setup My Email Now button to get to the Send Forms Preferences window (or click Edit➪Preferences and choose the Send Forms icon from the list on the left). In the My Preferences tab, click the Add button to display the Add Email Info dialog box. Configure your e-mail settings and click OK to save your changes and return to the My Preferences tab. You can add multiple webmail IDs (for example Yahoo, Gmail, or Hotmail/Live), or configure Microsoft Outlook or Mozilla Thunderbird to send QuickBooks e-mails if these programs are installed on your computer.

Exporting report data to Microsoft Excel

If you click the Excel button, QuickBooks displays the Send Report to Excel dialog box (see Figure 15-6). You can use this dialog box to create an Excel report that holds the same information as shown in the report. Select the Create New Worksheet radio button and then click the Export button. You can also get fancier by exporting a comma-separated values (CSV) file (these files can be opened by other electronic spreadsheet programs and by database programs), by exporting to a specific Excel workbook file, and by clicking the Advanced button to display another dialog box that lets you control how the exported information is formatted.

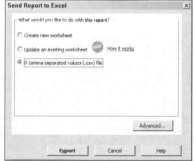

Figure 15-6:
The Send
Report
to Excel
dialog box.

A friendly suggestion, perhaps? Feel free to experiment with all the special exporting options. Just remember that after you export a QuickBooks report to a new, blank Excel workbook, you can do fancy stuff – special formatting and so on – there.

Here's a really cool feature: if you export and save QuickBooks data to a blank Excel workbook that you tailor with your own layout and formulas, you can update the QuickBooks data in the workbook without losing your custom formatting. Good stuff, isn't it?

The other buttons and boxes

If you want to see how the Hide Header, Collapse, and Dates stuff works, just play around. You can't hurt anything.

If you change the report dates, click the Refresh button to update the report. To set refresh options for reports, choose Edit⇨Preferences. Then click the Reports & Graphs icon in the list on the left and click the My Preferences tab if necessary. Click one of the Reports and Graphs options and then click OK.

Reports Made to Order

If you intend to print a large number of reports – and, more importantly, if you intend to print a large number of reports and show them to customers, investors, and other significant people – you want your reports to look good and to be easy to understand. As beauty is in the eye of the beholder, we are not going to get into the aesthetics of report layouts. What we are going to do is explain how you can make QuickBooks reports look exactly the way you want them to look.

Choose Edit➪Preferences. Click the Reports & Graphs icon in the list on the left and then click the Company Preferences tab to see the Preferences dialog box, as shown in Figure 15-7, for reports and graphs.

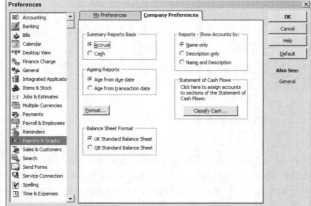

Figure 15-7: The Preferences dialog box for reports and graphs.

You need to be logged in to single-user mode as the administrator to change company preferences. Read how in Appendix C.

Here are your options:

- **Accrual:** *Accrual* is one of those cruel accounting terms that are hard to understand at first. If you select the Accrual radio button in the Summary Reports Basis panel, you tell QuickBooks to include all your transactions, sales, purchases, expenses, and so on, from the moment they're recorded, not from the time you receive or pay cash for them.

  Accountants follow the accrual method because it gives a more accurate picture of profits.

✔ **Cash:** If you select the Cash radio button, all the financial transactions in your reports are counted at the time you make your expense payments or receive your customers' payments.

✔ **Age from Due Date:** If you select the Age from Due Date radio button in the Ageing Reports panel, QuickBooks counts your expenses and invoices from the day that they fall due. Otherwise, QuickBooks counts them from the day they're recorded.

✔ **Format:** Click the Format button if you want to improve the look of your reports. In the Report Format Preferences dialog box that appears, as shown in Figure 15-8, you can use the Header/Footer tab to choose preferences for displaying the company name, the report title, the subtitle, and so on.

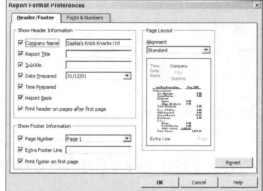

Figure 15-8:
The Report
Format
Preferences
dialog box.

✔ **Balance Sheet Format:** You probably to want to accept the default radio option (UK Standard Balance Sheet).

✔ **Reports – Show Accounts By:** You select a radio button in this group to indicate how you want QuickBooks to arrange account information on your reports: by name, by description, or by both name and description.

✔ **Statement of Cash Flows:** You click the Classify Cash button to tell QuickBooks how it should handle its accounts when it produces a picture-perfect statement of cash flows using generally accepted accounting principles. A suggestion? Leave this for your accountant.

You can use the Fonts & Numbers tab in the Report Format Preferences dialog box to choose preferences for displaying numbers, decimal fractions, and negative numbers. You also can fool around with different fonts and point sizes for labels, column headings, titles, and other things in your reports.

Click the Revert button in the Report Format Preferences dialog box to undo your customisation changes.

Processing Multiple Reports

Do you want to print several reports at once? No problem. Choose Reports⇨ Process Multiple Reports. When QuickBooks displays the Process Multiple Reports dialog box, as shown in Figure 15-9, select the group of reports that you want to print or display in the Select Memorised Reports From field.

Figure 15-9: The Process Multiple Reports dialog box.

Last but Not Least: The QuickReport

The QuickReport is one of the best kinds of report. You can generate a QuickReport from a list, from invoices and bills with names of people or items on them, and from account registers. QuickReports are especially useful when you're studying a list and see something that momentarily baffles you. Simply make sure that the item you're curious about is highlighted, click the Reports button, and choose the QuickReports command for the item from the drop-down list.

You can also right-click an item and choose QuickReport from the shortcut menu to create a QuickReport of the item. Or, highlight the item and press Ctrl+Q on your keyboard.

Figure 15-10 shows a QuickReport produced from the Accounts Payable register. We clicked the QuickReport button to display this transaction information for a supplier: the fictitious Stuff Galore.

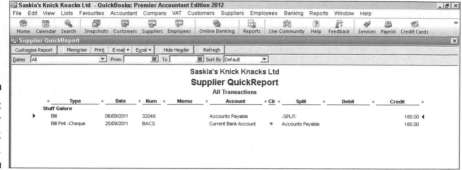

Figure 15-10:
A Supplier
Quick
Report.

Viewing the Company Snapshot

We saved the best for last. Here we want to tell you about the QuickBooks
Company Snapshot (Company⇨Company Snapshots). The Snapshot is the
QuickBooks version of a dashboard: in the space of one screen you can view
graphs and reports that give you immediate insight into how your business
is doing (see Figure 15-11). After all, nothing tells a story as well as a picture,
right?

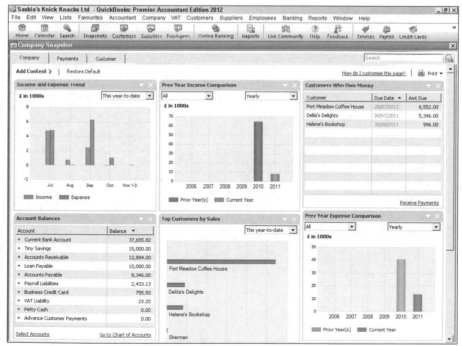

Figure 15-11:
The
Company
Snapshot
window.

There are in fact three Snapshots organised in three tabs: Company, Payments, and Customer (see Figure 15-11). The Company Snapshot shows, for example, income and expense trends, account balances, previous year income comparisons, top customers by sales, and so on. The Payments Snapshot contains information to help you manage your customer receipts, and the Customer Snapshot gives you useful data by customer, such as how long it takes on average for a specific customer to pay, sales summaries and histories, and so on.

Go on, spend some time exploring these snapshots; we think they are fantastic. What you'll find is that you can add or delete content, and move content around the page, so what you end up with is your own custom dashboard. And of course you can click buttons that take you straight to an activity, like Receive Payments. If you want to analyse something in greater detail, you can simply double-click a figure or column in a graph to QuickZoom, and view the underlying data.

Enjoy.

Chapter 16

Job Estimating, Billing, and Tracking

· ·

In This Chapter

▶ Turning on job costing and setting up jobs

▶ Creating estimates and estimate-based invoices

▶ Comparing budgeted, estimated, and actual job information

▶ Charging for time and out-of-pocket expenses

· ·

*Q*uickBooks has a feature that's very useful for business people – such as contractors, consultants, engineers, and architects – who do jobs or projects for their customers. QuickBooks has the capability to do simple project or job costing. This capability means that your business can create project or job estimates, track costs by project or job, and raise invoices by project or job.

In this short chapter, we describe the QuickBooks job costing feature. (Note: some features are not available in QuickBooks Pro and we'll point this out where that's the case.)

Turning On Job Costing

To turn on the job costing or estimating feature in QuickBooks, choose Edit➪ Preferences. Click the Jobs & Estimates icon on the left; click the Company Preferences tab; and then use the Do You Create Estimates? and Do You Do Progress Invoicing? radio buttons to tell QuickBooks whether, in fact, you want to do these things.

Note: progress invoicing refers to the practice (common to some construction and other project-based businesses) of invoicing a client or customer as work on a project progresses. In other words, rather than invoicing for the total amount at the very end of a project, you might invoice half the agreed-upon amount when work is roughly half done. And then you might invoice the remaining half of the agreed-upon amount when the work is finally finished.

Setting Up a Job

If you want to use QuickBooks job costing, your first step is to set up a job. For example, if you're a building contractor, you can use QuickBooks to track the invoices and costs of the remodelling jobs you do. You just need to set up a job every time you get ready to bid on a project.

To set up a job, first set up a customer in the usual way. Then set up a job also in the usual way. In Chapter 3, we describe how you do all this, so we don't repeat that information here. Just to save you time, however, all you need to do is choose Customers⇨Customer Centre to display the Customer Centre window, right-click the customer for whom you might do a job, and then choose Add Job from the pop-up menu. When QuickBooks displays the New Job window, describe the job by filling out the fields in the window that QuickBooks displays.

QuickBooks lets you categorise jobs as falling into several different status categories: Pending, Awarded, In Progress, Closed, and Not Awarded. As you might guess, you use these Job Status descriptions to categorise your jobs.

Creating a Job Estimate

In QuickBooks, job costing starts with an estimate. An *estimate* is just a list of the estimated costs you'll incur for some job you'll perform for some customer.

Assuming that you already created a job and told QuickBooks that you use estimates, here are the steps that you follow to create an estimate:

1. **Choose Customers⇨Create Estimates.**

   QuickBooks opens a Create Estimates form (see Figure 16-1), which bears an uncanny resemblance to the Create Invoices form that you've seen if you've worked with QuickBooks at all. (See Chapter 4 for more information about the Create Invoices form.)

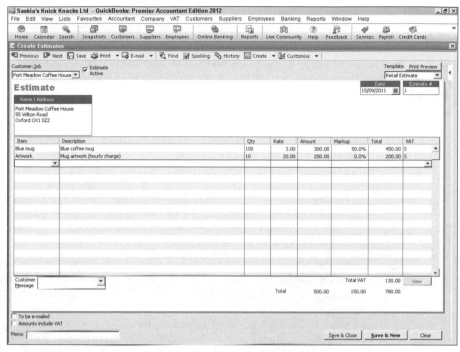

Figure 16-1:
The Create
Estimates
window.

Figure 16-1:
The Create
Estimates
window.

2. **Start filling in the blanks.**

   Choose the appropriate Customer:Job from the drop-down list at the top of the form. QuickBooks automatically fills in as much information as it can – usually at least the Name/Address text box – on the form.

   If you configured QuickBooks to track classes (as described in Chapter 3), the appropriate drop-down list shows up in the top centre of the form. Go ahead and use the box, if appropriate.

   Feel free to change the default settings – the Date and Estimate #, for example, using the Date Setting tricks that you can find in Chapter 4.

3. **Add the line items – details, details, details.**

   You fill in the details of a Create Estimates window in the same way that you fill in the details of a Create Invoices window. Read Chapter 4 if you have questions.

   One field that is unique to the Create Estimates window is Markup. The Markup field adds a specified percentage of the line item price total. Refer to Figure 16-1, where we specified one markup percentage as zero in the Markup column, so the Amount column values match the Total column values, and the other markup percentage as 50 per cent so the values shown in the Total column are 50 per cent greater.

In Chapter 3, we describe how to add items to the QuickBooks Items list. Each line item that you want to include on your job estimate needs to be described in the Items list. Note that because you often sell work to clients and customers by using, in part, an estimate, you'll typically want to include full descriptions of the items. (Construction contractors, for example, often use several lines of descriptive text to fully explain each item that shows on the estimate.)

4. **(Optional) Add any optional information.**

   Use any of the other boxes available in the Create Estimates window to collect and store additional information. For example, just as with the Create Invoices window, you can click the Customer Message drop-down list and choose or write a friendly message.

   You can also use the Memo field to write a note to yourself regarding the job. Or maybe add some notes about the screenplay that you've been thinking about pitching to the studios. Whatever suits your fancy.

If you want to include other fields and columns in the Create Estimates window, you can customise that window. You customise estimates in the same way as you customise an invoice. In Chapter 4, we talk a bit about how to customise invoice forms, so you may want to look there if you have questions about how to customise the Create Estimates form.

Before you print that estimate, remember that information in the Create Estimates window isn't the same information that appears on the written estimate. To see how the printed version looks, click the down arrow beside the Print button (located in the top row of icons) in the Create Estimates window, and choose Preview from the drop-down list. The result is a full-page image, shrunk to fit onscreen.

If you haven't saved your estimate yet, go ahead and click either the Save & New button or the Save & Close button.

To examine the estimate (or any onscreen QuickBooks form) more closely, either click the Zoom In button at the top of the Print Preview screen or move the mouse cursor over the image. When the cursor looks like a magnifying glass with a plus sign in it, click the left mouse button. Because you can **see** only part of the preview this way, use the scroll bars at the bottom and right of the windows to move around to the different areas.

Note that the magnifying glass now has a minus sign in it, and the Zoom In button toggles to Zoom Out. If you complete more than one estimate, you can use the Prev Page and Next Page buttons on the Print Preview screen to look at other estimates. When you finish, click the Close button.

When you get back to the Create Estimates window, click the Print button; QuickBooks Pro displays the Print One Estimate dialog box. Click Print to print the estimate without any further ado.

If you haven't used QuickBooks to print estimates before, you may need to set up your printer for this task first. To do so, choose File➪Printer Setup and then choose Estimate from the Form Name drop-down list. Specify the printer settings that you want for printing estimates. (This process works the same way as it does for printing other forms, such as invoices, as we describe in Chapter 4.) Click OK when you're done. The Print One Estimate dialog box that QuickBooks displays after you click Print in the Create Estimates window also works the same way as the Print One Invoice dialog box does. Read Chapter 4 if you need help with this dialog box.

Revising an Estimate

To revise an estimate, display the Create Estimates window, as described earlier in this chapter. Then click the Previous button (located in the row of icons at the top of the window) until you see the estimate.

Make your changes and QuickBooks recalculates all the totals. Smile. Imagine doing this task by hand – the recalculations, the looking up of prices, the retyping, the inordinate amount of wasted time. Making these changes automatically with QuickBooks doesn't quite beat a soft vanilla ice cream in the park on a sunny day, but it's pretty close.

You can keep only one estimate per job. After you click Save & New, any changes that you make automatically take the place of the old estimate. If you make changes to an estimate, though, you can tell QuickBooks to treat the revision as a change order. With a change order, the modifications to an existing estimate get added to the bottom of the estimate. Cool, right?

Turning an Estimate into an Invoice

You can easily turn the estimate into an invoice by following these steps:

1. **On the Customer Centre screen, select your customer.**

   QuickBooks shows you a list of transactions for the customer, including any active estimates.

2. **Double-click the estimate you want to work with.**

   The Create Estimates window opens. (Refer to Figure 16-1.)

3. **Click the Create button at the top of the window and select Invoice (in QuickBooks Pro it's the Create Invoice button).**

The QuickBooks Information window displays to tell you that the entire estimate has been copied and that you can edit the invoice by removing or adding items.

If you indicated that you might invoice a customer or client on progress, QuickBooks displays a different dialog box that asks whether you want to invoice the entire estimate or just some portion of the estimate. Answer the question by marking the appropriate option button. Then click OK. QuickBooks creates an invoice based on your estimate (see Figure 16-2).

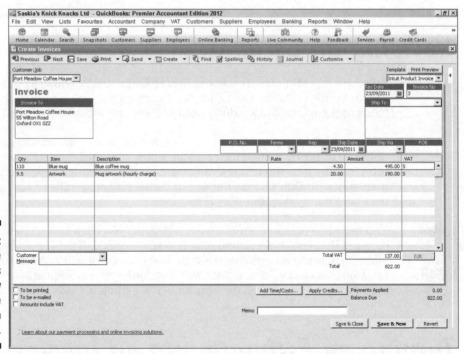

Figure 16-2:
The Create Invoices window with the data from Figure 16-1.

4. **(Optional) Make any necessary changes to the resulting invoice.**

The invoice that you see is a regular QuickBooks invoice, and you can edit it the same way that you edit any invoice.

5. **After you make all your changes, click Save & New or Save & Close to record the invoice.**

If you want to print the invoice instead, you can click the Print button (QuickBooks automatically saves the invoice before it prints it.)

In QuickBooks Premier, when you click the Create button in the Create Estimates window you can also select Sales Order or Purchase Order. While a purchase order (discussed in Chapter 7) is your commitment to buy from a supplier, a sales order is your customer's commitment to buy from you. You convert an Estimate into a Sales Order or a Purchase Order in the same way as you convert an Estimate into an Invoice. With a few mouse clicks you can record the items you need to buy from your supplier and start tracking the items you need to send to your customer. Pretty cool, isn't it? (***Note:*** Sales Orders are only in QuickBooks Premier.)

Comparing Estimated Item Amounts with Actual Item Amounts

In the previous paragraphs, we describe how you can take an estimate and create an invoice by using that estimate as a starting point. We also describe how you can edit the numbers that come from the estimate. Now, here's an interesting job costing point: QuickBooks prints reports – like the one in Figure 16-3 – that let you compare the item estimates shown on the original job estimates with the actual billed items shown on invoices.

Figure 16-3: An Item Estimates vs. Actuals report.

Saskia's Knick Knacks Ltd
Item Estimates vs. Actuals
September 2011

	Est. Cost	Act. Cost	Diff.	Est. Revenue	Act. Revenue	Diff.
Stock						
Blue mug	300.00	533.70	233.70	450.00	495.00	45.00
Total Stock	300.00	533.70	233.70	450.00	495.00	45.00
Service						
Artwork	200.00	0.00	-200.00	200.00	190.00	-10.00
Total Service	200.00	0.00	-200.00	200.00	190.00	-10.00
TOTAL	**500.00**	**533.70**	**33.70**	**650.00**	**685.00**	**35.00**

To produce such a report, choose Report Centre⊅Jobs, Time & Mileage⊅ Item Estimates vs. Actuals. QuickBooks displays a report that lets you compare estimated amounts with invoiced amounts. If you bid jobs by using estimates but must invoice with actual numbers, such a report is a great way to see how good a job you're doing in your estimating.

Charging for Actual Time and Costs

If you charge a customer for actual costs and hours, you need to track the costs and time when you incur the charges for them. You assign the cost to the job by entering the customer and job information into the Customer:Job column that's shown in the form window used to record a particular cost or time charge. For example, if you use the Enter Bills window (read Chapter 6) to record a bill for a particular job, you use the Customer:Job column on the Expenses or Items tab, to designate the job.

To charge a customer for costs or time that you recorded, follow these steps:

1. **Choose Customers⇨Create Invoices to open the Create Invoices window.**

2. **Change the name in the Customer:Job drop-down list to the proper customer.**

   This step is easy: Activate the drop-down list and choose the appropriate customer and job. If you assigned time or costs to this customer, the Billable Time/Costs pop-up window tells you that you have outstanding billable time and/or costs.

3. **Click the radio button for Select the Outstanding Billable Time and Costs to Add to This Invoice.** (If you decide to exclude these charges now, you can click the Add Time/Costs button on the invoice at a later point to include the charges in your invoice.)

   QuickBooks displays the Choose Billable Time and Costs dialog box. The dialog box already shows the costs and time charges that you assigned to this customer and job combination.

4. **Select the billable time and costs that you want to add to the invoice.**

   Check the time charges and costs that you want to invoice. Note that the Choose Billable Time and Costs dialog box provides different tabs for Time, Expenses, Mileage, and Items.

5. **(Optional, Expenses only) Indicate the markup.**

   The Expenses tab has a couple of extra fields at the top of the tab to indicate the Markup Amount or % and the Markup Account. If applicable, fill in the fields with the appropriate information. QuickBooks places a tick in the box next to Selected Expenses Are Taxable – ensure that this is the correct VAT treatment for your circumstances.

6. **(Optional) Indicate whether you want the charges to appear as a single item on the invoice.**

   If you want to avoid listing the gory details of the charges to your customer, check the Print Selected Time and Costs as One Invoice Item check box located in the bottom-left corner of the invoice. (***Note:*** if multiple VAT Codes are used for the charges, QuickBooks will display a summary of each VAT rate used in the body of the *printed* invoice.)

7. **Click OK.**

   After you have everything the way you want it, click OK. As if by magic – even if it was by your hard work and the sweat of your own brow – the invoice appears.

8. **(Optional) Add anything else you want to include on the invoice.**

   This invoice is a regular QuickBooks invoice, remember? You may want to click the down arrow beside the Print button and choose Preview from the drop-down list to make sure that only the job costs that you want to appear do appear.

9. **Click Save & New or Save & Close.**

   That's how you record the invoice.

After you record the invoice, the job costs that have been billed are removed from the Choose Billable Time and Costs window. You're finished. Breathe easier.

You can also track the amount of time that you or other employees spend on clients or customers. To turn on time-tracking, choose Edit➪Preferences, scroll down to and click the Time & Expenses icon, and then select the Yes radio button next to the question Do You Track Time?. After you do this, you can track the time that you spend on a client or customer by choosing Customers➪Enter Time➪Use Weekly Timesheet or Customers➪Enter Time➪ Time/Enter Single Activity. Either command displays an easy-to-understand window that lets you record time spent working for a particular client or customer.

Tracking Job Costs

To see the costs assigned or allocated to a project, use the Jobs, Time & Mileage Reports, which are available when you choose Reports➪Jobs, Time & Mileage. You can experiment with the different reports to see which provides the information in a format and at a level of detail that works best for you. For example, if you're invoicing customers by job and collecting cost data by customer and job, you can produce great job-profitability reports that show what you've made by job. Also note that you can budget amounts by customer and job (using the budgeting technique described in Chapter 13). If you do the extra work of budgeting by job, you can also compare actual job income and costs with budgeted job income and costs.

Chapter 17

File Management Tips

- -

- -

*O*kay, you don't need to worry about the data files in which QuickBooks stores your financial information. Pretty much, QuickBooks does all the dirty work. But that said, you do have a few housekeeping tasks to take care of. In this chapter, we describe these chores and how to do them correctly with minimal hassle.

Backing Up Is (Not That) Hard to Do

Sure, we can give you some tricky, technical examples of fancy backup strategies, but they have no point here. You want to know the basics, right?

The guiding rule is that you back up any time you work on something that you wouldn't want to redo. Some people think that a week's worth of work is negligible and others think that a month's worth of work is negligible.

Let's look at a pretty common scenario for backing up files. Say that you back up every week after you enter your data for the week. Then you stick the disk (you might use any removable disk, such as a USB flash drive or a writable CD) in your briefcase or bag, which you take home with you so that if something terrible happens (like a meteor hitting your office building), you don't lose both your computer and the backup disk with the data.

Sound like a pretty good system? Actually, this strategy has its problems:

- Because you back up weekly, you might have to re-enter as much as a week's worth of data if the computer crashes toward the end of the week. If you're someone with heavy transaction volumes – if you prepare hundreds of invoices or write hundreds of cheques each week, for example – you probably want to back up more frequently, perhaps every day.

- A second problem with this strategy is only remotely possible but still worth mentioning: if something bad happens to the QuickBooks files stored on your computer's hard drive as well as the files stored on the backup flash drive or CD disk, you'll be up the proverbial creek without a paddle. (After all, a removable disk is far more likely to fail than a hard drive and is easier to lose.) If this worst-case scenario actually occurs, you'll need to start over from scratch from the beginning of the year.

Some people, who are religiously careful, circulate three sets of backup disks to reduce the chance of this mishap. They also regularly move one copy off-site, such as to a safe deposit box. In this scenario, whenever you back up your data, you overwrite the oldest set of backup disks.

Say you back up your data every week, and your hard drive not only crashes, but also bursts into a ball of flames rising high into the night. To restore your files, you use the most recent set of backups – one week old, max. If something is wrong with those, you use the next-most-recent set – two weeks old. If something is wrong with those, you use the last set – three weeks old. This way, you have three chances to get a set that works – a nice bit of security for the cost of a few extra disks or storage devices.

Backing up the quick-and-dirty way

You're busy. You don't have time to fool around. You just want to do a passable job of backing up, and you've decided how often you plan to do it. Sound like your situation? Then follow these steps:

1. **Insert a blank disk/disc into the appropriate drive.**

   You can back up to any removable disk, including flash memory devices and writable CDs. However, note that Intuit (the maker of QuickBooks) now recommends that you do not use the QuickBooks backup command to move a backup file onto a CD. Instead, Intuit recommends you back up the file onto your hard drive and then use the Windows File Copy command to burn the file onto the disc. This workaround approach tends to solve some of the CD-writing problems people experience when backing up directly to a CD.

In fact you can back up to any fixed disk, such as your hard drive or a network disk, but the advantage of a removable disk is that you can store it in some other location. As a compromise, you can use a network disk. You typically don't want to use your hard drive (although this is better than nothing) because one of the disasters that might befall your QuickBooks data is a hard drive failure.

You can also back up your QuickBooks files to an online storage area. See the sidebar "Backing up files online" for more information.

2. **If you store data for more than one company, make sure that the company whose data you want to back up is the active company.**

Yes, we know that all your companies are active; we're hoping they're not dead in the water. Our point is that you want to back up the correct company. To find out whether the correct company is active, just look at the QuickBooks application window title bar, which names the active company. (If you don't remember setting up multiple files, don't worry. You probably have only one file – the usual case.)

3. **Choose File➪Create Back Up to begin the backup operation.**

QuickBooks displays the first Create Backup dialog box (see Figure 17-1).

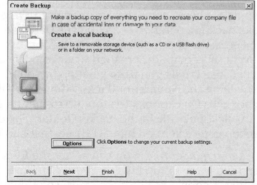

Figure 17-1: The first Create Backup dialog box.

If you use QuickBooks in multi-user mode, you need to switch to single-user mode before you back up your file. For more information on how to make this switch, see Appendix C.

4. **Describe how QuickBooks should back up your data file.**

Click the Options button. QuickBooks displays the Backup Options dialog box (see Figure 17-2), from which you specify how and when QuickBooks backs up your data file:

- *Pick a default location.* Specify where the backup file should be located. You can do this either by entering the pathname of the backup folder in the Tell Us Where to Save Your Backup Copies box (the hard way) or by clicking the Browse button and then using the Browse for Folder dialog box that Windows displays to pick a default backup location.

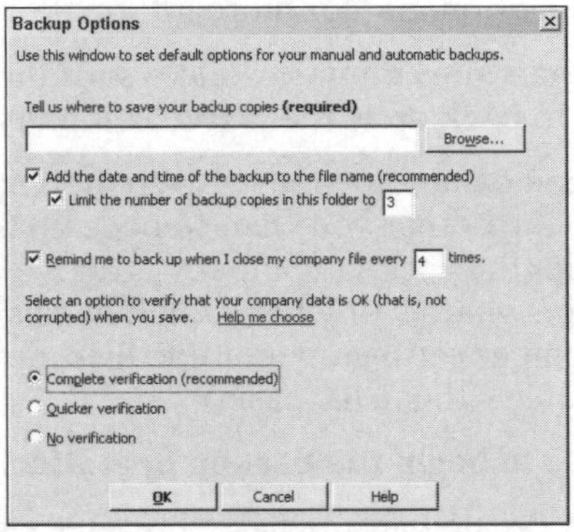

Figure 17-2:
The Backup
Options
dialog box.

- *Fine-tune the backup operation.* The Backup Options dialog box provides a couple of check boxes that you can use to fine-tune the QuickBooks backup operation. The Add the Date and Time of Backup to the File Name check box, if selected, does just what it says. (In the event of a computer crash, the backup date and time is very useful because it tells you from what point you have to redo work.) The Limit the Number of Backup Copies in This Folder To *[X]* check box tells QuickBooks to store up to that number of copies of your QuickBooks file in the backup folder. The default number of backup copies kept on hand is three; that should be fine.

- *Specify the backup reminder rule.* You can select the Remind Me to Back Up When I Close My Company File Every *[X]* Times check box to tell QuickBooks it should remind you every so often to back up. By default, QuickBooks reminds you every fourth time you close a data file, but you can replace the value in the text box to specify some other backup reminder frequency.

- *Select a data verification option.* QuickBooks provides three data verification options: Complete Verification (safe but slow), Quicker Verification (fast but not as thorough), and No Verification (saves you a bit of time now at the risk of huge problems later). The Complete Verification option is what QuickBooks (and we) recommend.

When you finish with the Backup Options dialog box, click OK. QuickBooks displays the second Create Backup dialog box (see Figure 17-3).

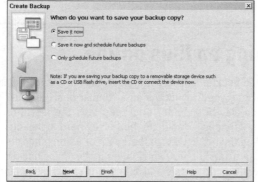

Figure 17-3:
The second
Create
Backup
dialog box.

5. **Determine when QuickBooks should back up your data file.**

   The second Create Backup dialog box provides radio buttons that you use to schedule when you want to back up. For example, to indicate that you want to back up on the spot, select the Save It Now radio button. Click Next. QuickBooks displays the Save Backup Copy dialog box (see Figure 17-4).

6. **Confirm the backup file location and name.**

   If you successfully completed Step 4, you already specified the appropriate folder location for the backup file. Just to be on the safe side, confirm that the filename and folder location shown in the Save Backup Copy dialog box are correct. If the folder location isn't correct, select a new folder location from the Save In drop-down list. If the filename isn't correct, edit the name shown in the File Name text box.

7. **Click Save.**

   QuickBooks backs up your data file and displays a message box that tells you it has backed up your file. The message also gives the backup filename and folder location.

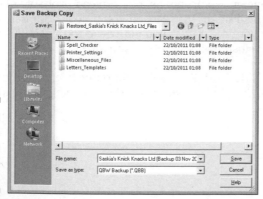

Figure 17-4:
The Save
Backup
Copy
dialog box.

Backing up files online

Nowadays there is another very good backup option to consider, and that's to back up your files to a secure online location. You may be familiar with or even already using services offered by the likes of Dropbox, Sugarsync, Carbonite, Mozy and so on (to name a few), where you can sign up for free (or paid) secure online storage space and back up your critical files or even your whole computer.

You can quickly and easily back up your data to an online space. Check with the individual service provider, but typically you install some software on your computer and then designate a folder on your computer which is "watched" so that each time you add a new file or folder to it, the file or folder is automagically backed up to your online backup space. One way to do it

is to ask QuickBooks to automatically back up your file on a regular basis to your "watched" folder and keep only the last three backups (as described elsewhere in this chapter). That way, in the event of a computer disaster, your files and folders in the online backup space are safe and sound, and you can download them to your computer. You never have to worry about losing your data ever again, nor do you have to remember to back up. Now that's pretty cool!

There is one **big bad warning** however: do not put your working QuickBooks file (the one that ends in the QBW file extension) in the "watched" folder. It can wreak serious havoc with your file, and mess up your data. Put only your backup copy (the file ending in extension QBB) in the "watched" folder.

Getting back the QuickBooks data you backed up

What happens if you lose all your QuickBooks data? First of all, we encourage you to feel smug. Get a cup of tea or coffee. Lean back in your chair. Gloat for a couple minutes. You, my friend, have no problem. You have followed instructions.

Okay, you may have one or two problems, but you can probably blame PC gremlins for those. If the disaster that caused you to lose your data also trashed other parts of your computer, you may need to reinstall QuickBooks. You also may need to reinstall all your other software.

After you gloat sufficiently (and piece your computer back together again if it was the cause of the disaster), carefully do the following to reinstate your QuickBooks data:

1. **Get your backup disk.**

   Find the backup disk you created and carefully insert it into the appropriate disk drive or USB port.

2. **Start QuickBooks and choose File➪Open or Restore Company.**

   QuickBooks displays the Open or Restore Company dialog box (see Figure 17-5).

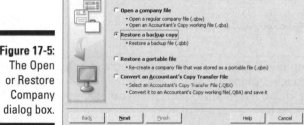

Figure 17-5: The Open or Restore Company dialog box.

3. **Indicate that you want to restore a backup copy of your QuickBooks data file. Then click Next.**

   How you do this is probably obvious, right? Select the Restore a Backup Copy option button.

4. **Identify the backup file that you want to use.**

   QuickBooks displays the Open dialog box (see Figure 17-6). (*Note:* depending on which folder viewing options you have enabled, your dialog box may look different; for example, you may see a list of files instead of icons.) If you know the company filename and location, you can enter this information in the boxes provided. If you don't know this information, use the Look In drop-down list to identify the drive that contains the file you want to restore. Then choose the backup file you want to restore and click Open. QuickBooks displays the Open or Restore Company dialog box (not shown) telling you that the next step (where you specify the restoration location) is pretty darn important. Click Next.

5. **Specify where the restored file will be located.**

   QuickBooks displays the Save Company File As dialog box (see Figure 17-7). Use the File Name text box and Save In drop-down list here to identify the file you want to replace. (If you work with multiple QuickBooks data files, make sure you choose the right one to replace.)

Figure 17-6:
The Open
dialog box.

If you know the company filename and location, you can enter this information in the text boxes provided. If you don't know this information, use the Save In drop-down list to make sure that you place the restored file in the correct folder on the correct drive.

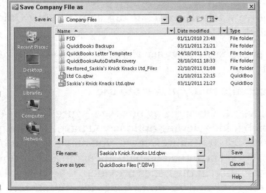

Figure 17-7:
The Save
Company
File As
dialog box.

6. Click Save.

If the file you're trying to restore already exists, you see a message box telling you so. Click Yes to overwrite and replace the file with the one stored on thc backup disk, or click No to keep the original copy.

QuickBooks may ask you for your password to verify that you have administrative permission to restore the file. Then, if everything goes okay, you see a message box that says so. Breathe a deep sigh of relief and give thanks.

Oops. We almost forgot:

- When you restore a file, you replace the current version of the file with the backup version stored on the backup medium. Don't restore a file for fun. Restore a file only if the current version is trashed and you want to start over by using the version stored on the backup disk.

- You need to re-enter everything you entered since you made the backup copy. We know. You're gutted. Hopefully, it hasn't been all that long since you backed up.

Working with Portable Files

QuickBooks includes a portable-files feature so you can more easily e-mail the QuickBooks data file to your accountant or your sister in Brighton. A *portable file* is a smaller, condensed version of the QuickBooks data file that contains only your financial data. Letters, logos, templates, images, and the transaction log file used by Intuit Technical Support to recover your data in the event of data damage are not backed up.

To create a portable file, choose File⇨Create Copy. When QuickBooks displays the first Save Copy or Backup dialog box, select the Portable Company File radio button, click Next, and then follow the onscreen instructions. The process, by the way, resembles the backup process described earlier in this chapter. It's quite convenient to save the file to your desktop from where you can attach it easily to your e-mail and send it out. After the other party receives the file, you can just drag your copy to the Recycle Bin. Your real file remains intact. (A portable file must typically be 10MB or less in size for transmission through most e-mail services.)

To open a portable file, a person (this could be your accountant or your sister in Brighton) should choose File⇨Open or Restore Company. When QuickBooks displays the Open or Restore Company dialog box (refer to Figure 17-5), this other person just specifies the file that he or she wants to open as a portable file and then follows the onscreen instructions.

Using an Audit Trail

For some curious reason, in the post-Enron world of accounting, people are much more interested in the QuickBooks Audit Trail feature. Because of this renewed interest, we will share the three things you need to know about using the QuickBooks Audit Trail feature:

✔ An *audit trail* is simply a list of changes. The QuickBooks Audit Trail – which is a simple report that lists the changes to the QuickBooks data file – lets you see who changed what. For example, you can filter the report (discussed in Chapter 15) to view a transaction such as a particular invoice and see if, how, when, and by whom it was changed.

✔ You don't have to turn on the Audit Trail feature. It's always on, baby.

✔ You can print the Audit Trail report by choosing Reports⇨Accountant & Taxes⇨Audit Trail.

Part V
The Part of Tens

The 5th Wave
By Rich Tennant

"The top line represents our income, the middle line is our stock, and the bottom line shows the rate of my hair loss over the same period."

In this part . . .

This part may be short, but it's packed with information. Here you find a ten-item (or almost ten-item) list of tips about QuickBooks and business formulas.

Chapter 18

Tips for Handling (Almost) Ten Tricky Situations

As your business grows and becomes more complex, your accounting does, too. We can't describe and discuss all the complexities you'll encounter, but we can give you some tips on handling (just about) ten tricky situations. In this chapter we'll take a look at depreciation, selling assets, drawing money out of the business, and repaying loans.

Entering Depreciation

In QuickBooks, you make journal entries by using the General Journal Entry window, which you get to by choosing Company⇨Make Journal Entries. If you don't understand double-entry bookkeeping but want to, take a gander at Appendix B.

To track the depreciation of an asset that you already purchased and added to the Chart of Accounts, you need two new accounts: a Fixed Asset type of (Balance Sheet) account called something like *Accumulated Depreciation* an Expense type (Profit and Loss) account called something like *Depreciation Expense*.

After you set up these two accounts, you can record the asset depreciation with a journal entry, such as the following one that records £1000 of depreciation expense:

	Debit	Credit
Depreciation Expense(a Profit and Loss account)	£1000	
Accumulated Depreciation (a Balance Sheet account)		£1000

If you have a large number of assets, keeping track of the accumulated depreciation associated with specific assets is a good idea. You usually do this outside QuickBooks, for example, in an Excel spreadsheet.

Selling an Asset

When you sell an asset, you need to *back out* (get rid of) the asset's account balance, record the cash (or whatever) that somebody pays you for the asset, and record any difference between what you sell the asset for and its value as a gain or loss.

If you purchase a piece of land for £5000 but later resell it for £4000, for example, you record the sale of the asset using a sales receipt and reverse the value of the asset using a journal entry. But you have to do some legwork before you can make these two entries. Follow these steps:

1. **Set up an Asset Disposal Gain account (of type Other Income) if you expect to make a gain on the sale or an Asset Disposal Loss account (of type Other Expense) if you expect to incur a loss on the sale.**

   In our example, you are making a £1000 loss on the sale, so you set up an Asset Disposal Loss account. Chapter 3 describes how to add a new account if you have trouble.

2. **Set up an Item (of Non-stock Part type) to use on the sales receipt. Call it something like Asset Sale.**

   Leave the Memo field empty because you can use this item for the sale of any asset (you add the description to the sales receipt.) Make sure you assign the right VAT Code; if you need to charge VAT, enter an "S" code, otherwise use the "Z" or "E" code, whichever applies to your specific circumstances. You specify either the Asset disposal Gain or the Asset Disposal Loss account (that you created in Step 1), for the item. Refer to Chapter 3 for help in adding the item.

3. **Now, create the sales receipt:**

    • In the Sold To field, enter the name of the person or business who is buying the asset.

    • Date the sale and – no surprise here – recall the Asset Sale item.

    • Select the bank account into which you are receiving the money in the Deposit To field. For example, if you are being paid in cash, select the Petty Cash account. (If you don't see the Deposit To field, that's a choice you need to enable. To tell QuickBooks to give you this choice, choose Edit⇨Preferences, scroll down to the Payments icon, click the Company Preferences tab, and then deselect the Use Undeposited Funds as a Default Deposit to Account option. After you make this change, QuickBooks adds buttons and a box to the lower-left corner of the Enter Sales Receipt.)

    So far you have recorded a credit of £4000 in the Asset Disposal Loss account and a debit of £4000 in the Petty Cash bank account.

4. **Hang in there, you're almost done. Next, you enter a journal to "back out" or "reverse" the asset from the books, as if you never bought it in the first place.** The journal to reverse the net book value of the asset looks something like this:

	Debit	*Credit*
Fixed asset		£5000
Asset Disposal Loss account	£5000	

You now have two entries in the Loss account. The first is a decrease (credit) of £4000 from the sale of the asset and the second is an increase (debit) of £5000 from backing out the value of the land, resulting in an overall loss of £1000.

Selling a Depreciable Asset

Selling a depreciated asset works almost identically to selling an asset that you haven't been depreciating. When you sell the asset, you need to back out the asset's account balance. You also need to back out the asset's accumulated depreciation (which is the only thing that's different from selling an asset that you haven't been depreciating). You need to record the cash (or whatever) that somebody pays you for the asset. Finally, you count as a gain or a loss any difference between what you sell the asset for and what its net-of-accumulated-depreciation (or *book value*) is.

This process sounds terribly complicated, but an example helps. Suppose that you purchased a £5000 piece of machinery and have accumulated £500 of depreciation thus far. Consequently, the fixed asset account shows a £5000 debit balance and the asset's accumulated depreciation account shows a £500 credit balance. Its net book value, in other words, is £4500. Suppose also that you sell the machinery for £4750 in cash. So overall you make a gain of £250.

To record the sale of this asset, you enter a sales receipt as described in the preceding section. This takes care of the £4750 cash received (a debit entry), and puts a credit entry of £4750 in the Asset Disposal Gain account.

Now you need to reverse the net book value of the asset, which you do using the following journal entry:

	Debit	Credit
Fixed asset		£5000
Accumulated Depreciation	£500	
Asset Disposal Gain	£4500	

If you were to look in the Asset Disposal Gain income account you'd see two entries: a credit (increase) of £4750 from the sale, and a debit (decrease) of £4500 for the net book value of the asset, resulting in an overall gain of £250.

Be sure to record the amount the asset depreciated for the year of the sale before you make the entry for the sale itself, so you have an accurate net book value. Otherwise it gives an incorrect value to the gain or the loss.

Repaying a Loan

In Chapter 8, we talk about how you enter a loan for the business, so we won't repeat it here. Eventually, however, you need to repay the loan. (You didn't know that?) To record loan payments, you need to split each payment between two accounts: the interest expense account and the loan payable account.

Suppose that you make £75 monthly payments on a £5000 bank loan. Also suppose that the bank charges 1 percent interest each month. You have set up a loan account (of type Other Current Liability) in QuickBooks to track the loan principal repayments and you call it, creatively enough, Bank Loan. You note that QuickBooks already has an expense account called Interest Expense.

You can enter the loan repayment either using the Write Cheques window, by filling in the top part of the cheque as usual (described in Chapter 6), choosing the bank name in the Pay to the Order of field, and entering the total amount of the payment. In the Expenses tab:

- ✔ Select the Bank Loan account in the first Account line.
- ✔ Choose the "O" VAT Code (the loan principal repayment is outside the scope of VAT) in the VAT column.
- ✔ Select the Interest Expense account in the second Account line.
- ✔ Choose the "E" VAT Code (the interest is a VAT-exempt entry).
- ✔ Click the Save & Close button.

Get the lender to provide you an amortisation schedule that shows the breakdown of each payment into interest expense and loan principal reduction. If this doesn't work, choose Banking➪Loan Manager. QuickBooks displays the Loan Manager window. If you click the Add a Loan button, QuickBooks collects a bit of information about the loan terms and builds an amortisation schedule for you. Note, too, that you can tell QuickBooks to remind you of upcoming loan payments and even to schedule the payments.

You can check your loan accounting whenever you get a loan statement from the bank. What the bank shows as the ending balance for a particular month should match what QuickBooks says is the balance for that month. To correct discrepancies between the loan balance that the bank shows and the loan balance that QuickBooks shows, make a general journal entry that adjusts both the interest expense and the loan principal at the same time. For example, if the loan balance is too low – say, by £8.76 – you need to increase the loan balance and decrease the loan interest expense using the following journal entry:

	Debit	**Credit**	**Explanation**
Interest expense	£8.76		Adjusts the interest expense by the same amount as loan balance changes
Loan payable		£8.76	Increases the loan principal balance to match the lender's statement

Writing off a bad debt

There may be (hopefully not many) times when a customer fails to pay you. You can write off the invoice as a bad debt and reclaim the VAT six months from the date you made the supply or invoiced the customer (whichever is later). To write off the bad debt you need to reverse the balance of the invoice in the accounts receivable account so that it no longer shows as being owed, record the net invoice amount as a bad debt expense, and reclaim the VAT amount. You do all this in one journal entry.

On 4 October 2011 you invoiced your customer £2,000 plus £400 VAT. On 4 April 2012 your customer still has not paid the £2,400 you are owed and you know you won't get paid. You make a journal entry (as shown in Figure 18-1) to record the bad debt.

Figure 18-1:
The Make General Journal Entries window showing a bad debt write-off entry.

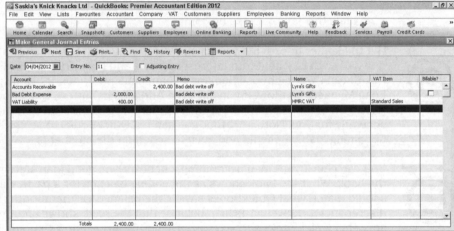

After you set up a new Expense type of account called *Bad Debt* (as described in Chapter 3), you make the journal entry as follows:

1. **Choose Company⇨Make General Journal Entry.**

   The Make General Journal Entries window is displayed.

2. **In the date field, enter the date of the bad debt (in our example that's 4 April 2012).**

3. **In the first Account line select the Accounts Receivable account and enter the gross amount (£2,400 in our example) in the *credit* column.**

   In the Name column enter the name of the customer.

4. **In the second Account line select the Bad Debt expense account and enter the Net amount (£2,000 in our example) in the *debit* column.**

   The £2,000 expense effectively reverses the £2,000 income from the sale. In the Name column enter the name of the customer and untick the check mark QuickBooks adds in the Billable? column.

5. **In the third Account line select the VAT Liability account, enter the VAT amount (£400 in our example) in the *debit* column, and select the Fuel Scale VAT Item.**

   QuickBooks automatically enters HMRC VAT is the Name column. In the VAT Item column select the same VAT item as applied to the original invoice (for example Standard Sales).

6. **(Optional) Add memos to each line of the journal to remind you later why you entered the journal (refer to Figure 18-1).**

7. **Click Save & Close to record the journal.**

Owner's Equity in a Sole Proprietorship

Actually, tracking owner's equity in a sole proprietorship is easy. If you told QuickBooks to set up a sole proprietor type of company during the QuickBooks Setup process, QuickBooks sets up three equity accounts in the Chart of Accounts: Owners Equity, Owners Drawings, and Share Capital account. You need to set up one more account, the Owners Capital Contributions account.

The balance of the Share Capital account should be zero provided that you entered your trial balance correctly in Chapter 3. It's a good idea to inactivate this account after you upload the trial balance.

To track the money you withdraw from the business, you can use the equity account called Owners Drawings; if you put money back into the business, use the Owners Capital Contributions account. Table 18-1 gives an example of owner's equity accounts in a sole proprietorship. Note that the numbers in brackets are negative values.

Table 18-1	An Example of Owner's Equity Accounts in a Sole Proprietorship
Account	***Amount***
Owners Equity	£8,000
Owners Capital Contributions	£5,000
Owners Drawings	(£2,000)
Share Capital	£0
Owner's Equity (total)	£11,000

Owner's Equity in a Partnership

QuickBooks also makes it very easy to track the equity for each partner in a partnership. To get you started, QuickBooks creates five accounts: Partner 1 Draws, Partner 1 Equity, Partner 2 Draws, Partner 2 Equity, and Retained Earnings. You need to create one more account for each partner, the Partner Capital Contributions account.

If you want to personalise the accounts, change the account names to something like Jane Smith Draws, Jane Smith Equity and so on. For each additional partner, you need to add his or her own set of Partner Draws, Partner Equity, and Partner Capital Contributions accounts.

Amounts that a partner puts into the business are tracked with the Capital Contributions account and amounts that a partner withdraws are tracked with the partner's Drawings account. The partner's share in the partnership's profits is tracked with the partner's Equity account.

The Retained Earnings account is where QuickBooks shows the accumulated profits (or losses) from prior years. This is often referred to as the *Reserves* account. (If you want to, you can rename the Retained Earnings account to Reserves.) You distribute profits from the Retained Earnings account into the individual partnership equity accounts according to the partnership agreement, which should say how the partnership income is distributed between the partners.

The partner's share of the partnership's profits gets distributed to the partner's Partner Equity account. Table 18-2 gives an example of owners' equity accounts in a partnership.

Table 18-2	An Example of Owners' Equity Accounts in a Partnership	
Account	*Partner 1's Amount*	*Partner 2's Amount*
Partner Capital Contributions	£5,000	£7,000
Partner Equity	£6,000	£6,000
Partner Draws	(£3,000)	(£4,000)
Retained Earnings	£0	£0
Equity (total)	£8,000	£9,000

Owner's Capital and Drawings Transactions

To record an owner's drawings from the business (for a sole proprietor or a partnership), use the Write Cheques window. Fill out the top part of the cheque as usual (described in Chapter 6). In the Expenses tab:

- Select the Owners Drawings (or Partners Drawings) account in the first Account line.
- Choose the "O" VAT Code (this payment is outside the scope of VAT) in the VAT column.
- Click the Save & Close button.

To record an owner's or partner's capital contribution to the business, use the Make Deposits window as follows:

- Select the bank account into which you are making the payment and the date of the receipt.
- Select the owner's name from the list of names in the Received From field.
- Select the Owners Capital Contributions (or Partners Capital Contributions) account in the From Account.
- (Optional) Enter a memo, a cheque number (if appropriate), and a payment method.
- Enter the amount in the Amount column.
- Click the Save & Close button.

Owners' Equity in a Limited Company

Yikes! Accounting for the members' equity in a company can get mighty tricky mighty fast. (In a limited company the owners are referred to as *members*. Don't ask.)

If you told QuickBooks to set up a limited company during the QuickBooks Setup process, QuickBooks sets up two of three required accounts in the Chart of Accounts: Share Capital and Members Equity. You need to add a third account, Dividends Paid:

 ✔ **Share Capital account**: this is where you specify the number and class of shares and the 'par value' of the shares. You get the par value amount by multiplying the par value per share by the number of shares issued. The par value of the stock is written on the face of the actual stock certificate and it's stated in the company's Articles of Incorporation.

 ✔ **Members Equity account:** this is where you track the business profits left invested in the business. (This is usually referred to by accountants as the *Retained Reserves* account.)

 ✔ **Dividends Paid account:** this is where you track the amounts distributed to shareholders in the current year. You need to add this account (of type Equity).

 You can only make a dividend payment if the business is in profit, and dividends cannot exceed the total profits of the business.

Table 18-3 shows an example of owner's equity accounts in a company.

Table 18-3	An Example of Owners' Equity in a Corporation
Account	*Amount*
Shareholders Equity	£5,000
Members Equity	£8,000
Dividends Paid	(£3,000)
Total Owners Equity	£10,000

Writing a Dividend Cheque

A dividend cheque is trivial to record in QuickBooks. As you might guess, you use the Write Cheques window. Fill out the top part of the cheque as usual (described in Chapter 6). In the Expenses tab:

 ✔ Select the Dividends Paid account in the first Account line.

 ✔ Choose the "O" VAT Code (this payment is outside the scope of VAT) in the VAT column.

 ✔ Click the Save & Close button.

Chapter 19

(Almost) Ten Secret Business Formulas

We have some good news and some bad news. The good news is that you can use some powerful formulas to improve your chances of business success and increase your profits. No, we are not joking. These formulas do exist. You can and should use them. And in the pages that follow, we explain the formulas and how to use them.

Now for the bad news: To use these formulas, you need to feel comfortable with a bit of arithmetic. You don't need to be a serious mathematician or anything, but you do need to feel comfortable using percentages and calculators. By the way, you can use the standard Windows Calculator, available from within QuickBooks by choosing Edit⇨Use Calculator, to work with these secret formulas.

Even if you're not particularly fond of (or all that good at) maths, we want to encourage you to skim this chapter. You can pick up some weird insights into the world of finance.

The First "Most Expensive Money You Can Borrow" Formula

Here's something you may not know: The most expensive money that you can borrow is from suppliers who offer cash or early payment discounts that you don't take. For example, perhaps your friendly office supply store offers a 2 percent discount if you pay cash at the time of purchase instead of paying within the usual 30 days. You don't pay cash, so you pay the full amount (which is 2 percent more than the cash amount) 30 days later. In effect, you pay a 2 percent monthly interest charge. A 2 percent monthly interest charge works out to a 24 percent annual interest charge – and that's a great deal of money.

Here's another example that's only slightly more complicated. Many, many suppliers offer a 2 percent discount if you pay within the first 10 days that an invoice is due rather than 30 days later. (These payment terms are often described and printed at the bottom of the invoice as 2% 10, Net 30.)

In this case, you pay 2 percent more by paying 20 days later. (The 20 days later is the difference between 10 days and 30 days.) Two percent for 20 days is roughly equivalent to 3 percent for 30 days (one month). So, a 2 percent, 20-day interest charge works out to a 36 percent annual interest charge. Now you're talking *serious* money.

Table 19-1 shows how some common early payment discounts (including cash discounts) translate into annual interest rates. By the way, we are a bit more precise in the calculations for this table, so these numbers vary slightly from (and are larger than) those given in the preceding paragraph.

Table 19-1	Annual Interest Rates for Early Payment Discounts	
Early Payment Discount	*For Paying 20 Days Early*	*For Paying 30 Days Early*
1%	18.43%	12.29%
2%	37.24%	24.83%
3%	56.44%	37.63%
4%	76.04%	50.69%
5%	96.05%	64.04%

Is it just us, or do those numbers blow you away? The 2 percent for 20 days early payment discount that you often see works out (if you do the maths precisely) to more than 37 percent annual interest. Ouch. And if you don't take a 5-percent-for-20-days-early payment discount when it's offered, you're effectively borrowing money at an annual rate of 96 percent. You didn't read that last number wrong. Yes, a 5-percent-for-20-days-early payment discount works out to an annual interest rate of almost 100 percent.

We want to make another couple of observations, too. Turning down a 1 percent discount for paying 30 days early isn't actually a bad deal in many cases. Look at Table 19-1. It shows that the 1 percent discount for paying 30 days early results in 12.29 percent. Sure, that rate is pretty high but it is less than for many credit cards and is less than for some small business loans. If you have to borrow money some other way to pay 30 days early, making an early payment might not be cost effective. Also, one of the VAT quirks of early payment discounts is that your supplier charges you VAT *as if* you took the early payment discount (whether you do or not). As a result you actually pay your supplier less (because the VAT is less), which can help out your cash flow.

The bottom line on all this is that early payment discounts, if not taken, represent one of the truly expensive ways to borrow money. We aren't saying that you won't need to borrow money this way at times. We can guess that your cash flow gets pretty tight sometimes (a circumstance that is true in most businesses, as you probably know). We are saying, however, that you should never skip taking an early payment discount unless borrowing money at outrageous interest rates makes sense.

Oh, yes. The secret formula. To figure out the effective annual interest rate that you pay by not taking an early payment discount, use this formula:

Discount % / (1 − Discount %) × (365 / Number of Days of Early Payment)

To calculate the effective annual interest rate that you pay by not taking a 2 percent discount for paying 20 days early, calculate this formula:

0.02 / (1 − 0.02) × (365 / 20)

Work out the maths and you get 0.3724, which is the same thing as a 37.24 percent interest rate. (Notice that the discount percentages are entered as their equivalent decimal values.)

The Scientific view of the Windows Calculator includes bracket keys that you can use to calculate this formula and the others we give in the chapter. With the basic calculator open, choose View⇨Scientific to switch to the Scientific view of the calculator.

The Second "Most Expensive Money You Can Borrow" Formula

You know that "most expensive money you can borrow" stuff that we talk about in the preceding section? The very tragic flip side to that story occurs when you offer your customers an early payment discount and they take it. In effect, you borrow money from your customers at the same outrageous interest rates. For example, if customer Joe Bloggs gets a 2 percent early payment discount for paying 20 days early, you, in effect, pay ol' Joe roughly 2 percent interest for a 20-day loan. Using the same formula we give for the first "most expensive money you can borrow" formula, the rate works out to 37.24 percent.

In some industries, customers expect early payment discounts. You may have to offer them, but you should never offer them willingly. You should never offer them just for fun. Borrowing money this way is just too expensive. A rate of 37.24 percent? Yikes!

Allow us to also offer a rather dour observation. In our experience, any time someone offers big early payment discounts – we've seen them as big as 5 percent – he's either stupid or desperate, and probably both.

The "How Do I Break Even?" Formula

We know that you're not interested in just breaking even. We know that you want to make money in your business. But knowing what quantities you need to sell just to cover your expenses is often super-helpful. If you're a one-person accounting firm (or some other service business), for example, how many hours do you need to work to pay your expenses and perhaps pay yourself a small salary? Or if you're a retailer of, say, toys, how many toys do you need to sell to pay your overhead, rent, and sales clerks?

You see our point, right? Knowing how much income you need to generate just to stay in the game is essential. Knowing your break-even point enables you to establish a benchmark for your performance. (Any time you don't break even, you know that you have a serious problem that you need to resolve quickly to stay in business.) And considering break-even points is invaluable when you think about new businesses or new ventures.

As you ponder any new opportunity and its potential income and expenses, you need to know how much income you need to generate just to pay those expenses.

To calculate a break-even point, you need to know just three pieces of information: your *fixed costs* (the expenses you have to pay regardless of business activity, the income that you generate for each sale, and the variable costs that you incur in each sale. (These variable costs, which are also called *direct expenses,* aren't the same thing as the fixed costs.)

✔ Whatever you sell – be it thingamajigs, corporate jets, or hours of consulting services – has a price. That price is your income per item input.

✔ Most of the time, what you sell has a cost, too. If you buy and resell thingamajigs, those thingamajigs cost you some amount of money. The total of your thingamajigs' costs varies depending on how many thingamajigs you buy and sell, which is why these costs are referred to as *variable costs.* A couple of examples of variable costs include hourly (or contract) labour and shipping. Sometimes, the variable cost per item is zero, however. (If you're a consultant, for example, you sell hours of your time, but you may not *pay* an hourly cost just because you consult for an hour.)

✔ Your fixed costs are all those costs that you pay regardless of whether you sell your product or service. For example, if you have to pay an employee a salary regardless of whether you sell anything, that salary is a fixed cost. Your rent is probably a fixed cost. Things like insurance and legal and accounting expenses are probably also fixed costs because they don't vary very much with fluctuations in your income.

Fixed costs may change a bit from year to year or bounce around a bit during a year. So maybe *fixed* isn't a very good adjective. People use the term *fixed costs,* however, to differentiate these costs from *variable costs,* which are those costs that do vary with the number of goods you sell.

Take the book-writing business as an example. Suppose that as you read this book, you think, "Man, these authors are having too much fun. Writing about accounting programs, working day in and day out with buggy beta software – yeah, that would be the life."

Further, suppose that for every book you write, you think that you can make £5,000, but you'll probably end up paying about £1,000 per book for such things as long-distance telephone charges, overnight courier charges, and extra hardware and software. And suppose that you need to pay yourself a salary of £20,000 per year. (In this scenario, your salary is your only fixed cost because you plan to write at home at a small desk in your bedroom.) Table 19-2 shows how the situation breaks down.

Table 19-2		Income and Costs
Description	*Amount*	*Explanation*
Income	£5,000	What you can squeeze out of the publisher
Variable costs	£1,000	All the little things that add up
Fixed costs	£20,000	Some place to live and food to eat

With these three bits of data, you can easily calculate how many books you need to write to break even. Here's the formula:

Fixed Costs / (Income – Variable Costs)

If you plug in the writing-business example data, the formula looks like this:

£20,000 / (£5,000 – £1,000)

Work through the maths and you get 5. So you need to write (and get paid for) five books per year to pay the £1,000 per book variable costs and your £20,000 salary. Just to prove that we didn't make up this formula and that it really works, Table 19-3 shows how things look if you write five books.

Table 19-3		The Break-Even Point
Description	*Amount*	*Explanation*
Income	£25,000	Five books at £5,000 each.
Variable costs	(£5,000)	Five books at £1,000 each.
Fixed costs	(£20,000)	A little food money, a little rent money, a little beer money.
Profits	£0	Subtract the costs from the income, and nothing is left.

Accountants use brackets to show negative numbers. That's why the £5,000 and the £20,000 in Table 19-3 are in brackets.

But back to the game. To break even in a book-writing business like the one that we describe here, you need to write and sell five books per year. If you don't think that you can write and sell five books in a year, getting into the book-writing business makes no sense.

Your business is probably more complicated than book writing, but the same formula and logic for calculating your break-even point apply. You need just three pieces of information: the income that you receive from the sale of a single item, the variable costs of selling (and possibly making) the item, and the fixed costs that you pay just to be in business.

QuickBooks doesn't collect or present information in a way that enables you to easily pull the income per item and variable costs per item off some report. Neither does it provide a fixed-costs total on some report. However, if you understand the logic of the preceding discussion, you can easily massage the QuickBooks data to get the information you need.

The "You Can Grow Too Fast" Formula

Here's a weird little paradox: one of the easiest ways for a small business to fail is by being too successful. We know. It sounds crazy, but it's true. In fact, we'll even go out on a limb and say that business success is by far the most common reason that we see for business failure.

"Oh, right", you say. "What are these guys on about?"

Let us explain. Whether you realise it or not, you need a certain amount of financial horsepower, or net worth, to do business. (Your *net worth* is just the difference between your assets and your liabilities.) You need to have some cash in the bank to tide you over the rough times that everybody has at least occasionally. You probably need to have some office furniture and computers so that you can take care of the business end of the business. And if you make anything at all, you need to have adequate tools and machinery. This part all makes sense, right?

How net worth relates to growth

Okay, now on to the next reality. If your business grows and continues to grow, you need to increase your financial horsepower, or net worth. A bigger business, for example, needs more cash to make it through the tough times than a smaller business does – along with more office furniture, more computers, and more tools and machinery. Oh, sure, you might be able to have one growth spurt because you started with more financial horsepower (more net worth) than you needed. But – and this is the key part – you can't sustain business growth without increasing your net worth. Now you may be saying things like "No way. That doesn't apply to me." But we assure you, it does.

As long as your creditors will extend you additional credit as you grow your business – and they should, as long as the business is profitable and you don't have cash-flow problems – you can grow your business as fast as you can grow your net worth. If you can grow your net worth by 5 percent yearly, your business can grow at an easily sustained rate of only 5 percent per year. If you can grow your net worth by 50 percent yearly, your business can grow at an easily sustained rate of only (only?) 50 percent per year.

You grow your business's net worth in only two ways:

- ✔ **Reinvest profits in the business.** Note that any profits that you leave in the business instead of drawing them out – such as through dividends or draws – are reinvested.

- ✔ **Get people to invest money in the business.** If you're not in a position to continually raise money from new investors – and most small businesses aren't – the only practical way to grow is by reinvesting profits in the business.

How to calculate sustainable growth

You can calculate the growth rate that your business can sustain by using this formula:

Reinvested Profits / Net Worth

We should say, just for the record, that this formula is a very simple *sustainable growth* formula. But even so, it offers some amazingly interesting insights. For example, perhaps you're a commercial printer doing £500,000 in yearly income with a business net worth of £100,000; your business earns £50,000 per year, but you leave only £10,000 per year in the business. In other words, your reinvested profits are £10,000. In this case, your sustainable growth is calculated as follows:

£10,000 / £100,000

Work out the numbers, and you get 0.1, or 10 percent. In other words, you can grow your business by 10 percent per year (as long as you grow the net worth by 10 percent per year by reinvesting profits). For example, you can easily go from £500,000 to £550,000 to £605,000 and continue growing annually at this 10 percent rate, but your business can't grow any faster than 10 percent per year. That is, you'll get into serious trouble if you try to go from £500,000 to £600,000 to £720,000 and continue growing at 20 percent per year.

You can convert a decimal value to a percentage by multiplying the value by 100. For example, 0.1×100 equals 10, so 0.1 equals 10 percent. You can convert a percentage to a decimal value by dividing the value by 100. For example, 25 (as in 25 percent) divided by 100 equals 0.25.

The sustainable-growth formula inputs are pretty easy to get after you have QuickBooks up and running. You can get the net worth figure from the balance sheet. You can calculate the reinvested profits by looking at the net income and deducting any amounts that you pulled out of the business.

We aren't going to go through the mathematical proof of why this sustainable-growth formula is true. It's our experience that the formula makes intuitive sense to people who think about it for a few minutes. If you aren't into the intuition thing or if you don't believe us, get a finance textbook, and look up its discussion of the sustainable-growth formula. Or do what all the kids today are doing – search online for *sustainable growth formula*.

The First "What Happens If . . . ?" Formula

One curiosity about small businesses is that small changes in income can have a huge impact on profits. A retailer who cruises along at £200,000 in income and struggles to live on £30,000 per year never realises that boosting the sales volume by 20 percent to £250,000 might increase profits by 200 percent to £60,000.

If you take only one point away from this discussion, it should be this curious little truth: if fixed costs don't change, small changes in income can produce big changes in profits.

The following example shows how this point works and provides a secret formula. For starters, say that you currently generate £100,000 yearly in income and make £20,000 per year in profits. The income per item sold is £100 and the variable cost per item sold is £35. (In this case, the fixed costs happen to be £45,000 per year, but that figure isn't all that important to the analysis.)

Accountants like to whip up little tables that describe these sorts of things, so Table 19-4 gives the current story on your imaginary business.

Table 19-4	Your Business Profits	
Description	*Amount*	*Explanation*
Income	£100,000	You sell 1000 thingamajigs at £100 a pop.
Variable costs	(£35,000)	You buy 1000 thingamajigs at £35 a pop.
Fixed costs	(£45,000)	All the little things: rent, your salary, and so on.
Profits	£20,000	What's left over.

Table 19-4 shows the current situation. Suppose that you want to know what will happen to your profits if income increases by 20 percent but your fixed costs don't change. Mere mortals, not knowing what you now know, might assume that a 20 percent increase in income would produce an approximate 20 percent increase in profits. But you know that small changes in income can produce big changes in profits, right?

To estimate exactly how a change in income affects profits, use the following secret formula:

Percentage Change × Income × (1 − [Variable Cost per Item / Income per Item])

From the sample data provided in Table 19-4 (sorry, this example is starting to resemble those story problems from secondary school maths), you make the following calculation:

0.20 × £100,000 × (1 − [35 / 100])

Work out the numbers and you get £13,000. What does this figure mean? It means that a 20 percent increase in income produces a £13,000 increase in profits. As a percentage of profits, this £13,000 increase is 65 percent:

£13,000 / £20,000 = 65 percent

Time for a quick observation: it's our experience that entrepreneurs always seem to think that they need to grow big to make big money. They concentrate on doing things that will double, triple, or quadruple their sales. Their logic, though, isn't always correct. If you can grow your business without having to increase your fixed costs, small changes in income can produce big changes in profits.

Before we stop talking about this first "What happens if . . . ?" formula, we want to quickly describe where you get the inputs you need for the formula:

- ✔ The percentage-change input is just a number that you pick. If you want to see what happens to your profits with a 25 percent increase in sales, for example, use 0.25.

- ✔ The income input is your total income. You can get it from your profit and loss statement. (In Chapter 15, we describe how you can create a profit and loss statement in QuickBooks.)

- ✔ The income per item sold and variable costs per item sold figures work the same way as we describe for the break-even formula earlier in this chapter.

The Second "What Happens If . . . ?" Formula

Perhaps we shouldn't tell you this, but people in finance usually have a prejudice against people in sales. And it's not just because people who are good at sales usually make more money than people who are good at finance. It's really not. Honest to goodness.

Here's the prejudice: people in finance think that people in sales always want to reduce prices.

People in sales see things a bit differently. They say, in effect, "Hey, you worry too much. We'll make up the difference in additional sales volume." The argument is appealing: you undercut your competitor's prices by a healthy chunk and make less on each sale. But because you sell your stuff so cheaply, your customers will beat a path to your door.

Just for the record, we love people who are good at sales. We think that someone who is good at sales is more important than someone who is good at finance.

But that painful admission aside, we have to tell you that we see a problem with the "Cut the prices; we'll make it up with volume" strategy. If you cut prices by a given percentage – perhaps by 10 percent – you usually need a much bigger percentage gain in income to break even.

The following example shows what we mean and how this strategy works. Suppose that you have a business that sells some thingamajigs. You generate £100,000 yearly in income and make £20,000 per year in profits. Your income per item (or thingamajig) sold is £100 and your variable cost per item (or thingamajig) sold is £35. Your fixed costs happen to be £45,000 yearly, but again, the fixed costs aren't all that important to the analysis. Table 19-5 summarises the current situation.

Table 19-5	Your Current Situation	
Description	**Amount**	**Explanation**
Income	£100,000	You sell 1000 thingamajigs at £100 a pop.
Variable costs	(£35,000)	You buy 1000 thingamajigs at £35 a pop.
Fixed costs	(£45,000)	All the little things: rent, your salary, and so on.
Profits	£20,000	What's left over.

Then business is particularly bad for one month. David, your sales guy, comes to you and says, "Boss, I have an idea. I think that we can cut prices by 15 percent to £85 per thingamajig and get a truly massive boost in sales."

You're a good boss. You're a polite boss. Plus you're intrigued. So you think a bit. The idea has a certain appeal. You start wondering how much of an increase in sales you need to break even on the price reduction.

You're probably not surprised to read this, but we have another secret formula that can help. You can use the following formula to calculate how many items (thingamajigs, in the example) you need to sell just to break even on the new, discounted price. Here's the formula:

(Current Profits + Fixed Costs) / (Income per Item – Variable Cost per Item)

From the example data provided earlier, you make the following calculation:

(£20,000 + £45,000) / (£85 – £35)

Work out the numbers, and you get 1300. What does this figure mean? It means that just to break even on the £85 thingamajig price, David needs to sell 1300 thingamajigs. Currently, from Table 19-5, you sell 1000 thingamajigs yearly. As a percentage, then, this jump from 1000 thingamajigs to 1300 thingamajigs is exactly a 30 percent increase. (Remember that David proposes a 15 percent price cut.)

Okay, we don't know David. He may be a great guy. He may be a wonderful salesperson. But here's my guess: David isn't thinking about a 30 percent increase in sales volume. (Remember, with a 15 percent price reduction, you need a 30 percent increase just to break even!) And David almost certainly isn't thinking about a 50 percent or 75 percent increase in sales volume – which is what you need to make money on the whole deal, as shown in Table 19-6.

Table 19-6	How Profits Look at Various Sales Levels		
Description	*1300 Units Sold*	*1500 Units Sold*	*1750 Units Sold*
Income	£110,500	£127,500	£148,750
Variable costs	(£45,500)	(£52,500)	(£61,250)
Fixed costs	(£45,000)	(£45,000)	(£45,000)
Profits	£20,000	£30,000	£42,500

In summary, you can't reduce prices by, say, 15 percent and then go for some trivial increase in sales. You need huge increases in the sales volume to get big increases in profits. If you look at Table 19-6, you see that if you can increase the sales from 1000 thingamajigs to 1750 thingamajigs – a 75 percent increase – you can more than double the profits. This increase assumes that the fixed costs stay level, as the table shows.

We want to describe quickly where you get the inputs that you need for the formula:

- ✔ The profit figure can come straight from the QuickBooks profit and loss statement.

- ✔ The fixed costs figure just tallies all your fixed costs. (We talk about fixed costs earlier in this chapter in the "The 'How Do I Break Even?' Formula" section.)

- ✔ The income per item is just the new price that you're considering.

- ✔ Finally, the variable cost per item is the cost of the thing you sell. (We discuss this cost earlier in the chapter, too.)

Please don't construe the preceding discussion as proof that you should *never* listen to the Davids of the world. The "cut prices to increase volume" strategy can work wonderfully well. The trick, however, is to increase the sales volume massively. Sam Walton, the late founder of Walmart, used the strategy and became, at one point, the richest man in the world.

The Economic Order Quantity (Isaac Newton) Formula

Isaac Newton invented differential calculus, a fact that is truly amazing to us. We can't fathom how someone could just figure out calculus. We could never, in a hundred years, figure it out. But we're getting off-track.

The neat thing about calculus – besides the fact that we are not going to do any for you here – is that it enables you to create optimal values equations. One of the coolest such equations is the *economic order quantity,* or *EOQ,* model. We know that this stuff all sounds terribly confusing and totally boring, but stay with us for just another paragraph. (If you're not satisfied in another paragraph or so, skip ahead to the next secret formula.)

Say that you buy and then resell 2000 cases of vintage South African wine every year. The EOQ model enables you to decide whether you should order all 2000 cases at one time, order 1 case at a time, or order some number of cases in between 1 case and 2000 cases.

Another way to say the same thing is that the EOQ model enables you to choose the best, or optimal, reorder quantity for items that you buy and then resell.

If you're still with us at this point, we figure that you want to know how this formula works. You need to know just three pieces of data to calculate the optimal order quantity: the annual sales volume, the cost of placing an order, and the annual cost of holding one unit in stock. You plug this information into the following formula:

$$\sqrt{(2 \times \text{Sales Volume} \times \text{Order Cost})} / \text{Annual Holding Cost per Item}$$

You buy and resell 2000 cases per year, so that amount is the sales volume. Every time you place an order for the wine, you need to buy an £800 round-trip ticket to Cape Town (just to sample the stock) and pay £200 for a couple of nights at a hotel. So your cost per order is £1,000. Finally, with insurance, interest on a bank loan, and the cost of maintaining your hermetically sealed, temperature-controlled wine cellar, the cost of storing a case of wine is about £100 yearly. In this example, you can calculate the optimal order quantity as follows:

$$\sqrt{(2 \times 2000 \times £1000)} / £100$$

Work through the numbers, and you get 200. Therefore, the order quantity that minimises the total cost of your trips to Cape Town and of holding your expensive wine stock is 200 cases. You could, of course, make only one trip to Cape Town per year and buy 2000 cases of wine at once, thereby saving travel money, but you'd spend more money on holding your expensive wine stock than you would save on travel costs. And although you could reduce your wine stock carrying costs by going to Cape Town every week and picking up a few cases, your travel costs would go way, way up. (Of course, you would get about a billion frequent-flyer miles yearly.)

You can use the Standard view of the Windows Calculator to compute economic order quantities. The trick is to click the √ (square root) key last. For example, to calculate the economic order quantity in the preceding example, you enter the following numbers and operators:

$$(2 \times 2000 \times 1000) \: / \: 100 = \sqrt{}$$

The Rule of 72

The Rule of 72 isn't exactly a secret formula. It's more like a general rule. Usually, people use this rule to figure out how long it will take for some investment or savings account to double in value. The Rule of 72 is a cool little trick, however, and it has several useful applications for business people.

What the rule says is that if you divide the value 72 by an interest rate percentage, your result is approximately the number of years it will take to double your money. For example, if you can stick money into some investment that pays 12 percent interest, it will take roughly six years to double your money because 72 / 12 = 6.

The Rule of 72 isn't exact, but it's usually close enough. For example, if you invest £1,000 for six years at 12 percent interest, what you really get after six years isn't £2,000 but £1,973.92.

If you're in business, you can use the Rule of 72 for a couple of other forecasts, too:

✔ **To forecast how long it will take inflation to double the price of an item, divide 72 by the inflation rate.** For example, if you own a building with a value that you figure will at least keep up with inflation, and you wonder how long the building will take to double in value if inflation runs at 4 percent, you just divide 72 by 4. The result is 18, meaning that it will take roughly 18 years for the building to double in value. Again, the Rule of 72 isn't exactly on the money, but it's pretty close. A £100,000 building increases in value to £202,581.65 over 18 years if the annual inflation rate is 4 percent.

✔ **To forecast how long it will take to double sales volume, divide 72 by the annual growth rate.** For example, if you can grow your business by, say, 9 percent per year, you will roughly double the size of the business in eight years because 72 / 9 = 8. (We are becoming kind of compulsive about this point, we know, but let us say again that the rule isn't exact, but it's very close. If a £1,000,000-per-year business grows 9 percent annually, its sales equal £1,992,562.64 after eight years of 9 percent growth. This figure really means that the business will generate roughly £2,000,000 of sales in the ninth year.)

Part VI
Appendixes

In this part . . .

Appendixes are like attics. Why? Authors use them to store stuff that they want to keep but don't know where else to put. The appendixes that follow provide instructions for installing QuickBooks, an overview of accounting, some help with how you share the QuickBooks data file in a multi-user setting, and information on how to print cheques.

Appendix A

Installing QuickBooks in Ten Easy Steps

● ●

*1*f you haven't already installed QuickBooks, get it over with right now:

1. Turn on the PC.

Find and flip on the computer's power switch. (Depending on which version of Windows 2000, XP, Vista, or 7 you're using, your screen may look a little different from the figures here. We're using Windows 7, by the way. Not that you care, or that it matters. . . .)

If you're installing QuickBooks on a computer running a professional or business edition of Windows, you may need to log on as either the administrator or a user with administrator rights. With the business flavours of the Windows operating systems, Windows security features require an administrator to install the QuickBooks program.

2. Get the QuickBooks CD.

Rip open the QuickBooks package and get out the CD (which looks exactly like the ones that play music).

You can also purchase QuickBooks directly from Intuit using the www. quickbooks.intuit.co.uk website and then download the software at the time of purchase. You need a fast Internet connection to download the QuickBooks software – the download requires close to an hour with a cable modem and even more time with a DSL connection. If you do download the software, click Save when the File Download window appears (don't click Open) and save the file to your computer desktop (or an easy-to-find location). Double-click the file you just downloaded to start unpacking the files, and then click Next to unpack the installation files. (***Note***: depending on your version of Windows, you may see Windows dialog boxes that you need to acknowledge to carry on.) When you see the "Welcome to QuickBooks" screen, click Next to begin and skip ahead to step 4.

3. **Insert the CD into your CD-ROM drive.**

   Windows recognises that you inserted the QuickBooks CD and displays a little message box that tells you "Welcome to QuickBooks!" Click Next to really get things started. (You may need to click Next again.)

4. **Indicate that you accept the QuickBooks licensing agreement and then click Next.**

   QuickBooks next asks whether you agree to play by its rules, as outlined in tedious detail in the licensing agreement displayed onscreen. Assuming you do – and you have to agree in order to install the software – select the I Accept the Terms of the License Agreement (But Only Because I Have No Other Choice) button and click Next.

5. **Select Custom and Network options and click Next.**

   When the Choose Installation Type window appears, select the Custom and Network option to tell QuickBooks more about how you'll be using the software.

6. **Describe any network sharing you plan.**

   When the Custom and Network Options window appears (see Figure A-1), describe whether you'll share the QuickBooks data file over a network. If you don't plan to use QuickBooks across your network, when asked you simply indicate that you'll use QuickBooks only on the computer onto which you're installing the software.

   You also have a couple of other options. You can install QuickBooks on the computer and make the QuickBooks data available to other computers on the network. And you can actually skip installing the QuickBooks software but can store just the QuickBooks data file on the computer.

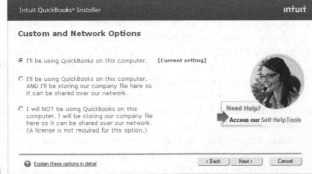

Figure A-1:
The Custom
and
Network
Options
window.

7. Provide the License and Product Number and then click Next.

When the License and Product Numbers window appears (see Figure A-2), enter these two bits of licensing information (they should be printed on a yellow sticker on the back of the CD sleeve, or sent to you via e-mail if you downloaded the software) and then click Next.

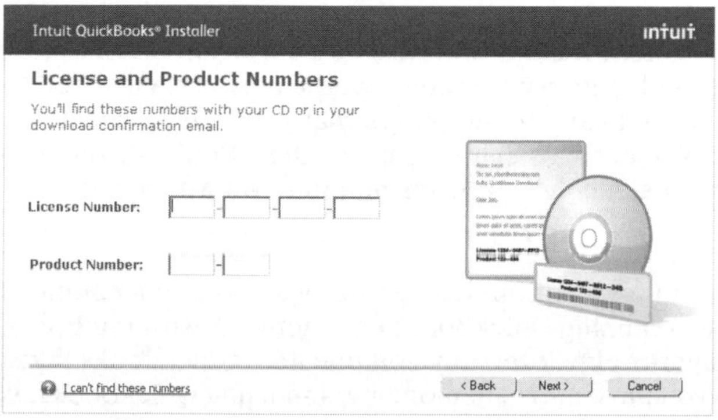

Figure A-2:
The License and Product Numbers window.

8. Select the installation location and then click Next.

When the Choose Installation Location appears, click the Next button to use the Intuit default installation location. (The default installation location is fine for 999 of 1000 users.)

You don't have to choose the suggested installation location. You can, instead, choose to have the QuickBooks program and data files stored in some other location. We don't talk about this option here because most people won't want to (and shouldn't) make this customisation. What's more, if you're someone who can safely customise the QuickBooks installation location settings, you don't need our help with figuring out how this change works.

9. Begin the installation.

The installation program tells you, at long last, that it's ready to begin as soon as you click Install. Click Install. While the installation program runs, you can see a little bar that shows your progress.

If you need to cancel the installation at any time, just click Cancel. QuickBooks warns you that the setup is incomplete. That's okay; just start the setup from scratch next time around.

10. Take 15–20 minutes or so to contemplate the meaning of life or get a drink of water.

11. **When the Install program finishes, click Finish.**

> Congratulations. You're finished with the installation. You have a new item on the Programs menu and probably new shortcuts on your desktop.

Now that you've installed QuickBooks you may want to flip to Chapter 2 and find out how to register the program. You'll probably want to register QuickBooks before you begin using it.

If you work on a network and want to share a QuickBooks file stored on one computer with another computer on the network, you need to install QuickBooks on all the other computers that you want to use to work with the file. *Note:* You need a separate copy of QuickBooks – from the three-pack version, for example – for each computer on which you want to install QuickBooks.

By the way – and we mention this just because we had a couple of clients ask about this – running QuickBooks on a network with multiple QuickBooks users isn't super-tricky or terribly complicated. QuickBooks takes care of the hard stuff. If you have more than one person using QuickBooks, you owe it to yourself (and your business) to set up a network and then purchase and install multiple copies of QuickBooks. Read Appendix C for more information.

Appendix B

If Numbers Are Your Friends

You don't need to know much about accounting or about double-entry bookkeeping to use QuickBooks, which, as you know, is most of its appeal. If you're serious about this accounting business or serious about your business, consider finding out a bit more; setting up QuickBooks and understanding all the QuickBooks reports will be easier, and you'll be more sophisticated in your accounting, too.

Just because the accounting in this appendix is a little more complicated doesn't mean that you can't understand it. To make this whole discussion more concrete, we use one running example. We hope it helps you out! If nothing else, it'll inspire you to get into the rowing–boat-hire business.

Keying In on Profit

Start with the big picture. The key purpose of an accounting system is to enable you to answer the burning question "Am I making any money?"

Accounting is that simple. Really. At least conceptually. So, throughout the rest of this appendix, we just talk about how to calculate a business's profits in a reasonably accurate but still practical manner.

Let me introduce you to the new you

You just moved to Scotland for the laid-back living and fresh air. You live in a cottage on Raith Lake. To support yourself, you plan to purchase several rowing boats and hire them to visiting fishermen. Of course, you'll probably need to do quite a bit of fishing, too, but just consider it the price you pay for being your own boss.

The first day in business

It's your first day in business. About 5 a.m., old Peter Gruntpaw shows up to deliver your three rowing boats. He made them for you in his barn, but even so, they aren't cheap. He charges £1,500 apiece, so you write him a cheque for £4,500.

Peter's timing, as usual, is impeccable. About 5:15 a.m., your first customers arrive. Mr. and Mrs. Hamster (pronounced "ohm-stair") are visiting from Edinburgh. They want to catch the big fish. You're a bit unsure of your pricing, but you suggest £25 per hour for the boat. They agree and pay £200 in cash for eight hours.

A few minutes later, another couple arrives. The Gerbils (pronounced "go-bells") are very agitated. They were supposed to meet the Hamsters and fish together, but the Hamsters are rowing farther and farther away from the dock. To speed the Gerbils' departure, you let them leave without paying, but you're not worried. As the Gerbils leave the dock, Ms. Gerbil shouts, "We'll pay you the £200 when we get back!"

Although you don't hire out the third boat, you do enjoy a sleepy summer morning.

About 2 p.m., the Hamsters and Gerbils come rowing back into view. Obviously, though, a problem has occurred. You find out what it is when the first boat arrives. "Gerbil fell into the lake," laughs Mr. Hamster. "Lost his wallet, too." Everybody else seems to think that the lost wallet is funny. You secretly wonder how you're going to get paid. No wallet, no money.

You ask Mr. Gerbil whether he will come out to the lake tomorrow to pay you. He says he'll just post you a cheque when he gets home to Edinburgh. Reluctantly, you agree.

Look at your cash flow first

We just described a fairly simple situation. But even so, answering the question "Did I make any money?" won't be easy. You start by looking at your cash flow: You wrote a cheque for £4,500 and you collected £200 in cash. Table B-1 shows your cash flow.

Table B-1	The First Day's Cash Flow	
	Cash In and Out	*Amount*
Add the cash.	Money from Hamsters (pronounced "ohm-stairs")	£200
	Money from Gerbils (pronounced "go-bells")	£0
Subtract the cash.	Money to purchase rowing boats	(£4,500)
Equals your cash flow:		(£4,300)

To summarise, you had £200 come in but £4,500 go out. So your cash flow was –£4,300. (That's why the £4,300 is in brackets.) From a cash-flow perspective, the first day doesn't look all that good, right? But does the cash-flow calculation show you whether you're making money? Can you look at it and gauge whether your little business is on the right track?

The answer to both questions is no. Your cash flow is important. You can't, for example, write a £4,500 cheque unless you have at least £4,500 in your bank account. Your cash flow doesn't tell you whether you're making money, though. In fact, you may see a couple of problems with looking just at the cash flow of the rowing boat hire business.

Depreciation is an accounting gimmick

Here's the first problem: If you take good care of the rowing boats, you can use them every summer for the next few years. In fact, say that the rowing-boat-hire season, which runs from early spring to late autumn, is 150 days long and that your well-made rowing boats will last ten years.

✔ **You can probably hire out the rowing boats for 1500 days.**

(One-hundred-and-fifty days per year times ten years equals 1500 days.)

✔ **Each rowing boat costs £1,500.**

The depreciation expense for each rowing boat is only £1 per day over 1500 days. That's a whopping £3 for all three boats.

Do you see what we're saying? If you have something that costs a great deal of money but lasts for a long time, spreading out the cost makes sense. This spreading out is usually called *depreciation.* The little £1 chunks that are allocated to a day are the *depreciation expense.*

Accountants use the terms *cost* and *expense* to mean distinctly different things. A *cost* is the price that you pay for something. If you pay Peter Gruntpaw £1,500 for a rowing boat, the rowing boat's cost is £1,500. An *expense,* on the other hand, is what you use in a profit calculation. The little £1 chunks of the rowing boat's £1,500 cost (that are allocated to individual days) are expenses.

If this depreciation stuff seems wacky, remember that what you're really trying to do is figure out whether you made any money your first day of business. And all we're really saying is that you shouldn't include the whole cost of the rowing boats as an expense in the first day's profit calculation. Some of the cost should be included as an expense in calculating the profit in future days. That's fair, right?

Accrual accounting is cool

You don't want to forget about the £200 that the Gerbils owe you, either. Although Mr. Gerbil (remember that the name is pronounced "go-bell") may not send the cheque for several days, or even for several weeks, he will pay you. You earned the money.

The principles of accounting say that you should include sales in your profit calculations when you earn the money and not when you actually collect it. The logic behind this include-sales-when-they're-earned rule is that it produces a better estimate of the business you're doing.

Different names, same logic

We don't see any point in hiding this nasty little accounting secret from you: accountants call this cost-allocation process by different names, depending on what sort of cost is being spread out.

Most of the time, the cost allocation is called *depreciation.* You depreciate buildings, machinery, furniture, and many other items as well. Allocating the cost of a natural resource — such as crude oil that you pump, coal that you dig, or minerals that you extract — is *depletion.* And allocating the cost of things that aren't tangible — franchise agreements, copyrights, and patents, for example — is *amortisation.*

Say that the day after the Gerbils and Hamsters hire the rowing boats, you have no customers, but Mr. Gerbil comes out and pays you £200. If you use the include-sales-when-they're-earned rule – called *accrual accounting* – your daily sales look like this:

	Day 1	Day 2
Sales	£400	£0

If you instead use *cash-basis accounting* (in which you count sales when you collect the cash), your daily sales look like this:

	Day 1	Day 2
Sales	£200	£200

The traditional accrual-based accounting method shows that you have a good day when you hire two boats and a terrible day when you don't hire any boats. In comparison, when you use cash accounting, your sales record looks as though you hired a boat each day, even though you didn't. Now you know why accrual accounting is a better way to measure profit.

Accrual accounting also works for expenses. You should count an expense when you incur it, not when you pay it. For example, you call the local radio station and ask the people there to announce your new boat-hire business a couple times for a fee of £25. Although you don't have to pay the radio station the day your announcement airs, you should still count the £25 as an expense for that day.

Now you know how to measure profits

With what you now know, you're ready to measure the first day's profits. Table B-2 is a profit and loss statement for your first day in business.

Table B-2	A Profit and Loss Statement for the First Day	
Description	*Amount*	*Explanation*
Sales	£400	Hire money from the Hamsters and Gerbils
Expenses	£3	Three rowing boats × £1/day depreciation
Depreciation	£25	Radio advert
Advertising		
Total expenses	£28	Depreciation expense plus the advert
Profit	£372	Sales minus the total expenses

Although the first day's cash flow was terrible, your little business is quite profitable. In fact, if you really do make about £370 per day, you'll recoup your entire £4,500 investment in less than three weeks. That's quite good.

Some financial brain food

Now that you know how to measure profits, we can fill you in on some important conceptual stuff:

- **You measure profits for a specific period of time.**

  In the rowing–boat-hire business example, you measured the profits for a day. Some people actually do measure profits (or they try to measure profits) on a daily basis. Most times, though, people use bigger chunks of time. Monthly chunks of time are common, for example, as are three-month chunks of time *(quarters)*. And everybody measures profits annually – if only because the government makes you do so for tax purposes.

- **When people start talking about how often and for what chunks of time profits are measured, they use a couple of terms.**

  The year that you calculate profits for is the *financial year*. The smaller chunks of time for which you measure profits over the year are *interim accounting periods*.

  You don't need to memorise these new terms. But now that you've read them, you'll probably remember them.

- **The length of your accounting periods involves an awkward trade-off.**

  Daily profit and loss calculations show you how well you did at the end of every day, but you have to collect the data and do the work every day. And preparing a profit and loss statement is a great deal of work.

We made the example purposefully easy by including only a few transactions. In real life, you have many more transactions to worry about and account for.

✔ **If you use a quarterly interim accounting period, you don't have to collect the raw data and do the arithmetic very often, but you know how you're doing only every once in a while.**

To us, checking your profits only four times per year isn't enough. A lot can happen in three months.

In the Old Days, Things Were Different

If you're new to the arithmetic and logic of profit calculation – which is mostly what modern accounting is all about – you won't be surprised to hear that not all that long ago, most people couldn't and didn't do much profit calculating.

What they did instead was monitor a business's financial condition. They used – well, actually, they still use – a balance sheet to monitor the financial condition. A *balance sheet* just lists a business's assets and its liabilities at a particular point in time.

Say that at the start of your first day in the rowing–boat-hire business – before you pay Peter Gruntpaw – you have £5,000 in your bank account. To make the situation interesting, £4,000 of this money is a loan from your mother-in-law and £1,000 is cash that you invested in your business.

Here's a key to help you understand the balance sheets and cash flow in this section:

✔ A business's *assets* are composed of things that the business owns.

✔ *Liabilities* consist of the amounts that the business owes.

✔ *Equity* is the difference between the business's assets and its liabilities. Interestingly, equity also shows the money that the owners or shareholders or partners have left in the business.

✔ If you correctly calculate each of the numbers that go on the balance sheet, the net assets (that's total assets less total liabilities) value always equals the owner's equity value.

Your balance sheet at the beginning of the day looks like the one in Table B-3.

Table B-3   The Balance Sheet at the Beginning of the Day

Description	Amount	Explanation
Total Assets	£5,000	The bank account balance. Your only asset is cash, so it's your total, too.
Total Liabilities	£4,000	The loan from your mother-in-law. Your only liability is the loan, so it's your total, too.
Net assets	£1,000	The total assets less total liabilities.
Owner's equity	£1,000	The £1000 you put in, equal to the Net assets.

If you construct a balance sheet at the end of the first day, the financial picture is only slightly more complicated. Some of these explanations are too complicated to give in a sentence, so the paragraphs that follow describe how we got each number.

Even if you don't pay much attention, we recommend that you quickly read through the explanations. Mostly, we want you to understand that if you try to monitor a business's financial condition by using a balance sheet, as we've done here, the picture gets messy. Later in this appendix, we talk about how QuickBooks makes all this stuff easier.

Table B-4 shows the balance sheet at the end of the first day.

Table B-4   The Balance Sheet at the End of the Day

	Description	Amount
Assets		
	Cash	£700
	Receivable	£200
	Rowing boats	£4,497
Total assets		£5,397
Liabilities		
	Payable	£25
	Loan payable	£4,000
Total liabilities		£4,025

	Description	Amount
Net assets		**£1,372**
Owner's Equity		
	Capital	£1,000
	Reserves	£372
Owner's equity		**£1,372**

Cash, the first line item shown in Table B-4, is the most complicated line item to prove. If you were really in the rowing–boat-hire business, of course, you could just look at your bank account. But if you were writing an appendix about being in the rowing–boat-hire business (as we are), you'd need to be able to calculate the cash balance. Table B-5 shows the calculation of the cash balance for your rowing–boat-hire business.

Table B-5	The First Day's Cash Flow		
Description	**Payment**	**Deposit**	**Balance**
Initial investment		£1,000	£1,000
Loan from mother-in-law		£4,000	£5,000
Rowing-boat purchase	£4,500		£500
Cash from the Hamsters		£200	£700

The £200 receivable, the second line item shown in Table B-4, is the money that the Gerbils owe you.

The third line shown in Table B-4, the rowing-boats balance sheet value, is £4,497. This is weird, we grant you, but here's how you figure it: you deduct from the original cost of the asset all the depreciation expense that you charged to date. The original cost of the three rowing boats was £4,500. You charged only £3 of depreciation for the first day, so the balance sheet value, or net book value, is £4,497.

The only liabilities are the £25 that you owe the radio station for those new business announcements (shown on the seventh line in Table B-4) and the £4,000 that you borrowed from your mother-in-law (shown on the eighth line in Table B-4). We won't even ask why you opened that can of worms.

Finally, the owner's equity section of the balance sheet shows the £1,000 that you originally contributed (see line 10 in Table B-4) and also the £372 you earned (see line 11 in Table B-4).

It's not a coincidence that the net asset value (that's total assets less total liabilities) equals the total owner's equity value. If you correctly calculate each of the numbers that go on the balance sheet, the two totals are always equal.

A balance sheet lists asset, liability, and owner's equity balances as of a specific date. It gives you a financial snapshot at a point in time. Usually, you prepare a balance sheet whenever you prepare a profit and loss statement. The balance sheet shows account balances for the last day of the financial year and interim accounting period. (Hey, it's kind of cool that after only a few pages of this appendix, you're reading and understanding such terms as *financial year* and *interim accounting period.*)

What Does an Italian Monk Have to Do with Anything?

So far, we've provided narrative descriptions of all the financial events that affect the balance sheet and the income statement. We described how you started the business with £5,000 of cash (a £4,000 loan from your mother-in-law and £1,000 of cash that you yourself invested). At an even earlier point in this appendix, we noted how you hired out a boat to the Hamsters for £200 and they paid you in cash.

Although the narrative descriptions of financial events – such as starting the business or hiring a boat to the Hamsters – make for just-bearable reading, they are unwieldy for accountants to use in practice. Partly, this awkwardness is because accountants are usually terrible writers. But an even bigger problem is that using the lots-and-lots-of-words approach makes describing all the little bits and pieces of information that you need difficult and downright tedious.

Fortunately, about 500 years ago, an Italian monk named Luca Pacioli thought the same thing. No, we're not making this up. What Pacioli really said was, "Hello? Is anybody in there? You have to get more efficient in the way that you describe your financial transactions. You have to create a financial shorthand system that works when you have a large number of transactions to record."

Pacioli proceeded to describe a financial shorthand system that made it easy to collect all the little bits and pieces of information needed to prepare income statements and balance sheets. The shorthand system he described? *Double-entry bookkeeping.*

This system enabled people to name the profit and loss or balance sheet line items or accounts that are affected and then give the pound value of the effect. The profit and loss statement and the balance sheet line items are *accounts.* You need to remember this term.

A list of profit and loss statement and balance sheet line items is a *chart of accounts.* You might already know this term from using QuickBooks.

Pacioli also did one wacky thing: He used a couple of new terms – *debit* and *credit* – to describe the increases and decreases in accounts:

- ✔ **Debit:** Increases in asset accounts and in expense accounts are *debits.* Decreases in liability, owner's equity, and income accounts are also debits.

- ✔ **Credit:** Decreases in asset and expense accounts are *credits.* Increases in liability, owner's equity, and income accounts are also credits.

Keeping these terms straight is a bit confusing, so see Table B-6 for help.

We're sorry to have to tell you this, but if you want to use double-entry book-keeping, you need to memorise the information in Table B-6. If it's any consolation, this information is the only chunk of data in the entire book that we ask you to memorise. Or, failing that, dog-ear this page so that you can flip here quickly.

Table B-6	The Only Stuff in This Book That We Ask You to Memorise	
Account Type	*Debits*	*Credits*
Assets	Increase asset accounts	Decrease asset accounts
Liabilities	Decrease liability accounts	Increase liability accounts
Owner's equity	Decrease owner's equity accounts	Increase owner's equity accounts
Income	Decrease income accounts	Increase income accounts
Expenses	Increase expense accounts	Decrease expense accounts

And now for the blow-by-blow

The best way to help you understand this double-entry bookkeeping stuff is to show you how to use it to record all the financial events that we discussed thus far in this appendix. Start with the money that you invested in the business and the money that you foolishly borrowed from your mother-in-law. You invested £1,000 in cash, and you borrowed £4,000 in cash. Here are the double-entry bookkeeping transactions – the *journal entries* – that describe these financial events.

Journal Entry 1:	To record your £1000 investment	
	Debit	*Credit*
Cash	£1,000	
Owner's equity		£1,000

Journal Entry 2:	To record the £4000 loan from your mother-in-law	
	Debit	*Credit*
Cash	£4,000	
Loan payable to mother-in-law		£4,000

 If you add all the debits and credits in a journal entry, you get a *trial balance*. A trial balance isn't all that special, but you use it to prepare profit and loss statements and balance sheets easily. If you add the debits and credits shown in journal entries 1 and 2, you get the trial balance shown in Table B-7.

Table B-7	Your First Trial Balance	
	Debit	*Credit*
Cash	£5,000	
Loan payable to mother-in-law		£4,000
Owner's equity		£1,000

This trial balance provides the raw data needed to construct the rowing–boat-hire business balance sheet at the start of the first day. If you don't believe this, take a peek at Table B-3. Oh, sure, the information shown in

Table B-7 isn't as polished. Table B-7 doesn't provide labels, for example, that tell you that cash is an asset. And Table B-7 doesn't provide subtotals showing the total assets less total liabilities (equal to £1,000) and the owner's equity (also equal to £1,000). But it does provide the raw data.

Take a look at the journal entries you'd make to record the rest of the first day's financial events:

Journal Entry 3:	To record the purchase of the three £1500 rowing boats	
	Debit	**Credit**
Rowing boats (fixed asset)	£4,500	
Cash		£4,500

Journal Entry 4:	To record the boat hire to the Hamsters	
	Debit	**Credit**
Cash	£200	
Sales		£200

Journal Entry 5:	To record the boat hire to the Gerbils	
	Debit	**Credit**
Receivable	£200	
Sales		£200

Journal Entry 6:	To record the £25 radio advert	
	Debit	**Credit**
Advertising expense	£25	
Payable		£25

Journal Entry 7:	**To record the £3 of rowing boat depreciation**	
	Debit	*Credit*
Depreciation expense	£3	
Accumulated depreciation (fixed asset)		£3

To build a trial balance for the end of the first day, you add all the first-day journal entries to the trial balance shown in Table B-7. The result is the trial balance shown in Table B-8.

Table B-8	**The Trial Balance at the End of the First Day**	
	Debit	*Credit*
Balance sheet accounts		
Cash	£700	
Receivable	£200	
Rowing boats – cost	£4,500	
Accumulated depreciation		£3
Payable		£25
Loan payable		£4,000
Owner's equity		£1,000
Profit and loss statement accounts		
Sales		£400
Depreciation expense	£3	
Advertising expense	£25	

The trial balance shown in Table B-8 provides the raw data used to prepare the balance sheet and profit and loss statement for the first day.

If you look at the accounts labelled *Balance sheet accounts* in Table B-8 and compare these with the balance sheet shown in Table B-4, you see that this trial balance provides all the raw numbers needed for the balance sheet. The only numbers in Table B-4 that aren't directly from Table B-8 are the subtotals that you get by adding other numbers.

If you look at the accounts labelled as *Profit and loss statement accounts* in Table B-8 and compare them with the profit and loss statement shown in Table B-2, you see that this trial balance also provides all the raw numbers needed for the profit and loss statement. Again, the only numbers in Table B-2 that aren't directly from Table B-8 are the subtotals that you get by adding other numbers.

Blow-by-blow, Part II

If you understand what we've discussed so far in this appendix, you grasp how accounting and double-entry bookkeeping work. We want to show you about half a dozen more transaction examples, however, to plug a few minor holes in your knowledge.

When you collect money that you've invoiced, you record the transaction by debiting cash and crediting receivables (or accounts receivable). In the rowing–boat-hire business, you make this basic entry when Mr. Gerbil later pays you the £200 that he owes you for the first day's hire.

Journal Entry 8: To record a payment from a customer	Debit	Credit
Cash	£200	
Receivable		£200

Don't record a sale when you collect the cash. The sale has already been recorded in Journal Entry 5. When you pay the radio station for the advert, you record the transaction by debiting accounts payable and crediting cash.

Journal Entry 9: To record your payment of £25 to the radio station	Debit	Credit
Payable	£25	
Cash		£25

The one other thing we want to cover – ever so briefly – is *stock accounting.* Accounting for items that you buy and resell or the items that you make and resell is a bit trickier, and we don't have room to go into a great deal of detail.

When you buy items to resell, you debit an asset account, often named Stock. If you purchase 300 of the £10 thingamajigs that you hope to resell for £25 each, you record the following journal entry:

Journal Entry 10: To record the cash purchase of thingamajigs

	Debit	Credit
Stock	£3,000	
Cash		£3,000

When you sell a thingamajig, you need to complete two tasks: record the sale and record the cost of the sale. If you need to record the sale of 100 thingamajigs for £25 each, for example, you record the following journal entry:

Journal Entry 11: To record the sale of 100 thingamajigs for £25 apiece

	Debit	Credit
Receivable	£2,500	
Sales		£2,500

You also need to record the cost of the thingamajigs that you sold as an expense and record the reduction in the value of your thingamajig stock. That means that if you reduce your stock count from 300 items to 200 items, you need to adjust your stock's value. You record the following journal entry:

Journal Entry 12: To record the cost of the 100 thingamajigs sold

	Debit	Credit
Cost of goods sold	£1,000	
Stock		£1,000

The cost of goods sold account, by the way, is just another expense. It appears after the income accounts on your profit and loss statement.

How does QuickBooks help?

If you keep (or someone else keeps) the books for your business manually, you actually have to make these journal entries. When you use QuickBooks to keep the books, however, all this debiting and crediting business usually goes on behind the scenes. When you invoice a customer, QuickBooks debits accounts receivable and credits sales. When you write a cheque to pay some bill, QuickBooks debits the expense (or the accounts payable account) and credits cash.

In the few cases in which a financial transaction isn't recorded automatically when you fill in an onscreen form, you need to use the General Journal Entry window. To display the General Journal Entry window, choose Company➪ Make General Journal Entries. You use the General Journal Entry window to create journal entries. An example of one of these noncash transactions is depreciation expense.

QuickBooks automatically builds a trial balance, using journal entries that it constructs automatically and any journal entries that you enter by using the General Journal Entry window. If you want to see the trial balance, just choose Reports➪Accountant & Taxes➪Trial Balance. QuickBooks prepares balance sheets, profit and loss statements, and several other reports by using the trial balance.

Appendix C

Sharing QuickBooks Files

· ·

In This Appendix

▶ Understanding how QuickBooks works on a network

▶ Installing QuickBooks for use on a network

▶ Setting up permissions

▶ Selecting multi-user mode

▶ Working with a shared QuickBooks file

· ·

*O*kay, here's a cool deal: Within QuickBooks, you can set up user permis-sions, which enables you to specify who has access to which areas of your QuickBooks files. In fact, you can also work with your QuickBooks file on a network and in a multiple-user environment by using a powerful feature called *record locking*.

If you work on a network and need to use or just want to find out about the QuickBooks network features, read this appendix. If your computer isn't con-nected to a network, but you want to designate unique permissions for differ-ent people by using a QuickBooks file on a single computer, read the section, "Setting Up User Permissions", later in this appendix. And if you're the only one using QuickBooks, you can skip this appendix.

Sharing a QuickBooks File on a Network

Two important features power the QuickBooks multi-user network capability: user permissions and record locking. The *user permissions* feature lets mul-tiple users of a QuickBooks file have unique permissions settings to access different areas of QuickBooks. The *record locking* feature allows more than one person to log on to and work with a QuickBooks file at the same time.

User permissions

QuickBooks enables you to set user permissions so that you can give differ-ent QuickBooks users different privileges. For example, Jane Owner may be able to do anything she wants because, metaphorically speaking, she's The Boss. Joe Clerk, though, may be able only to enter bills. Joe, a lowly clerk of perhaps dubious judgment and discretion, may not have the ability to view the company's profit and loss statement, print cheques, or record customer payments. This idea makes sense at a practical level, right? In a situation where a bunch of people access the QuickBooks file, you want to make sure that confidential information remains confidential.

You also want to make sure that people can't intentionally or unintention-ally corrupt your financial records. For example, you don't want someone to enter incorrect data (perhaps because they stumble into some area of the QuickBooks program where they have no business). And you don't want someone fraudulently recording transactions – such as fake cheques – that they can cash.

I think that if you reflect on this user permissions stuff, you'll realise, "Hey, yeah, that makes sense!" So, we're not going to talk a bunch more about it. Let us conclude by making a couple of general observations about how you decide which user permissions are appropriate:

- **Data confidentiality:** This issue probably has the most to do with your management philosophy. The more open you are about stuff, the less you probably have to worry about people snooping for stuff. I want to point out, however, that payroll is always a touchy subject. If everybody knows what everyone else is paid, some interesting discussions occur – but you already knew that.

- **Data corruption:** You need to know that people usually apply two gen-eral rules about data corruption:

  - Don't give people access to tools they don't know how to use. That's asking for trouble.

  - Make sure that no one person can muck around unsupervised in some area of the accounting system – especially if that person records or handles cash.

If at all possible, employ a buddy system whereby people do stuff together so that people always double-check – even if only indirectly – other people's work. Maybe Joe records a bill, for example, but Jane always writes the cheque to pay the bill. Maybe Raul records customer invoices but Chang sends them out. Maybe Saul records cash receipts but Beth deposits them. You see the pattern, right? If two people deal with a particular economic event – again, especially one that involves cash – it's a really good idea for Joe and Jane, Raul and Chang, and Saul and Beth to look over each other's shoulders.

Just what is a network, anyway?

A *network* is a set of connected computers so that the people who use the computers can share information. Uh, well, this is somewhat self-serving, but let me say that if you don't currently use a network, *Networking For Dummies,* 9th Edition (Doug Lowe), *Home Networking* *For Dummies,* 4th Edition (Kathy Ivens), and *Wireless Home Networking For Dummies*, 3rd Edition (Danny Briere, Pat Hurley, and Edward Ferris) explain how to set up a small business network in a couple of hours and live to tell about it.

Record locking

The easiest way to understand record locking is to compare it with the other variety of locking: *file locking.* Most other programs that you use – perhaps every one but QuickBooks – use file locking. What file locking means is this: If one person on the network has, for instance, a word-processing document open, nobody else on the network can open that document. Others may be able to open a copy of the document that they can save on their computers, but they can't edit the original document. The operating system locks the original document (the file) so that only one person can fool around with the file at a time. This locking ensures the integrity of the data and the changes that people make to the data. (If this business about ensuring integrity seems weird, think about the difficulty of making sure that both people's changes end up in a word-processing document that both people are editing simultaneously.)

Record locking works differently. With record locking, more than one person on the network can open and edit the same file at once, but only one person can work with a specific record.

A *record* is a part of a file. For example, in a file of bills that you owe to suppliers, the file is the entire collection of bills. The individual bills are records within the file and more than one person can open the file of bills. Individual bills, though – the individual records that make up the file – are locked when a person grabs a record.

This information may be a bit confusing, but differentiating between files and the records *within* a file is what makes sharing files possible. In QuickBooks, for example, if Jane is entering one bill for the Alpha Company in a file, Joe can edit a bill for Beta Corporation because the two bills are different records. However, Jane can't – because of record locking – fool around with the Beta Corporation bill that Joe is editing. And Joe can't – again, because of record locking – fiddle with the Alpha Company bill that Jane is entering.

Restated more generally, no two people can edit the same record in a file at the same time. Record locking enables employees to use a file in a multi-user environment because it lets more than one person work with a file.

Installing QuickBooks for Network Use

To install QuickBooks for network use, you must first install QuickBooks on all the computers on the network that need to access and work with the QuickBooks file. This task isn't tricky. You don't need to install QuickBooks in any fancy way to be able to share QuickBooks files.

You need to purchase a copy of QuickBooks for each computer that's going to run the program. If you have three computers on which you want to use QuickBooks, you need to buy three copies of QuickBooks. Or, you could buy the special three-license version of QuickBooks. If you attempt to install a single copy of QuickBooks (with a single key code) on multiple computers, QuickBooks won't allow two computers using the same key code to share a file in multi-user mode.

When you create the file that you want to share, you need to make sure that you store the file in a location where the other QuickBooks users can access it. That is, you may need to store the file on a server. You can also store the file on a client computer as long as you designate sharing permissions for either the folder or the drive on which you save the QuickBooks file.

Another important thing: Whoever creates the QuickBooks file automatically becomes the file administrator. The *file administrator* has access to all areas of the file and sets up the other file users, so you don't want just anybody setting up the QuickBooks file. Either the business owner or the head of accounting is well suited for this job. In any case, the person who sets up the file should be trustworthy, regularly around the office, and easy to reach for any questions or problems that arise. And this person probably should have a strong background in accounting. See the following section for more details.

Choosing a good password

The administrator has access to all areas of QuickBooks, so picking a good password is especially important. Other users (especially those with higher levels of access permission) also need to select their passwords carefully.

A good password is one that you can easily remember but that other people can't easily guess. Combinations of letters and numbers are the best way to go. For example, use a random number combined with the name of your favourite restaurant (as long as you don't walk around all day muttering "Number nine, number nine, number nine" and raving about your love of this particular eatery). Avoid using telephone numbers, family names, and family dates (such as the birthday of a family member). And *absolutely do not* use banking PINs.

One last tip: QuickBooks lets you create passwords from 0 to 16 characters in length. As a general rule, choose a password that's five or more characters long.

Setting Up User Permissions

You can tell QuickBooks who else will use the file and set permissions for these other people in the User List dialog box, as shown in Figure C-1. To display this dialog box, choose Company⇔Set Up Users and Passwords⇔Set Up Users.

Figure C-1:
The User List dialog box.

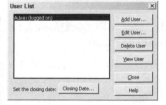

1. **Click the Add User button.**

   Doing so displays the Set Up User Password and Access dialog box (see Figure C-2). You use this wizard to add new users and specify passwords.

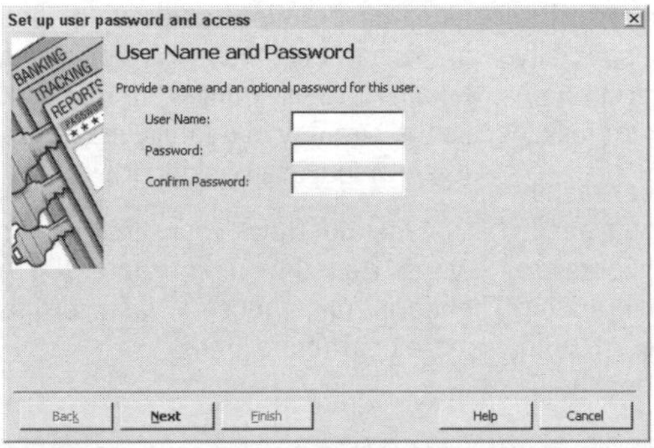

Figure C-2:
The Set
Up User
Password
and Access
dialog box.

2. **Type a username and password for the additional person whom you want to be able to use the QuickBooks file; type the password again in the Confirm Password text box.**

   Re-entering the password confirms that you typed the password correctly the first time.

   From this point, when someone opens the QuickBooks file, QuickBooks asks for a username and password. So for another person to access the QuickBooks file, he or she must enter the username and password that you set.

3. **Specify the user's access level: All Areas of QuickBooks, Selected Areas of QuickBooks, or External Accountant.**

   Select the access level that best matches the user you're describing and then click Next. An owner, by the way, should have access to All Areas of QuickBooks so she can do anything she wants.

   If you choose Selected Areas of QuickBooks, the wizard will guide you through a series of screens in which you can describe in more detail what the user can and cannot do. The last page of the wizard shows you an overview of the user's permissions. Click the Finish button to return to the Set Up User Password and Access dialog box.

4. **(Optional) View access for a user.**

   You can view a particular user's access rights in the Set Up User Password and Access dialog box. Just highlight the person's name in the User List and click the View User button. QuickBooks then displays a table of the different areas of QuickBooks and the activities (Create, Print, Reports) that the user can perform (see Figure C-3).

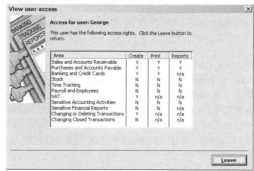

Figure C-3:
The View
User
Access
dialog box
for user
George.

A user can log on and open a QuickBooks file from any computer on the network as long as the computer has QuickBooks installed and has network access to the QuickBooks file. If a person attempts to open a restricted area or perform an unauthorised action, QuickBooks displays a message box indicating that the person lacks the permissions necessary to perform the action.

Individual users can specify and save their preferences for working with QuickBooks. For example, a user can decide to display and even customise the QuickBooks Icon bar or set options for graphs, reminders, and warnings. Users can access their preference settings by choosing Edit➪Preferences. Select an area by clicking an icon (such as General) on the left. Click the My Preferences tab, if it isn't already selected.

Specifying Multi-User Mode

For more than one person to work with a QuickBooks file at one time, users must work with the QuickBooks file in *multi-user mode*. The first person who opens the file needs to specify multi-user mode for others to be able to open the file. To specify multi-user mode, choose File➪Switch to Multi-User Mode. You can tell that you're working in multi-user mode because the QuickBooks title bar indicates so. When other people open the QuickBooks file, it automatically opens in multi-user mode. For a user to work in single-user mode, the other users must close the QuickBooks file, and the user wanting to work in single-user mode may need to choose File➪Switch to Single-User Mode.

Working in Multi-User Mode

Sharing a QuickBooks file over a network involves a couple of tricks. First, you need to make sure that no one who is in single-user mode is using the file that you want to open. If someone is and you try to open the file, QuickBooks displays a message indicating that someone is using the company file in single-user mode. Tell the person to switch to multi-user mode and then click Try Again.

As soon as you begin creating or editing a transaction, QuickBooks locks the transaction. This way, no one else can edit the transaction while you work on it. You can tell whether you have a transaction open in edit mode by what QuickBooks indicates on the title bar at the top of the form: QuickBooks displays Editing Transaction on the title bar. Other users can open the transaction while you are in edit mode, but they can't make changes to it until you're finished.

For example, if you attempt to edit a transaction that your co-worker Harriet already has open in edit mode, QuickBooks displays a message that reads (and here, we paraphrase), "Excuse me, mate? Harriet is working with that transaction. You need to come back later."

Appendix D

Printing Cheques

- -

*W*e have to be honest with you. We were not sure whether to include this section at all, as many businesses are using online banking nowadays rather than writing cheques by hand or using preprinted cheques. And this trend is on the rise for good reasons – it's fast, convenient and saves trees.

Having said that, there may be those among you who swear by using preprinted cheques (we used to, too). And it certainly beats writing a bushel of cheques by hand! So here we tell you how to print cheques you have queued up in QuickBooks, regardless of the method you used to generate these cheques: the Write Cheque window, the Pay Bills window, or running the payroll (discussed in Chapter 12) to generate employee pay cheques.

By the way, we are making two assumptions. The first assumption is that your printer is talking nicely to your computer. The second is that you have bought your stack of preprinted voucher or standard cheques or both types. (Yes, you have to buy them. To order them, click Help⇨Add QuickBooks Services in QuickBooks; in the web page that displays, click the link More about QuickBooks Stationary. In the second web page that displays, click the link Buy Cheques Online. It takes about three weeks from the time you place your order to receive the cheques because your bank needs to approve them, but refill orders take only about ten days.)

Aligning Your Printer

Before you print your first cheque, you need to align your printer to the cheque page. Now this is pretty similar to how you align an invoice, and we discuss this in excruciating detail in Chapter 4, but we'll give you the abbreviated version here because there are some important differences.

1. **Choose File⇨Printer Setup, and select Cheque/Payroll Payment from the Form Name drop-down list (see Figure D-1).**

   You may have to scroll up in the Form Name list: Cheque/Payroll Payment is the first item listed.

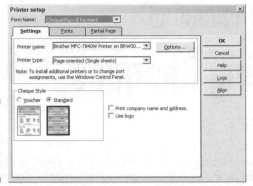

Figure D-1:
The Printer
Setup dialog
box.

2. **Select your printer in the Printer Name field, and accept the Printer Type default of Page-oriented (Single sheets).**

3. **Select the appropriate Cheque Style (if you use both types of cheques then you'll have to go through the alignment process for each type of cheque, as described in the next step).**

   Now you're cooking. This step is where you get to make a real choice.

   • *Voucher cheques* include a standard cheque at the top and two voucher remittances that fill the rest of the page. When you select the Voucher option, QuickBooks prints one remittance of the payment (including bill date, number, original and payment amounts) that you include with the standard cheque and a second copy of the remittance which you keep for your records. This is a good choice for Bill Payments.

   • *Standard cheques* are three to a page. This is well suited to paying employees where you don't need the voucher because you give a payslip instead.

4. **Click the Align button.**

   Different windows appear, depending on your cheque style selection in step 2:

   • *Voucher cheques*: In the Fine Alignment window, click the Print Sample button to see what you need to change (if anything), and then come back to this window and fine tune the way the cheque prints by clicking the arrows next to the vertical and horizontal boxes to move the position of the printed text on the page. When your printed sample lines up well with the voucher page, click OK to save your settings and return to the Printer Setup window.

- *Standard cheques*: In the Align Cheques window, first select the type of page you're adjusting, and then go through the same process of aligning each type of page as described for voucher cheques.

5. **Click the Partial Page tab of the Printer Setup dialog box and then select a Partial Page Printing Style.**

Fortunately, some graphics appear; otherwise, you wouldn't have a clue what these options are, would you? Suppose that you feed two cheques to the printer, but the cheque sheets have three cheques each. You have a leftover cheque.

Thanks to this option, you can use the extra cheque. Select one of the options to tell QuickBooks how you plan to feed the cheque to the printer – vertically on the left (the Side option), vertically in the middle (the Center option), or horizontally (the Portrait option). You feed cheques to the printer the same way that you feed envelopes to it.

6. **Click the OK button to save your settings and exit.**

Printing Cheques by the Bushel

Say you recorded a bunch of Cheques marked To Print (using the Pay Bills or Write Cheque windows) or ran the payroll and have a bushel of Payroll Payments marked To Print. Now you need to print them. After you load some blank cheques into your printer, follow these steps:

1. **Choose File⇨Print Forms⇨Cheques (or Payroll Payments).**

You see the Select Cheques to Print dialog box, in which you select the cheques you want to print (see Figure D-2).

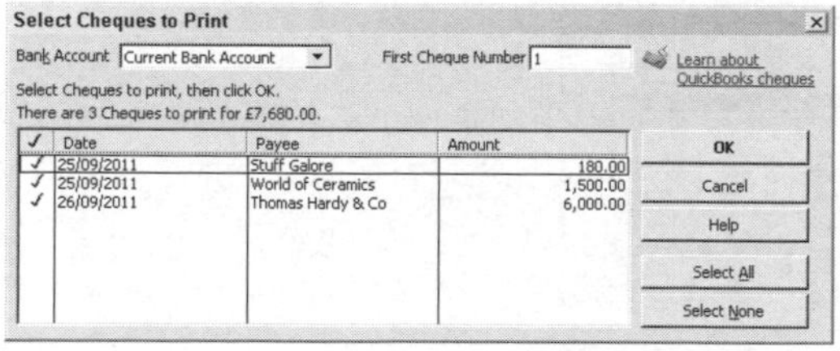

Figure D-2:
The Select
Cheques to
Print dialog
box.

✓	Date	Payee	Amount	
✓	25/09/2011	Stuff Galore	180.00	
✓	25/09/2011	World of Ceramics	1,500.00	
✓	26/09/2011	Thomas Hardy & Co	6,000.00	

Select Cheques to Print
Bank Account | Current Bank Account | First Cheque Number 1 | Learn about QuickBooks cheques
Select Cheques to print, then click OK.
There are 3 Cheques to print for £7,680.00.
OK | Cancel | Help | Select All | Select None

2. **Select the bank account in the Bank Account field.**

If you don't see the cheques you expect to print, make sure you have the correct bank account selected in the Bank Account field.

3. **Enter (or double check) the first cheque number to be printed, in the First Cheque Number field.**

    This is one is critical to get right!

4. **Click to remove the check marks next to the cheques that you don't want to print and then click OK.**

    All the cheques are selected at first, which is fine if you want to print them all. If not, click the check marks next to the cheques that you don't want to print so that QuickBooks removes the check marks. If you want to print only a few of the cheques, click the Select None button and then click next to the cheques that you want to print so that QuickBooks places a check mark in the column.

    When only the cheques that you want to print have check marks, click OK to continue. QuickBooks, happy with your progress, displays the Print Cheques dialog box (refer to Figure D-1). Here, you see the settings that you chose when you first told QuickBooks how to print cheques.

5. **Either click Print to accept the default settings, or make changes in the dialog box and then click Print.**

    You can change the settings in this dialog box if you want them to be different. Any changes that you make for a particular batch of cheques don't affect the default settings. The next time you print a cheque, your original settings appear again.

    If you're printing a partial page of cheques, enter the number of cheques on the first page in the Number of Cheques on First Page text box.

    QuickBooks prints the cheques, and then you see the Print Cheques – Confirmation dialog box (Figure D-3).

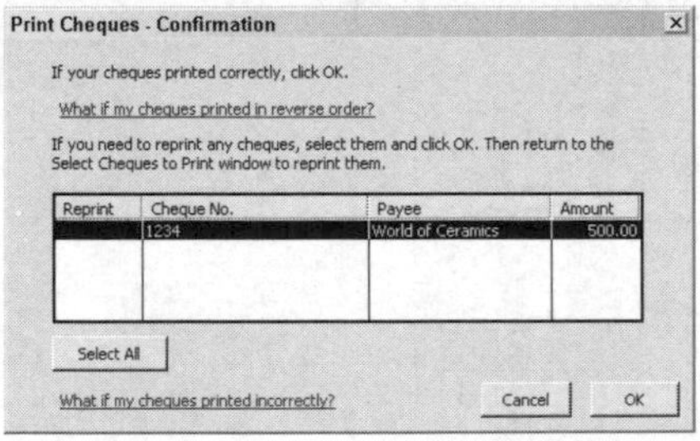

Figure D-3:
The Print
Cheques –
Confir-
mation
dialog box.

6. **Review the cheques that QuickBooks printed; then do one of the following:**

   - *If QuickBooks printed the cheques correctly,* answer the Did Cheque(s) Print OK? question by clicking OK.

   - *If QuickBooks didn't print a cheque correctly,* type the number of the first incorrectly printed cheque in the text box and then click OK. In this case, repeat the steps for cheque printing. Note, though, that you need to reprint only the first bad cheque and the cheques that follow it. You don't need to reprint good cheques that precede the first bad cheque.

   Don't forget to write **VOID** in large letters and permanent ink across the front of incorrectly printed cheques. Then file the cheques for safekeeping. (*Do not* throw them away.) To record the voided cheque in QuickBooks, see Chapter 8.

   If the numbers of the cheques that you need to reprint aren't sequential and are, in fact, spread all over creation, print one at a time, giving QuickBooks the correct cheque number each time.

   If your cheques came out all right, take the rest of the day off. Give yourself a raise while you're at it.

7. **Sign the printed cheques.**

   Then – and we guess you probably don't need our help here – sign and post the cheques.

Index

● *Ɗ* ●

FOR DUMMIES®

Making Everything Easier!™

GADGETS

978-1-1180-2444-7

978-1-1180-3671-6

978-1-1180-2445-4

MAC OS X LION

978-1-1180-2205-4

978-1-1180-2206-1

978-1-1180-2772-1

PROGRAMMING LANGUAGES

978-0-470-37173-2

978-0-470-92996-4

978-0-470-52275-2

Amazing Android Apps For Dummies
978-0-470-93629-0

AutoCAD 2012 For Dummies
978-1-118-02440-9

BlackBerry PlayBook For Dummies
978-1-118-01698-5

Blender For Dummies, 2nd Edition
978-0-470-58446-0

Creating Web Pages All-in-One For
Dummies, 4th Edition
978-0-470-64032-6

Digital SLR Cameras and Photography
For Dummies, 4th Edition
978-1-118-14489-3

Facebook For Dummies, 4th Edition
978-1-118-09562-1

HTML, XHTML & CSS For Dummies,
7th Edition
978-0-470-91659-9

iPad 2 For Dummies, 3rd Edition
978-1-118-17679-5

Laptops and Tablets For Seniors For
Dummies, 2nd Edition
978-1-118-09596-6

Mac Application Development
For Dummies
978-1-118-03222-0

Macs For Dummies, 11th Edition
978-0-470-87868-2

Nikon D5100 For Dummies
978-1-118-11819-1

QuickBooks 2012 For Dummies
978-1-118-09120-3

Samsung Galaxy Tab 10.1
For Dummies
978-1-118-22833-3

Twitter Marketing For Dummies,
2nd Edition
978-0-470-93057-1

WordPress Web Design For Dummies
978-0-470-93503-3

Windows Phone 7 Application
Development For Dummies
978-1-118-02175-0

FOR DUMMIES®

Making Everything Easier! ™

FOR DUMMIES

Making Everything Easier! ™

The ultimate beginner guide to the groundbreaking music service, Spotify!

978-1-1199-5234-3